Deschutes
Public Library

D1005959

LEFT TO THEIR OWN DEVICES

LEFT TO THEIR OWN DEVICES

LEFT TO THEIR OWN DEVICES

*How Digital Natives Are
Reshaping the American Dream*

JULIE M. ALBRIGHT

Foreword by THOMAS DOLBY
Musician, technology innovator, and author of The Speed of Sound

Prometheus Books
59 John Glenn Drive
Amherst, New York 14228

Published 2019 by Prometheus Books

Left to Their Own Devices: How Digital Natives Are Reshaping the American Dream. Copyright © 2019 by Julie M. Albright. All rights reserved. No part of this publication may be reproduced, stored in a retrieval system, or transmitted in any form or by any means, digital, electronic, mechanical, photocopying, recording, or otherwise, or conveyed via the internet or a website without prior written permission of the publisher, except in the case of brief quotations embodied in critical articles and reviews.

The lines from "Song." Copyright © 2016 by the Adrienne Rich Literary Trust. Copyright © 1973 by W. W. Norton & Company, Inc., from *Collected Poems: 1950–2012* by Adrienne Rich. Used by permission of W. W. Norton & Company, Inc.

Stanley Kunitz, "The Layers," from *The Collected Poems of Stanley Kunitz*, W. W. Norton and Company, Inc., 2002

"Let Us Be Men" from *The Complete Poems of D. H. Lawrence* by D. H. Lawrence, edited by Vivian de Sola Pinto & F. Warren Roberts, Copyright © 1964, 1971 by Angelo Ravagli and C. M. Weekley, Executors of the Estate of Frieda Lawrence Ravagli. Used by permission of Viking Books, an imprint of Penguin Publishing Group, a division of Penguin Random House LLC. All rights reserved.

Cover image © Getty Images
Cover design by Nicole Sommer-Lecht
Cover design © Prometheus Books

Trademarked names appear throughout this book. Prometheus Books recognizes all registered trademarks, trademarks, and service marks mentioned in the text.

The internet addresses listed in the text were accurate at the time of publication. The inclusion of a website does not indicate an endorsement by the author or by Prometheus Books, and Prometheus Books does not guarantee the accuracy of the information presented at these sites.

Inquiries should be addressed to
Prometheus Books
59 John Glenn Drive
Amherst, New York 14228
VOICE: 716–691–0133 • FAX: 716–691–0137
WWW.PROMETHEUSBOOKS.COM

23 22 21 20 19   5 4 3 2 1

Library of Congress Cataloging-in-Publication Data

Names: Albright, Julie M., 1962- author.
Title: Left to their own devices : how digital natives are reshaping the American dream / Julie M. Albright.
Description: Amherst : Prometheus Books, 2019.
Identifiers: LCCN 2018050608 (print) | LCCN 2018060067 (ebook) | ISBN 9781633884458 (ebook) | ISBN 9781633884441 (hardback)
Subjects: LCSH: Mass media and youth—United States. | Digital media—Social aspects—United States. | Information technology—Social aspects—United States. | Diffusion of technology—United States. | American Dream. | BISAC: SOCIAL SCIENCE / Demography. | PSYCHOLOGY / Social Psychology. | COMPUTERS / Social Aspects / Human-Computer Interaction.
Classification: LCC HQ799.2.M352 (ebook) | LCC HQ799.2.M352 .U63 2019 (print) | DDC 302.23/10835—dc23
LC record available at https://lccn.loc.gov/2018050608

Printed in the United States of America

CONTENTS

FOREWORD

by Thomas Dolby

It's the dirty little question no one wants to know the answer to: *Would I be happier if I threw away my phone?*

Heaven forbid the answer is "Yes!" That's a scenario I can't bear thinking about. I've invested in every version of that darn phone, all the way back to V1. I salivated over each upgrade announcement, then rushed out to buy the new model, even knowing it would probably be buggy and overpriced. I strayed to the "dark side" for a brief spell in 2009, after reading a comparative review in the *New York Times*, and made the switch to a famous Korean brand. So unwise! My life was hell for two months. I felt like I'd had a limb amputated. What a blessed relief to rummage for my old device in the bedside drawer, power it up, and watch it install the latest OS.

My phone is like a prosthetic extension of my hand. My entire world's in there. (Or in the iCloud? I'm confused. . . .)

I love technology. I have a fetish for the latest, geekiest device. Yet there's always this little voice nibbling away at my subconscious: *You'd be better off without it. Delete your Facebook and Twitter. Unplug, before it's too late. Go for a walk in the park. Breathe the air. Talk to actual people! Make goo-goo faces at babies!*

If you feel you're going slowly insane, Julie M. Albright's book is the comforting voice of reason. *Left to Their Own Devices: How Digital Natives Are Reshaping the American Dream* looks at the roots of our society's addiction to the small screen and asks those questions we're loath to ask, in a warm and human way. So, whether you're struggling with your own Android dependency, conflicted about your teenager's first iPhone, or just wishing you had more time to read detective novels and learn salsa dancing and do the crossword with Gran, this book is packed with wisdom and understanding—and you'll probably feel a lot better by the end of it.

Professor Thomas Dolby
Johns Hopkins University
Baltimore, MD

ACKNOWLEDGMENTS

This book has been many years in the making. It was written across multiple cities, five countries and three continents. I first tested out the notion of "coming untethered" on an audience that organizer Bruce Armstrong Taylor described as a "hard-bitten tech crowd" in New York City in the winter of 2017. I wanted to see if the ideas resonated. A lively discussion followed my keynote; afterward, folks queued in a line for twenty-five minutes to speak to me. I noticed two tall men standing in that line, chatting among themselves. Looking back now, thinking about those two executives actually waiting over twenty minutes in a line to talk to me brings tears to my eyes. That day changed my life. My heartfelt thanks to you, Mr. Peter Gross and Mr. Christian Belady, for your continued support and encouragement. You have inspired me ever since I gave that talk on that snowy winter's day. Thanks, too, to George Rockett, Scott Foley, Giovanni Zappulo, Kurtis Friesen, Tom Winter, Maxine Chang, and the rest of the Data Center Dynamics conference team for your continued support.

Creating this work was certainly not an individual endeavor: I owe a great debt of gratitude to my wonderful agent, Mark Gottlieb of Trident Media Group in New York City, who believed in this project from the start. I'd like to thank also my editor at Prometheus Books, Steven L. Mitchell, for staying the course and for challenging me throughout. I know the work is stronger because of your efforts. Special thanks to you, Alexander Pournelle, for your feedback on early drafts. You lifted this project to a new level. Thanks, too, to the rest of the Prometheus team, including Lisa Michalski, Jill Maxick, Hanna Etu, Nicole Sommer-Lecht, Jade Zora Scibilia, and Cate Roberts-Abel for all your contributions.

This is a work of narrative nonfiction, inspired by artists, designers, composers, and writers then and now, from F. Scott Fitzgerald and R. W. Emerson to current writers Tod Goldberg, Jeff Eyres, Natashia Deon, and Lee Michael Cohn. Special thanks to David Ross and my spiritual guide, Mick Scott, for keeping me sane along the way.

My warmest thanks to Dean Nelson, Simon Allen and Jeff Omelchuck, Oliver Jones, Eddie Schutter, and Maricel Cerruti of Infrastructure Masons, for taking me into the fold and for all your support and good cheer.

I'd like to thank my colleagues at USC—especially Margaret McLaughlin, who believed in me from the start. You are a beautiful and graceful role model, and I wouldn't be here without you. Special thanks to my colleagues Don Paul, Edward Maby, James Moore, and Neil Siegel from the Viterbi School of Engineering. Thanks, too, to Stan Rosen, Dan Lynch, Brett Sheehan, Ed McCann, Oliver Mayer, Peter Exline, Clay Dube, Mina Chow, Erica Watson-Currie, and Victor Currie for your enduring friendship and support. Thank you, too, to Eddie North-Hager and Jim Key for your deft publicity support throughout the years.

I want to thank friends and other contributors to this project: First, Steven Meloan. You are the heart and soul of this project. You so graciously loaned me your parents, so we could retrace their steps toward the American Dream, your brother, Michael, providing us comic relief along the way. Your digital native son showed us where we are now. I'm glad we've been on this journey together. Thank you to Ryan Singer, Ed Maguire, Andy Grignon, Bill Tai, Alexis Dickerson, Alan W. Silberberg, Mr. and Mrs. Michael Daniel Williamson, Mr. and Mrs. Larry Singer, Ethan Anderson, Donavan Freberg, Brian Hayashi, Warren Whitlock, Lance Mayfield, Paul Boutin, Sarah Farley, Todd Terrazas, Woody Lewis, Barry Caplan, Ann Greenberg, Constanza Blondet, Ariel Jalali, Julio Fernandez, and Buzz Bruggeman for your contributions and inspiration. A heartfelt thanks to the artists and writers who took me in and inspired me while I worked on this project: Franklin Vagnone and Johnny Yeagley in New York City, and Jean-Luc Lienard and Noemie Le Menn in Paris. Thank you to Steven Moss and Gaynell Albright for your ongoing support and prayers. Robyn Mattison: You showed up in our lives at just the right time with your big heart, sharp wit, and guidance. Thank you, Dad, for all of the things you taught me about art, fashion, architecture, design, and New York. And for that Dave Brubeck album you left behind. Much of your spirit is woven into this project. I wish you were here to see it.

Lastly, and most important—thank you, my beloved brother, Brad. I am excited we can go on this journey together. Thank you for your unflagging support and enthusiasm. I appreciate you more than you'll ever know. We will never be untethered.

INTRODUCTION

*Gatsby believed in the green light, the orgiastic future that
year by year recedes before us. It eluded us then, but that's no
matter—tomorrow we will run faster, stretch our arms further.
. . . And one fine morning—So we beat on, boats against the
current, borne back ceaselessly into the past.*
                    —F. Scott Fitzgerald, *The Great Gatsby*, 1925

NEW YORK CITY, MID-MORNING.
THE UPTOWN 5 FROM BROOKLYN

A petite woman in her mid-fifties boards the train at Church Street, her face partially obscured by her large, white, Jackie O–style sunglasses. Her dark hair is styled into a polished bob; her skinny jeans, folded up neatly to Capri length, show off her pert figure. She stops midway into the car, facing the pole directly in front of the door, while her friend, frumpier, slightly overweight, and a bit winded from the walk, takes a seat on the side. The doors close and the train lurches forward; the dark-haired woman is suddenly thrown backward, her mouth opening into a sudden, silent O of shock. As she falls back, her arms flail outward toward the pole, and I see the flash of a Tiffany charm bracelet on her left wrist just as her toes lose contact with the floor. Houston, we have liftoff. She wraps her fingers around the pole just in time, pulling herself upright to regain her balance. She then shouts excitedly to her friend, "We have to hang on!" a little too late for that public service announcement.

The cardinal rule of subway riding is that you either have to hang on or stand sideways, feet far enough apart to brace yourself against any sudden movements. Posters above the riders helpfully point this out. I smile as a I read one that says, "The poles are for your safety, not your latest routine," with an illustration of a sideways stick figure in full pole-dance spin. Facing forward, if you're not hanging on, you're guaranteed to be thrown by the sheer velocity of the train. It's a simple law of physics. The woman decides to relocate to a seat next to her friend—enough excitement for one day. We barrel on. The subway bangs about on the tracks like a can suddenly sent skidding down the street by the eager toe of a grinning kid in a summer game of Kick the Can. The woman's friend must've read a guidebook telling her that New Yorkers dress in head-to-toe black; though garbed thusly, she somehow still manages to look like a tourist, the pedestrian cut of her clothes more Kohl's than Bergdorf Goodman. She shouts over the din, "Where are we now?" The woman with the bobbed hair turns to search the walls that circle the platform behind her. She spots a word reflected back in sparkling, square, tiny black tiles, and with a satisfied smile spreading across her face she turns back and proclaims assuredly, "Canal!" The man seated between them is mustachioed, with a thick head of carefully coiffed black hair (no doubt a source of pride) and a beer gut. He's also dressed in head-to-toe black (likely at his wife's suggestion), with matching black leather sensible shoes with cushioned soles, no doubt in anticipation of the extra walking they'll be doing in the city. The man has the stocky build of a tradesman—a mechanic or a pipe fitter or a man who pours concrete for a living. His thick, weathered hands grip a large, unfolded paper map; hunched over it, oblivious to the women's conversation, he struggles to get his bearings on the fly—the Meriwether Lewis of this urban expedition. Like the eighteenth-century gentleman's skill of starting a fire using flint and steel from a tinderbox, map reading is quickly becoming a lost art, now largely confined to Eagle Scouts and older folks. Four out of five young people can't even read a paper map anymore; instead, they rely on Siri and Waze and Google Maps to get them to their destinations.[1] Some can't even tell the time on an analog clock. For Millennials, digital is always the preferred interface over analog.

The train hurtles onward, the din getting louder as we reach full speed, the tunnel amplifying the roar. Things are quiet again as we approach Spring Street Station. A sudden whir of air is expelled, and we begin to slow. The brakes scream, the train lurches to a halt; doors fly open with a loud bang, and the conductor's flattened voice, unintelligible, announces the station. The subway is a battleground of noises, all competing for one's attention. The train quickly staggers off again, reaching full speed in a matter of seconds; squeals, a solid whir, and some strange, high-pitched tone emanates from somewhere. The brakes scream again. We come to another halt, the doors open—quieter this time, for some reason. People shuffle in and out. Though at least twenty or more people come and go, it's surprisingly quiet—most are wearing soft-soled walking shoes. The doors slam closed again, and off we go. The man never looks up from his map.

Riding the subway is the quintessential New York City experience. It is the great equalizer, as *everyone* rides the subway—people of every age, race, and class stand or sit in close proximity, sometimes uncomfortably so during the busier times of day. In these moments, there is no such thing as personal space. As a sociologist, I find the subway endlessly fascinating, as it provides an ever-changing snapshot of the city's now nearly eight and a half million people, or what we sociologists call a "sample" of New York's diverse population. It's a bit like one of those digital picture frames where, each time you look, a different image appears. The subway here mirrors urban scenes played out daily in other American cities: commuters head to work or head home or head out for the evening in Washington, DC, on the Metro; in Boston on the "T"; and in the San Francisco Bay Area on the BART. Millennials (those aged approximately twenty-two to thirty-seven in 2018, that is, born between roughly 1981 and 1996) tend to be increasingly urban and less interested in driving or owning a car, and hence are more inclined to ride public transportation. The sights and sounds and smells of the subway (e.g., urine, sweat, freshly washed hair, cologne) are certainly not romantic, but for many, they—combined with the constant din of taxi horns honking and the white-noise whir of traffic—serve as the soundtrack of the city. This is the subway known to New Yorkers since the beginning of the transit system here, when the first subway car rattled its way down the tracks at 2:34 p.m. on October 27, 1904, with Mayor George B. McClellan symbolically standing at the wheel as engineer. The *New York Times* marked the occasion with the giddy headline "McClellan Motorman of First Subway Train" in its October 28 morning edition. A crowd of between six and seven thousand people had to be held back by two or three hundred police officers, as they pushed to be among the first to ride as soon as the ribbon was cut. When the line of policemen parted, the crowd eagerly ran toward the subway tunnel, paying a nickel apiece to be a part of the excitement, thereby avoiding the horse-and-buggy frenzy clogging the streets aboveground. The entire city took part in the festivities: factories blew their whistles; tugboats, steamships, and cargo boats tooted their horns; and church bells pealed in greeting and celebration. The opening of the subway line marked a new era in New York City, and the invention of the modern "commuter."

One hundred and fifteen years later, the subway chugs resolutely on; meanwhile, the industrial era that produced it has given way to the digital era. The

Millennial commuters aboard are now largely immune to the cacophony of the subway, sequestered away within their own highly curated digital bubbles, staring at cool glass screens. Connected to smartphones; wearing earbuds or large, over-the-ear headphones like the popular Beats by Dre in candy-hued tones of raspberry, green, or electric blue; they tune out the world, focusing instead on the bass line of Kendrick Lamar's or Drake's or Taylor Swift's or someone else's latest hit song. Heads bowed, they sit or stand hunched over their screens, heedless of the world around them, multitasking; two thumbs always at the ready, they shift constantly between reading, texting, scrolling, and going through their playlist—choosing, deleting, commenting, liking, checking messages, sharing, replying. This silent freneticism is occasionally punctuated by a smile or laughter, but most of the time the dominant expression is a blank-faced stare. They rarely look up or look around—their interaction is not human to human, but human to screen. Life is lived mediated. These behaviors go on endlessly throughout the day and night, unimpeded by work, meals, conversations, school, or any other potential distraction—even driving. At mealtime, cell phones sit at the ready, face up on breakfast, lunch, and dinner tables across the country; quick glances at them punctuate every meal. Here on the subway, frequent "dings" ring out, indicating the arrival of yet another text message. When one ring sounds, I see multiple people check their phones, unsure if it's theirs—hoping that it is. They are like Pavlov's dogs salivating at the sound of the bell in anticipation of food. Each time the cell phone's alert is played, it triggers the brain to release a little shot of dopamine, the "feel good" drug that lifts the mood and relieves pain; this "reward" mechanism ensures repeated behavior. And repeat they do: the highest-frequency cell phone users touched, tapped, or swiped their phones an unbelievable 5,427 times a day.[2] For many Millennials and those younger, these behaviors are self-reinforcing and addictive, becoming for many, to use Karl Marx's words, the new "opium of the people." The average child aged eight to eighteen now spends an average of 7 hours and 38 minutes per day, or more than 53 hours a week, "media multitasking" across various digital screens. So as never to miss a text, tweet, Facebook update, Snap, Instagram post, or—streaming video on Facebook or Periscope—now more than 70 percent of Millennials sleep with their cell phones beside them (as compared to only a third of Baby Boomers).[3]

We reach 14th Street at Union Square Station. The tall, hip-looking African American young man next to me is wearing Beats headphones in a shocking violet color. I can hear the bass and the faint, muffled chorus of Kendrick

Lamar's "Swimming Pools (Drank)."[4] The young man bobs his head in time as he shuffles between his playlist and the frequent text messages that keep coming in. He quickly texts back before checking his Instagram feed and then returns to iTunes. This circular behavior is repeated over and over during the few minutes as I stand next to him. Looking around, I do a quick visual survey of the car: Half the people in the car who appear to be under thirty are staring at screens. No one over fifty is looking at a screen—instead, they're either sitting quietly, contemplating their day, perhaps, or else they're looking around, looking at each other, talking, or if alone, some are reading a print newspaper or magazine like the *New Yorker*. Seated across the car from me is a gentleman in khakis, a blue oxford shirt, and tie, whose hair is thinning and grey. In his hands I see the familiar *New York Times* Fashion & Style section with a large photo of a rail-thin model, head turned to the left, haughtily looking down at the audience from the catwalk in a form-fitting, high-necked, modern-looking, lace-embellished dress, her chestnut hair pulled tightly away from her face in a high ponytail. It's Fashion Week in New York City.

There's a tactile pleasure in reading the Sunday *Times*, and typically a ritual to it. My father, like many of his generation, read the Sunday *New York Times* religiously every week. We'd walk down to what the locals called Don's Market on Balboa Island to pick up the hulking, three-inch-thick, several-pound bundle, haul it back home, and then we would go about sorting it into its various sections: the Front Page, the Business section, Sports, Technology, and so on. Weeding out the editorial from the advertising inserts, he'd pull out and set aside the slick, full-color glossy Style magazine, to save it for last—the cupcake of his literary feast. Picking up a section, the pages seemed huge to me. I remember the feel of the newsprint between my fingertips, the smell of the pages, and the blackness of the still-wet ink staining my fingertips. I remember trying to be careful not to get any ink on my clothes (or on Grandma's couch!). Turning the pages created a soft whooshing sound and a puff of breeze that would blow up a few wisps of the baby hair circling my face. I voraciously ate up the society pages. I knew all of the New York society women by face: Nan Kempner, Anne Bass, Pat Buckley, Mercedes Kellogg (later Bass, after she married wealthy oilman Sid Bass, Anne's ex)—always dressed in fabulous designer gowns and jewels, attending various charities and benefits. A few pages in, the corners would begin to collapse, sagging toward my face—a quick snap brought them back into line, the pages standing up straight again, one against the other, like a garrison of paper soldiers coming to attention.

These kinds of pleasurable sensual experiences are beyond most Millennials' weekly repertoire, since they get their news on cool glass screens via Facebook or Twitter or through reruns of *The Daily Show* on Hulu—if they catch the news at all. One young woman who was interviewed for a story on NPR said, "Newspapers are for old people." Paper newspapers and magazines have been struggling to survive for some time now in the wake of digital media: In 2009, the *Times*'s circulation dropped below one million, to 980,000, for the first time since the 1980s. In 2013, the paper stopped offering lifetime tenure to its reporters, a leading indicator of the uncertainty of traditional news media's future. Some papers are even turning to robots to write routine stories as a cost-cutting measure—covering everything from corporate earnings reports to baseball scores.[5] Years ago, no one foresaw that reporters' bylines would read, "Lois Lane, Ex-Machina." Digital media's impact on bookstores has also been seismic: From 1991 to 2011, over 1,100 bookstores closed their doors forever. Meanwhile, newsstand sales of print magazines have tumbled by half since 2007.[6] These changes are occurring at an increasingly fast clip, leaving "digital immigrants" or Luddites from the Silent Generation (those born before World War II) and even some Baby Boomers scrambling to keep up. Many don't even try. Yet perhaps the thrill of the "new shiny toy" of Kindles and other ebook readers is beginning to dim, as recent reports show that independent bookstores are beginning to make a comeback again.[7]

Our train screeches to a halt at my stop, 42nd Street. I get off and climb the stairs to the outside world. The bright light of the sun reflects off the grey-white winter clouds and buildings, blinding me for a second. I blink until my eyes adjust, unlock my phone to check the compass, then turn to head off toward the New York Public Library. Walking down the street, I pass a group of young people, all walking with heads bowed, staring at screens. It reminds me of that famous illustration of the Evolution of Man, shown evolving from knuckle-dragging ape to upright *Homo sapiens*. It seems now we've somehow devolved a few steps backward with the head bowed, hunched-over, "phone checking" position. Almost every young person is wearing earbuds or Beats headphones, so if you were to say hello to one or ask a question, you'd likely be met with an unacknowledged silence.

This digital immersion of sight and sound impedes their situational awareness—that is, the awareness of what's around them that has enabled our species to survive all these years by being alert to any danger in the immediate surroundings. A nice-looking kid about nineteen in a blue wool sweater, Zac Efron haircut, and earbuds has stopped directly in the middle of the sidewalk at the intersection of 42nd and 5th, completely oblivious to what's going on around him. Teams of people make their way around him like salmon avoiding a human rock in an urban stream. I walk by and stare right at him, hard, as I pass—he never looks up. This lack of situational awareness can be dangerous. In fact, some cities are now putting crosswalk lights in the pavement to catch the eye of downward-looking younger pedestrians, in the hope of avoiding accidents for those whose eyes are glued to their phones.[8] Untethering from the sights and sounds of the physical world around them allows Millennials and younger persons to focus on their own digital bubble, a curated world of their own creation, hooking in and out of outside reality when and how they please. I see this all of the time at the university where I work. One of my recent year-end evaluations from the students said I had "made eye contact during class, and it made me very uncomfortable." Unmediated interaction now seems alien to many in this crowd.

This assumed "naturalness" of digitally mediated interactions reminds me of the story of the fish in water: Two young fish are swimming along and eventually encounter an older fish swimming toward them. The older fish nods and says, "Morning, boys. How's the water?" The two young fish swim on for a bit; eventually, one looks over at the other questioningly and says, "What the hell is water?" For Millennials and those younger, digital connectivity *is* their water. A study by Cisco Systems found that half of the Millennials they surveyed say they cannot live without the internet, and a third say it is as important to them as food, air, or water. Half say it's close to that important.[9] Connectivity has become so vital that losing it seems like a life-threatening emergency. In the summer of 2014, Facebook went down, and so many people called the 911 emergency line in Los Angeles that an officer from the LA County Sheriff's Information Bureau took to Twitter to, say, "Facebook is not a law enforcement issue, please don't call us about it, we don't know when Facebook will be back up!"[10] A seventeen-year-old girl even hung herself after her parents banned her from Facebook so she would spend more time on her studies. "Is Facebook so bad?" her suicide note read, "I cannot stay in a home with such restrictions as I can't live without Facebook."[11]

This kind of digital immersion is generationally uneven: many older Americans don't own smartphones, use apps, or have profiles on social media. Walt, the owner of the boat next to mine in Marina del Rey, is one of these: at seventy-six years old, he's a curmudgeonly former Korean War fighter pilot, computer coder, and, later, assistant district attorney. One day Walt held his iPhone high in the air, waving it at me from his boat, saying, "You see these apps? I don't know what nine-tenths of 'em do, and I don't wanna know. I just wanna get rid of 'em all. I'm not an app trier." Walt doesn't text and doesn't have a profile on Facebook or elsewhere on social media. I offered to show him how the apps work, but he just wasn't interested.

Walt is not alone in his views: a vast majority of people his age, the Silent Generation, don't own smartphones. The disconnected Walts of the world, compared with the hyperconnected Millennials, are examples of the social fractures at hand between the digital haves and have-nots in society, fractures that are opening up along generational lines. This is not simply a matter of having or not having a device; instead, this digital divide encapsulates an entire constellation of cultural capital and technological savvy that goes hand in hand with living immersed in a digital culture, resulting in major differences in their ways of relating to and experiencing the world. This fracture is more than simply differing use of electronics; it, instead, signals the emergence of separate *cultures*, with very different behaviors, social rules, and value propositions. The effect of this will be tectonic, dwarfing that of the Industrial Revolution or the invention of the printing press. The resultant untethering from well-established cultural values and behaviors extends well beyond the digital realm. As a reaction to difficult economic circumstances and bolstered by these new social technologies, Millennials are disconnecting from what has been termed by many the American Dream, and they are doing so in droves. They are rewriting the rules of the social contract. This untethering has massive implications for the economic, social, and political future of our country, but these changes don't stop at the borders of the United States. What we're talking about here is unhooking from traditional social structures and ways of doings things at a global scale, facilitated by digital technologies, or what technologists call "disaggregation."[12] It signals the emergence of an untethered world. Let's take a look at a few examples.

(1) Silicon Valley: The Hacker Hotel

Adulthood, as defined by the General Social Survey—a large-scale survey conducted every two years by the National Opinion Research Center—is the achievement of five major milestones: leaving home, finishing school, becoming financially independent, getting married, and having a child.[13] Americans in the past have considered these milestones tantamount to attaining the American Dream, and a majority achieved them by age thirty-two. In the post–World War

II period, most Americans reached adulthood in their teens or early twenties. Today, Millennials are taking much longer to reach adulthood; one can wonder at this rate if they will at all. Now, many Millennials are unhooking from this dream altogether. Social media has opened up new worlds to be seen and aspired to. For some it is a cotton-candy world where everything seems possible. In this context, the American Dream may not be the major milestones sought by prior generations—that is, the achieving of specific life stages or the acquiring of certain items like a house or a spouse—but rather, they may be seen as the atmosphere in which everyone has the basic freedom to attain their aspirations, whatever those may be. Rather than a strictly defined set of milestones, it is a pastiche of creativity, entrepreneurship, experience, and chutzpah, alongside a disaggregation of the traditional ways of doing things. Take Cory, for example; he is currently living this new America Dream. Though almost thirty-five, he could easily pass for seventeen. At our last meeting at a restaurant in Portland, Oregon, the waitress refused to serve him alcohol after he'd forgotten his ID in his hotel room. Sandy-haired, nerdy, and bespectacled, Cory cuts a slightly rumpled figure in an oversized suit that hangs a bit awkwardly from his rail-thin frame, giving him the appearance of a boy in his father's clothing. Fast-thinking, fast-talking, and incessantly checking his phone, Cory lives with forty other young men in their twenties (and a handful of women) in a "hacker hotel" in San Francisco called 20Mission—a glorified frat house for techies. Others like it have sprung up in Brooklyn and even in Medellín, Colombia. There's even a catamaran now, traversing the world, called *Coboat*, whose owners describe the typical workday as, "waking up to the rocking of the ship, then grabbing a delicious breakfast in the sun before launching into the day's work. Meetings and brainstorming are interrupted only by diving and sunbathing, and you watch the sunset over drinks with your fellow coworkers."[14] Life is just one big vacation.

At 20Mission in the Bay Area, life is just one big frat party—if the frat was for engineers. Their promotional video shows a party attended by a large number of guys in hoodies and jeans, and a small handful of girls. 20Mission brands itself as a creative space for entrepreneurial activities, touting daily contact with "engineers, graphic designers, photographers, videographers, brand consultants, and well-connected Silicon Valley entrepreneurs."[15] This access to cultural capital combined with high-speed internet means potential residents will have "every resource at [their] fingertips." 20Mission, *Coboat*, and other similar shared live/work spaces like them claim to promote community, idea exchange, and a healthy dose of work-life balance. Striking that balance can be hard, though, in this atmosphere. Cory told me they had to cut the parties down at 20Mission to once a month and move them off-site because the constant late-night partying and all of the people showing up was becoming "too much." In addition to unhooking from the house with the white picket fence, Cory has also unhooked from the idea of becoming an "educated person." He says about school, "The concept of doing [school] work solely to be evaluated and discarded instead of being useful for something I could never motivate myself to do ... [and] I found work much more fulfilling."[16] With billionaire college-dropout role models such as Bill Gates, Steve Jobs, and Mark Zuckerberg, college—with its high tuition and residual back-breaking student-loan burden—now seems a barrier to success, rather than a stepping-stone toward it. Young folks like Cory do not have the benefit of the G.I. Bill to pay their way through college, as did many returning World War II veterans, and the price of tuition has skyrocketed. The student-debt load is a burden that many will never get out from under. The public educational system, developed as a way to prepare workers for factory labor, has remained largely unchanged since its inception in the industrial era. Now, it appears woefully unprepared to educate an emerging digital workforce. Many young people are eschewing education for an entrepreneurial dream or to pursue a neo-bohemian life as a barista or Uber driver or even as seasonal farm workers on organic farms around the world. Compared to Boomers, a higher percentage of Millennials report having taken some college course work (65 percent of twenty-five- to thirty-four-year-olds have some college experience, compared to 59 percent of Boomers aged forty-five to sixty-four), and a new high of 88 percent of young people in 2015 completed their high school degree. Yet, while degree seeking has risen, it seems that with grade inflation and a focus on standardized testing, educational standards have fallen, leaving younger workers unprepared.[17] With the digital transformation of the workforce, many jobs that previously didn't require higher education now do. One study estimates that by 2020, 65 percent of all jobs in the American economy will require education beyond high school.[18] Take manufacturing as an example: German manufacturing company Siemens advertised 800 positions at its new plant in Charlotte, North Carolina, in 2016. Ten thousand applicants showed up for 800 positions, yet, as the *New York Times* reported, fewer than 15 percent of the applicants were able to pass a reading, writing, and math screening test geared toward a ninth-grade education. In 1965, the United States was number one in education for college-level degrees among industrialized nations. Now, it's fallen to tenth. The United States ranks thirty-second in literacy and dead last in math out of thirty-five countries surveyed by the Organization for Economic Cooperation and Development for their Adult Skills Survey.[19] Despite this evidence to the contrary, many still believe that America is "best in the world" in these areas.

Marriage is another aspect of the American Dream losing its luster among Millennials. Cory, like many of his cohort, has no plans to marry—ever. With the ready availability of a myriad of new dating apps like Tinder and Feeld (previously known as 3nder, which is used to set up threesomes—and moresomes), monogamy may seem passé, when ordering up a new and exciting romantic or sexual partner is as easy as ordering a pizza. As Jamie Varon put it in her blog:

> When we choose—if we commit—we are still one eye wandering at the options. We want the beautiful cut of filet mignon, but we're too busy eyeing the mediocre buffet, because choice. Because choice. Our choices are killing us. We think choice means something. We think opportunity is good. We think the more chances we have, the better. But, it makes everything watered-down. Never mind actually feeling satisfied, we don't even understand what satisfaction looks like, sounds like, feels like. We're one foot out the door, because outside that door is more, more, more. We don't see who's right in front of our eyes asking to be loved, because no one is asking to be loved. We long for something that we still want to believe exists. Yet, we are looking for the next thrill, the next jolt of excitement, the next instant gratification.[20]

Cory's Facebook status proclaims that he's "in an open relationship." His girlfriend's status says the same. When I ask about it, he says that he's dating her and they're both dating another girl. The end game here isn't to "find the one" and marry—it's polyamory. A quick search of Meetup groups revealed hundreds for those seeking a polyamorous lifestyle in major cities like Los Angeles and New York. But perhaps surprisingly, they also exist in smaller bedroom communities like Boulder, Colorado; Albuquerque, New Mexico; and Orange County, California. Several of these groups boast a membership of over 2,500. Cory explained:

> I want love. . . . I want growth. I just also want to be free to explore exciting new relationships and where they take me. The popular idea of serial monogamy involves dumping a wife when you get the hots for a younger colleague. I prefer a more flexible framework. I think it makes for [a] better ability to commit.[21]

Cory sees his girlfriend every day since they live in the same building; she frequently posts pictures of them together, having drinks, going to a new ramen restaurant or sampling a charcuterie plate in some new hip Bay Area trattoria. They look like any other smiling, happy couple. Seeing the photos, I asked Cory why he doesn't commit, since they seem to get along fine. His answer was:

> I can love someone . . . have children, and fund trusts for grandchildren. These are useful commitments. Committing to only having one fun, romantic, or sexual relationship at any given time is not useful. There is an increasingly large group of people in San Francisco and NYC that are starting to see polyamory as the thing that happens after you settle down, instead of until.[22]

At this rate, the untethered life isn't so much a Hemingway-esque moveable feast as it is a life of endless appetizers. It seems that for many, the slow-moving, long-lasting commitments linked to the American Dream are becoming outdated. A 2014 survey found that half of Americans who once believed in the American Dream (defined as the belief that if you work hard, you'll get ahead) think it no longer exists. That thirty-year mortgage and "till death do us part" seem like forever when spin cycles rotate at the speed of on-demand digital technologies. Computer experts call the time it takes for something like a video to load on your phone the "latency time." Online viewers of videos now will leave if the video takes more than two seconds to load. Clearly, those who grew up as digital natives now desire a no-latency life. Yet commitments to things like a marriage or a mortgage or a college degree take time, focus, and attention—things that are in short supply these days. Given these changes, it seems that the American Dream now may not mean achieving specific life-stage milestones or acquiring certain items like a house or a car, as was the case for those living in the 1950s, but rather, it may be that the dream is more diffuse; perhaps it becomes the atmosphere itself in which everyone perceives that they have the basic freedom to attain their aspirations, to be anyone, or be anywhere—leading a life that plays well on Instagram.

(2) St. Barts, the Untethered Workforce, and "Microlives"

> *I have walked through many lives,*
> *some of them my own . . .*
>
> —Stanley Kunitz, "The Layers,"
> from *The Collected Poems of Stanley Kunitz*, 2002

Caitlin is another young person living this New American Dream. I sat down at the table on the patio at Marina del Rey's Killer Cafe across from her. She's a new acquaintance of mine, a writer from San Francisco who had been introduced to me on Facebook by a mutual friend. She struck me as warm and friendly, with a slightly impish grin; her intelligent eyes sparkling behind red cat-eyed glasses, were framed by a full mane of long, wavy, two-toned steel-grey hair. She looked every bit the San Francisco hippy in her flowing cotton Indian dress and Birkenstocks; the unmistakable aroma of patchouli wafted toward me, reminiscent in my imagination of the Summer of Love.[23] Caitlin is a digital nomad and homeless; she supports herself through writing and remote digital bookkeeping. We exchanged pleasantries about the weather, then dove into a discussion about her current living situation. She was very open to talking about it. She said she's on her way back to the Bay Area for a brief visit for a writer's event, then off to Norway and Iceland. After that is yet to be determined. At the time of our interview, Caitlin divided her time between housesitting, CouchSurfing, and Airbnb. Caitlin said she gave up all her "stuff" about three years ago, emptying her storage unit by selling what she could and giving the rest away to friends. She's at the moment a permanent digital nomad. Though at first it was a bit traumatic, she ultimately found giving away all of her stuff to be "freeing." Being on the road like a modern-day Jack Kerouac gives her the peace to write, she says. I ask her if there are any downsides. She thinks a moment, then admits that it can get lonely at times; that being gone means she can't put in the time it takes to maintaining her relationships, so some friends have begun to drift away. She admits, though, that she actually likes to leave a place when people get too close, too comfortable. When people want to "drop by" it interrupts her work, she says, so she's glad to be on to the next city or town. She lives like an urban anthropologist, exploring her latest city, getting to know the natives and their customs, and all of the cool places to go, then she leaves before she gets too embedded, or before she "goes native," as anthropologist call it. She suddenly asks, "Do you know the poet Adrienne Rich?" Of course I do. On her shoulder, I see the words, "If I get lonely . . ." tattooed there in blue ink. "I have part of her poem 'Song' tattooed on my body," she told me. "The rest is across my back. Look it up after you leave here," she said. I did. It seems to encapsulate Caitlin's nomadic lifestyle:

> You want to ask, am I lonely?
> Well, of course, lonely
> as a woman driving across country

day after day, leaving behind
mile after mile
little towns she might have stopped
and lived and died in, lonely.[24]

Noelle Hancock is another example: Untethered from marriage and home-ownership and unhooked from the thirty-five-year career typical for many Baby Boomers, she's been able to pull up the tent stakes and explore many bohemian "microlives," as I call them, a riff on what user experience, or UX designers (i.e., those who design the digital interfaces that you see when you use apps, etc.) and some sociologists call "microinteractions," or subtle moments centered around accomplishing a single task. Microlives can be thought of as time-limited living in a particular setting, before moving on to the next "life" in some other place, documenting on Instagram or Facebook shopping at a flea market in Paris, posing for a selfie in front of Angor Wat, or floating in the warm waters off of Mykonos in the Greek Isles. After seeing an image of a white, unspoiled sandy beach with swaying palm trees on her computer screen, Noelle quit her $95,000-a-year writing job in New York City, bought an airplane ticket, and left. As she put it, "Why couldn't I? With no professional obligations or boyfriend, I was completely untethered for the first time in my life."[25] She now scoops ice cream for a living on the gorgeous Caribbean island of St. Barts, spending her time off swimming, snorkeling, and watching sunsets with friends. She's now pondering a move to Europe.

"Sharing economy" sites like CouchSurfing and Airbnb, TaskRabbit, and HelpX facilitate these microlives by allowing people to digitally coordinate gig work, room, and board. Freed from the burdens and responsibilities of their own homes and families, the Untethered Generation can up and go on a whim. It's no wonder YOLO (You Only Live Once) and FOMO (Fear of Missing Out) have become the rallying cries for this generation. While sharing assets, many Millennials also feel that they're building a community or making a new friend in the process—key values for this generation.

For Millennials, growing up in the Great Recession (2007–2009) has lead them to value experiences over the acquisition of things, a virtue born of necessity, but which has far-reaching implications for the economy, particularly for shopping malls and luxury brands that have been built upon the Boomer tendency toward conspicuous consumption. Older businesses that missed the changing zeitgeist of this newly emerging economy are facing serious losses or are even failing. Long-standing brick-and-mortar stores like RadioShack, Macy's, and Polo Ralph Lauren are shuttering their doors, leaving malls struggling to survive. A 192-year-old building housing the iconic department store Lord & Taylor on 5th Avenue in New York City was recently sold to WeWork for transitory coworking spaces for untethered workers. Gump's, the 157-year-old San Francisco Bay Area landmark, has recently declared bankruptcy.[26] Meanwhile "virtual" companies like Amazon and eBay that deliver desired products right to the consumer's door through the touch of an app—some within an hour or less—are thriving. Other tech companies facilitate "sharing," borrowing, or renting, even for clothes. Why buy, when you can "Rent the Runway" for 20 percent of the cost, and have something new to wear for every occasion? Other brands have tapped into this "I want it now" sensibility driven by the fast spin of digital technologies—like those that deliver to the door to satisfy the desire of "hype beasts" for the latest athletic gear (one area where sales have continued to be strong). Athletic wear brands like Neek Lurk's Anti Social Social Club, Supreme, Off-White, and Fear of God are popular and fast-moving; Kanye West's Yeezy Calabasas shoe collection of 2017 sold out in five minutes.[27] As Ismael, a Latino songwriter and producer from Los Angeles put it,

> Social media has taken it to another level because trends, influence, and cultures are no longer restricted by location thanks to the advent of the internet. Anyone around the world can see what's "in," what's "hip," what's "cool," and mimic it. Moreover, my generation and even younger are really into online shopping. So even if, say, a kid wants this dope SUPREME hoody but doesn't have a tangible store near them, they can easily buy online. And social media has also given the power of "influencer" to anybody. So social media drives this culture of hype beast because more kids will buy this s— hoping to get more followers, views, clicks, likes. It's the whole "insta model" model but for fashion influencers.[28]

Allyah, an African American environmentalist in her mid-thirties, believes that Millennials are still very status-oriented, but that they are spending in other markets. She says, "I think Millennials spend a lot on food and experience, but they don't like the 'chain store' experience for the most part. They like to be pandered to in an artisanal or faux artisanal way. Also, spending a lot on fashion makes [a] little less sense, because you can get inexpensive facsimiles, and discard them when the winds shift. They like status-y tech, though. Or anything that signifies that they are an early adopter of something."[29]

McDonald's has been one of the most visible victims of these "changing winds" in recent years. The largest fast-food chain in the world for over sixty years now—with 36,000 restaurants in 100 countries, having served 69 million people—has been faltering.[30] It's trying to reinvent itself from a one-size-fits-all industrial food producer to the faux artisanal "customizable world" desired by younger consumers for a limited number of items. Meanwhile, "fast casual" competitors like Chipotle and Starbucks, sensitive to the new, on demand, customizable marketplace, are booming. For Chipotle, digital ordering and delivery has led to higher than average checks, landing them higher profits. Chipotle's digital users are up 65 percent from a year ago.[31] Scores of such examples of these kinds of transformations of the social, political, and business environments exist.

Playing a game they can't win after the economic downturn beginning in December 2007 (the Great Recession being the worst since the Great Depression of the 1930s), and its recovery since (or lack thereof for many middle-income or low-income Americans), Millennials are rewriting the rules. Millennials are the largest generation to come along since the Baby Boomers and are the largest group in both the workforce and consumer market since 2015. Due to their sheer numbers alone, their values, behaviors, and attitudes matter. Millennials are young, tech-savvy, and—increasingly—non-white. This combination of changing socio-demographic factors, their population size, and their tendency to want everything filtered through a digital interface means that they will leave an indelible mark on society.

Enabled by mobility and digital connectivity, the sum total of these changes represents the emergence of a new social contract with vast implications for the social, economic, and political environments whose impacts will be as significant and far-reaching as that of the printing press of the Industrial Revolution. I refer to these changes as a whole as the "Untethered Society." I define coming *untethered* as

> a condition in which ties to people, places, jobs, traditional processes, and organizing structures in society—like churches and political parties—are being weakened, broken, and displaced by digital hyperconnectivity.

Although untethering is increasing in scope across socioeconomic and generational lines, it is manifesting most notably among Millennials and those younger. An estimated 5,527,000 young people between the ages of sixteen and twenty-four are now living life untethered in the United States, totally disconnected from work or school.[32] This represents about 13 percent, or about one in seven American youth today, more than the population of thirteen states. In certain cities, like Philadelphia, the number of eighteen- to twenty-four-year-olds totally disconnected from work or school (i.e., not attending either) is as high as 25 percent. Most of the states with the highest youth disconnection rates are located in the South and Southwest, including Arizona, New Mexico, Louisiana, Alabama, and South Carolina.

Like Captain Edward Smith of the *Titanic* powering along, full steam ahead, in the "unsinkable ship," many Boomers (and those older) see only the tip of this iceberg but do not fully grasp the magnitude of the impact of what's ahead. Failing to plan ahead, and an overreliance on the "unsinkability of the ship"—we know how that story ends. The Untethered Society isn't simply about devices in hands or the number of text messages sent per month or the 1.44 billion monthly active users on Facebook or a few kids dropping out of high school. The Untethered Society represents a new set of technologies and behaviors coming together to create a new social DNA, and with it a new set of social problems and challenges to businesses and other institutions. The Untethered Society is the socio-genetic underpinning of a new constellation of behaviors, values, norms, and ideals for the Millennial generation and those following it—a double helix of technology and behavior that is reshaping the evolution of society going forward.

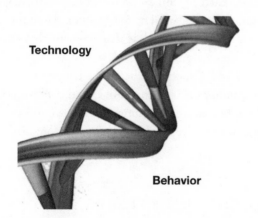

Figure 1. Double helix of technology and behavior. (Image created by the National Human Genome Research Institute, an agency of the National Institute of Health.)

Like the dinosaurs before them, large and seemingly entrenched social, financial, and political systems are unraveling and being reconfigured as a result of this coupling, with some going extinct altogether. This double helix of behavior and technology is the genetic code for the social trends of the future—trends that have far-reaching global implications to reconstitute consumer behavior, political outcomes, home, and hearth—and, indeed, the structure and workings of our very nation-state. Millennials aren't simply shunning a long-standing, traditional concept of the American Dream—they're hacking it. Groups like ISIS have already figured out how to tap into the Untethered Generation—with brutal viral videos of both beheadings and increasingly violent acts and recruitment videos that look like highly produced video games that speak to a young, untethered (male) audience who grew up gaming. Such moves leave traditional political structures at a loss for a response. This is a war being fought—and lost—in social media. It is survival of the digital fittest. Recent polls show a loss in confidence in institutions in the United States, ranging from political parties to the banks, from churches to marriage, and homeownership and family, most notably among Millennials.[33] What's happening here? How and why are more and more Americans, particularly younger Americans, untethering from the American Dream?

I visited Shanghai to talk about the untethering of Millennials in America. After my talk, many in the audience came up to me, saying they were experiencing the same phenomenon there in China with their Millennials, despite the fact that Facebook, Twitter, and other social media sites popular in the United States are banned in that country. I realized at that moment that becoming untethered isn't just a US phenomenon but, instead, we're entering a new era of an increasingly untethered world. Cybernetic theory has taught us that change is destabilizing until a new equilibrium is reached. An Untethered Society, then, is ultimately an unstable one. Entrenched institutions that don't understand the changes underway and that don't evolve to address them may potentially go the way of the dinosaurs.

TRIAD OF TECHNOLOGICAL IMMERSION

The Untethered Society represents an uncoupling and reconstitution of the social contract, in sometimes unexpected and surprising ways. Our reliance upon and embeddedness within technological systems is growing. I have developed a theoretical framework for understanding the phases of these changes, which I am calling the "Triad of Technological Immersion." It is an organizational scaffolding for the stages of technological and behavioral development. These stages are not sequential but, rather, operate simultaneously as each technological phase makes its appearance at various points of time and spreads, from its introduction and adoption by early adopters through to becoming a fully mature technology with widespread adoption by the general population. The stages behave like a symphony, where the strings come in, then the woodwinds rise up, then the brass joins in, while all eventually operate together in (hopefully) a harmonious way. Yet while these technological systems may operate as intended, there are also unintended and disruptive consequences of each that will have widespread impact on society and on human lives. These are the three stages: (1) the Untethered Society, (2) the Internet of Me, and (3) the Internet of Them.

The first stage is the Untethered Society, which we are in now, where there is a ubiquity of digitally enabled mobile devices. During this stage, there is an increasing desire for a digital interface; behaviors revolve around connectivity and there is a simultaneous *unhooking* from traditional social structures, processes, and institutions (like marriage, buying a house, having children, buying a car, having a long-term career—all aspects of what many have considered the American Dream prior to this point in time). This is our current stage of technological immersion. All this connectivity has fueled a plethora of social behaviors, from online dating to the formation of social movements (e.g., the Arab Spring, #OccupyWallStreet, #MeToo, etc.), and it has allowed many old friends to reconnect to one another via social networks. All of this connectivity has a dark side, however: as more behaviors are conducted and documented online in social media and other places, more and more data is gathered, allowing the development of computerized behavioral models that can be used in increasingly sophisticated ways to persuade or even manipulate audiences based upon their likes, fears, and psychological profiles, as seen in the recent Cambridge Analytica scandal with Facebook.[34]

Next to emerge is the Internet of Me (some call this "the Internet of Self"). This is happening now with the Internet of Things (IoT) and "smart" systems in which there is an increasing intersection between physical systems and an array of objects—from light bulbs connected to your smartphones to Alexa and Google Home to connected automobiles and smart homes—all connected via digital and information technologies. Examples include the smart grid, an array of sensors and smart-home technologies like the Nest thermostat that can be controlled from your smartphone. In the Internet of Me, environments are customizable to your preferences—the temperature and lighting are adjusted to the way you like it when you come home; perhaps your favorite music is playing when you walk through the door. This is the stage that is now beginning to emerge on a larger scale and will continue to do so with smart, connected cities in the future, where more and more things become "digitized" and connected to the internet. The Bolt light bulb from Misfit is one example: taking cues from a clip-on device on your body, it simulates a slowly brightening sunrise based on your sleep/wake patterns.[35]

The last stage on the horizon is what I call the Internet of Them. In the prior stages, humans were in the loop, in terms of controlling the technologies (e.g., pushing a button on your app to hail a cab or have dinner or groceries arrive, or setting your preferences for the lights to come on or the proper temperature for the air-conditioning or furnace at a certain time of day). In this stage, intelligence becomes embedded in devices and acts autonomously, spinning away from human control. It is human *out* of the loop. An increasing number of "things" have their own embedded artificial intelligence. They can "learn" and get smarter without human intervention, and they make decisions on their own. They will increasingly "talk to" and coordinate with other intelligent objects and agents, like autonomous cars communicating with one another to coordinate driving on the road. Examples include chatbots that will simulate their owners or others through "synthetic personalities," intelligent robotics, and automated workers. Eventually, as some researchers believe, these intelligent agents will achieve what has been called the singularity, a stage at which they exceed human intelligence and capabilities for certain tasks. For example, IBM's computer Watson recently was able to diagnose a rare form of cancer that had stumped a panel of human doctors.[36] In the Internet of Them phase, intelligent agents are linked and inter-operative, working alongside and cooperatively with other intelligent agents, interdependent with other smart systems. The social and human impact of this ranges from the positive, like artificial-intelligence-enabled robots that can help tend to our increasingly greying population, to the more troubling, including mass layoffs and "the end of jobs" for many workers in those parts of the economy in which automation can replace human labor. These impacts may well span beyond the factory walls and into white-collar sectors including law, medicine, accounting, and other fields. A key factor differentiating this from earlier technological innovations, which many people fail to account for, is the exponential increase in the pace of change. The chart below shows the adoption rates of various technologies, and the time it took for them to reach majority adoption in American households. For example, compared to the time it took steam power, on average, to saturate a country (about one hundred years) or electrification (about sixty years), it could take only about sixteen years for the internet to fully saturate a country.

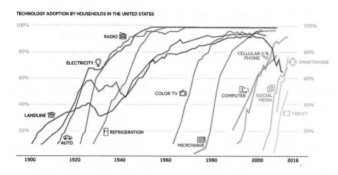

Chart 1. Consumption Spreads Faster Today. (The Visual Capitalist.)

Technological disruption is faster now, making it more difficult for people to keep up with and adapt to these new technologies. With the spread of robotics, automation, and artificial intelligence, some are simply bound to be left behind, the detritus of the digital divide.

The aim of this book is to start a conversation about the impacts that digital devices and the constant connectivity to them is having on society. This book will begin to explore in more depth the various social and psychological impacts of our increasingly technology-embedded lives, and the fractures taking place because of it, focusing on the first of these stages, the Untethered Society. I'll attempt to address a number of questions about the impact of ubiquitous, connected digital technologies on our social world and lives, to begin the conversation, including:

What challenges do we face as we enter an increasingly untethered world?

What does it mean when a generation grows up where reality is filtered through a digital interface? In relationships, what impact will an endless sea of attractive and available others online have on relationships, marriage, and the family?

How are businesses being impacted by a digital-first consumer and workforce? How do they need to change to adapt?

What will it mean for human brains when more and more "physical" work is simulated, and more cognitive work is transferred to digital devices? What impact do digital devices have on learning, memory, and the ability to think and focus?

For every movement, there is a countermovement. What counterforces are emerging in response to untethering? In what ways are people beginning to resist the Untethered Society and reconnect to physicality, nature, the body, and so on?

And, last, what changes are afoot as we enter an increasingly untethered world?

But, first, how did we get here? How did we become tethered in the first place, and when did everything change?

CHAPTER 1

BECOMING TETHERED: THE AMERICAN DREAM

Americans forever imagine the lands further off are still better than those upon which they are already settled. . . . If they attained Paradise, they would move on if they heard of a better place farther west.
—Lord Dunmore, Royal Governor of Virginia, 1744

MAY 8, 1945. 10 DOWNING ANNEX, LONDON

Prime Minister Winston Churchill reached over and picked up the navy-blue leather-bound notebook he'd set down on the bedside table; he opened to the page he was working on when his secretary, John Miller Martin, interrupted him with the telegrams. He opened the one from Clementine, his wife first. Lady Churchill was in Moscow, having been dispatched there to deliver a burden of gratitude to the Soviets in the form of both aid and goodwill in her role as chairman of the Red Cross Aid to Russia Fund. Hearing of Germany's surrender, she cabled her husband immediately, saying, "All my thoughts are with you on this supreme day, my Darling. It could not have happened without you."[1] The second telegram was from US President Harry S. Truman. It read, "With warm affection, we hail our comrades-in-arms across the Atlantic." May 8 was the president's sixty-first birthday. In a few hours he would write to his mother with news of the German surrender: "Isn't that some birthday present?"[2]

After reading the telegrams, Churchill took his breakfast in bed: a poached egg, toast with butter and jam, cold chicken, milk, and grapefruit, followed by a whiskey soda and a cigar. He took a sip of his morning whiskey, lit the cigar with a big match, took a puff, then settled back to work. He often composed his speeches in bed, and today would be no different. He felt comfortable there and knew no one would bother him, save Mr. Martin, his private secretary. He found it easier to concentrate there than in the War Office with all its interruptions.

Churchill turned his attention back to the notebook and read the sentence again quietly to himself, "This is your victory!" The words, written in his usual rather-flat cursive style in black ink with his favorite fountain pen, were still damp on the page. He turned the first line of the speech over in his head. Churchill knew he had to strike just the right note: celebratory, yet somber—there was still far too much work to be done to repair the damage incurred during the Blitz of Hitler's Luftwaffe. Starting in September 1940, London was bombed for fifty-six days. More than a million homes were destroyed. Industrial centers, ports, and other strategic locations were targeted, as were civilians. Churchill had just rung off the telephone with Lord Woolton, the Minister of Food, whom he'd called to make sure there was enough beer in London for a proper celebration before he made the big announcement. The minister assured him there was. Churchill knew full well that his people would waste no time hoisting a pint to celebrate after six hard-fought, war-torn years. Both the rationing and the nightly black-outs had taken their toll on most Londoners' morale. Churchill knew his people had grown war-weary and were ripe for celebration.

After scrawling out the final lines, Churchill got up and rang for his valet, Frank Sawyers, to come help him get ready for his public appearance. He then set off down the hall and descended the set of stairs that led to the basement War Room for the penultimate time. Technicians were already there shuffling about, checking the microphone for the official announcement, which had been set for 3:00 p.m. Churchill was late and a bit irritable; he shouted at the sound engineer, "Pull down that blind!" then blew his nose rather loudly, leaving the crowd of typists and private secretaries tittering in the hallway, their ears pressed to the Cabinet Room door to hear the announcement. At 3:40 p.m., Churchill finally leaned forward and began, "My dear friends," he said, "This is your hour . . ." The cheers outside could be heard all the way into the basement.[3]

Later that night, Churchill reached over the papers stacked neatly on the big wooden desk in the ministry and picked up another of his fat, hand-rolled Cuban cigars. They had become a kind of trademark for him; he was never without one. He had developed an affinity for them in Cuba in 1895. Bored, he had taken a trip there, seeking "vital action" as a military observer. Upon arriving in Havana, he indulged in sweet oranges and cigars for days. Churchill clipped off the cap with his cutter, opened his mouth and bit down on the pungent cigar, lit the end, then sent a dark blue-grey ring of the thick, rich smoke lazily skyward. At 5:40 p.m., Churchill and some of the men from his cabinet walked out onto the balcony. Below, twenty thousand Londoners shouted, chanted, danced, and sang the national anthem. The scene could only be described as an outpouring of pure joy. On the balcony, the jubilation was palpable. Other ministry men and their staffs jostled for position on adjacent balconies to get a look at the growing crowd. People had heard the radio announcement, and news had traveled fast via word of mouth and through special editions of the papers that were flying out of the hands of the boys excitedly hawking them on every street corner. The crowd quickly swelled to over fifty thousand strong. Churchill lifted his hat, then set it down and lifted his fingers in a "V for Victory" sign. The crowd roared and broke into a spontaneous round of "For He's a Jolly Good Fellow." Eventually, darkness fell, and klieg lights were trained upon the balcony. Churchill took the cigar out of his mouth, and, smiling, tentatively began to address the cheering crowd below. "God bless you all!" he began. The crowd cheered and waved. Some held up Union Jacks; others hitched women or children up atop their broad shoulders to allow them a better view. Servicemen waved blown-up condoms tied to sticks they'd bought from street vendors (balloons were still in short supply due to the rubber shortage). Big Ben rang and church bells pealed along in celebration. Roused by the crowd's enthusiasm, Churchill bellowed, "THIS IS YOUR VICTORY!" The crowd shouted back, "NO, IT'S YOURS!" and began to cheer again. Churchill looked at his men, then began again in a measured tone, "God bless you all. This is YOUR victory. It is the victory of the cause of freedom in every land. In all our long history we have never seen a greater day than this. Everyone, man, or woman, has done their best. Everyone has tried. Neither the long years, nor the dangers, nor the fierce attacks of the enemy, have in any way weakened the independent resolve of the British nation." He closed the speech with another, "God bless you all."[4]

On the other side of the Pacific, President Truman awoke at 6 a.m. from a restless sleep. Though victory was in hand in Europe, America was still caught in a deadly struggle with the Japanese. This was no time for Americans to let their guard down. Just twenty-eight days into his fourth term, President Franklin D. Roosevelt had died suddenly of a cerebral hemorrhage, just as the war he'd led for nearly two terms was drawing to a close. Vice President Truman was unexpectedly sworn in as president just two hours after the announcement that Roosevelt had died. It was bittersweet, then, that Truman—and not Roosevelt—would be the one to deliver the message to the American people on this momentous occasion that Germany had surrendered. At 8:15 a.m., Truman sat down at his desk in the Oval Office. Today's announcement would be restrained; there would be no Churchill-esque victory signs, no celebrations. His wife, his daughter, and a few aides were in chairs clustered around his desk. Truman admonished the reporters that there would be no speculation or news releases of any kind before 9 a.m.—plenty of time for most people to begin their work day and carry on with their normal routines. He wanted the celebrations contained. We were, after all, still at war, and Japan had proven a formidable enemy. The Oval Office was jammed with reporters. Truman began reading the announcements, "This is a solemn but glorious hour. I wish that Franklin D. Roosevelt had lived to see this day. . . . General Eisenhower informs me that the forces of Germany have surrendered to the United Nations. The flags of freedom fly all over Europe. For this victory, we join in offering our thanks to the Providence which has guided and sustained us through the dark days of adversity and into light. . . . It's celebrating my birthday today, too."[5] "Happy Birthday, Mr. President!" the reporters chimed in, chuckling. He smiled and went on to read a second press release regarding Japan, saying, "Much remains to be done. The victory won in the West must now be won in the East." He paused a moment, then looked at the reporters, with a serious expression, and said, "I want that emphasized time after time, that we are only half through." He continued, "If I could give you a single watchword for the coming months, that word is work, work, and more work. We must work to finish the war. Our victory is only half over." Truman's tone reverberated in reports across the nation. Many cities ordered the immediate shuttering of liquor stores and taverns, to avoid drunken celebrations. There was much more work to be done. Work, work, and more work.

The war raged on. Yet in a strange way, it brought people together, if only for the simple reason that all had sacrificed: Whether rich or poor, Northern or Southern, Democrat or Republican, the war became the great equalizer. All had been impacted, from sending young men to war via the national draft to rationing, recycling, and other war efforts at home. The Office of War Information issued a series of graphic posters to encourage this "all hands on deck" approach, with slogans like "Use It Up—Wear It Out—Make It Do—or Do Without!"[6]

Food was one area hard-pressed during the war, due to the strain of feeding over sixteen million troops. President Roosevelt was quoted in 1943 saying that, "Meats and fats are as much munitions in this war as are tanks and aeroplanes."[7] Groceries remained in short supply, including cheese, butter, margarine, silk, nylon, canned milk, jams, jellies, shortenings, and oils. In 1941, Roosevelt appointed Leon Henderson to the unenviable position of "price czar" in the newly formed Office of Price Administration to help stabilize prices and ration foods to avoid hoarding and shortages. Housewives were given ration booklets that contained stamps for many items—from rubber products to sugar and coffee—which they took with them to the local grocer. The grocer would then remove a number of stamps from the booklet when items were purchased. Once the monthly allotment of stamps was gone, no more of the particular item was to be had until the next month's stamps were issued. Henderson's seemingly arbitrary and mysterious rationing and price-control methods frustrated both producers and consumers alike. Prices and point values could fluctuate widely from week to week, meaning housewives had to juggle both ration points and cash budgets on the fly. Other times, ingredients like sugar or red meats were simply not available. The government began to issue cookbooks like, *Recipes to Match Your Sugar Ration* or *Eating for Victory* to help housewives keep pace. One issued by Pillsbury Flour called *How to Bake Fightin' Food* promised recipes to "keep your family fit," using "meat extenders, sugar savers, fruit extenders, vegetable extenders, and many [recipes] for non-rationed food."[8] The government rolled out public-relations campaigns to help manage the shortages, calling for "Meatless Tuesdays" and "Wheatless Wednesdays."

Meat was particularly scarce during the war. Many housewives turned to hot dogs to satisfy their family's appetites. When those grew scarce, manufacturers began to adulterate them to stretch the meat, filling them with soybeans, potatoes, or cracker meal. The Committee on Food Habits was formed to figure out how to change America's eating habits. Noted anthropologist Margaret Mead and psychologist Kurt Lewin were tapped to join the council, which was sponsored by the Department of War, to consider ways to enact widespread behavioral change around food. The difficulty in that effort lay in the fact that food isn't merely sustenance but is also laden with many varied personal, cultural, and sometimes religious meanings. Taking this into consideration, rather than trying to enact radical change in Americans' diets (which was bound to fail), the committee suggested instead "small changes" like encouraging the substitution of organ meats uncommon in most American's diets, meats like liver, brains, intestines, and sweetbreads "for variety." To this end, the government issued cookbooks, and community cooking classes sprung up to teach housewives how to prepare these "variety meats." Advertisements began to appear for meats like rabbit that said, "No Meat Stamps Required." Ads in popular magazines like *Life* suggested that eating these unusual meats was "patriotic." Americans begrudgingly went along with these changes, yet many began to question the food-ration system, which seemed to have a sort of "feast or famine" quality about it. Certain foods—like potatoes or eggs—would disappear completely, then reappear in a glut, giving consumers the sense that there was no rhyme or reason to the system, which weakened people's resolve.[9]

Americans were also encouraged to plant "victory gardens"—food-producing gardens in their own homes. Government PR campaigns told them that "Food Is a Weapon;" Posters featuring slogans like "Plant Your Victory Garden—Food Is Fighting" and "Make Your Rations Go Further" encouraged food conservation and the growing of one's own food. Newsreels screened before films in theaters taught Americans forgotten skills like sowing seeds and using pesticides to kill predatory bugs. Featuring the headline, "Of Course I Can," one poster showing a young woman, arms overloaded with home-canned jams, was aimed at encouraging young women to practice the mostly lost art of canning. Americans got the message and pulled together to "do their part." By war's end, nearly fifty-five million victory gardens had been planted.

Other consumer items were also in short supply. Before stepping down as price czar in 1942, Henderson ordered a moratorium on the sales of all civilian cars and trucks. Detroit auto production facilities were converted to military production to aid the war effort, building aircraft engine parts, scout vehicles, and cannon barrels instead of cars. Production was curtailed on metal office furniture, radios, phonographs, vacuum cleaners, washing machines, and sewing machines. Metal was a key ingredient for artillery, tanks, and other war machinery, but also for the millions of canteens needed for soldiers on the front lines.

Rationing even went so far as to specify the amount of wool one could use to make a man's suit: In 1942, the War Production Board called for "streamlined suits by Uncle Sam," effectively forbidding the production of the long, wide-lapelled zoot suits popular with African American and Latino youth. The result was the infamous Zoot Suit Riots that broke out in June 1943. For a week, thousands of servicemen stationed in California—including Marines, Navy men, and soldiers—stalked and beat up local Latinos—some as young as twelve or thirteen years old—because they felt that the extra fabric required to make the zoot suits was wasteful and unpatriotic. One hundred fifty Latinos were injured in the melees, and another five hundred were arrested for charges ranging from "vagrancy" to "rioting." Similar riots broke out in other cities across the nation.[10]

THE TURNING POINT

One forty-five on the morning of August 6, 1945, marked the turning point: Colonel Paul W. Tibbets Jr. fired up the engines on the four-propeller Boeing B-29 Superfortress bomber. At 2:00 am, he and his crew rolled down the runway in the *Enola Gay*, named after Tibbets's mother, accompanied by both navigation and photography planes. At 8:15:15 a.m. local time, the airplane lurched as it released its 9,700-pound cargo—the devastating "Little Boy" nuclear bomb, which contained the equivalent of 16,000 tons of dynamite. Sixty thousand Japanese were killed instantly. Even though it was by then over ten miles away, the plane that dropped the bomb was pummeled by a 2.5 G shock wave from the blast.[11] Sergeant Joseph Stiborik, the radar operator on the mission, remembers the crew sitting in stunned silence. The co-pilot, Captain Robert Lewis, was the only one who spoke, uttering the words, "My God. What have we done?"[12] Between 90,000 and 146,000 Japanese would die as a result of the bombing. Yet despite the massive fatalities and injuries, the response from Japan was only silence. Two days later, Major Charles Sweeney fired up the engines on another Superfortress bomber, the *Bockscar*, on the island of Tinian, some 1,500 miles south of Japan. Sweeney and his crew took off at 3:47 a.m., armed with a second nuclear warhead, nicknamed "Fat Man." Their destination: Nagasaki.

NEW YORK, CAFE ZANZIBAR

Life on the mainland rumbled on. Unbeknownst to many, the explosion of the American Dream was on the near horizon. With a dearth of consumer goods available to buy, many attended local dance halls to pass the time. Others stayed home, listening to live broadcasts of big band remotes from the big cities. On this particular night, the show broadcast from Cafe Zanzibar in New York City. The announcer's familiar smooth voice rang out steady and true as he announced this week's episode of the big band show. Listeners across America—many who tuned in faithfully every week—heard him say something like, "This program is coming to you from Cafe Zanzibar on Broadway in New York City, where we bring you the Prince of Hi De Ho, Mr. Cab Calloway, who will entertain you with some hot shot razz-ma-tazz."[13] Cafe Zanzibar was one of the hottest nightclubs in the city, and one of the few that welcomed a mixed audience of black and white patrons. The war had begun to change the status quo between blacks and whites in America: African American servicemen had enjoyed a rare degree of respect and near-equality while serving in the armed forces, spear-headed by the Tuskegee Airmen, the first group of black pilots ever trained by the Air Force. These airmen had an impeccable record: Over the course of two hundred missions, they'd never lost a bomber to enemy fire. Their symbol was the Double V, which stood not only for victory abroad, but for victory at home as well, against the social ills of racism, discrimination, and Jim Crow preva-lent at the time.[14] These social changes reverberated back to the States, changing many people's views on race relations.[15] At the same time, the so-called New Negro sensibilities begun during the Harlem Renaissance began to gain popu-larity through popular radio shows. Also, network radio had spread since the Depression, affording these musicians both new venues and new audiences for their live shows.

First opening its doors on Broadway between 50th and 51st in Man-hattan in 1943, Club Zanzibar billed itself as the "Home of the Stars," fea-turing "sepia" chorus girls called the Zanzibeauts who were "the most beautiful around."[16] Unlike some of the other popular clubs at the time, the Zanzibar accepted "mixed" black and white audiences, which lead to its success with both orchestras and the public. The club owners advertised aggressively, offering air-conditioning that "has Mother Nature beat all hollow" and a $2 dinner, giving patrons the opportunity to sit inside on a hot summer's night, watch the band, and dance before and after dinner—all of which made it a popular date spot. The Zanzibar was a big success, prompting its owners to negotiate a move to a bigger space down the street at 49th and Broadway and to rename it "Cafe Zan-zibar." The new venue offered three shows a night, packing in as many as 350 guests at a time. Cafe Zanzibar hosted some of the biggest names in big band, swing, and jazz of their time, including Duke Ellington, Ella Fitzgerald, Count Basie, and Louis Armstrong.[17] That night, the heavy gold velvet curtains parted, and out stepped Cab Calloway—one of the most popular bandleaders of the day. The audience cheered in delight. With his wide smile and high-energy showmanship, Cab was a crowd favorite. Sporting a wide-lapelled zoot suit; a well-groomed mustache; and long, straight, glossy black hair that he loved to swing, he grinned as the orchestra swung into the peppy "Foo a Little Bally-Hoo." Striding down the stairs, his legs snaked out this way and that, giving the distinct impression he might just be made out of rubber. Reaching the ground floor, Cab broke into an exuberant tap dance as he sang, grinning and mugging for the audience. The crowd went wild, and more couples crammed themselves onto the already-packed dance floor, joining a frenzy of kicking legs, flying arms, and twirling skirts. White and black couples danced the Lindy Hop and Jitterbug side by side, bumping up against each other in a whirlwind of sweat and passion. The women's twirling skirts flew up like morning glories, revealing flashes of large white underpants underneath. The energy was palpable, and lots of happy laughter and bright smiles filled the room.

Since the Depression, big band remotes broadcast from places like Cafe Zanzibar had become a popular form of entertainment. Radio stations liked them because they were popular and relatively cheap to produce. The shows garnered wide audiences nationwide, with many tuning in faithfully each week to hear the latest music from the big cities. This night was not to be the typical weekly broadcast, however: At 1:30 a.m. (ET), the music suddenly fell silent, and the announcer broke in with an urgent-sounding, breathless announcement, repeating it several times, as if even he couldn't believe what he was saying: "From the Mutual Newsroom in New York: Tokyo Radio says acceptance of Potsdam Proclamation coming soon. I repeat: Tokyo Radio's acceptance of Potsdam Proclamation coming soon."[18] The excited voice of a man shouting the news to someone, perhaps on the phone, can be heard in the background. Chaos then erupted: Someone shouted, "No, No!" perhaps uncertain the news was really happening. The announcer then said, "One moment please," followed by a long pause. Finally, the announcer continued his announcement with an imploring tone: "Please, I repeat this bulletin—Tokyo Radio says acceptance of Potsdam Proclamation coming soon. The bulletin from San Francisco—Tokyo Radio said today that an Imperial message accepting the Potsdam Proclamation would be forthcoming soon. . . . For the news, listen to your Mutual station."[19] The orchestra horns blared up in a wild swing. The news was out: Japan would surrender; World War II was over. That night, the celebration at the Zanzibar lasted well into the night.

KEEPING UP

The idea of the American Dream was iterated and developed over time. Though it had been implied in the various stories about "the Land of Eden" sent back to those who remained in Europe by the original settlers who sought a better life in the New World, the actual concept of the American Dream wasn't articulated until several hundred years later, in 1931. It was then that historian James Truslow Adams named and described it in an essay:

> The American Dream that has lured tens of millions of all nations to our shores in the past century has not been a dream of merely material plenty, though that has doubtlessly counted heavily. It has been much more than that. It has been a dream of being able to grow to fullest development as man and woman, unhampered by the barriers which had slowly been erected in the older civilizations, unrepressed by social orders which had developed for the benefit of classes rather than for the simple human being of any and every class.[20]

One aspect of this early America Dream that has abided to this day is the notion of "keeping up." First coined by Arthur R. "Pop" Momand in 1913 in a *New York Globe* cartoon strip called *Keeping Up with the Joneses*, the phrase at once articulated and mocked American's aspirational hopes. It is still used overtly or is alluded to even to this day, from advertisements featuring "the good life," to music videos starring blinged-out rappers, to the Insta accounts of the Rich Kids of Instagram, to the reality show *Keeping Up with the Kardashians*.[21] "Keeping up" has become a trope for couples keeping an eye on their neighbors' and friends' places in the race for conspicuous consumption. A popular bumper sticker from the 1980s, which evolved into license-plate frames, capturing this sensibility reads, "He who dies with the most toys, wins."[22]

But what exactly are people keeping up *with*? What are the markers that they (or we) have "made it"? Ask most older Americans to define the American Dream, and they'll tell you some version of: being married, having a career, and owning a home with a white picket fence, 2.5 kids, a dog, and a car. Achieving these goals signaled to others that you'd "made it" as an adult. This idea of the American Dream stands in as a kind of shorthand for what sociologists call "social mobility"—that is, the ability to move up in the world from even meager social class beginnings. There are of course variations on the Dream: How *big* your house is, the type and make of your car, whether your job entails a corner office and a title, how beautiful or handsome or successful your spouse is, how well-groomed and spoiled your children are, what private school they attend, where your family vacations, and so on. Having the children in a private versus public elementary school, for example, is a sign of status flaunted by some parents' license-plate frames affixed to their luxury import cars or name-dropped at parties to signal status. These days the tuition at some of the more prestigious private elementary schools can rival that of a good college. Parents fret over getting their kids into the "right" kindergarten, which is thought to ensure "future success for junior and unrivaled cachet right now for Mom and Dad."[23] The idea is that each generation can do a little bit better than their parents.

THE GOLDEN AGE OF THE AMERICAN DREAM

The end of the Second World War and the return of the troops marked the moment in this country when we were most "tethered" to this Dream. Sociologists refer to this period as "the golden age of the family," since the return of the troops after the end of the war and the end of years of sacrifice on the home front breathed new life into marriage and family in the 1950s. The GDP in the United States had dropped by 20 percent during the Great Depression that preceded our entry into World War II, which brought with it an economic growth of 2.5 percent per year for the United States from 1950 to 1973. African Americans lagged behind these gains, as it took the passage of the Civil Rights Act in 1964 for them to attain full representation in skilled jobs. National figures then show a sharp upward shift in relative black incomes between 1965 and 1975.[24] Taking a longer view, the post-industrial years represented the sharpest economic growth in history.[25] The post–World War II years were the boom years. After the hardship of the war both at home and abroad, and the years of separation, couples were exuberant the hostilities had ended, and they were eager to start their families.

Veterans, upon their return from the European and Pacific theaters had much to celebrate. They came home to exuberant crowds and ticker-tape parades, an economy that would soon be booming, and love in the air. Prior to the war, America's financial situation was dire. The Depression and the Dust Bowl of the 1930s had left 16 million people floundering; many ended up homeless and jobless as the nation's industrial production fell 44 percent from 1929 levels. Scores of farmers faced foreclosure on their farms, and banks failed. Local governments strained at the seams, trying to provide relief.[26] America's "exceptionalism" rose at the end of the war, when the United States ended up in what may have been seen in the long view as a historically unique position. The Marshall Plan channeled $13 billion into a massive European recovery, guaranteeing a market for US-produced goods that propelled the economy. At the same time, much of Europe's and Japan's industrial base had been destroyed, leaving the

United States with little to no outside manufacturing competition. China had also been hit hard, after eight war-torn years of the Sino-Japanese War. This perfect storm put the United States in a position of economic dominance, in control of capital worldwide, ushering in what some have called the golden age of capitalism. This clear US economic advantage lasted until the early 1970s. It was a time when, for many, "America was great." It was the apex of what many considered the American Dream.

Servicemen and their families benefited greatly during the postwar boom years: The Servicemen's Readjustment Act of 1944, commonly referred to as the "G.I. Bill," gave them a "leg up" to the American Dream as never before or since. The bill offered them everything from low-cost mortgages to loans to start businesses, to tuition to enroll in college.[27] Millions took advantage of this opportunity, enrolling in colleges and training programs, and buying newly built tract homes in the suburbs. Women who had turned out to work in military munitions and related manufacturing and other positions during the war effort were encouraged to "return to their normal roles" as housewives and mothers in these newly built suburban tract homes. Betty Friedan, author of *The Feminine Mystique*, described the zeitgeist of the moment, saying:

> Millions of women lived their lives in the image of those pretty pictures of the American suburban housewife, kissing their husbands goodbye in front of the picture window, depositing their station wagons full of children at school, and smiling as they ran the new electric waxer over the spotless kitchen floor. . . . Their only dream was to be perfect wives and mothers; their highest ambition to have 5 children and a beautiful house, their only fight to get and keep their husbands. They had no thought for the unfeminine problems of the world outside the home; they wanted the men to make the major decisions. They gloried in their role as women and wrote proudly on the census blank: "Occupation: housewife."[28]

Anna "Jeri" Leukering was one such woman. Her father owned the feed and grain store of Round Knob, Illinois, as well as the general store, and the local post office in a town of fewer than one thousand people. Yet despite her father being a relative mogul in this small town, Jeri dreamed of getting out, of leaving the small-town life behind to pursue new, exciting adventures in the big city. Despite Jeri's parents' warnings that they'd end up in the "white slave trade," Jeri and her girlfriend Rhea hatched a plan and caught a Greyhound bus out of nearby Metropolis to start a new life in New York City. Three days later, they arrived. They dreamed of staying at the Barbizon, the famous Manhattan women's hotel that had housed many a star of stage and screen, as well as noted writers.[29] Young women of the day dreamed of becoming "Barbizon Girls," selected on criteria including looks, dress, and demeanor. The "girls" then entered a sorority-like atmosphere, supervised by the watchful eyes of hotel "House Moms." Both men and cooking in the rooms were strictly forbidden. Unfortunately, the Barbizon was out of their price range. They instead checked into the lower-priced Allerton Hotel for Women on East 57th Street, but they weren't there long. They soon found an apartment in bohemian Greenwich Village for $40 a month (the equivalent of about $500 a month in today's dollars). Rhea found a job as a receptionist on Wall Street, and Jeri ran the cosmetics counter at Saks Fifth Ave in Midtown. One afternoon, a handsome young man in uniform strolled in. Spotting the attractive chestnut-haired woman behind the counter, Taylor Meloan quickly strode up and feigned bewilderment at all of the choices. He told Jeri he needed help picking out a perfume for his girlfriend. She recommended a small bottle of Guerlain "Shalimar." He smiled, paid the bill, and left with his purchase. In reality, there was no girlfriend; the entire thing had been a ruse quickly concocted to speak with the comely girl behind the counter. A few days later, Taylor returned, saying he and the girlfriend had broken up, and he gave Jeri the perfume. He then asked her to dinner, and she accepted. After a few months of dating, Taylor proposed, and they were married a few months later in a small civil ceremony.[30]

The Meloans were the typical Mr. and Mrs. America of the time, the "every family" of the postwar era. Like millions of other servicemen, Taylor Meloan was ready to claim his stake in the American Dream. After the war, Taylor and Jeri moved back to St. Louis, where he used the G.I. Bill to pay for college. It provided a monthly stipend for tuition, books, fees, and living expenses. He earned a bachelor's degree in business, followed by an MBA, then finally a doctorate from Indiana University. Along the way, they had had two boys, Steven and Michael.

In 1960, the newly minted Dr. Meloan piled his wife, the two young boys, and all their belongings into their new white station wagon in Bloomington, Indiana, and headed for Los Angeles. Dr. Meloan had accepted a plum job as chair of the Business Department at the University of Southern California, an opportunity that would be unheard of right out of graduate school today. The Meloan boys were excited about this new adventure: Shows like *Leave It to*

Beaver and *The Adventures of Ozzie and Harriet* had given them the impression that life in LA would be clean, orderly, and pleasant, with sunny skies, mani-cured lawns, and little conflict. The three-day trip from Indiana to Los Angeles afforded much time for the boys' anticipation to grow. They were headed for the Cloud Motel as a temporary home in Downtown LA. The Cloud was decorated in the popular midcentury modern style, from its bright-orange bedspreads, to the matching orange Eames-style chairs lined up at the bar, to the giant orange triangle-shaped sign outside, which was topped by a white, cloud-like oval that framed the word *Cloud*.

In *On the Road*, writer Jack Kerouac described his stay in a similar hotel in LA, though in much bleaker terms than the boys' imaginations:

> I could hear everything, together with the hum of my hotel neon. I never felt sadder in my life. L.A. is the loneliest and most brutal of American cities; New York gets godawful cold in the winter but there's a feeling of wacky comrade-ship somewhere in some streets. L.A. is a jungle.[31]

Ultimately the Meloans' arrival would turn out to be more like Kerouac's jungle than the sanitized homogeneity of *Leave It to Beaver*. Steven recounts the family's arrival in LA:

> At the Northwest corner of Pershing Square in Downtown L.A., there once stood a diner—"Googies." That was where we arrived, fresh from the mid-west. Our Ellis Island. It had been a long, hard drive for everyone, in our boat-like 1960s-era Mercury. My parents could only cover a few hundred miles a day—because my brother and I were always hungry, or bored, or needed to pee. After a half-day of driving, my father would finally give-in, check us into a road-side "Motor Hotel," where we would swim, eat burgers, bounce like monkeys between beds in the musty room, and then finally fall into exhausted sleep. The final stretch had seemed an eternity of highway—parched plains, tin-badge sheriffs wanting payments for (we suspected) manufactured infractions . . . and the haunted moonlit expanse of the Mojave Desert. My parents had purchased an aftermarket air-conditioner for our new car—a rare luxury for the time. But because of it, the car was endlessly overheating. Knowing nothing about such things, my college-professor father opened the hood, cars roaring past us in the starry night. He pulled out his handkerchief, loosening the radiator cap, unleashing a boiling geyser of water that blew nearly ten feet into the air. My mother applied Vicks VapoRub (there in case my brother or I fell ill) to his badly

blistered forearm, and we continued on into the desert expanse. So, after all that, it was a relief to have finally arrived—to be in Los Angeles. We pulled in at midnight off the Harbor Freeway, our legs stiff, our butts numb. Rolling down the windows brought a distant roar of traffic, which I imagined to be the ocean. The summer breeze carried with it the smell of oranges and dust, and other new and indefinable things. And Downtown L.A. wasn't much back then, almost a ghost town by night. My brother whispered over to me, "It's not very nice here, is it? Not like Indiana." My mother peered out into the solitary darkness, involuntarily gathering her coat around her. I watched her tired face lit in pale fluorescence, reflected in the car's window glass.[32]

The Cloud was home for the Meloans for several months, until they closed escrow on one of the newly built tract homes in the LA suburb of Hawthorne. The Meloans liked that it was safe, near a school, and that there was a big backyard for the boys to play in. The neighborhood showed signs of other families living there: bikes littered the lawns of several nearby homes, and a house across the street and one three doors down had installed basketball hoops over the garage. It seemed like a wholesome place to raise kids and start a new life.

Dr. and Mrs. Meloan settled in quickly. The boys made friends with the neighbor kids, and the Meloans hosted frequent cocktail parties for Dr. Meloan's USC colleagues. Dr. Meloan was the most educated man on the block—most of the other neighborhood men were blue-collar working-class folks or skilled craftsman. The short Italian fellow next door, Mr. Rossi, worked as a tailor in the men's department at the Macy's in the South Bay Galleria. At the time, even someone on a tailor's salary could afford to buy a house in LA, while supporting a stay-at-home wife and two children. Now, the average price of a home in that area is $689,000,[33] necessitating a yearly income of $133,164 to afford it, which is far more than the average tailor's salary of $31,000 a year.[34] Most Americans during this time could gain a foothold in the American Dream, and fully 60 percent of adults owned their own home.

Millions of veterans like Dr. Meloan received federal loan guarantees to buy homes, get college educations, start families, and get their stake in the American Dream. From 1944 to 1952, the Veterans Administration backed nearly 2.4 million home loans for war veterans.[35] By the end of the 1950s, one-third of Americans lived in the suburbs. Eleven of the twelve largest cities in America experienced notable declines in population, as suburban tract housing became the rage.[36] Cars had been scarce during the war years, due to the rationing of rubber, steel, and other components, and the use of auto makers' factories for war production. As Detroit got back into the car business again, car makers encouraged Americans to get rid of their older vehicles and buy new "family wagons." Advertising and year-over-year radical design changes in automotive features and car bodies encouraged Americans to scrap their older models and buy new. By 1960, Americans owned more cars than all the rest of the world put together. Station wagons became popular to transport large families from the suburbs into the cities.

Marriage rates during this time reached an all-time high, with annual rates of 143 out of 1,000 single women marrying each year (up from 99 out of 1,000 in the 1920s). People also married younger: the average age of a person at their first marriage dropped to 22.5 years for males and 20.1 for females, down from 24.3 for males and 21.5 for females in 1940.[37] Couples were also eager to start families, resulting in the "baby boom." Most women became pregnant with their first child within seven months of their wedding, and family size increased sharply as a result. The average woman had 3.09 children in 1950; the rate peaked in 1957 at 3.77; then dropped slightly to 3.65 children per family in 1960. Between 1940 and 1960, the number of families with three children doubled, and the number of families having a fourth child quadrupled. The four million children born per year during the 1950s postwar expansion in America became the largest generation in history. By the end of 1964, almost 77 million Baby Boomers had been born.[38]

Perhaps because of the atrocities of war, maybe as a result of their newfound family life, or perhaps encouraged by Cold War anti-communist sensibilities, conformity to a relatively narrow set of American values was encouraged.[39] Church membership skyrocketed, and thousands of new congregations were formed. Millions of dollars went into building new cathedrals: Americans spent a whopping $409 million between 1940 and 1950 for new church construction. About 43 percent of the public attended church before the war; by 1950, more than 55 percent were members of religious groups, a figure that would increase to 69 percent by the end of the 1950s. Between 1945 and 1949, Catholics baptized one million infants a year. "Sinful" relationships, like homosexuality, single motherhood, or cohabitation, resulted in social ostracism, condemnation, or—in the case of the McCarthy Trials on "Anti-Americanism" and the FBI surveillance of gay bars and suspected gay citizens—legal repercussions.

THE WOLVES OF WALL STREET
AND THE FALL OF THE AMERICAN DREAM

An integral part of the American Dream since its inception has been a perceived sense of social mobility: the idea that if you work hard, you can "move up the ladder" and get rich or at least achieve your personal goals. Many of the biggest scions of industry did just that, hailing from modest backgrounds: Standard Oil's John D. Rockefeller's father owned farmland; shipping and railroad scion Cornelius Vanderbilt was the son of a ferry captain; Andrew Carnegie, founder of US Steel, was the son of a weaver.[40] These and other early American industrialists were the personification of the rags-to-riches story, building their fortunes during a time of great expansion of infrastructure and industry in America. This idea of social-class mobility reached a zenith in the 1980s and early '90s, the end of which signaled the denouement of the modern Tethered Society, and the end of the industrial era as we knew it in America. Social mobility had stalled for most since the 1980s.[41] We were at the dawn of the digital era, though no one knew it yet, and everything was about to change.

The 1980s were a time of free-flowing money, fueled by cocaine, alcohol, and fast living. "Greed for life" was the mantra at the time of men like Michael Milken, the junk-bond king who earned over \$1 billion over four years at Drexel Burnham Lambert.[42] Excess in everything was the norm: The economy was booming, celebrated at drug-fueled parties at discos like the famous Studio 54 in New York City, which, at the time, was the epicenter of the social scene for the who's who of socialites.[43] The 1987 film *Wall Street* captured the spirit of the era: Gordon Gekko, played by Michael Douglas, was modeled after Michael Milken. In the film, Gekko says:

> Greed, for lack of a better word, is good. Greed is right. Greed works. Greed clarifies, cuts through, and captures, the essence of the evolutionary spirit. Greed, in all of its forms; greed for life, for money, for love, knowledge, has marked the upward surge of mankind and greed, you mark my words, will not only save Teldar Paper, but that other malfunctioning corporation called the USA.[44]

Stratton Oakmont's Jordan Belfort, who was played by Leonardo DiCaprio in the 2013 film *The Wolf of Wall Street*, was another character cut from the same cloth as Gordon Gekko with one difference—he was real. This film, which was based on Belfort's memoir of the same name, follows Belfort and his merry band of Brooklyn blue-collar meat-salesmen-cum-stock-brokers on their cocaine- and quaalude-fueled sexual escapades taking place at their corporate offices on Long Island. The film re-creates their unscrupulous insider trading and fraud devised to keep the party going. Belfort, Milken, and later Bernie Madoff (the former non-executive chairman of the Nasdaq Stock Market who carried out the largest Ponzi scheme in US history) could be viewed as Adam Smith's "Masters of Mankind" who pursued their own "vile maxim," which he defined as, "all for ourselves, and nothing for other people."[45]

The American Dream has been for a great many people a kind of shorthand for happiness, promising a golden path to contentment: As Gordon Gekko's monologue suggested, greed could fulfill the evolutionary spirit of humankind. This wasn't invented in the 1980s, however; the United States was based on the notion. Founding Father Samuel Adams suggested that owning property is a veritable "law of nature."[46] Yet over time it has become apparent to many that the Hollywood version of the American Dream has always far exceeded reality, so much so that real life was bound to disappoint. And it did. Feminist writer Betty Friedan deftly chronicled this undertow of disappointment in the suburbs in her seminal 1960s book *The Feminine Mystique*. She interviewed her college contemporaries—housewives at the time—from the exclusive Smith College thirty years after graduation. She found that many expressed a kind of nagging ennui, which they tried to chase away with booze and prescription drugs, a condition Friedan termed "the problem that has no name." As Friedan described it:

> The problem lay buried, unspoken, for many years in the minds of American women. It was a strange stirring, a sense of dissatisfaction, a yearning that women suffered in the middle of the twentieth century in the United States. Each suburban wife struggled with it alone. As she made the beds, shopped for groceries, matched slipcover material, ate peanut butter sandwiches with her children, chauffeured Cub Scouts and Brownies, lay beside her husband at night—she was afraid to ask even of herself the silent question—"Is this all?"[47]

For many male Baby Boomers hitting a midlife crisis, "the problem" has many times expressed itself as conspicuous consumption. As research psychologist and author Jesse Bering put it: "My first encounter with this tragic illness was my mother informing me that, 'your father is having a midlife crisis' after he suddenly bought a horse and left her for a younger woman. . . . The most frequent symptoms of this disease, I gathered from television, were a shiny new convertible (or prize-winning stallion), a toupee, and the unshakable delusion that one is now attractive to twenty-year-old co-eds."[48] The middle-life crisis and the ennui of suburban life were depicted in the troubling but brilliant Academy Award–winning film *American Beauty*.[49] In it, Kevin Spacey portrays Lester Burnham, an office worker in the middle of a midlife crisis who (stereotypically) buys his dream car and becomes infatuated with a beautiful blond high-school cheerleader, played by Mena Suvari. The movie's screenwriter, Alan Ball, echoed Betty Friedan's "problem that has no name" when he described the film, saying, "I think as human beings we have a spiritual need to live an authentic life. You see so many people that strive to live the unauthentic life and then they get there and wonder why they're not happy. We continue to have more and more distances between us and the natural world."[50] Both the *American Beauty*–style midlife crisis described by Ball and Friedan's "problem that has no name" rendered problematic the view of many that the American Dream and its perceived central tenet, conspicuous consumption, leads to a life of happiness. With the emphasis on consumption to trigger in onlookers (e.g., neighbors, other family members, colleagues, etc.) what's been called "invidious comparison" (inspiring envy, hostility, or contempt), the ability to consume became intertwined with one's sense of self, identity, self-esteem, and social status. Marketers and Hollywood filmmakers have been all too keen on selling this version of the American Dream to the nation—as the golden road to happiness, to be found right around the corner with your next purchase.

For those seeking social mobility via the American Dream, it seemed like happiness would be found around that next golden corner. Beginning with the gold-rush pioneers and the frontiersmen who came out West to stake their claims, the land was fertile. There were no harsh winters on the coast of California like there were in New York or Chicago or St. Louis. No shoveling snow. No blinding blizzards. This was a happy place of sunshine, smiles, and the promise of newfound riches: the American Dream within easy reach. Yet, not everyone made it: many gold miners returned to St. Louis, Boston, and other points eastward, downtrodden and empty-handed. Later, many hopeful "stars" looking to be discovered ended up staffing local restaurants and coffee shops in LA, which remains a place where you'll find the most attractive waiters, waitresses, and baristas in the world. Others, immigrants from places like Topeka, Kansas, or Monroe, Louisiana, who came to Los Angeles hoping for their "big break" might end up in Chatsworth—shooting for the small screens of the porn business. Wanna-be tech entrepreneurs can be found sleeping forty to an apartment at places like 20Mission in San Francisco, where young, mostly male digerati hope to become the next Mark Zuckerberg. Few achieve it. Yet they dream on, hoping their dreams will come true.

Real life of course could never live up to the hype of the Hollywood culture machine. In the real LA, everything's a little smaller, a little grayer, and a little less bright. More than 48 million tourists visited Los Angeles in 2017.[51] Many of those no doubt found out that what writer Gertrude Stein said was right—there's no "there there." Many are surprised to find that Los Angeles is not a city at all but, rather, a loosely attached web of suburbs, each with vastly different styles and demographics: from Latino working-class East LA to African American Long Beach to gay West Hollywood to the wealthy, largely Jewish neighborhood of Beverly Hills. Downtown, cranes dot the horizon on every street of LA, which is currently undergoing a renaissance. Nearby is the legendary Sunset Boulevard, where rockers like the Doors, the Rolling Stones, Neil Young, and the Eagles performed at places like the Troubadour and the Whisky a Go Go before they achieved their dream. Now referred to as "the Boulevard of Broken Dreams," Sunset Boulevard is also home to the famed Chateau Marmont where John Belushi, chasing the ultimate high, overdosed on a "speedball" of cocaine and heroin in the 1980s. In her essay on Sunset Boulevard, Laura Barton points out the many homeless people now haunting the street after dark, creating a tableau straight out of the *Night of the Living Dead*. She says:

> To walk Sunset is to be struck not only by the deliberately outlandish characters but by the many mentally disturbed people on its sidewalks: the woman rooting through bins who growled on approach, the man masturbating in a car park, the slink-eyed souls muttering darkly to themselves on street corners.[52]

Hollywood Boulevard has become a caricature of the American Dream. A tin can and neon version of what it once must have been. It is a dingy, dirty place that stinks of urine and body odor; is peopled by hucksters clad in Batman, Superman, Darth Vader, or Captain Jack Sparrow costumes—even Marilyn Monroe makes an appearance at times—offering (and sometimes coercing) to pose for pictures with tourists for a tip. After nightfall, many of the streets are deserted, save for the homeless, the schizophrenic, and the heroin-addled, muttering to themselves while digging through trash bins to find their next meal, or begging from random passerby, some becoming violent when rebuffed. These are the souls who have lost their dream; others never had it to begin with. Some have simply given up on ever having a stake in the American Dream; drugs have become the default path for the hopeless. This scene is repeated nightly in other cities, notably in San Francisco, ironically on the doorsteps of some of the wealthiest tech companies in the world. These examples are indicative of how the American Dream has always been more of an ideal than an achievable reality for many. Now, with growing income inequality and changing values in reaction to that, coupled with new digital technologies, the dream itself is changing. Yet as we gain new possibilities, we also lose something in this changing cultural zeitgeist: For many, the dream was their North Star.

THE PULL FACTOR OF THE AMERICAN DREAM

Being tethered to the dream was always more than just consumption: it gave people something to look forward to, something to work toward. Our own personal North Star. Whether that dream was to meet a husband or wife, buy a home or car, or start or enlarge a family, the American Dream, however conceived, gave people hope and something on the horizon to navigate toward, their goals and dreams acting as a "pull factor" toward the future. Being tethered also meant people had a stake in the game in their communities: people cared about their neighbors and took an active interest in their neighborhood, their homeowner's association, and the local government. That thirty-year mortgage was a grounding force in people's lives; they weren't just passing through. The much-sought-after long-term career meant that parents could pay the bills and keep their children in the local schools with their friends. It also meant that homeowners were concerned about the proposed bond levies that would repair the roads nearby, or if new bins would be coming to help sort the trash for recycling. Ownership meant you cared about how the lawns looked and what colors the neighbors painted their houses. In many neighborhoods, families lived there for generations: people would see their neighbors growing up, getting married, and having kids of their own. Neighbors would see each other in church each week. The middle class meant more than simply acquisition; it also meant a kind of rootedness in the suburban outskirts of town, which lent themselves to social and psychological stability for inhabitants. Being tethered meant people were woven into a social fabric that served as a stabilizing factor for them, for their community, and for the broader society.

Early sociological studies lend support to the stabilizing factor of our social structures. One of the foundational books in the field of sociology is *Suicide* by Émile Durkheim. Though written in the 1800s, the book was the first to discern sociological patterns of how one's ties to the social fabric can impact one's individual behavior. It underscored the importance of being woven into the social fabric.[53] Durkheim found differences between Protestantism and Catholicism in terms of suicide rates, with Protestants committing suicide more often. Durkheim surmised that this is because Catholics are more connected to the social fabric via more frequent church going, and thus have a tighter connection to the church and its doctrine, which serves as a kind of prophylactic against mental illness and suicide. Durkheim's work was seminal because it was one of the first to show systemic causes of individual behavior.[54] He believed that small, close-knit communities are better able to regulate behavior and that collective activity gives purpose and meaning in life. He characterized two kinds of suicide that are pertinent to our current social clime: anomic suicide and egoistic suicide. In *anomic suicide*, a person experiences a sense of disconnection from society and a feeling of not belonging that results from weakened social cohesion. Anomie occurs during period of serious social, economic, or political upheaval, which results in quick and extreme changes to society and everyday life. In such circumstances, people might feel so confused and disconnected that they choose to commit suicide.[55] Anomic suicide is related to a quickened pace of change which leaves people unable to keep up. Technological change is one such fast-moving social driver. As technological innovations continue to develop—particularly those that impact people's livelihoods, like the rising tide of artificial intelligence and automation that threatens to displace wide swaths of workers from their jobs, it can cause such quick economic and social upheaval. These kinds of changes can set the stage for anomic suicide to occur, as people's coping mechanisms for dealing with change may begin to fail them due to the increased pace of changes and rising hopelessness as they are unable to see a productive future for themselves.[56]

The second form of suicide identified by Durkheim is *egoistic suicide*. In this type, suicide happens when people feel totally detached from society. In ordinary circumstances, people are integrated into society by work roles, ties to family and community, and other social bonds. When these bonds are weakened through loss of family or friends, the stabilizing social fabric unravels, and the likelihood of egoistic suicide increases.[57] This is happening as younger people increasingly untether from marriage, families, neighborhoods, religious institutions like churches, and other similar stabilizing social structures. Now, viewed through this lens, it makes more sense why suicide has become the second most frequent cause of death among eighteen-to-thirty-four-year-olds in the United States (the leading cause of death is accidents).[58]

Durkheim's work set the stage for what sociologists later called "control theories," which were developed to explain deviance in society, particularly among juveniles. The idea was that certain social structures like family, church, and community act as "controls" on an individual's negative or "deviant" behaviors. Control theories tell us that being tethered to these social structures makes for a more stable individual and society. In this view, social institutions serve to communicate and reinforce shared values, which are then internalized and act as controls on the behavior of the individual.[59] It is the very institutions that transmit these values—families, religious institutions, political parties, and so on—that are eroding now among younger generations. William Reckless's version of a control theory includes both pushes and pulls to deviancy, pushes being things that keep people away from deviant behavior, and pulls being those that draw people toward it. In his "containment theory," pushes and pulls are buffered by inner and outer containments. Inner containments include self-concept, goal orientation, frustration tolerance, and norm commitment. Outer containments refer to elements outside the individual, such as the social environment where the individual resides, which is linked to community norms and values.[60] Clearly, community norms and values are much easier to transit and maintain in smaller, close-knit communities than in the diverse and diffuse environment of big cities, where young people are now flocking in a growing global trend of urbanization. As of 2015, over 83 percent of people in the United States live in urban environments.[61]

Research on Reckless's control theory found that a lack of goal orientation and availability of meaningful roles predicted deviant behaviors. Given the diminishing availability of meaningful work for many, particularly the less educated and blue-collar workers, and the subsequent diminishment of other social roles, including those of husband or wife, church deacon or other religiously oriented status, homeowner, parent, and so on, it would follow that younger people who are coming untethered from these important social roles may find themselves at loose ends. Idle hands may indeed be the devil's workshop. Deviance includes not only criminal behavior but also drug use. The current opioid crisis in this country is one example of the rise in deviance, a crisis law enforcement professionals have called "unprecedented."[62] According to the Drug Enforcement Administration, heroin use has tripled from 2007 to 2014, and the use of prescription opioids has shot up 240 percent in drug-poisoning deaths since 1999.[63] In 2016, nearly out of every 100,000 people between the ages of twenty-five and thirty-four died of a drug overdose. That's almost a 50 percent increase from the rate of overdose fatalities in that age group in 2014, when about 23 out of every 100,000 deaths was the result of a drug overdose. Between 2015 and 2016, the death rate for people in that same age group rose by more than 10 percent. Drug overdose deaths are increasing in the suburbs and areas outlying the cities, areas left behind in a growing digital economy and untethered world dominated by cities. Given the linkage between untethering—from jobs and from other stabilizing social structures like marriages—and the hope and future orientation social roles bring, it is perhaps not surprising that the highest opioid overdose death rate in the country is in an area hardest hit by job elimination: the coal country of West Virginia.[64]

A notable recent reaction to untethering has been a nostalgic desire to return to simpler times, captured in Donald Trump's campaign slogan "Make America Great Again." Unfortunately, despite people's attempts to return to earlier, simpler times, that genie has left the bottle, making a return difficult if not impossible for younger generations. By the end of the 1980s, the high-flying economic party was over, setting the stage for now. Studio 54 would be closed; bond trader Michael Milken would receive a ten-year jail sentence for insider trading (of which he served two years) and be barred for life from securities trading; while the Wolf of Wall Street, Jordan Belfort, would spent twenty-two months in jail and would be ordered to repay his investors over $110 million stolen from them in so-called "pump and dump" penny stock schemes carried out in boiler rooms filled by up to one thousand brokers at a time. In the 2000s, Bernie Madoff was arrested for the largest financial fraud in US history, stealing billions—millions of which came from his own Jewish community. Famed Nazi hunter, Holocaust survivor, and Nobel Peace Prize winner Elie Wiesel lost his entire life's savings in the scam. In 2009, seventy-one-year-old Madoff was sentenced to 150 years in prison, effectively a life sentence. None of his close family members attended the sentencing hearing. His son Mark, who had been his right-hand man at the business and had been plagued by swirling rumors and innuendo about his involvement in the swindle, committed suicide exactly two years after his father's arrest, leaving behind his wife of six years, Stephanie, and their two small children. Madoff's other son, Andrew, died four years later of mantle cell leukemia.[65] Diane Henriques, covering the case for the *New York Times*, wrote that this case was larger than Bernie Madoff himself, that in fact, "the Madoff case seemed to put an entire era on trial—a heady time of competitive deregulation and globalized finance that climaxed last fall in a frenzy of fear, panic and loss."[66] The reverberations of this changing economic climate continue to impact the country to this day, in the form of distrust in institutions among many younger digital natives who grew up in or after these times.

The era was on trial, and it lost. The party is now over, not just for Madoff and Belfort and their ilk, but for the vast majority of everyday citizens who had counted on what they thought of as the American Dream. Globalization has offshored many of the jobs that had greeted the servicemen returning home after World War II. There has been a notable decline in permanent, salaried jobs with benefits and retirement, and an escalation of part-time and temporary "gig" jobs, as well as a decline in union participation—severing the previous era's social contract between employer and employee. An Oxford University study found that nearly half of jobs will be eliminated in the next twenty years by automation, a process that is already well underway.[67] Millennials are also saddled with an undue burden of $1.4 trillion in student loan debt, a debt some may never be able to repay. The average college graduate in 2016 left school $37,172 in debt.[68]

An analysis of income inequality in the United States by economists Peter Lindert from the University of California, Davis, and Jeffrey Williamson from Harvard University found that from the early days of near income equality at the time of this country's founding, income inequality has now hit historic levels, greater in fact in the United States than in any other wealthy nation in the world.[69] As Williamson, the study's author, said, "We went from one of the most egalitarian places in the world to one of the least."[70] Social mobility seems a quaint remnant of the past, as wealth consolidates in the hands of fewer and fewer individuals and multinational corporations. Some, like MIT professor Noam Chomsky, have even begun to write the *Requiem for the American Dream*.[71] Americans may never be tethered again in the way we were during the postwar period, due to the confluence of circumstances that gave the United States and its citizens a unique social and economic advantage at the time, the parameters of which we are unlikely to see again. Although changing economic circumstances from post–World War II through the 2000s began to change the complexion of American society, it wasn't until the introduction of the internet-enabled iPhone in 2007 that seismic changes in society really began.

CHAPTER 2

SYNCHRONIZATION AND HARMONIZATION

As much as I love how the Internet and social media have democratized things, it also means that if it is your nature to gossip, to construct your own reality, that it's much easier than it ever was before, and it creates a lot of distraction and a lot of media fragmentation. So let's celebrate the empowerment that having access to a lot of information has been facilitated by new media, but let's also remember that truth and a sophisticated understanding of the issues we all face [are] also important.

—Shepard Fairey, artist, quoted in the
Hollywood Reporter, September 25, 2016

Cruising through the streets of Los Angeles in the mid-1990s, my eye wandered over the ornamentation of the architectural gems along my route to work. Having an interest in historic preservation, I noticed the elaborate architectural details of the classical Beaux-Arts-style 1920s-era buildings in Downtown: Modeled after French and Italian palazzos of the sixteenth century, many were abandoned or had fallen into disrepair. I had recently relocated from Miami, where I was a member of the Historic Preservation Society, whose aim it was to preserve and restore the many Art Deco hotels and other buildings lining Ocean Drive on South Beach. Compared to the whimsical, soft, undulating lines and playful pastel colors of Miami, Los Angeles architecture is much more austere, masculine, and formal in style. At the Fine Arts building on 7th and Figueroa, with its decorative arches and scrollwork carved out of sand-colored stone, festooned with fanciful griffins, gargoyles, and birds, visitors are watched over by two supine, draped classical male figures representing Sculpture and Architecture. Further south on Olympic is the imposing grey facade of the Italian palazzo-style Standard Oil Building. Built in 1924, it served as the regional headquarters for John D. Rockefeller's vast oil empire. At its zenith, Standard Oil controlled over 90 percent of the world's oil refining, causing the Ohio Supreme Court to declare it an illegal monopoly and order its dissolution. After the dismantling, Rockefeller's net worth was an estimated $336 billion, making him the wealthiest American of all time.[1] Over the entryway of the Standard Oil Building is a bas relief of classical figures reminiscent of the ascendant Roman Empire. The central figure is Athena, her left hand holding a protective shield, her right gesturing toward a toga-draped woman whose arm rests on a gear. On her left, a seated, nude, Olympian-style man pulls a lever. Two angels float behind them on either side, holding torches to light their work. The figures are flanked by two wooden oil derricks. Given that one translation of the name Athena is "moral intelligence," the scene seems to suggest the moral and God-given uprightness of the industrial era in general and the oil business in particular. The size, quality of finishing materials, and decorative detailing of this building and others reflect the power and prosperity of ancient Greece or Rome, while simultaneously evoking the hope and promise of the Los Angeles oil boom. Rockefeller was a devout Christian who attended church in New York, read the Bible daily, tithed, and even held regular Bible studies at his home, so the symbolic nod to moral uprightness and religion at the entryway to his building were reflections of his own personal values.[2]

Continuing south to the corner of Broadway and 11th, one comes across the sunflower-yellow and bright-blue tiled domes of the Herald Examiner building. Commissioned by William Randolph Hearst and designed by Julia Morgan (who also designed Hearst Castle), its garish ornamentation and exotic Spanish-Moorish style cut a dissonant figure more suited to Morocco when compared with the classicism and restraint of the rest of the Downtown area. All of these buildings are the physical embodiment of the values emerging out of the industrial era. They celebrate religiosity and industry, capitalism and wealth, and the success of the scions of the oil and financial markets. The frequent references to classical art, architecture, and the exotic are signals of the sophistication and cultured tastes of the social class positions of the occupants and owners.

My mind temporarily transported to another era by these stately older buildings, I was startled to see an incongruous image staring down at me from the fourth-floor wall of one of these buildings. It was a stylized yet imposing black-and-white face. I soon saw another on telephone pole nearby, with the word *OBEY* printed below it in capitalized, bold white type on a bright red background. I wondered who made them and what they meant. This same anonymous, imposing figure of André the Giant would soon appear in urban downtowns across the United States. The message was unclear, its maker unknown. The "OBEY Giant" campaign became a sort of modern-day Rorschach test, where one could project onto it one's own meaning. I half expected some new record announcement, or a concert of some kind to be announced, but no such announcement came. Clearly it was the work of a street artist making some kind of Orwellian statement about political or corporate power or something, with *OBEY* implying the need for resistance, yet the ambiguity of that power and the route to resistance remained a mystery.

Figure 2. OBEY Giant, by Shepard Fairey, 1990. (Image used with permission of Shepard Fairey.)

The ambiguity of the image turned out to be intentional. Its creator, Shepard Fairey, revealed that he was inspired by Marshall McLuhan's notion that the medium is the message. Fairey said the campaign was meant to evoke curiosity and cause people to stop and question their relationship with their surroundings. Shepard's stickers and the work of other urban artists, including taggers and graffiti artists, are a visible manifestation of the changing cultural zeitgeist. Stickers slapped onto the sides of skyscrapers and other urban architecture or spray-painted "tags" or graffiti painted in the dead of night represent urban teens and young adults giving the finger to traditional power structures to which they don't belong. It's a way for them to also assert, "I matter. Like your corporate or family name, here's my name, my work, on the building. I exist too." Laura Shillington, who teaches a course on urban nature and environments at John Abbott College in Montréal, has said, "the act of producing graffiti interrupts normative ways of being and living in the city."[3] Although he wouldn't become a household name for at least ten years after the OBEY Giant sticker campaign, Shepard Fairey's work was about to be disruptive to the normative ways of living on a much larger scale.

In 2008, with a short run of hand-screened posters, Fairey took to the streets and the internet to sell the latest edition of posters he had made. They featured a young African American senator from Chicago gazing out from the frame, looking upward and seemingly into the future, with the word *PROGRESS* emblazoned underneath. The entire run of 350 posters sold out in less than fifteen minutes.[4] Initially, the Barack Obama campaign wanted nothing to do with Fairey's posters. Yet within weeks of their first release, campaign representatives contacted Fairey, requesting another run with a new word underneath: *HOPE*. The Obama Hope graphic became one of the most recognizable political images in history. *New Yorker* art critic Peter Schjeldahl called it "the most efficacious American political illustration since 'Uncle Sam Wants You.'"[5] Prints of it now hang in the Smithsonian, the Museum of Modern Art, the Los Angeles County Museum of Art, and the US National Portrait Gallery, among others.

Fairey's "Hope" poster likely helped Obama win the election. It was a breath of fresh air blowing through the political landscape, especially when compared to campaign posters of the past, whose red, white, and blue Americana style had become trite, stereotypical, predictable, and easily forgotten. The "Hope" image encoded the language of the street, evoking hip-hop and skaters, urban youth and popular culture, and an outsider perspective. As such, it quickly caught the imagination of American youth because it *felt* different and seemed to embody the values they sought, having lost much of their hope in entrenched institutions, including politics, which had failed them and their parents so badly growing up. Tapping Shepard Fairey to style what would become the iconic image of the

Obama campaign was a stroke of genius, yet it was controversial since Fairey's renegade street art and bold stickers and posters were usually posted illegally. In spite of this controversy, his image quickly became the visual symbol of Barack Obama's first campaign. This campaign, and by default, this presidential hopeful, was clearly different than Establishment Washington, DC. Obama's young base was composed of the children of 9/11, the banking crisis, and the real-estate meltdown; they grew up with a cynicism toward institutions and an economy that some would argue failed to protect them and their parents from harm.

Figure 3. Obama "Hope" poster, by Shepard Fairey, 2008.
(Image used with permission of Shepard Fairey.)

The Republican ticket, headed by the much older Arizona Senator John McCain, vastly underestimated the power of social media to "rally the troops." Youthful voters are the least likely to watch traditional TV now and are the most likely to be on social media. McCain's team played it straight, running a traditional campaign. His campaign manager, Rick Davis, sent out an email saying, "Barack Obama has played the race card, and he played it from the bottom of the deck. . . . It's divisive, negative, shameful and wrong."[6] This type of negative campaigning played as "business as usual" in Washington, DC, particularly among younger voters. Obama's positive message of "Hope," on the other hand, resonated because it was exactly what Millennials were seeking. For many twenty-somethings, Obama represented the face of their generation, reflecting the changing demographics of the nation. Millennials as a cohort are much more diverse than their older Gen X or Boomer counterparts, so there was a convergence between age and diversity among this group of voters. Most political campaigns depend on the establishment of credibility and trust among voters, and Obama vibed with the eighteen-to-twenty-nine crowd. They responded in droves, rallying in teams of grassroots volunteers, organized via social media to email, call, and knock on doors in important swing states to evangelize for him. This same youthful enthusiasm spilled into the polling booths, spurring the largest under-twenty-nine voter turnout since the early 1980s, reaching a new watermark. An estimated 23 million young adults under thirty came out to vote during this campaign, representing a boost of 4 to 5 percentage points from the 2004 election, and 11 percentage points higher than the 2000 election.[7] Although exit polls confirmed that those under thirty didn't solely bring Obama across the finish line, many twenty-to-thirty-year-olds became enthusiastic political evangelists, convincing their parents and grandparents, neighbors and complete strangers by phone and door-to-door canvassing, spreading the word that this new candidate represented a fresh breeze of hope to lift the country from the depths of economic and social despair.

The Obama campaign was the first truly social-media-leveraged presidential campaign. His campaign managers throughout the country understood the power of social media to mobilize voters. It represented a major shift in how campaigns are marketed and how volunteers and donors are mobilized. This campaign spoke the language of untethered voters: it was visual, graphic, quick, and digital. Obama's "Hope" campaign was pre-memeified, that is, already ready to share on social media, appearing on millions of Facebook profile photos. It soon spread virally to other social media sites, giving Obama a free advertising lift. Using social media turned out to be the best way to bring in voters who were historically less likely to come out to vote, namely, younger and minority voters. The 2008 Obama campaign resulted in 3.1 million individual contributors and a grassroots movement of more than 5 million volunteers. In the election itself, 66 percent of voters under thirty voted for Obama, which is the largest age disparity since polling began in 1972.[8]

Buoyed by "Hope" in the 2008 campaign, younger voters soon became disenchanted, let down when Obama hit "politics as usual" within the beltway of Washington, DC, as he became unable to enact some of the sweeping changes he promised during his energetic campaign, including an emphasis on global warming, universal healthcare, and a reform of mandatory minimum sentences for federal drug violations.[9] In the 2012 reelection campaign between Obama and Republican candidate Mitt Romney, youthful voter turnout (i.e., the eighteen-to-twenty-nine age group) dropped from 51 percent in 2008 to 45 percent, a full 6 percentage points.[10] Disappointed and disillusioned, younger voters simply untethered from the political process, while other age-group turnouts remained stable. Despite the disappointing turnout, Obama won reelection still lifted by the youth vote, making it clear that engaging younger voters is critical for winning important elections. Still, the tide of young voters coming out to support candidates has receded over time: In 1964, 51 percent of youthful voters aged eighteen to twenty-four voted; in 2012, only 38 percent did.[11] The 2008 election represented an anomaly, a brief uptick in the generally downward trend among new and recent potential voters in this age group. The 2018 midterm election saw an increase in voter turnout similar to the initial Obama campaign, which was boosted by a Get Out the Vote push online by the teen survivors of the Parkland, Florida, high-school shooting; a live-streamed celebrity Get Out the Vote event; and celebrity Taylor Swift urging her 112 million Instagram followers to vote, among others, leading to a 188 percent surge in young voter turnout.[12]

Politics, like everything else, is being transformed by digital technologies. Political-party affiliation has been impacted, as Millennials in record numbers are disengaging from the politics of their parents, that is, Democratic or Republican Party affiliation, and instead are declaring themselves Independents, with most clearly left of center.[13] Being majority non-white and hit particularly hard by the Great Recession, these younger voters are unhooking from the political-party identity altogether; they hook in or out depending upon the issue or candidate.

Many are beginning to question the necessity of the political nation-state altogether: to them, hyper-local or global governance is all that matters, demonstrating that they have shifting and evolving definitions of both governance and community. John Zogby, founder of the well-known Zogby Poll refers to them as "First Globals," because Millennials are the generation most likely to consider themselves "citizens of the world." Sixty-one percent of them have a valid passport and are ready to go.[14] The youth of today have grown up with cable television networks such as CNN and MSNBC, as well as instantaneous world news and the global internet. Possessing an international perspective and interacting with friends abroad is second nature to them. Movements like Occupy Wall Street have shown that even relatively privileged American youth are willing to forego individual advantages in pursuit of the greater good. Although younger voters tend to be more idealistic than those older, in the postwar era, after the Cold War and McCarthyism, socialism largely lost its luster in America, as most Americans were employed with benefits, the G.I. Bill and two-week paid vacations. As one of the founders of the New Left movement in the 1960s, University of Michigan student Tom Hayden wrote the Port Huron Statement, a manifesto for the Students for a Democratic Society (SDS), a radical student group that was mainly energized by anti–Vietnam War and pro-civil-rights efforts on college campuses.[15] Later, 1968, in "Two, Three, Many Columbias," Hayden took a more direct swing at capitalism and inequality when he wrote that "the student protest is not just an offshoot of the black protest—it is based on authentic opposition to the middle-class world of manipulation, channeling and careerism. The students are in opposition to the fundamental institutions of society."[16] Despite the initial fervor of Tom Hayden and the Students for a Democratic Society, the New Left movement of the 1960s and '70s largely fizzled out, remaining a fringe movement and never gaining widespread appeal.

In recent years, the tides seem to be turning: First, it was demonstrated by their strong support for Bernie Sanders's 2016 campaign for president.[17] Sanders's platform rested on ideals such as universal healthcare, combating climate change, and providing free education—all issues deeply important to many Millennials.[18] More recently, a 2016 Harvard University survey of eighteen-to-twenty-nine-year-olds revealed that half of them don't support capitalism, and, perhaps surprisingly, a full third support socialism. The words that Millennials in the study most associated with capitalism were greed, corrupt, and control.[19] By these indicators, it seems the younger generation has moved markedly away from the 1980s Gordon Gekko mantra of "Greed is Good," from the film *Wall Street*, toward a motto more like Google's former slogan "Don't Be Evil" (which has now transformed into *Alphabet* and "Do the Right Thing"), seemingly rejecting many of the failed policies and the economy they've inherited from older generations.

SYNCHRONIZATION AND HARMONIZATION

The shift in values underway can be linked to our changing media landscape. Marshall McLuhan, Shepard Fairey's muse and a well-known professor of culture and communications, famously stated that "the medium is the message," by which he meant that there are both personal and social consequences of any medium. Books were one of the earliest technologies for conveying information.

Handwritten in Latin, Greek, or other native languages on sheepskin or papyrus by scribes, their expense and rarity limited their ownership to the wealthy or the clergy. Consequently, the vast majority of pre-Enlightenment Europeans were illiterate. After the invention of the printing press, books ushered in individualism in the sixteenth century, since reading is largely a silent, personal activity. They also encouraged nationalism, since they could be printed in native languages of English, French, Italian, Spanish, German, and others, rather than in the scholarly languages of Greek or Latin. The advent of broadcast media later represented another paradigmatic shift. Radio and television had two key effects: *the synchronization of time* and *the harmonization of values*.

The introduction of radio in the twentieth century reintroduced tribalism in America, since it was typically consumed in groups. As McLuhan puts it, compared to the individualism fostered by print media before it, "Radio had done just the opposite in reviving the ancient experience of kinship webs of deep tribal involvement."[20] Radio took off in 1920 after the November broadcast of the presidential election featuring Republican William G. Harding and Democrat James M. Cox on station KDKA in Philadelphia. By 1930, 60 percent of American households had a radio in their homes.[21] The San Francisco journal *Radio* published this account of the impact of the "wireless" on families:

> There is radio music in the air, every night, everywhere. Anybody can hear it at home on the receiving set, which any boy can put up in an hour. One of these sets cost less than a phonograph. With that can be heard grand operas, orchestras, phonograph music, market reports, press summary, sermons, and speeches. All that is needed is a hundred-foot clear span of copper wire, a couple of batteries and a cabinet set that can be bought from a radio dealer in every town.
>
> No better investment can be made as to a means for making a home more attractive to the entire family. Radio brings fathers and sons together on a common basis of mutual interest. Any phonograph selection will be played by request to the operator in charge of the sending station. No home is complete without radio.[22]

Families tuning in each week would hear, "Who knows what evil lurks in the hearts of men? The Shadow knows!" These words, a sinister laugh, and a few stanzas of Saint-Saens's *Omphale's Spinning Wheel* launched *The Shadow* radio show every Sunday night. Other radio dramas like *Dick Tracy* and *Gunsmoke*, classical music shows like *The Voice of Firestone*, and musical variety shows like *The Grand Ole Opry* also garnered big followings, as well as situation comedies like *Amos 'n' Andy*. Radio dramas sparked listeners' imaginations, with vivid descriptions and sound effects created live in studio via miniature doors that could be slammed, stretches of metal that could be vibrated to create the sound of thunder, and cellophane that when crunched up close to the microphone simulated the pleasing sound of a crackling fire. Wednesday nights at 8 p.m. brought family programming that supported family values in the form of shows like *One Man's Family*, which aired from 1932 to 1959. Listeners could also tune into big band remotes, to hear the soothing sounds of the Waldorf-Astoria Orchestra, broadcast live from their New York ballroom. The average listener at the time tuned in to hear such programming for four hours a day. Families would gather around the radio in the evenings and on weekends to enjoy entertainment and news together. People would host "radio parties" for friends to gather in each other's homes to eat, drink, and listen to popular radio shows. Extended family would gather to listen to weekly shows like the Gillette *Cavalcade of Sports*. "Variety shows," which evolved from early vaudeville acts, were also popular. Families would schedule their activities around popular radio shows and news broadcasts, timing dinner to catch them and synchronizing their time. Since recording methods weren't widely available in the early days of radio, radio had to be consumed live, when it aired.

President Franklin D. Roosevelt recognized the power of radio and took to the airwaves in the 1930s for a series of folksy "fireside chats," during the Great Depression, leading up to America's entrance into World War II. These broadcasts enabled him to bypass antagonistic newspapers and speak directly to the people. "My friends . . ." he would begin, as if addressing each family member personally as they huddled close to the radio. The chats appealed not only to patriotism, but also to the listener's faith, as God or Providence was invoked at the end of almost every speech. People tuned in religiously to hear Roosevelt's reassuring words, spoken in simple, plain language that anyone could understand. Roosevelt's radio audiences averaged 18 percent during peacetime, and 58 percent during the war. His address of May 27, 1941, in which he declared an unlimited national emergency in response to Nazi Germany's threats, was heard by 70 percent of the radio audience. The top-rated radio shows of the time were lucky to get 35 percent of the audience.[23]

Television came along in the late 1940s, first spreading throughout well-to-do homes by the beginning of the 1950s. Because televisions were expensive, few homes had them, and even fewer could be found outside of major cities like New

York or Chicago. Residents of Bozeman, Montana, or De Smet, South Dakota, could do little more than read about television in the early days. Once again, like the heydays of radio, relatives, friends, and neighbors would synchronize their time, gathering for "TV parties" to watch a show together. Early TV was a mechanism for broadcasting programming created by various sponsors: Gillette Blades, Firestone Tires, and General Electric, to name a few. Their messages were both overt and subtextual, including those that encouraged an emerging consumer culture. These TV shows were consumed by millions of Americans en masse at the same time each week. In an era before digital video recorders (DVRs) or streaming content, people had to organize their schedules around the broadcast time of their favorite shows. This forced people to come together in tribal groups to consume the content collectively. Since there were few channels to choose from in those early days, large swaths of the American public tuned into the same content on a weekly basis, with the net result being a harmonizing of values. Much of that content supported a narrow set of values centered around the American Dream and the nuclear family via shows like *Leave It to Beaver*, *The Donna Reed Show*, and *The Adventures of Ozzie and Harriet*. These domestic comedies presented a standardized version of conservative family values. The shows focused on white, middle-class families, and although the majority (nearly 60 percent) of families at the time were middle-class, the shows did not reflect the more than 50 percent of black families who remained poor.[24] These shows all featured similar themes: intact, white nuclear families in which men and women performed traditional gender roles—woman were stay-at-home wives and mothers (with neatly styled hair, wearing dresses, aprons, and often pearls); the men were strong, rational breadwinners. Any family problem could be solved within the span of a thirty-minute show, and each show ended on a moral lesson. These shows depicted life in the suburbs as harmonious; homes were tidy and organized, and their inhabitants lived relatively stress-free lives.

The result was a harmonizing of values across a wide swath of American households. There were only three networks at the time, and not the thousands of channels and choices available now on network TV, cable TV, and streaming services like Netflix, Amazon, Hulu, YouTube, and others. Now, both synchronization and harmonization are beginning to breakdown, as we amuse ourselves to death with our connected devices and social media. Neil Postman foreshadowed this moment in his foreword to his book *Amusing Ourselves to Death*, where it is Aldous Huxley's dystopian views of the future that have begun to come true, and not, as everyone feared, George Orwell's:

We were keeping our eye on 1984. When the year came and the prophecy didn't, thoughtful Americans sang softly in praise of themselves. The roots of liberal democracy had held. Wherever else the terror had happened, we, at least, had not been visited by Orwellian nightmares. But we had forgotten that alongside Orwell's dark vision, there was another—slightly older, slightly less well known, equally chilling: Aldous Huxley's *Brave New World*. Contrary to common belief even among the educated, Huxley and Orwell did not prophesy the same thing. Orwell warns that we will be overcome by an externally imposed oppression. But in Huxley's vision, no Big Brother is required to deprive people of their autonomy, maturity and history. As he saw it, people will come to love their oppression, to adore the technologies that undo their capacities to think.

What Orwell feared were those who would ban books. What Huxley feared was that there would be no reason to ban a book, for there would be no one who wanted to read one. Orwell feared those who would deprive us of information. Huxley feared those who would give us so much that we would be reduced to passivity and egoism. Orwell feared that the truth would be concealed from us. Huxley feared the truth would be drowned in a sea of irrelevance. Orwell feared we would become a captive culture. Huxley feared we would become a trivial culture, preoccupied with some equivalent of the feelies, the orgy porgy, and the centrifugal bumblepuppy. As Huxley remarked in *Brave New World Revisited*, the civil libertarians and rationalists who are ever on the alert to oppose tyranny "failed to take into account man's almost infinite appetite for distractions." In *1984*, Huxley added, people are controlled by inflicting pain. In *Brave New World*, they are controlled by inflicting pleasure. In short, Orwell feared that what we fear will ruin us. Huxley feared that what we desire will ruin us.[25]

Though Postman's 1985 foreword predated the digital era, mobility (e.g., cell phones, laptops, tablet devices), and social media, his notion that it was Huxley's view of the future and not Orwell's that would predominate turned out to presage our current situation. A study by the Pew Research Center found that by 1994, the values of Democrats and Republicans had largely converged. Yet by 2014, in the era of digital technologies and social media, they are more disparate than ever.[26] The truth online gets concealed in a sea of distractions, coupled with fake news and fake people spreading it ("bots"), designed to create division and stoke dissent, further driving people apart as their beliefs and values seem to diverge.

THE SIX EMERGING VALUES OF THE UNTETHERED

Although the internet at first seemed like an antidote to the mind-numbing "one size fits all" consumerist worldview presented by radio and later television, with the maturation of social media, Huxley's view of the future seems to be coming true, where we adore the very technologies that undo our capacities to think. The enhanced ability of each person to "curate" or select their own news feed around their particular values and beliefs—and to structure their friend-ship networks in alignment with these values and beliefs using social media, particularly on Facebook—means that each person can create echo chambers of news and information that can contribute to the larger social aspects of group-think, self-reinforcing (mistaken) beliefs, and the fragmentation of larger soci-etal values. In these informational echo chambers, "fake news" can quickly be memeified (i.e., turned into funny or informational graphics that can be quickly shared on social media), amplified, and shared. The key here is for you not to be taken by surprise by these reactions, but, rather, to account for them. New types of values are emerging, facilitated by our digital connectivity, associated with young, untethered adults, values that are also beginning to spread to connected individuals of other generations. These are as follows.

(1) Plug Life: The Desire for a Mediated World

The cornerstone of untethered values is the desire for a digital interface. A survey by Frisch's, owners of Big Boy Restaurants, found that a third of eighteen-to-twenty-four-year-olds use the restaurant drive-through because they don't want to "deal with" a human.[27] Andy Puzder, the CEO of Hardee's and Carl's Jr. fast-food restaurants, says that, "Millennials like not seeing people. I've been inside restaurant[s] where we've installed ordering kiosks ... and I've actually seen young people waiting in line to use the kiosk where there's a person standing behind the counter waiting on nobody."[28] They'd rather use an Uber or Lyft app to call a car than physically hail a cab, and text or email someone than make a call. Twice as many teens (55 percent) text their friends every day, while only a quarter see their friends in person.[29] A majority of fourteen-to-sixteen-year-olds (66 percent) say their bedroom is the number one place they spend free time, mostly on social media or gaming.[30] Only a third mentioned going to a friend's house. Life is lived mediated. It's common to see young friends sitting next to each other or in the same room now, texting each another, rather than talking.

Digital natives now value internet connectivity so much that a third say it is as vital to them as food, water, or air; and half say it's close to that important.[31] Half of college students and young employees surveyed would rather lose their wallet or purse than their smartphone or mobile device. Connectivity has become so important that 83 percent of Millennials now sleep beside their cell phones, so as never to miss a message, and half of them look at it the first thing when they wake up in the morning.[32] Many text after going to bed, and are sleep-deprived as a result. A Cisco Systems study of eighteen-to-twenty-nine-year-olds found that, for many, keeping up-to-date on Facebook is more important than dating, spending time with friends, listening to music, or going to a party.[33] Twenty percent are even using their smartphones during sex. Connectivity has become so important that not having their smartphone within arm's reach—or in hand—feels like a limb is missing. Two out of five say they feel "anxious, like part of me is missing" if they can't check their smartphone constantly, and a majority say they could not live without the internet.[34]

(2) Experiences versus Acquisitions

"Status symbols"—that is, expensive designer items such as clothing, jewelry, high-end automobiles, and the like—have been one way for prior generations to show they can "keep up with the Joneses" by emulating the tastes and styles of higher classes.[35] Status acquisition and the conspicuous show of wealth has long been a key value and driver of behavior for Baby Boomers. The big house, the big car, the attractive spouse or significant other (and possibly children) were all signs that a person had "made it." In the post-recessionary digital era, where one's lifestyle is visible to others through an endless array of photos and videos on social media, the acquisition of *things* as status symbols has given way to *experiences* as the aspirational value. Seventy two percent of Millennials would now rather spend money on experiences than on things, leading some to call this the "experience economy."[36] And if you think about it, acquisition of a status item is pretty generic—anyone with the means (or a credit card) can purchase that exact same item—but experiences are one-offs, unique. Cameras built into smartphones combined with social media has amplified this desire for experiences, and for documenting them. A survey of over two thousand Millennials found that 61 percent of them are influenced to travel to a destination by its potential for Instagram-friendly snaps, and nearly a third (29 percent) would veto a holiday destination if they were unable to post about it on social media.[37]

That amazing red-sand cave you took a selfie in, or the waterfall you hiked up to on Kauai, or the endless waves of sand dunes you saw that looked like Mars on your African safari are unique to you; the exact experience (and photograph) is yours and can be replicated but never duplicated. Of course, this drives one-upmanship behaviors, as people seek out the more-unique and the more-extreme selfies, photos, and videos.

The shift away from consumer culture is having devastating effects on the retail industry: One impact is that stores that don't cater to online shoppers are starting to shutter their doors. Even fashion, a historically cyclical set of consumer goods, has been impacted by digital technologies. It used to turn on a slower spin cycle, with three to four new collections per year (typically Fall, Spring, and "Cruise"). Now, newer brands like Zara, Uniqlo, H&M, Topshop, and others are churning out cheap "fast fashion" at a rate of ten to fifteen or more collections a year, according to Tasha Lewis, a professor at Cornell University's Department of Fiber Science and Apparel Design.[38] Old-school brands that aren't adapting to these new trends are struggling: Fashion stalwart Ralph Lauren is closing his flagship Manhattan Polo Store even though he hired an alum from fast fashion's H&M in a last-ditch effort to reshape the brand to appeal to younger consumers. The constant photographing of outfits on Instagram and other social media helps drive this quicker oscillation of fast fashion, and it fuels a constant desire for new outfits, particularly among women. Some are ordering new clothes, shooting selfies in the them, then returning them to retailers with liberal return policies like Nordstrom, an action the fashion industry has dubbed "The Selfie Effect."[39]

Major mall anchor stores are closing their doors: Neiman Marcus, at 109 years old and the top of the food chain in terms of luxury goods, was sold twice in the last twelve years.[40] Older Boomers are slowing their own spending, and younger buyers aren't as interested in purchasing things to signal wealth, which makes businesses that depend on the value of conspicuous consumption unsustainable, or, at the very least, frequently challenged to reinvent themselves. The exception to this pattern for young adult consumers is electronics, particularly iPhones, which are the new status symbol, since this group looks to smartphones for social cache, and sportswear, including collectible athletic shoes and wear, as opposed to the traditionally more formal fashions offered by the couture houses of fashion.

(3) Transactors versus Owners

Burning Man, the tech version of the 1960s hippie Summer of Love, takes place each year around Labor Day weekend on the playa at Black Rock Desert, 120 miles outside of Reno, Nevada. The organizers have instilled a "no cash/no vending" policy during the event. On their event FAQ, they say:

> Burning Man has survived and flourished through sharing, trading and the giving of the gift of yourself. We have found the buying and selling of goods is a distraction to connecting and creating relationships. Selling is a transaction-based activity. Other than the Cafe and ice in Center Camp, there is NO VENDING at Burning Man. Participants who are found vending will be asked to leave.[41]

This "no cash policy" of sharing and borrowing, as opposed to owning, is a key value for Millennials. They are exuberantly embracing the "sharing economy," becoming borrowers of others' assets, facilitated by smartphones and social networking. For them, it's a world of "everything as a service." Millennials are, per capita, less likely to own assets compared to their Boomer counterparts, including such assets as houses and cars. Sites like CouchSurfing, where subscribers offer free housing to travelers, as of August 2018 has a reported 14.0 million registered users in 200,000 cities.[42] The average age of a "CouchSurfer" is twenty-eight. Millennials are the age cohort most likely to say they have used sites like CouchSurfing, Airbnb, or Uber—peer-to-peer sharing networks—to save money, to offer a service, or to receive a service from a stranger.

It's not just houses or cars that are being rented—luxury clothing and accessories are available for loan on sites like Bag Borrow or Steal, and dresses can be rented for a night via Rent the Runway. These sites and others like them make available luxury goods, clothing, and accessories that would often be out of Millennials' financial reach. This "sharing economy" has also become a way that cash-strapped Millennials can eke out a living or supplement a low-paying, entry-level job—whether as a driver for Uber or Lyft, or through renting a room, a couch, or even the floor, through Airbnb—and still have a new outfit for one night on Instagram. Ride-sharing services like Uber and Lyft have been one of the most notable of the transactor versus owner shifts. When going out for an evening with friends, Millennials use ride-sharing services 70 percent of the time. Furthermore, they use such services much more frequently than other generations, with 15 percent saying that they use them as often as two to five times per week, citing the ease of use and short waiting time for a car. By comparison, 69 percent of other generations say they summon cars once a month or less often.[43]

Groups are popping up to support new sharing models for living and working, enabling people to "borrow" or rent assets, rather than own them. One of these is Flip, a company which advertises sublets, that touts on its website that "long-term leases are for old people."[44] A group of real-estate developers, event planners, and others in New York City are developing a new model of community based on co-living and sharing called the Assemblage. They describe themselves as:

> A community of individuals who believe the world is at the verge of a col-
> lective conscious evolution; transitioning from a society defined by indi-
> vidualism and separation into one of mutual interconnectedness. To make
> collaboration possible across all fields of human endeavor and develop new
> synergistic approaches, our members will have access to co-working, living and
> social spaces in New York City and around the world.[45]

The digital world has also been subjected to this same kind of *transactor versus owner* transformation. One example is the open-source software movement (OSS), where software is often given away for free to be re-coded and used as the user sees fit. Sites like Creative Commons allow for the free sharing and reuse of art, music, photography, and other digital works, with proper attribution to their creators. As of 2017, Creative Commons hosts nearly 1.5 billion licensed works.[46] Other sites, like Wikipedia, depend on the free updating and editing of entries. Contrary to people's fears that the entries wouldn't be accurate, several studies have found that the "free encyclopedia that anyone can edit" is actually as accurate as professionally hosted databases and the *Encyclopedia Britannica.*[47] WikiLeaks, founded by hacker Julian Assange in 2006, facilitates the sharing of restricted or classified documents by leakers and whistleblowers; it continues to grow in importance as a tool wielding significant political influence. Sites like YouTube depend on content shared for free, and people now watch one *billion* hours of YouTube videos per day and share three hundred hours of video every minute. Of people aged eighteen to forty-nine, one in eight tunes in to watch YouTube videos every month.[48]

For now, these "alternative lifestyles" appeal mostly to young, urban, college-educated consumers. Yet in the future, with the possible automation of many jobs, leading to a possible "end of work" on the horizon, borrowing and sharing may end up being more a necessity than a desire.

(4) Don't Care How, I Want It Now
(or How Veruca Salt of *Charlie and the Chocolate Factory* Was Just ahead of Her Time)

Digital technologies spin fast: we get news on demand at the touch of an app, without having to wait for the six o'clock news to come on. With Amazon Prime, we can order groceries with the touch of an app. Postmates, Grubhub, or Uber Eats can bring dinner to our home or office in minutes; we only ever have to leave our couches or desks to answer the door. With Uber or Lyft, a car will show up to take us wherever we want to go. We can walk outside in many cities now and grab a bike or an electric scooter to take us to our destination, and leave it wherever we want, without a care of what happens to it when we're done. Some restaurants are experimenting with ways to tap into this "I want it now" sensibility: Chipotle has experimented with on-call drone delivery of burritos at Virginia Tech, while 7-11 and Dominoes are trying it in Australia. Postmates promised fifteen-minute food delivery in Manhattan, based upon a limited menu, but then scrapped it. Uber Eats is still experimenting with instant delivery, delivering a Blink 182 curated salad in two minutes in Manhattan.[49]

Tapingo is another company tapping into young consumers' desire for a digital interface and the "I want it now" mind-set. Available on or near college campuses, Tapingo allows students (and others who have the app) to cut in the line at local Starbucks or other participating restaurants by ordering and paying ahead with the app. Their time "dealing with" a human is minimized. When they enter their local Starbucks or other participating vendor, they walk up to a special Tapingo counter, grab their drink or food, and go. Tapingo founder and CEO Daniel Almog observes, "Your phone should know what kind of coffee you like and make sure it's available for you—where you need it, when you need it."[50] Tapingo is currently doing 25,000 transactions a day at eighty-five universities. It has recently expanded its offerings to include the drugstore chain Walgreens, which aims to deliver to students at their apartments or dorm rooms.[51] As younger digital natives expect things quickly and have less desire or comfort with face-to-face interactions, such mediated experienced will likely become the preferred means for obtaining food, drinks, groceries, and other purchases.

(5) Green Is Good

Younger, hyperconnected Millennials are also the generation most likely to value "green," and to be environmentally conscious. Though largely not active environmentalists compared to their older cohorts, they are more likely to pay for eco-friendly products, "fair trade," and eco-friendly or minimalist packaging for food and products. The 2018 Princeton Review's College Hopes and Worries Survey, surveying 10,958 college applicants and their parents, found that a majority (63 percent) said that having information about colleges' commitment to environmental issues would contribute "strongly," "very much," or "somewhat" to their application/attendance decisions.[52] I have taught a couple of courses at the University of Southern California related to energy, environment, and sustainability. One of my USC engineering students, Kevin Chan, is a first-generation American of East Asian descent. His liminal identity of "betweenness"—between the American and Asian cultures—lead him to quiet moments of contemplation in nature during visits to family in China, which gave him the opportunity to reflect upon issues larger than himself. For him, sustainability is a core value. He said:

> The languages and cultures of East Asia began to be something that fascinated me. It is at once foreign and familiar. It is an identity that I hold, but not yet fully realize. My visits to East Asia to visit family and relatives were always marked with this half-identity. The language I could not speak fluently, the mannerisms I could not emulate flawlessly, the culture I could not embrace entirely. It was not long before I realized that I could not communicate as accurately as I did in Los Angeles, and so I tended to talk less and contemplate more. My eyes turned up to the sky often. The megacities of China seemed to have a near-constant dreariness to them. The sky would often be obstructed by a layer of cloud or haze, and even when the skies were clear, they would be too clear. The night sky would be almost devoid of stars, just a black curtain veiling the entire cityscape. Light pollution and carbon emissions made it so that I could not see anything beyond the gray ambience. But I knew that beyond this were the starry skies and all the celestial wonders in space that sparked my first real interest in science. When I was young, astronomy was full of ephemeral objects that captured my imagination. There were the moons, planets, stars, nebulae, and galaxies. There were black holes, red and white dwarfs, and blue supergiants. Each seemed to have their own personality, each playing a part in the cosmic narrative. Yet, all of them were in some sense removed from reality.

Forever unreachable and intangible, it can be easy to lose sight of the grandeur they can elicit. But as I moved toward the outskirts of the cities and into the rural villages, pinpricks of light started fazing—and then pouring—in. To stand there, head tilted back and eyes toward the heavens, it's hard not to contemplate about the universe, the world we live in, and ourselves. Those were the contemplations that led me down the path of science. If astronomy and cosmology seek to piece together the actors and narrative of the universe, then the geosciences are attempting to do the same with Earth. Upon the Earth, a parallel narrative unfolds—the story of life. Evolutionary history tells the tale of not only endeavors in nature and the anatomical and physiological arms race between predators and prey, but also mutual growth and symbiosis. Underlying everything is the chemical and physical properties that form the grammatical laws and compositional structure of the universe. As a whole, it forms a complex yet elegantly interwoven story. But living in a community known for being a hub for artists and creators alike, just being the reader is not enough; we write the stories. If the history of this Earth is one long narrative, the chapter that humanity is writing now is hinting at a dismal end. Engineering is a powerful pen that we have developed in writing the history that we create. But in our ferocity to industrialize, humanity has consumed much of the resources it needs to prosper. The ink that we use to write with is smearing across the pages. Though engineering is a powerful tool, it is just that: a tool. And the supply of ink is running out. How is humanity to continue their story? Continue writing at the current pace and be faced with an abrupt ending? Write less forcefully and conserve the supply of ink for several more pages? Perhaps hopefully find an alternative renewable source of ink? Sustainability is a concept to embody the myriad of ways to prolong humanity's existence on Earth and to thrive while doing so. It is literally to sustain ourselves and maintain our first-world quality of life in the long term. It is the ability to continue to write while minimizing wasteful smearing and ink blots that pollute the pages. As a consequence of the goal of sustainability, other subplots naturally follow.[53]

Such enhanced "green" value is likely to follow digital natives into their careers, as 80 percent of Millennials surveyed showed a preference for working for a company with clear sustainability and corporate social responsibility policies.[54]

(6) Customizable World

Mr. Potato Head was the original customizable toy, first marketed by Hasbro for the World War II–generation kids. In the original version, kids had to supply their own potato for the "head" to which they stuck on plastic hair, eyes, nose and mustache, and a corncob pipe to make the cartoonish character. The industrial era ushered in the process of assembly-line production, a process that would be used in many manufacturing settings. It resulted in a period of mass homogenization, beginning with Henry Ford's assembly line for improving the production of automobiles. McDonald's was an outcome of that, when Ray Croc first applied Ford's industrial methods of rationalization and bureaucratization to food production, a process George Ritzer termed "McDonalidization."[55] The war years of 1941 to 1945 were hard for Americans. Nothing came easily, food wasn't readily available, and ingredients were rationed and ran out quickly in the stores. In the postwar period, anything that signaled "convenience" was a ready respite from the grueling days of the war. A hot meal was available in minutes from McDonald's under the easily recognizable Golden Arches—an okay burger, delicious, salty fries, and a creamy milkshake or Coca-Cola. By 1962, McDonald's had sold its millionth burger. TV dinners also became popular at the time. Developed by C. E. Swanson in 1953, TV dinners came in aluminum trays that could be heated in the oven. The first TV dinner was a Thanksgiving dinner—turkey, mashed potatoes, frozen peas, corn-bread stuffing, and peaches, apples, or a dessert. These sold for 98 cents. The value of "convenience" was key. The dinners fit nicely on a "TV tray," a small foldable table for one that could be pulled up to the sofa so a meal could be enjoyed while watching popular TV shows.

In recent years, a backlash against this kind of mass uniformity has begun. We are increasingly living in a customizable world. Social media has made it possible for each individual to personalize his or her world, a mirror of narcissism reflected back to him or her. The untethered are coming to expect commodity and service providers to personalize products and services to their unique needs and desires. They're used to customized information streams, and following or friending people they are interested in. If they don't like it, they can simply hide, unfollow, unfriend, or block. It's no longer a "one size fits all" world. Monique, a Latina college student in Los Angeles, talks about how customization is an everyday part of her life now:

Customization plays out in my life daily. . . . It even plays out in almost every-one's life I would say. Every day we get to dress ourselves how we want, do our hair how we want, or even apply makeup. We get to choose how we want to portray ourselves or want people to view us through how we look. It goes with the same thing for online. When I use my social media, I get to choose who I want to see my post or who I want to accept request from. I also get to cus-tomize what content I chose to display on my social media. Customization is a major key in social media because we get to choose what picture we want to put up, if it looks cute, or if the angle and lighting is right. All these are types of ways [. . .] we chose how we display ourselves to the world. On my social media I rarely use my name, I customize it by using my nickname [. . .] and [deciding] what picture I use as my cover photo.[56]

Starbucks was one of the first to pick up on this new value shift: the one key element being that at the end of each order, they ask, "What is your *name*?" Psychological and neuropsychological research has shown that one's own name both draws attention and activates areas in the brain not activated by the names of others.

"Kurt?" the barista calls out over the soothing electronic beats and falsetto voice of a Massive Attack song playing unobtrusively in the background. "Venti iced Americano with a Ristretto shot, three pumps of white mocha, three pumps hazelnut, half and half, and whipped cream?"

"That's me!" Kurt, a tall, wiry fellow around thirty with long, stringy blond hair and a goatee, steps forward to get his specialty concoction. This is something he does up to three times a day, according to my former assistant, who worked as a manager at Starbucks. Starbucks is using social media sites including Twitter, Facebook, and Foursquare to engage with customers, not only to announce new or special products, but also to quickly act on customer's complaints and com-pliments. Starbucks also has a discussion forum called MyStarbucksIdea, where customers can make suggestions for new drinks or products. In the first two months of its launch, some 41,000 new ideas were contributed, some of which have since been implemented and are now part of the company's product and service range.[57] In this way, Starbucks promotes and maintains a personalized relationship with its customers by creating an active online community. That, coupled with the customizing of the product to suit the customer's desire, has been key to its continued success. Starbucks understands the untethered con-sumer; it's now streaming it's stores' music on Spotify, which is available on users' smartphones, tablet devices, or laptops, thereby keeping the emotional connection and relationship going with its customers after they leave the store.

THE END OF TRUST AND THE
EMERGENCE OF THE DARK ARMY

The deregulation of the mass media has contributed to the fragmentation of values we are seeing now, and the coalescing into increasingly divisive tribes. Tribalism and its shared social meanings date back to the earliest days of humans. It's what may have given *Homo sapiens* an advantage. From the myth of twins Romulus and Remus suckled by a she-wolf and the founding of the Roman Empire to the Declaration of Independence, upon which the colonies of America built their new country,[58] shared myths have enabled people to coalesce and form complex cities and societies. Shared myths are based on a shared communications structure. In small bands of people, such communication can be spread orally, through storytelling. As societies grow, they must be codified or written down to spread the common understanding in a homogeneous way, and over longer distances. In modern times, first the telegraph, followed by radio and then television, spread the word in the United States; with them came a common culture and shared values.

A few years ago, I sat outside on a hard, white folding chair in the quad at USC, one of thousands anxiously awaiting the appearance of Mr. Robert F. Kennedy Jr., attorney and nephew of slain president John F. Kennedy. Mr. Kennedy had come to campus to talk to the standing-room-only crowd as a representative of Waterkeeper Alliance, his project to save the waterways of the United States from corporate waste and runoff ranging from chemicals to waste generated by industrial pig farming. As he began to speak, I recognized the unmistakable bone structure, the Massachusetts accent, and familiar cadence of his father, Attorney General Robert F. Kennedy. Mr. Kennedy spoke about the Environmental Protection Agency and several specific cases in our national parks where corporations had dumped chemicals in rivers, sometimes tens of thousands of gallons. His book on the subject, *Crimes Against Nature,* released shortly after his appearance, became a *New York Times* bestseller. Both his passion and the panache of the Kennedy name brought particular attention to this issue.[59]

Though I was somewhat familiar with issues surrounding the environment, what caught my attention was an area I knew nothing about: the fact that the news outlets used to have a social compact with the public that served to inform the citizenry so that they had the best available information when it came time to vote. Prior to the 1970s, television news was regulated by the Federal Communication Commission. At that time, the news had to be presented "objectively," airing multiple sides of an issue, regulated by something called the fairness doctrine. Enacted by the FCC in 1949, the view was that news stations were trustees of the social contract and as such they had an obligation to viewers and listeners to present divergent points of view—particularly on controversial subjects—in order to educate the public on matters important to their communities and to the nation.[60] In 1971, the FCC expanded this social contract by mandating that stations actually seek out controversial topics and air information on them to educate the public. Thus, early television was seen as a way to educate viewers on matters of social importance, by presenting controversial topics and offering multiple points of view on those topics. In the 1940s, the FCC also had established the Mayflower doctrine, which banned editorializing by television stations.[61] By 1971, the FCC made license renewal for radio and television stations contingent upon submitting evidence that they had in fact sought out and reported on issues important to the community. Another key communication legislation was the Communications Act of 1937. This act made it mandatory that politicians seeking election be given equal time on stations. This was federal law, enacted by Congress, while the Mayflower doctrine and the fairness doctrine were FCC policies. All of these regulations and laws were put into effect in an attempt to make sure that the media were evenhanded in their approach to stories important to communities and that no political party was given an inordinate amount of airtime on radio or TV. The goal was an educated public when it came to important stories and issues of the day, so that voters could make informed decisions when voting. In 1969, the US Supreme Court upheld the FCC's right to enforce its fairness doctrine on the grounds that the scarcity of the broadcast spectrum created a need for such regulation.[62]

Another key regulation specific to politics was the equal-time rule.[63] This dated back to the first broadcast law in the United States, the Radio Act of 1927. As a kind of "Golden Rule of Radio," the 1927 act ensured that no political candidate would dominate the burgeoning radio domain, by mandating that if a radio station sold or gave time to a candidate, the opposing candidate would be able to buy or be given equal time. With the advent of television, this law was adapted and became Section 314 of the Communications Act of 1934.

Media ownership was also previously more strictly regulated by the FCC: The Local Radio Ownership Rule and National TV Ownership Rule held that a broadcaster could not own television stations that reach more than 35 percent of the nation's homes.[64] In 1946, the Dual TV Network Ownership Rule was enacted, which prohibited a major network from buying another major network. And, finally, in 1964, the Local TV Multiple Ownership Rule prohibited a broadcaster from owning more than one television station in the same market, unless there were at least eight stations in the market.[65] The mass media has often been referred to as the Fourth Estate, meaning it wielded a kind of unrecognized power of its own, in contrast to the three estates of the realm: the clergy, the nobility, and the commoners. In modern times, the Fourth Estate was thought to serve the public as a kind of check and balance against the power of the three branches of government. The FCC regulations were meant to protect that role, so that a single corporate interest or individual could not wield too much political power by holding too much sway over the information being channeled to the public.

In the 1960s, television became a major force in American politics, as the 1960 Kennedy–Nixon debate so sharply demonstrated. Kennedy was the first "TV president." During his debate with Richard Nixon, Kennedy appeared telegenic, poised, and attractive, with hands folded neatly in his lap and legs crossed, exuding the casual ease of a gentleman of his social class and stature. Nixon, on the other hand, came across as awkward and ill at ease; his five-o'clock shadow and shifty-eyed demeanor telegraphed to the audience a clear lack of confidence in the presence of the regal Kennedy. Polls conducted after the debates were fascinating; they showed the powerful effect of what "looking presidential" would do for a candidate: Those who listened to the debate on the radio had the clear perception that Nixon had won, while those watching the sweating, nervous performance of Nixon on TV felt that Kennedy had won. Later, Kennedy's assassination and its aftermath would be watched by millions of people around the world; Jackie Kennedy's blood-stained pink Chanel-style suit and John John Kennedy saluting his father's coffin would become icons seared into the grieving nation's collective mind, brought to them by television.

Gallup polls have been tracking Americans' trust in the media since 1972. That trust reached an all-time high during the years when Walter Cronkite anchored the CBS *Evening News*, after his detailed reporting on Vietnam and the Watergate scandal. Families would gather around the "set" to hear Cronkite deliver the news. Children were often admonished to keep quiet and pay attention to what was being said. "Uncle Walter," as he came to be known, became the most trusted man in America. His trust level—due to his gravitas and integrity—was higher even than that of the president. Trust in the media reached an all-time high in 1976, with a 72 percent majority expressing a high level of trust.

During the 1980s, the "fairness" and evenhandedness of the media envisioned by its early regulators began to unravel, with the eventual unintended consequence of vastly diminished trust. In 1987, President Ronald Reagan vetoed a bill that would have made the FCC's fairness doctrine federal law. He felt that such a law would create a "chilling effect" among journalists, and that it was an unconstitutional affront to First Amendment rights. He stated upon vetoing the bill, "In any other medium besides broadcasting, such federal policing of the editorial judgment of journalists would be unthinkable."[66] In 1981, the number of television stations any single entity could own grew to twelve, and by 1987, the fairness doctrine was eliminated. Deregulation continued when President Bill Clinton signed the Telecommunications Act of 1996, which lifted the forty-station ownership cap. Soon after, just five companies—Viacom, the parent of CBS; Disney, owner of ABC; News Corp; NBC; and Comcast controlled 75 percent of all free prime-time viewing.[67] With deregulation, the public "commons" aspect of the Fourth Estate had eroded. Perhaps as a result, Americans' trust in the media has sunk to a new low: 26 percent of those aged eighteen to forty-nine (down from 36 percent last year) and only 38 percent of those aged fifty and older (down from 45 percent) say they have a great deal or fair amount of trust in the media. Art Smith of the Gallup Poll explained these finding by saying, "When opinion-driven writing becomes something like the norm, Americans may be wary of placing trust on the work of media institutions that have less rigorous reporting criteria than in the past."[68]

Ecologist Garrett Hardin has discussed the degradation of a common resource available for the public good—be it land, water, or air—in his essay, "The Tragedy of the Commons."[69] Using the parable of a cattle farm, he says that each cattle rancher is motivated by his own interests to expand his herd, yet as each does, the cattle tend to overgraze the land, leading to the eventual demise of the cattle, an unintended consequence of unbridled expansion and self-centeredness. In Hardin's view, it is not the fact there is a commons that is the problem. Rather, it is an *unregulated* commons that leads to tragedy for all. Hardin's notion of the tragedy of the commons can be applied to our current media milieu, in that the mass news media can be seen as a kind of virtual commons. The deregulation of the media has led to a tragedy of the commons in the digital era. First, since media consolidation has taken hold, news media have had to "brand" themselves to compete in an unregulated market, which drives news shows to the poles of the political spectrum so that networks like Fox, CNN, and MSNBC can carve out niche audiences of right- or left-wing adherents. Their "biases" are readily apparent, and without the balancing factors of the fairness doctrine or the equal-time rule in place, trust in the Fourth Estate has dropped, reaching an all-time thirty-year low in 2016, with only 40 percent believing that the broadcast news media can be trusted to report the news fully, accurately, and fairly.[70]

Traditional TV watching has plummeted in recent years with the advent of on-demand streaming using desktop computers, laptops, tablets, and even smartphones. As a result, Millennials are unhooking in droves from traditional news media. A Pew Research study in 2015 found that fully 61 percent of Millennials look to Facebook as their main source of news. Only 37 percent get it from watching traditional local network news. Others get their news from YouTube, Reddit, Instagram, or other social media sources. The two highest-rated sources for news in the United States for Millennials, following Facebook, are Fox News and Google News. Analysts have looked at several factors for engaging a social, untethered audience, including the use of memes, that is, sound-bites, imagery, or text that is quickly and easily translatable to digital and accessible to mobile-connected audiences, capturing fleeting attention in a few seconds.[71]

Social media gives people the ability to "curate"—that is, to pick, choose, and organize—the information they receive, dividing them into "communities of interest" of similar individuals to themselves, in which ideas and political viewpoints can be self-referential and group-reinforced, like an echo chamber in which like-minded ideas are amplified. Dissenters are often chided, called names, unfriended, and blocked. In his article on politics and Facebook for the *New York Times* Magazine, John Herrman reported on hundreds of insulated, politically specific groups with names like Occupy Democrats, the Angry Patriot, US Chronicle, Addicting Info, RightAlerts, Being Liberal, Opposing Views, Fed-Up Americans, American News, and hundreds more.[72] Some of the pages have millions of followers; many have hundreds of thousands. One of his interviewees, Rafael Rivero, a left-leaning young man who was on a pro–Bernie Sanders page, turned his attention to anti-Trump memes. "It's like a meme war, and politics is being won and lost on social media," he said. Tech entrepreneurs who are social media savvy (with bank accounts swollen by new media profits) are well aware of the power of memes to sway opinion. One such entrepreneur is the founder of Oculus VR (which designed a virtual-reality headset called Oculus Rift), Palmer Luckey, who sold his company to Facebook for $2 billion. Luckey found himself in hot water when it became known that a group he supports, Nimble America, a 501(c)4 nonprofit that bills itself as politics for the younger social media crowd, had spent its time creating and propagating anti-Hillary memes and viral content.[73] Luckey said that "we've proven that sh*tposting is powerful and meme magic is real." He and his tech crowd realized that the old saw, "Perception *is* reality" has never been truer than it is today for the digital native.

The almost hermetically sealed ideology bubbles online coupled with branded mass media news makes it so that one never has to tolerate an opposing view, much less resolve a difference; one can maintain the illusion of moral superiority of a political point of view by surrounding oneself with like-minded individuals who confirm one's biases. Bill Clinton, talking with Trevor Noah on *The Daily Show* noted this trend, saying that, "America has come so far . . . we're less racist, sexist, homophobic, anti-specific religion than we used to be. We have one remaining bigotry, we don't want to be around anybody who disagrees with us."[74] Social media is allowing the creation of information silos that allow people to coalesce into self-referential interest groups, blocking out dissenters or those offering disparate interests. It's the very definition of groupthink, the idea that groups—lacking dissenters entirely or silencing dissenting voices—can self-direct into disaster.

Malevolent actors have already found ways to utilize these fractures, with a "divide and conquer" strategy, in the United States precisely because of our current lack of a shared, cohesive culture and myth. Using advanced analytics, groups like Cambridge Analytica were able to micro-target specific small groups and subtly influence them. Cambridge Analytica and its group of cognitive and data scientists guided both the Trump campaign and the Brexit movement in the United Kingdom to their sudden and surprise victories.[75] Information has since come out that Russia, too, was in the mix, using "bots" or simulated people online, to target key swing states, amplifying messages on Twitter and Facebook, and spreading disinformation about Hillary Clinton—enough so that Trump may well have won the election in states expected to go to Clinton. This caught the Clinton campaign off guard, as they assumed she had a clear advantage in these must-win states, so she didn't even bother to campaign there. With the help of sophisticated computer modeling and polling, Cambridge Analytica and the Russians were able to create the illusion of a shared mythology by creating fake people trumpeting a particular message to specific voting groups who were most vulnerable to being swayed by the message, for example, those who may exhibit higher levels of anxiety. Fifty thousand bots on Twitter alone shared fake and divisive election messaging, spreading misinformation and propaganda.[76] African American voters were dissuaded from voting due to a Facebook "dark post" campaign (visible only to the receiver) that painted Hillary Clinton as a racist:

> Trump's digital team created a South Park-style animation of Hillary Clinton delivering the "super predator" line (using audio from her original 1996 soundbite), as cartoon text popped up around her: "Hillary Thinks African Americans are Super Predators." Then, Trump's animated "super predator" political advertisement was delivered to certain African American voters via Facebook "dark posts"—nonpublic paid posts shown only to the Facebook users that Trump chose, to encourage voter suppression.[77]

Wall Street Journal reporter Christopher Mims reported that one day in August, Trump's campaign pushed "dark posts" to Facebook users that led to 100,000 different web pages, each micro-targeting a different segment of voters. Other voters likely changed their votes when influenced by a swarm of bots amplifying the message that Hillary Clinton was sick, and possibly suffering from a terminal illness. Haitians were told that Clintons and their cronies "cashed in" on Haiti when hundreds of thousands lay dead after the 2010 Haiti earthquake.[78] Cambridge Analytica is said to have collected five thousand data points on every citizen in America now, meaning it could create extremely targeted campaigns tied to people's very specific fears and interests, from animal rights and abortion, to immigration and guns.[79]

The unraveling continues, as the doors are flung open wide on users' data, allowing for more and more sophisticated behavioral models to be built: House Republicans in March 2017 voted to approve legislation that would allow internet service providers to sell people's browser data without their consent, undoing prior Obama-era FCC rules aimed at protecting internet users' privacy. Access to such data will mean that these same techniques can be used with many more data points on individuals. The result is that a finer- and finer-grain sieve can be established in which specific user fears can be amplified. They do this by targeting certain users via a combination of direct advertising and large numbers of "bots" (i.e., fake people online) who can get into conversations on social media to propagate fake news and misinformation to confuse voters. These bots, or fake people, can then sway conversations via the applied pressure of the group on individuals. This is no longer advertising; it's something social psychologists call "social influence."[80] Research in social psychology has shown that most people are prone to conform to group pressure, rather than resist it (a point I'll explain in more detail shortly). Perhaps ironically, some Millennials see this environment as limiting their choices in a seemingly endless sea of information. Luis, a Latino college student in Los Angeles said:

> I believe that this Wild West media [environment] must be entered cautiously, similarly to how one would venture vigilantly into the [actual] Wild West. With the proliferation of "bots" and fake news, misinformation can easily be consumed as real information. No longer is one safe to assume that a story is true; however, it was never safe to make that assumption. Keep in mind the media tactic of fear . . . that violence projected from mass media makes the viewer fear the world and makes it seem more dangerous. With the advancements of social media allowing it to constantly penetrate our lives, it can now collectively target individuals with greater intensity, making it almost impossible to not be influenced by it. Indeed, people have no/little choice in the information that they are exposed to, thus they have limited options in what they can believe in.[81]

Social influence and the pressure to conform to the group is unbelievably strong; it probably helped us to survive as a species, since it motivates us to conform to what the group is doing. Studies on the dynamics of the pressure individuals feel to conform were conducted by social psychologist Solomon Asch in the 1950s. In his groundbreaking studies, he showed that even in the case of an unambiguous "test" the *majority* of people are likely to go along with the crowd than to stand alone on their own convictions.[82] Though developed in the 1950s, the same studies have been replicated more recently, and the findings still hold true. Asch's studies were elegantly simple: He arranged to have a group of eight undergraduate "confederates" who were in on the aims of the study, and one person who wasn't, the test subject. The nine people were gathered together in a lab at Swarthmore College, and the test subject was told he was there for a study on perception. All were shown a set of three lines of various sizes, all in a box on the right side of a large white sheet of paper. Each line was labeled A, B, or C (see figure 4).

Then they were asked which line, A, B, or C, matched the length of a line in another box, on the left side of the paper. There was nothing ambiguous about the answer. In the example shown in figure 4, one can clearly see that the matching line is C. The subjects would go from left to right, calling out their best assessment of which of the three lines matched the "test line" on the left. The three comparison lines were of markedly different sizes, so there was a clear match to the test line. The first couple of rounds, all of the confederates would give the correct response, as would the test subject. But after the third round or so, the confederates were told to go along with whatever the first person said, which was an obviously incorrect response.

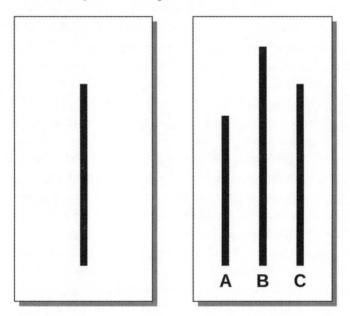

Figure 4. Asch conformity experiment. (Image from Wikimedia Creative Commons; author: Fred the Oyster; licensed under CC BY-S.A 4.0.)

Amazingly, over the twelve critical trials, about 75 percent of participants conformed to the incorrect answers of the group at least once, and only a quarter never conformed. Yet only 1 percent chose the wrong answer when there was no social pressure to provide an incorrect answer, clearly showing that the test was not confusing and participants knew they were choosing the incorrect answer in the group trials. The key takeaway here is this: Social pressure is an incredibly powerful force. It can be used to push people to conform *even when they know they are giving the wrong answer.* Other studies have found that people are even more likely to conform when the situation is ambiguous, in other words, when they're not 100 percent sure what is going on. For example, in a setup similar to the Asch study, confederates would sit in a room filling with smoke, and the test subject, the majority of the time, would sit there right along with them. This tendency to conform is what can now be easily exploited online, as people's social lives are increasingly lived online. Only now we can fake the confederates. With the advent of artificial intelligence and bots, the Asch conformity experiments can be carried out at scale, as (potentially) malevolent or manipulative actors cause people to change their opinions, or even their votes. Unleashing a swarm of tens, hundreds, thousands, or even millions of "bots," (real-seeming online "people" who are actually nothing more than virtual robots) coded with a mission to amplify false information, can be used to pressure those who don't conform into aligning their opinions, votes, and so on. I call this the Dark Army. The implications of leveraging Asch's conformity learnings in the digital arena using human-seeming imitation groups of programmed bots is troubling indeed. Cambridge Analytica, has been said to possess approximately 5,000 data points on every single adult in America. "From that trove of data, it is able to identify the most persuadable voters and send them targeted messages at key times in order to move them to action."[83] Cambridge Analytica connected a well-known psychological test called the OCEAN with Facebook likes, which enables them to build very specific, targeted, and sophisticated computer models to target people in very specific ways. It's like the Asch experiment on steroids.[84] OCEAN stands for *openness, conscientiousness, extraversion, agreeableness,* and *neuroticism,* or what psychologists refer to as the Big Five. Based on those five dimensions, companies can form a remarkably accurate profile of what drives an individual's behavior.[85] Knowing this, targeted ads or, going forward, bots armed with this information, can penetrate online conversations and begin to sway unwitting social media users, using Asch-style social pressure; and, more importantly, they can target those with higher levels of anxiety by focusing on the very things these people are most anxious about. The influencers can then take advantage of the trust the users have in their social network, amplifying fake news, which their friends will share among their friendship network, and so on. This is how the divide-and-conquer strategy is implemented, by leveraging the trust in social networks.

With mass media as the Fourth Estate hobbled as a check and balance to power, and audience trust eroded, people may understandably turn to those they know when seeking trustworthy information. McLuhan predicted this turn during the television era of 1969, saying that the "instant nature of electric-information … is decentralizing—rather than enlarging—the family of man into a new state of multitudinous tribal existences."[86] His prediction has come to fruition since then with the degradation of the "mass" media, the invention of the internet, and the widespread adoption and use of social media. As trust in large-scale institutions erodes due to assaults from detractors, people may turn to "who they know" as a reaction to the communications they receive, while political and social infrastructures crumble around them. The strategy worked before, and it will likely work again. The key is now: Rather than a few "confederates" in a room in the Asch conformity studies persuading one person, bots can amplify the message by the tens of thousands or even millions, persuading voters in key swing areas, for example. They can "friend" people on social networks and lie in wait until the moment they are deployed. At this point, there is little recourse, save for the identification of Russian-generated profiles. What we need now are stronger trust markers—indicating the provenance of data and the provenance of identity, for example, telling us from where and whom information came. Facebook is attempting to address this by putting biographical info of the author and links along with articles, to help people research where their information is coming from, to determine whether it is from a trusted person and/or source. Twitter is addressing the problem by slashing fake accounts—so far, to the tune of 70 million in two months in the summer of 2018 alone.[87] Facebook is also trying to identify and close suspicious accounts, shutting down 583 million fake accounts in just the first three months of 2018.[88] The trouble is that new agents of the Dark Army are likely even now infiltrating people's social networks, building trust, and lying in wait for their moment to be activated.

Clearly, this is an atmosphere that is beginning to erode trust in everything: What is real or what is fake is becoming increasingly harder to discern. This renders "adulting" much more difficult, given that young people are coming of age within the context of a fast-paced and sometimes-confusing digital environment. Online, teens and young adults are presented with a seemingly endless array of choices available at the touch of an app, for living, working, and playing. This sea of choices, combined with the fast churn of social media and online life, make the "'til death do us part" marriages and thirty-year mortgages of their parents' and grandparents' day seem like an eternity. Having so many choices has diminished many young people's willingness (or even interest) in choosing—or committing to—anything. The road to adulthood now has become muddied, the path, unclear.

CHAPTER 3

THE UNTETHERED ADULT

Until one is committed, there is hesitancy, the chance to draw back, always ineffectiveness.

Concerning all acts of initiative and creation, there is one elementary truth, the ignorance of which kills countless ideas and splendid plans: that the moment one definitely commits oneself, then providence moves too.

All sorts of things occur to help one that would never otherwise have occurred. A whole stream of events issues from the decision, raising in one's favour all manner of unforeseen incidents, meetings and material assistance which no man could have dreamed would have come his way.

I learned a deep respect for one of Goethe's couplets:

Whatever you can do or dream you can, begin it. Boldness has genius, power and magic in it.

Begin it now.

—William H. Murray,
The Scottish Himalayan Expedition, 1951

GREENWICH VILLAGE, NEW YORK CITY

"It's a bit small," Roy said with a wince, as he unlocked the door to the apartment in the West Village, my home for the next few days. Roy was drawn to New York by his dream of the bright lights of Broadway ever since he caught the acting bug in high school. Yet moving to Manhattan and "making it there" proved much more difficult than the dream. Tall, whippet-thin, with dark hair, light eyes, and pale skin, Roy's protruding round ears give him a bit of a mouse-like appearance. After his acting career failed to launch, he took a job as a "Genius" at the Apple Store in Midtown Manhattan, renting out his room on Airbnb to make ends meet, staying with his girlfriend whenever guests arrived. Roy seemed friendly but harried as he rushed through a tour of the tiny, windowless living room and kitchen. When he swung open the door to "my room," I caught my breath, seeing how cramped it really was: The queen-sized bed literally filled the whole room side to side; the only free space was a small, one-foot-by-four-and-a-half-foot area at the end of the bed to turn around in. Stepping inside, I was overwhelmed for a moment by the smell of sweat, men's cologne, and worn shoe leather. My head swum for a second, and I searched for something to anchor me in the claustrophobic space. Regaining my bearings, I realized the room was actually a Pinterest-worthy marvel of urban organization: every square inch was utilized and neatly organized. A small shelf jutted out from the wall next to the bed to hold a glass of water or a cell phone. An Elfa closet system on the wall across from the bed held a small TV, surrounded by shelves of Roy's clothes, all neatly folded and arranged by color and season. Winter coats hung in descending order on the back of the door. The bed itself was jacked up on risers so high that, even at five feet nine, I literally had to jump to get in. Had I been any shorter, I'm not so sure I would have made it. Rows of shoes lined the shelves underneath. I was thankful for the windows overlooking the Avenue of the Americas, which gave me some breathing room in this tiny space. Outside, the news was winter. Framed by a graceful, black, wrought-iron Juliet balcony, I could see everyday life persisting below despite the snow. Trucks pulled up and men hustled things to and fro through the snowbanks, into stores across the street. People wended their way past on the sidewalk, bundled up in scarves and hats and shiny black Hunter boots against the cold, many had sweatered dogs ambling alongside. Roy rushed out after pointing out the travel-sized bottles of shampoo and conditioner he'd left for me on the bed. Sitting neatly next to the shampoo, atop the instructions he'd written, was a small orange origami flower he'd apparently folded himself. I picked up the tiny bit of incongruous sunshine on this grey, wintery day and turned it between my thumb and forefinger for a closer look, then stepped back outside the room to look around. All three bedrooms opened onto a windowless living room. On one side, large, opaque plastic storage boxes full of neatly folded clothes were stacked floor-to-ceiling against the wall. A breakfast bar jutted out from the wall across from the kitchen. It served as a dining table, the Elfa storage shelving system below it neatly holding their silverware, glasses, and dishes. Pegs under the kitchen cabinets kept oft-used spoons, spatulas, and other equipment visible and at the ready. A collection of small pans cascaded down the right side of the cabinet.

A single diminutive and oddly angled bathroom hid behind the kitchen; it contained the smallest bathtub I had ever seen. More like a half-tub, it was so tiny that only a small child could stretch out in it. Roy had three roommates, and all three shared this tight space; a comparable apartment in Los Angeles would be a rental for one. The room next to mine housed another Airbnber: Pale-skinned and strawberry-blond, Iris had come to New York for an internship at the Guggenheim. Although polite and pretty, she always seemed preoccupied with ... something. It seemed so strange that none of the roommates were ever there, and instead, two transient visitors occupied their space. Next week, two new transient roommates would meet in this tiny space.

Roy, his roommates, and Iris are all typical untethered adults: young, professional, urban, and on the move; they'd rather rent than own and are increasingly living single. According to the 2010 US Census, almost half (46.3 percent) of Manhattan households contain a single occupant, with some neighborhoods rising as high as two-thirds singles.[1] This uptick in single adults is not unique to Manhattan but is instead indicative of a larger trend sweeping the nation, as Millennials postpone or avoid getting married altogether.

Forming relationships, getting married, and having a family were well-established aspirational goals for earlier generations. For many women, getting married and having a family was *the* goal. Couples at the end of and after World War II prided themselves on getting married and buying a home in the suburbs, with 2.5 children, a dog, and a station wagon in the driveway. These were not only markers of adulthood but also symbols that one had achieved the American Dream. Marriage and establishing a family home are two of the stepping-stones in a series of milestones that together sociologists call the "transition to adulthood." Sociologists Richard Settersten Jr. and Barbara Ray have studied this transition for decades and have identified five key "markers" of adulthood; These are: completing school, leaving home, becoming financially independent with a full-time job, marrying, and having a child.[2] Settersten and Ray are now seeing a shift in the achievement of these milestones compared to earlier generations, saying:

> By the 1950s and 1960s, most Americans viewed family roles and adult responsibilities as being nearly synonymous. For men, the defining characteristic of adulthood was having the means to marry and support a family. For women,

it was getting married and becoming a mother; indeed, most women in that era married before they were twenty-one and had at least one child before they were twenty-three. By their early twenties, then, most young men and women were recognized as adults, both socially and economically.[3]

Young people in their twenties and into their thirties are now untethering in large numbers from the traditional markers of adulthood, choosing instead to experience what can be thought of as an extended period of adolescence. Because the markers have moved, the road to adulthood has become fraught with anxiety, as the path becomes unclear. Writer Julie Beck put out a call to readers of the *Atlantic* to gather their stories of the rocky and uncertain road to adulthood; Maria Eleusiniotis was one who responded. Her anxiety is palpable as she discusses the dizzying array of choices available to her now, making the achievement of adulthood difficult:

> At 28, I can say that sometimes I feel like an adult and a lot of the time, I don't. Being a Millennial and trying to [be an] adult is wildly disorienting. I can't figure out if I'm supposed to start a non-profit, get another degree, develop a wildly profitable entrepreneurial venture, or somehow travel the world and make it look effortless online. Mostly it just looks like taking a job that won't ever pay off my student debt in a field that is not the one that I studied. Then, if I hold myself to the traditional ideal of what it means to be an adult, I'm also not nailing it. I am unmarried, and not settled into a long-term, financially stable career. Recognizing that I'm holding myself to an unrealistic standard considering the economic climate and the fact that dating as a Millennial is exhausting, it's unfair to judge myself, but I confess I fall into the trap of comparison often enough. Sometimes because I simply desire those things for myself, and sometimes because [of] Instagram. My ducks are not in a row, they are wandering.[4]

Like Maria, many Millennials' "ducks" are wandering. Millennials themselves are wandering from job to job, home to home, and relationship to relationship. Digital technologies serve as the connective tissue that keeps their networks intact. The reconstitution of their social networks from analog to digital allows more degrees of freedom of movement away from any specific physical locality and a wider base of friends. Most folks from previous generations didn't wander farther than eighteen miles from their mother.[5] On the other hand, almost a quarter now haven't left home at all, whether as a financial necessity or as a way to simply enjoy the comforts of childhood a little while longer.[6] This represents a marked move away from the path to adulthood traversed by previous generations. In 1960, by age thirty, 77 percent of women and 65 percent of men had achieved all five of the markers of adulthood. By the year 2000, fewer than half of all thirty-year-old women and a third of the men had. A recent study of young adults (ages eighteen to twenty-five) and their romantic relationships found that the most prevalent "group" was composed of those who said they were postponing a serious relationship until their midtwenties or even later. Approximately 10 percent of the group had yet to experience a romantic relationship of at least three months' duration by age twenty-five. These findings prompted the researchers to suggest that perhaps the definition of what the "normal" steps toward adulthood even are needs to be revised.[7]

In 1950, marriage was the main socially approved context for having sex and bearing children; young women who found themselves pregnant and unwed at that time were often sent to "homes for unwed mothers" to discreetly give birth and give the child away for adoption. This practice was common from the beginning of the 1900s well into the 1970s, when it finally fell out of fashion. By 1960, the end of the post–World War II era, which is often referred to by sociologists as the "golden age of the family," 73 percent of the time when households had children, both a husband and a wife were present. From 1960 to 2016, the number of children living with a single mother tripled, from 9 to 26 percent.[8] Now, that is changing. Cherie is one example of these trends: Smart, with a pretty smile and a good sense of humor, she successfully completed her undergraduate degree, then went on to complete a master's degree in social work. She quickly landed her first job in Los Angeles and got to work on accumulating her "hours" toward her counseling license, which she also completed. Soon after, she began posting nervous "countdown to social work license exam day" notes on Facebook. The day she joyfully announced that she had passed her licensure exam, she also announced that she was pregnant. Soon afterward, professionally taken, happy photos of the proud parents showed up on my Facebook newsfeed. Cherie's face glowed happily as she showed off her expanding belly, looking up lovingly at her boyfriend, who gazed down proudly with a broad smile. She and her boyfriend were neither engaged nor married. No plans were announced for either event, and to this day, even though she's since given birth to a healthy and beautiful baby girl, Cherie remains single. She's just one example I've seen of several of my former students who are educated, urban, professional, in their late twenties, and having kids but not getting married. Folks from earlier generations in this situation would have had a "shotgun marriage"—the man would be pressured to marry the woman he had impregnated, typically under the coercion of her father's shotgun. The shotgun marriage now seems a quaint remnant of the past, as having children out of wedlock increasingly becomes the new normal. Cherie and her boyfriend are but two of the many faces of this seismic shift underway in untethering from marriage and a traditional family structure in the United States among digital natives. Marriage continues to be postponed: By 1971, half of the US population was married by the age of twenty-five; nowadays, it's just one out of ten, a record low.[9] The median age (i.e., mathematical middle) when adults first marry also continues to rise: In 2016, it was age 29.5 for men and 27.4 for women, up from ages 23.7 and 20.5, respectively, in 1947.[10] The chart below illustrates these changes.

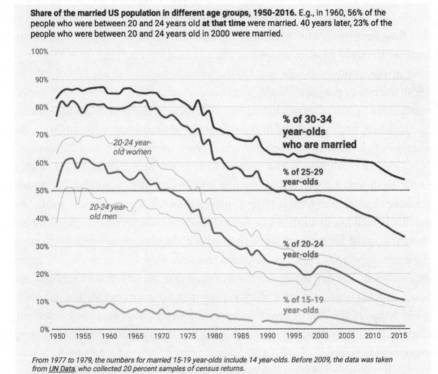

Share of the married US population in different age groups, 1950-2016. E.g., in 1960, 56% of the people who were between 20 and 24 years old **at that time** were married. 40 years later, 23% of the people who were between 20 and 24 years old in 2000 were married.

% of 30-34 year-olds who are married

20-24 year-old women

% of 25-29 year-olds

20-24 year-old men

% of 20-24 year-olds

% of 15-19 year-olds

From 1977 to 1979, the numbers for married 15-19 year-olds include 14 year-olds. Before 2009, the data was taken from UN Data, who collected 20 percent samples of census returns.

Lisa Charlotte Rost, Datawrapper • Source: American Community Survey • Get the data • Created with Datawrapper

Chart 2. Share of the US Population in Different Age Groups, 1950–2016. (Chart from Lisa Charlotte Rost, Datawrapper; source: American Community Survey.)

One reason for these changes may be that digital life spins fast, resulting in time compression. Marriage to someone "'til death do us part" may seem like forever in this fast-spinning world, or it may simply be too "adult" for those who want to postpone adulthood. Twenty-six-year-old comedian and YouTube star Jenna Mourey, better known by her YouTube nickname "Jenna Marbles," has almost 19 million subscribers to her weekly video blog (vlog). On one, she suggests postponing marriage until middle age, saying:

> I have a hard time wrapping my brain around what your f—ing hurry is [when] eighteen-year-olds, twenty-one-year-olds are getting married. . . . Why, dude, why? And that's kind of a rhetorical question; I understand there's lots of reasons why, but the way I look at it is—your theoretically gonna be with that person forever. . . . Why do you need to get married, like, now? Why can't you get married when you're, like, sixty? That's kind of cute. My aunt got married for the first time when she was fifty-two. That s— was f—ing awesome. I have a lot of respect for people that are together for like ten years or fifteen years and they're, like, "Hey dude, you wanna f—ing get married?" Because to me what's important is having that commitment. You don't need a ring, you don't get a dress, you don't need any of that—it's all kind of, like, symbolic of the commitment, but you can certainly have the commitment without all of that.[11]

Twenty-nine-year-old Henya, another social media influencer, who is also a vegan author, said on her vlog (i.e., video blog) that she used to fantasize about meeting "the one" every single day, as a result of watching lots of romantic movies and TV shows as a teen. Having not yet met that person, she has given up on the idea of the American Dream. She seems to hold a pragmatic view of what marriage is about—apparently it's about having someone to drill a hole in a wall when you need it, a task she says she can accomplish some other way. She says:

> You know, it's very, very, hard to imagine someone, like, forty or fifty years old—without a partner. Like, what's life without being married? What's life without being in an American house with a car in the backyard in the garage and, like, a living room and the husband drinks beer? I do not feel like in today's media definitely, and back then, no one ever portrayed a single person above the age of, like, twenty. . . . But my point is I had no idea whatsoever that there's an actual thing. . . . People can just be by themselves and just live by themselves and not have a partner for, like, the rest of their lives. And I know it's really stupid, but I just recently at twenty-eight got to the conclu-

sion that I realized that it is possible to just spend your life without finding the one, without being in a relationship. . . . I feel like—especially women—we're kind of taught that [we're] incomplete without a man. In particular, there are so many things, supposedly, that women can't do, like fix the leak in the sink or drill a hole in the wall or do all these sort of things—which is bulls—. For example, I'm fifty years old and I'm single and I live in a house and whatnot and I need someone to drill a f—ing hole in the wall, I can ask my brother, I can ask my neighbor. . . . There's so many other things I can do to get that need of mine met. . . . It doesn't mean that I have to be married to someone that would, you know, do these things for me.[12]

Postponing marriage isn't simply a shift in behavior. Instead, it signifies a major shift in values around marriage and family. Another leading indicator of this is that Millennials have now surpassed every other generation in terms of single motherhood. In 2016, 8.6 million households were headed by a single mother with a child younger than eighteen years; of those, 4 million mothers were Millennials.[13] The share of never-married mothers among all single mothers has increased from 4 percent in 1960 to 44 percent in 2011.[14] By 2010, fully 57 percent of births to Millennials aged twenty-six to thirty-one were out of wedlock (though, overall, births to teens and young women in their twenties is down).[15] The reasons for being a single mother have also changed. In 1960, it was usually the result of either the death of a spouse or a divorce; then, 95 percent of newly single mothers had in fact been married.[16] Now, only half of single mothers have ever been married, and many are choosing to become pregnant before, or instead of, getting married. Some women who plan to live single are even turning to sperm banks to have children alone, as "single mothers by choice" when a partner is unavailable or unwilling to have children.[17] Others are postponing or eschewing parenthood altogether. An emerging trend among young women in their twenties is to get their fallopian tubes tied to prevent conception—ever. Martin Varsavsky, the CEO of Prelude Fertility, said he's also seen young men in their late twenties and early thirties coming in to get their sperm frozen or to get a vasectomy so they can enjoy sex without having to use condoms to prevent unwanted pregnancies.[18]

Another marker of adulthood and aspect of the American Dream that is changing is the dream of buying the house with the white picket fence. Home buying is down, reversing a trend that began at the founding of our country. Property ownership was a key attractor for pioneers to the New World. After the Industrial Revolution, homeownership, and particularly owning a home in the newly built suburbs, became a key goal for a growing middle class. Owning a home indicated you'd "made it," while putting down roots in a neighborhood ensured you were part of a community: It meant you had neighbors you could go to to borrow a cup of sugar, neighbors who you could help you out in a crisis, and there were other kids your kids could play with. A neighborhood meant there were people you could socialize with, people you would see in church every Sunday. People you could trust. Some families remained in the same home for generations. There was a rootedness about it that lent family members a sense of stability, identity, and purpose. At the turn of the century, 44 percent of twenty-nine-year-olds owned their own home. Now, only 35 percent of those in that same age group are homeowners. A common accolade used to describe upstanding men of prior generations was that they were "pillars of the community." Pillars are stabilizing forces, steadfast and immovable—the polar opposite of the untethered. Now, the British and Australian press have taken to calling untethered stateside Millennials "Generation Rent," while National Public Radio described this phenomenon as "the slamming door of homeownership."[19] Lack of commitment to marriage and family plays a role in this, as does the burden of student debt. Time compression also warps younger digital natives' sense of the pacing of life: For younger potential homebuyers, 30 years, the length of a typical mortgage, seems like an eternity. Many don't know what they want to do five years from now, much less thirty. Also, embittered by the housing crisis, when many saw their parents' houses go underwater (they owed far more than the house was actually worth), many Millennials became dubious of the notion that homeownership builds wealth.[20] Others don't want to spend forever in one place: Todd, a young tech entrepreneur I know from Los Angeles, has moved four times in the past year alone—out of choice, not necessity. He's now considering a move to Spain. There seems to be an internal churn going on in folks like Todd that mirrors the churn of new posts on social media, a kind of mental or emotional restlessness. Todd has told me he gets bored and always wants something new, on the assumption that something (or someone) better may be just around the corner. His attitude reflects a line from Jamie Varon's essay on Millennial dating: "Outside that door is more, more, more. . . ."[21]

Cars have been another cornerstone of the traditional middle-class American Dream. That new station wagon in the driveway after the war signaled to your neighbors that you'd "made it." As suburbs were built farther and farther outside of metro areas, cars became a necessity to commute to work in the city.

As urban flight pushed more people out and away from nearby suburbs to those farther away and even to small nearby towns, the car became more of a need than a want. Yet in recent years, the desire to own a vehicle has fallen away for many digital natives. Today, many Millennials are migrating to urban centers and giving up cars in light of the growing ubiquity of car-sharing services like Lyft, Uber, Zipcar, or EVShare. In some urban areas, electric shareable scooters, like Bird and Lime, can be borrowed with one click on an app and left anywhere once the ride is done. Getting a driver's license used to be a much-anticipated stepping-stone toward adulthood for teenagers. Now, only 69 percent of teenagers have a driver's license, down from 90 percent in 1983. Many don't even know how to drive. In the year 2000, only 21 percent of fourteen-to-thirty-four-year-olds were without a driver's license, but by 2010 it had increased to 28 percent, representing an increase of over 33 percent. Fewer younger people are buying cars now as a result. The share of new vehicles purchased by sixteen-to-thirty-four-year-olds was down by 6 percentage points between 2000 and 2015.[22] Carmakers are scrambling to figure out how to adapt to these changing values and behaviors. Some are turning to a "borrowing" model that matches the desire for the new among digital natives. Cadillac is one of these. Its new luxury-car subscription service, BOOK by Cadillac, allows customers to return their car and check out a new one up to eighteen times a year.[23] Need an SUV for the weekend? Just bring in your two-seater sedan and swap it out, for a mere $1,500 a month. Now that services like Amazon Prime, DoorDash, and Uber Eats deliver ready-made food to your door; meal-delivery programs like Blue Apron, Hello Fresh, and Plated send right to your door in a refrigerated box everything that you need to create a meal; alcohol shows up from Saucey; and dog walkers are available from Wag!, it seems like the cost of owning and maintaining a vehicle is less urgent and, indeed, less appealing—if not even an unnecessary burden in an on-demand, "touch of an app" society. Not to mention the fact that the cost of garaging a car in many cities is exorbitant.

This general lack of desire for long-term commitments is starting to spill into other areas that typically entailed some kind of long-term contract. Gyms, mobile-phone service providers, rental property owners, and others are starting to recognize this shifting value set and are responding by offering "no contracts/ no commitments" to entice younger buyers who seem to think that commitments are for old people. Lack of desire for commitment is becoming one of the hallmarks of this generation and those younger.[24]

UNTETHERED RELATIONSHIPS: "BECAUSE CHOICE"

Another reason for Millennials' lack of desire for commitment is that there are simply too many choices. In terms of relationships, the vast array of choices on social media and dating apps can be both enthralling and overwhelming. On dating apps like Tinder, people have become commodified objects of consumption, where they are rated, accepted, or rejected, usually based on appearance, in an oversaturated dating market.[25] The availability of so many choices literally at one's fingertips on apps can diminish one's desire to commit altogether. The churn rate of relationships now has escalated: the average adult relationship now lasts just over two years.[26] Part of this can be linked to dating apps that facilitate the "hookup" culture of casual sex, like Grindr and Tinder, where one "swipes right" on a photo to indicate interest (a mutual right swipe leads to an introduction on the app). Others, like OkCupid, Bumble, or Match.com, promise that you can meet a mate—or in the case of eHarmony, even a soulmate—if you're willing to endure a four-hour onboarding survey, that is. On Facebook, people are ditching their spouses for the excitement of rekindling a high-school flame. Online dating is now the third most common way people of all ages to meet their spouses, and the second most popular way for those over the age of fifty. The most popular online dating company, Match Group (owners of Match.com, PlentyOfFish, OkCupid, and Tinder), reported 7.43 million paid members in 2018, nearly double its 2014 numbers.[27] Apps that facilitate hookups and "instant" matching using swiping, like Tinder, Grindr, and Bumble, are proving popular with younger daters. Half of Tinder's users are younger than twenty-six.[28] Compare that with eHarmony's average user, who has typically skewed older, between thirty-three and fifty-four years old, with many attracted by the promise of meeting a longer-term "soulmate."[29]

I remember my first visit to the eHarmony offices: Lining the wall of a hallway on one side were hundreds of snapshots and Polaroids of happy couples. On the opposite wall were hundreds of photos of babies. When I asked about them, the executive I was working with said they were couples eHarmony had matched who'd gotten married, and the babies were the result of those matches. My friend Peter Sanger is now one half of one of these couples; he met his wife, Melissa, on eHarmony. He told me he's never been more compatible with anyone in his life. With over five hundred marriages a day, I'm sure eHarmony will soon be needing more wall space. For some, online dating can be ideal, including the busy mothers with small children, the widowed, or older daters who have aged out of the club scene. It can also be a godsend for the shy or socially awkward, since the social "cost" of approaching others online is lowered: The humiliating walk of shame after being shot down by someone in front of a crowd of people in a bar is eliminated, since the embarrassment of rejection is rendered private online. For digital natives who prefer mediated conversations, online dating would seem to make perfect sense.

THE INTERNET AS OTHER

Yet for every "soulmate" who has met someone on a dating app, there is also evidence that online dating is a double-edged sword. Despite its ability to match-make couples who may never have met otherwise, the internet can also tear people apart, undermining committed relationships by providing an endless array of attractive potential mates for romantic or sexual encounters, not to mention pornography of every stripe. As such, it becomes a kind of omnipresent "Other" that can undermine people's willingness to commit to or sustain a monogamous relationship. The "Internet as Other" may more profoundly impact younger users, due to their more frequent use of digital devices. Jamie Varon, in her essay "This Is How We Date Now," discusses the effect the perception of an endless sea of choices has had on her and her fellow Millennials:

> Our choices are killing us. We think choice means something. We think opportunity is good. We think the more chances we have, the better. But, it makes everything watered-down. Never mind actually feeling satisfied, we don't even understand what satisfaction looks like, sounds like, feels like. We're one foot out the door, because outside that door is more, more, more. We don't see who's right in front of our eyes asking to be loved, because no one is asking to be loved.[30]

Common sense tells us that this seemingly endless array of attractive others for romantic partnerships or "hookups" would make finding a compatible mate easier. Yet, paradoxically, having more choices actually makes it even harder to choose. This was demonstrated in the now-classic "jam study" by consumer psychologists Sheena Iyengar and Mark Lepper. They set up a table in a store, giving shoppers a choice of twenty-four different varieties of gourmet jam to try. After the jam tasting, shoppers were given a coupon for a discount on a jar of jam. The next day, the researchers presented shoppers with only six choices of jam before they were given the discount coupon. It turns out that on the days when shoppers were given more choices, they were only one-tenth as likely to buy *any* jam, compared with the days when they were given fewer choices.[31] This inability to choose in the face of a vast array of options has been called "choice overload." In the realm of romantic relationships, choice overload has been linked to an inability to choose a romantic partner. Studies have also found that having more choices diminishes people's willingness to tolerate a partner's flaws or transgressions, particularly for men. The appearance of more choices of available attractive romantic partners also predicts breakups and divorce.[32]

Those who are less skilled at forming relationships can also find a place for themselves online. Socially awkward, lonely young men have found a ready tribe of like-minded others with whom to air their grievances and plot revenge against women whom they perceive as having wronged them. These "incels" (short for "involuntarily celibates," for their lack of success with women) foment hostility online against women whom they blame for denying them their perceived "right" to sexual intercourse.[33] Self-styled gurus have found a willing audience among these young men, promising them surefire skills for sexual conquest. Neil Strauss's bestselling book *The Game* provided a glimpse into the underground world of aspiring "pickup artists," where gurus like "Mystery" (real name Erik von Markovik) teach socially awkward young men such lessons as how to avoid awkward silences and boring conversations. The Mystery Method website guarantees success to these desperate young men, saying, "These 2 simple tactics guarantee that ALL your conversations are exciting!" and "What to say and do once a woman is over at your house to make her feel comfortable enough to go into your room . . . and jump into your bed!"[34] One popular technique is to "neg" young women, that is, to offer a semi-insulting compliment or to insult them outright (e.g., "Hey, your roots are showing."), to improve the young man's chances of "scoring" by lowering her self-esteem.[35] An entire pickup artist subculture has developed with online groups, meetups, bulletin boards, and expensive in-person seminars focused on training aspiring pickup artists in techniques that can include elements of neurolinguistics programming (NLP) or even hypnosis.[36] Because many young digital natives have less experience now with face-to-face interactions, due to escalating screen time, these pickup-artist gurus will continue to be in demand. Although their seminars address the right problems, their passive-aggressive, superficial, "pick-up-and-dump" approach will ultimately leave young men holding an empty relationship bag—perhaps the wrong end goal for the lonely.

The endless sea of choices online is also beginning to destabilize existing relationships. As Varon put it in her essay, "We're always one eye wandering at the options."[37] Dating apps and social media act as a constant reminder to people that alternatives to their current relationship exists at the touch of a button, which contributes to relationship instability. This "Internet as Other" provides an unprecedented level of ease of access to sexual gratification and extramarital affairs. Online, people can easily and discreetly "test out the waters" before leaving a relationship. Clandestine affairs can be started at a relatively low social or financial cost on websites or apps explicitly designed for that purpose, many of which target men—sites like Ashley Madison provide matchmaking for affairs, or what it calls "discreet married dating."[38] The tagline on its website matter-of-factly declares, "Life is short. Have an affair." Other sites targeting men for affairs include Sugar Baby/Sugar Daddy websites like Sugardaddie.com or Seeking.com. On these sites, "Sugar Daddies" are encouraged to trade money and presents for no-strings-attached sex with younger women. On SugarBook .com, under "What it means to be a Sugar Baby," the site explains, "The Sugar Baby is an individual seeking mentorship, financial support, or general companionship under the terms of an agreed-upon arrangement. She could be a single mom, someone seeking assistance with month-to-month expenses, or simply a goal-focused woman who seeks a higher class of life. Business aside, genuine feelings of love and long-term relationships often form."[39] It goes on to say that college students make up a large portion of Sugar Babies on the site, and that they "often benefit from the mentorship, generous allowances, exotic vacations and shopping sprees across the globe," which also gives the men an idea of what to expect. Many of the women on these sites claim to be "paying their way through college," positioning them as "nice college girls," as opposed to prostitutes, thereby shifting the sex-work aspect of the Sugar Baby/Sugar Daddy relationship into the realm of more traditional courtship and marriage, where trading beauty for money is a well-established and accepted practice.

The impacts of social media and dating apps and websites on preexisting relationships are beginning to emerge: In the United States, the diffusion of Facebook between 2008 and 2010 has been correlated with an increase in the divorce rate during that same time period.[40] Furthermore, family lawyers have seen an increase in the number of divorce cases involving social networks in recent years.[41] Meanwhile, one in seven people says he or she has considered divorce because of a spouse's questionable activity on Facebook, Skype, Snapchat, Twitter, or WhatsApp.[42] Younger unmarried users say that social media negatively impacts their relationships by making them "too visible" to others (69 percent), and a quarter said that this can evoke jealousy.[43] Given the myriad of romantic choices in their pocket (or hand) at all times, young people now may be less inclined to work through the rough patches in their relationships, turning instead to dating apps to seek out some new, imagined "more perfect"—and frictionless—other online. Dating then becomes not a means to an end (i.e., not a way to find "The One") but instead an end in itself, an endless carousel of superficial experiences.

The end result of coming untethered means coming unmoored from the stability of things like committed relationships. The ephemeral nature of romantic relationships may be contributing to the marked increase in psychological disturbances seen among teens and young adults in recent years. In 2013, 95 percent of college-counseling-center directors reported seeing a greater number of students with severe psychological problems than they had in the previous years.[44] Several college counselors have told me they've seen students come in for anxiety around social media, sometimes because they are cyberstalking their exes, then becoming distraught when the ex starts to date someone new. There's an "in your face" quality about all of this now, which previous generations never had to deal with when they were coming of age. For college students, time spent online may actually be a symptom of the depression or anxiety they are feeling. "Digital isolation" creates a vicious cycle, diminishing their social circles, which leads to the unintended consequence of raising levels of loneliness and stress, which then feeds their depression and anxiety.[45] Other unintended consequences of excessive time spent online among college students include neglect of their academic work, which can lead to failure in school, lowered GPAs, and—once again—heightened levels of anxiety.[46] Other side effects include neglected domestic responsibilities, financial problems, and increased substance use, including tobacco and alcohol.[47]

RESHAPING THE AMERICAN DREAM

The move away from committed relationships and other connections to stabilizing social structures (e.g., homeownership, religion, etc.) necessarily means a reshaped trajectory of adulthood. The American Dream has always been aspirational, yet now, what one aspires to is changing. In the 1980s, a popular bumper sticker read, "He who dies with the most toys wins," capturing the competitive and consumerist aspects of the dream. Now, those aspirations are changing. Fabrice Grinda's story is indicative of this changing zeitgeist. Grinda is the digital era's answer to Jordan Belfort's 1980s *Wolf of Wall Street*. At forty, Grinda's net worth hovered somewhere north of $100 million. His angel investments ranged from Uber to Alibaba to the sales app Letgo. Like many men approaching middle age, Grinda suddenly had a midlife crisis. Yet unlike many men of the Baby Boomer generation before him, who would typically react to it by buying a sports car to show off their wealth and success, or by growing their hair long and starting a new workout routine in an effort to hang on to their waning masculinity, Grinda did the exact opposite: He began to purge his life of all of the "things" he had acquired in his boom days, including his $50,000-a-year butler, a twenty-acre estate in Upstate New York, a $300,000 McLaren sports car, and a beautiful $13,000-a-month *pied-à-terre* in Manhattan. He donated all of his furniture to a Manhattan thrift shop and gave his kitchen wares to a local church before setting off to travel, CouchSurfing-style, flopping with friends in Miami, Paris, Nice, and elsewhere—armed only with a stash of cash, a suitcase, and a backpack containing fifty items, including two pairs of jeans, a bathing suit, and ten pairs of socks.[48]

Fabrice soon proved an overbearing and unwelcome houseguest, talking loudly and disrupting his friends' sleep patterns while imposing on their wives to do his laundry. He now lives out of rented hotel rooms and Airbnb apartments. In one interview, he said, "My home is where I am, and it doesn't matter if it is a friend's place or a couch or the middle of the jungle or a hotel room on the Lower East Side."[49] He then added, "But I realize that most of humanity, especially women, don't see it that way." According to the "old Dream," Fabrice had "made it"; yet he gave most of it away in an attempt to recapture his youth, by emulating younger, untethered, nomadic Millennials.

My friend Robert is another example. A bright and successful Gen Xer living in Dallas and working in the healthcare-technology industry, he had a posh apartment overlooking Main Street, decorated with an impressive collection of modern art and home furnishings. Active in local philanthropy, he also sat on the board of a nearby art museum. Around four years ago, he married Lacy, a Millennial accountant who hailed from another town in Texas. Within a year, they gave it all up to chase their dream of wanderlust and adventure. Both quit their jobs; he sold the glamorous condo and liquidated his car, motorcycle, and art collection to fund the dream. Living out of backpacks, they first hiked the Pacific Crest Trail—which stretches 2,650 miles from Mexico, along the Sierra Mountain chain, all the way north to British Columbia—depending on "trail angels" along the way for things like snacks and water. They stopped only occasionally at Airbnb cabins for a once-in-a-while splurge of a steak dinner, craft beer, or glass of good California Central Coast Cabernet, and a warm shower. Currently hiking in Nepal, they have no clear future plans to "settle down" at all. In fact, Robert just got his first haircut in twenty months, his former short, conservative, corporate haircut long ago giving way to a long-haired style he refers to as "trail hippy." The couple are photographing and writing about their adventures on their blog, *Modern Gypsy Tales*.[50]

Clearly, Robert and his wife had more resources to "up and wander" than the typical digital nomad. Others not so financially situated are flying by the seat of their pants, pursuing a digital-nomad lifestyle by CouchSurfing, staying in cheap hostels, or finding other live/work situations to support their time on the road. In June 2018, I stayed in a hostel in San Francisco to get a firsthand look at some of these untethered digital nomads. I stayed in a dorm room with three other girls for $64 a night, instead of choosing the more expensive but private room, to get the full, immersive experience. I arrived to the shared room of four bunk beds, only to be met by the contents of someone's luggage splayed across the floor around the room's only sink. A girl sitting on the top bunk across from me apologized for the mess. I asked her how she was doing, and with a grimace she replied, "Not very good. I didn't know San Francisco was going to be so expensive. . . . My housing with my friend fell through, and I'm totally out of money. I'm going to have to fill up on the [free] breakfast tomorrow morning!" The next day, her glum mood lifted as she excitedly told me about a new job she'd been offered from the Workaway site. She'd just come from a yoga and "sacred-sexuality" retreat in New Mexico, and before that was caring for horses at a ranch. She would soon be on her way to her next work adventure, an organic vegetable farm in the Sonoma area. The Workaway website and another, HelpX, give volunteers the chance to work on tasks ranging from farming to home renovation, running a bed and breakfast, or providing childcare, typically done for room and board. This particular girl told me she had been on the road doing Workaway gigs for a year. She seemed to have no intention of stopping any time soon.

Why does untethering from the traditional American Dream, as illustrated by these cases, seem to be the new normal? For clues, one might look at the context that Millennials and those younger grew up in. Rather than simply a case of "maturity lag," the trifecta of a weakened economy, having grown up in a "risk society" where uncertainty was the rule, and the ubiquity of digital connectivity all seem to be contributing to a new cynicism toward the stability, and indeed, desirability, of traditional social structures. Instability and change seem to be encoded in their social DNA, the product of childhoods plagued by uncertainty that left an indelible mark on their beliefs and values: Parents lost long-held jobs in the Great Recession, shattering the notion of a "job for life"; major banks failed; families lost their homes during the Fannie Mae / Freddie Mac mortgage crisis; divorce tore apart half their homes. When the Twin Towers fell on 9/11, it shook many young people's confidence that the government could protect them. All of these events left them with a shattered sense of trust in social institutions and instilled an abiding sense of anxiety. Given this background, it is understandable that very little seems safe, predictable, or even certain. In response, many digital natives are choosing to live life unhooked from what are, in fact, stabilizing social institutions, including marriage and the family, religion, homeownership, and political parties. Because they are the largest cohort in history, it matters greatly that Millennials are disconnecting from the social fabric in droves, partly because of their influence on other generations.[51] For them, less truly is more. Or so it seems.

Untethering from home and hearth has impacts beyond changing individual lives. Cities are beginning to come up short when it comes to available housing, as family structures change and more people are choosing to live alone. New York City is one of these. The mayor of New York and local real-estate developers have responded by rethinking housing, since apartments there are now more often inhabited by a single adult living alone, as opposed to a young family. Though cramped, Roy's apartment that I stayed in is absolutely palatial when compared to New York's newest rental units. These "micro apartments" range in size from 260 to 360 square feet, about the size of a typical college dorm room. Further trying to appeal to digitally immersed untethered people, they come with an online roommate-matching program. These tiny units consist of a living space, a small kitchenette, and a balcony. These "affordable" micro apartments opened March 2016 on the gentrifying East Side of Manhattan's Kip's Bay, rent for between $2,000 and $3,000 a month. Normal monthly rent is between $2,550 and $3,140 for units in the square-footage range of these micro apartments. The project is already fully rented out, with 60,000 applicants and an extensive waiting list.[52] San Francisco is another city plagued by high rents and an influx of thousands of single tech workers. It is considering permitting even smaller units, perhaps as small as 150 square feet, about the size of a walk-in closet. One such high-density micro apartment building has already opened in San Francisco's SOMA district; its 230-square-foot tiny lofts rent for $2,237 a month.[53] Escalating rents driven by the Silicon Valley tech boom have driven some from apartments altogether: One young man is living in a wooden box in a friend's living room; another has chosen to live inside the back of a repurposed 128-square-foot cargo truck with no running water, bathroom, or electricity, in the parking lot of Google.[54] He showers at the Google gym, eats his meals in the company dining room, charges his laptop at work during the day, and uses a small, battery-powered camping lantern in the van for light at nighttime. Driving down the street in Palo Alto near the Facebook headquarters recently, I saw an entire fleet of older-model RVs parked along the road, clearly serving as housing on the cheap for those who had come to Silicon Valley for the tech boom, or for those working in supporting roles. An entire hashtag (#vanlife) has emerged on Instagram, where people share their tricks and tactics for living in a van or an RV, a lifestyle we'll explore more later.

Another living situation emerging in response to untethering is co-living in "adult dormitories." Some venture capitalists are calling this "the future of cities."[55] One of these is *Common*. With several locations, including one in the hip Williamsburg district of Brooklyn, Common offers hip, curated, and stylish buildings and provides a turnkey approach to living. The buildings offer everything from yoga studios and movie screening rooms, to cleaning supplies and a weekly cleaning service. These "dorms" are decorated with hip, modern furniture from Restoration Hardware; all you need to do is bring your duffle bag of clothes, electronics, and toiletries, and you're home. Rather than rent, these communities emphasize "membership," as if the living space were a private club. As a former faculty in residence at USC, I lived in the dorms with students and a rotating staff of three residential advisors (known a RAs) for seven years. What Common is offering sounds exactly like student living in college dorms at a private university. The Common website shows a group of happy residents out on a ski trip, advertising that "Each week, your House Leaders host a get together in one of the five beautiful common areas. Each month, the entire NYC Common community does something fun together out in the neighborhood."[56] Common features individual bedrooms but shared living spaces and kitchen/ dining areas, extending the "college experience" of adolescence into adulthood. Most importantly, there's no commitment. The Common website emphasizes, "With just one day's notice, you can move to another room at Common Havemeyer or any other Common home, anywhere."

Hotels and furniture designers are also responding to these changing sociodemographic trends, looking to modernism and its "less is more" aesthetic for inspiration. This phrase, "less is more," was first uttered by the famous "starchitect" Ludwig Mies van der Rohe (a member of the influential German Bauhaus movement) to describe modern design and a minimalist aesthetic that influenced everything from architecture to furniture to product design, beginning in the 1930s.[57] His favored "mid-century modern" style has been making a comeback lately in urban centers. Its pared-down, "cool" aesthetic, devoid of ornamentation, seems to embody both the promise of technology and the "travel light" aesthetic of the untethered urban dweller. Young German designer Till Könneker recently reimagined modernism in a line of pared-down, multiuse furniture for untethered urban dwellers living in small spaces. Könneker's talks about how his designs were created in response to his own challenge of living in a tiny studio apartment:

> I moved into an apartment studio without storage room. So, I made a minimalist cube design with a shelf for my vinyl collection, my TV, clothes, and shoes. On the cube is a guest bed and inside the cube is a lot of storage space. . . . A house is not really flexible, but we can re-think the space and furniture inside. I believe useful furniture must be adaptable to the needs of the user.[58]

Könneker's "Living Cube" is part storage unit, part furniture. It is both efficient and sleek—an inspired marriage of both form and function. IKEA is also responding to the untethered zeitgeist by offering a "small spaces" collection, which packs plenty of form and function into modern-day tiny apartments and homes. IKEA describes the vision for this line on its website:

> Small ideas are about finding and using hidden spaces and choosing furniture that does more than one thing. It's about being creative, a little rebellious and doing what you dream about no matter how much or how little space you have.[59]

Their appeal to "rebelliousness" is clearly targeting a youthful buyer, and IKEA gets that demographic. Its nightstands have built-in wireless charging stations that will appeal to power-hungry Millennials, 83 percent of whom sleep with their cell phones.[60] IKEA's wireless charging products include a bed-loft combo; a desk; two bedside tables; and floor, table, and work lamps—all embedded with wireless chargers for mobile devices. IKEA has traditionally targeted people with thin wallets and quickly realized that the number one value to that customer now is 24/7 connectivity, which relies on power. It identified the pain point—the need to charge the critical mobile devices allowing uninterrupted connectivity—and created the solution. Hotels are also beginning to react to these changing preferences, offering smaller rooms with free Wi-Fi, communal spaces to work, and such technophilic amenities as keyless room entry and a smartphone app that lets guests adjust the room temperature or make restaurant reservations without talking to a human.[61]

Millennials are untethering in droves from other social structures that used to give people a sense of identity, community, and belonging, including churches and political organizations. According to a study of over 35,000 adults by Pew Research, they are the largest group not attached to any particular religious organization, with almost a third reporting no religious affiliation at all, which is up 10 percentage points since 2007.[62] Compare that to just 16 percent of Baby Boomers and 9 percent of the Silent Generation. There are a couple of factors impacting their decision to steer clear of these institutions. For one thing, there is a strong correlation between being married and attending church; Millennials' staying singles longer is one driver of their lowered interest in churchgoing. Having children is also related to churchgoing; since having kids is also on the decline, this too plays into the trend of lessened church attendance.[63]

Millennials are also untethering from political parties at three times the rate of the Silent Generation, and almost twice that of Boomers. Fully 50 percent of Millennials claim to be political independents now, versus 37 percent of Baby Boomers, and only 9 percent of the Silent Generation.[64] One reason seems to be that the extreme polarization of political parties we have seen in recent years, driven by a combination of branded news media and social media "tribes" has turned them off. Their aversion is so strong that almost 90 percent said they would never consider running for office, and most avoid talking about politics altogether.[65]

THE SINGULARITY MEETS HER

As digital technologies progress and artificial intelligence gets more sophisticated, people may untether from human relationships altogether, creating vexing new issues and challenges as people, laws, and policy scramble to keep up. Kids growing up now will deal with next-generation technologies as they grow up, in the form of various digital assistants such as IBM's Watson and others. These technologies are sure to bring further disruption to the established social order, as they facilitate (for some) a complete untethering from intimate and romantic human relationships. The enlarging sphere of the Internet of Things (IoT) will bring with it an intensification of these trends. Digital immersion will expand via connected smart homes (including apartments) and a plethora of intelligent devices (including smart, autonomous vehicles), all controllable by the user's smartphone or an interface like Amazon's voice-controlled Echo electronics using the Alexa command. The Internet of Things is another step away from analog life, toward an always-on, digitally mediated, interconnected world. It will be so pervasive that some are calling it "the Internet of Everything." The interfaces to "everything" are still evolving from flat-screen apps toward three-dimensional autonomous "agents" that have an intelligence of their own, part of what I call "the Internet of Them." One company, Gatebox, is on the cutting edge of this movement. Rather than a graph or a faceless, disembodied voice like Amazon's Alexa, they have imagined an interface to this world in the form of a virtual "wife," an attractive, three-dimensional, holographic girl, in the Japanese hentai style like the popular Sailor Moon. The girl will not only turn on and off your lights, stereo, heater, or AC, but will also send text messages to the lonely, single, urban dweller it serves throughout the day, texts like, "Have a nice day," "I miss you," or "Come home early," thus simulating a real-life "wife" at home.[66] One male follower on Gatebox's Facebook page said about her:

> I just found my perfect wife. She is amazing . . . no sex though but I have 2 hands, and she never complains or nags . . . ever. And the best thing is when I get sick of her I can just sell her on eBay.[67]

In a world where swiping right on a cell phone has become a primary way young people meet, where relationships are as ephemeral as a disappearing pic on Snapchat, a virtual wife you can "sell on eBay" when you get sick of her seems to fit the short attention span of many in this fickle, no-commitments-wanted demographic.

In 1993, noted science fiction author and computer scientist Vernor Vinge predicted that "within thirty years, we will have the technological means to create superhuman intelligence. Shortly after, the human era will be ended."[68] As we draw nearer to the future he termed the "singularity," we'll need to consider the very real ramifications of the convergence of robotics, artificial intelligence (AI), virtual reality (VR), and humans. As the lines between machines and humans blur, we need to redefine both legally and socially what it means to be in a relationship.

Filmmakers are already beginning to grapple with these questions. In the 2013 sci-fi movie *Her*, Theodore Twombly (played by Joaquin Phoenix), a lonely, melancholic urbanite, spends his days writing emotional prose for virtual clients. Upon booting up his new "OS1" operating system, he is surprised by its friendly-sounding female voice, complete with emotional inflections, personality, and a sense of humor. Samantha (from the Aramaic term for "listener") or Sam, as she calls herself, is a marvel of machine learning: she listens and learns and responds in the same way humans do when they are developing an intimate relationship. Samantha and Theodore begin very much like any online relationship, with lots of back-and-forth communication and quickly deepening feelings. In the film, the filmmaker is essentially asking the audience to consider whether, in an increasingly untethered society like the United States, where one in five suffers from persistent loneliness, it is so far-fetched to imagine that a lifelike digital being like Samantha could be the object of someone's romantic affections.[69] One young man, Bryan, differentiated between meeting in real life and having a completely virtualized dating experience using a VR dating app:

> It depends on what you want from a dating site. If you want to meet in real life then yes, a real dating site is probably just as good, if not better. However, if you wanted a VR dating experience only, you'd go to a VR dating site. I would expect.[70]

Another young man, Jeffrey, was more interested in a replacement model, carrying on VR relationships purely in VR, with no intention of transferring them to face-to-face reality. For him, VR becomes a way to experience a form of idealized relationship and intimacy, while minimizing any potential "negative" real-life struggles. He said:

> All of these programs already provide an immersive way to talk to people and their avatars and activities are far more advanced than yours. However, what's not currently available is a way to match a user with another user who specifically wants to have a date-like experience, one on one, and private. A VR relationship . . . for people who want to date in VR but not in real life. As for actually meeting in real life, hmmm, that would be a really bad idea. There's nothing worse than falling in love with this person behind an idealized avatar only to meet in real life and discover you've been having feelings for a 4 ft 6

transgender truck driver. What happens in VR should stay in VR. I myself would not mind a VR relationship. Meet a girl in VR, swaps stories, ask about each other's day, be supportive etc., but never, ever meet or see each other. That way the relationship stays idealized. I strongly suspect it's inevitable that something like that will happen, although right now VR is definitely a boy's club with men outnumbering women.[71]

Bryan talked about VR being attractive because it eliminates the financial pressures of having to provide for a wife in the real world. Yet the emotions of disappointment for him were very real when his VR chat companion turned out to be married in real life, putting an end to his fantasy relationship:

Actually, life is a lot cheaper if you're single. If I had to justify my VIVE purchase and additional new PC purchase to a wife or girlfriend I doubt they'd be happy about it. I'm single and without someone wanting new shoes, bigger house, holidays, etc., saving money is not hard. Yes, most of the women I meet in VR are not single and it's hard to find women in VR in the first place. That's why I don't think internet dating will be a thing for quite some time. Yet I see the appeal. I was talking to a woman the other day on VRchat. A perfectly nice and pleasant conversation between mature people, and then she mentioned she was married and I felt disappointed. Despite the fact she was 15 years younger than me and in a different country it had felt as if I had been talking to some girl I had met at a function in real life.[72]

Already, some virtual reality "dating simulator" games exist where (mainly) guys can interact with Asian young women, like with VR Kanojo. Some young men are "dating" and already falling in love with virtual girlfriends. One can choose clothes from a virtual dresser before interacting with the girl in a 3-D apartment and playing games like darts to unlock the next level. On the couple of YouTube simulations that I saw, one young man (the YouTube influencer PewDiePie) immediately looked up the girl's skirt; another grabbed her breasts within the first moments of the game beginning.[73] The girl in the game was outfitted in a sexy short German dirndl, complete with waist cincher and push-up bra. An inspection of the demo for another of these VR love games, LovinVR, shows a pretty rudimentary experience, where disembodied heads float in a room. Players are given the possibility to play a game to get to know each other, one of which is to ask "embarrassing questions." Another game was to discuss "controversial topics," where couples would talk about their views on such hot-button issues as abortion.[74] Clearly, VR simulations of human relationships like this one would benefit from the input of someone more well versed in human relationship dynamics, as opposed to a VR game coder. Such games could be useful, however, as training platforms for the socially anxious to practice their dating skills, to help them develop better flirting and conversational skills with potential real-life romantic partners.

The future of artificially intelligent agents and their enlarging relationships with humans will transform how we think about relationships themselves. In the movie *Her*, Samantha and Theodore's simulated relationship eventually hits the rocks due to her disembodied state, since the relationship couldn't be consummated. But what if that weren't the case? It's not hard to imagine that modern robotics combined with AI could result in highly intelligent silicon, human-seeming robots like those depicted in the film *Ex Machina*.[75] Might such an embodied partner—customized to precisely match one's sexual "type"—blond, redhead, or brunette; black, white, Asian, or Latina; small- or large-busted; green-eyed or brown, and so on—be appealing? The costs associated with artificial companionship run high now, as silicon dolls currently without built-in robotics and artificial intelligence run an average of $6,500 each; although, as is the case with Moore's law, the price should come down over time.

Other questions and issues will arise as these realistic, human-seeming machines come into our homes, adding complexity to marriage and family dynamics while further untethering people from human-to-human relationships. Such moral conundrums run the gamut; for instance, if a wife comes home to find her husband having "relations" with the robotic nanny, is he technically cheating? Cities including Toronto, Canada, are allowing the opening of robot sex brothels, the social impacts of which are yet unknown.

The fast-spinning development of digital technologies is beginning to conflict with some of the slower, long-evolved human anthropological, psychological, and sociological needs for companionship, intimacy, identity, and belonging. The challenge in this high-churn, digitally connected, "always on" atmosphere is to slow down, to take the time to seek true intimacy and real self, rather than swiping for more, more, more—to realize that there is value in commitment, to being tethered to something. It provides an anchor point for stability. Being woven into the social fabric is an important contributor to both emotional and physical health. Unfortunately, given the endless sea of romantic partners and lifestyle choices on addictive social media and gamified dating apps, committing to anything is easier said than done.

Kids are now growing up digital. Those who are currently children will be the first generation to grow up not only where there always was an internet and connected mobile devices, but also voice-controlled intelligent agents like Amazon's Alexa, Apple's Siri, Google's Home, or Gatebox's virtual wife. For these kids, interacting with an intelligent agent will become a routine and unremarkable part of their daily lives. It may even come to be viewed as the same as interacting with a human, or perhaps even be preferred, since, unlike a human, these digital agents will cater to their every wish or desire without imposing needs or desires of their own. What unintended consequences will emerge for kids and teens who are growing up from infanthood staring at screens, where more and more of life is digital, virtualized, and simulated? Since we know the first few years are the most critical in shaping a child, setting the foundation for his or her life, what will it mean that their earliest relationships are with artificially intelligent virtual agents like Alexa or Google? How might this impact the development of their personalities? What about their empathy for others? Some impacts of growing up digital we know. Others will remain to be seen.

CHAPTER 4

GROWING UP DIGITAL

The world is broken and the people who know how to put it back together are dead or have been put out to pasture. The poet and psychologist Robert Bly predicted this, in his book, The Sibling Society. I'm not a huge fan of everything Bly says, but I like his take on the dangers of having a lack of real elders. In his older, pre-internet books, he speaks of a coming "horizontal culture," where we look to each other for guidance, instead of the veterans who've seen this all before. The tribe cannot look to the tribe for help, it must look to wise council, to the medicine people, the shamans, the great grandmothers and wizards. The wizards are gone. Many factors are at play, but the internet, in its total flattening of the world, has created perpetual lost teenagers of us all, looking into a tiny box for likes, and finding the holes in our hearts growing like chasms of forgotten footing.
—Donavan Freberg, photographer, Facebook post, 2017

"It always kills me to see a family out for a meal, and everyone at the table is cast in the glow of a screen, ignoring each other," Andy Grignon, one of the original members of the iPhone development team, lamented.[1] The first phone call on any iPhone from Steve Jobs—ever—went to Andy. "I can't speak for the rest of the original iPhone team," he went on, "but I know I wouldn't ever want what we ended up with today. This thing was just supposed to be a kick-ass web browser that played music and made phone calls." Andy had posted a picture on Facebook of his kids at the "kids' table" in a restaurant. All four kids sat slack-faced, elbows on the table, staring at iPhones. No one was interacting with anyone else, each mesmerized by his or her own screen. Unfortunately, he'd captured the image of many family dinners today. One night while out to dinner in Los Angeles, I was seated next to a family with a boy who was about seven. The boy's mesmerized wide eyes and frozen smile were lit by the blue glow of a cell phone, the tinny music emanating from the device hanging cloyingly in the air like bad perfume. The grandma next to him sat slumped over in defeat, a glum look on her face as she stared off into space. Clearly, she'd come with the hope to interact with the boy, but he was having none of it. Grandma is oh-so-boring compared to the excitement of the cartoon or game on the screen. The relentless electronic nursery rhymes emanating from the device at this dinner drowned out all hope of conversation. The family ate in sullen silence, their dinner hijacked by the phone. Mealtime is important for kids' socialization into both language and social expectations for their behaviors. One study of two hundred families found that positive communications during family mealtimes predicted higher child quality of life.[2] An ad for XFinity Wi-Fi addresses this problem. It first shows an array of family dinners across history, normalizing the pre-device family meal as a time for reconnecting, sharing, and communing together. Then comes the modern family: suburban, middle-class, and digital; Dad and kids sit at the dinner table, staring at devices. Mom surveys the scene and with a swift touch of an app on her phone, expertly shuts off the Wi-Fi. The teen girl says "Hey," and points at her screen. "I paused it," Mom replies, then she says with a cheery tone, "So how is everyone?" They all immediately get down to the business of dinner.[3] This is not how it usually goes in real life, of course. Teens are the most likely age group to think it's fine for children to use their cell phones during meals.[4] The majority (58 percent) of adolescents and young adults aged eighteen to twenty-four say they text during a family meal, and 87 percent say they'd text at a funeral.[5] It seems nothing is sacred anymore. Several moms I know say they have to text or call their kids to even get them to come down for the family dinner. I once gave a talk at a local museum in LA; afterward, one mom came up to the microphone in the Q & A and said she'd called her son for dinner; he answered the call, said, "wrong number," and hung up on her.

Kids under ten now have not only never known a world without the internet but also have never known a world without digital *mobility*, that is, without internet-enabled devices like smartphones, laptops, or tablets. As I have already mentioned in a previous chapter, babies now are picking up digital skills even before acquiring language, as myriad "baby with iPad" videos on YouTube will attest.[6] Tim, an engineer and father of four, said of his kids:

All my kids picked up the iPhone and iPad early. My 16-month-old understands swiping/scrolling. My other three picked it up early as well. My 6- and
8-year-olds are pretty good on them. They also use the computer for homework. They started that in kindergarten.[7]

Tim's kids are typical of most in the United States these days. By 2013, 72
percent of children under the age of eight had used a mobile device for playing
games, watching videos, or using apps, almost double the number (38 percent)
when compared to 2011. Ninety-eight percent of all households with kids under
age eight not only have a mobile device but also a TV,[8] which parents say is
"always" or "almost always" on, making glowing screens, background noise, and
stimulation a constant. The average kid under eight now spends two hours and
nineteen minutes a day gazing at a screen. For lower-income kids, that number
is even higher. In homes with a yearly household income under $30,000, kids
under eight spend nearly three and a half hours a day staring at screens. By
comparison, kids from higher-income homes making more than $75,000 a
year spend only an hour and fifty minutes staring at screens. Researchers from
Common Sense Media attribute different situational factors as reasons for this
disparity, including having a mother who is working and can't monitor the
amount of screen time.[9] One of the mothers in their study said to the researcher,
"all she can do is call every few hours and ask, 'Have you eaten? Have you done
your chores?'" In a sense, the device becomes a digital babysitter. In other cases,
kids may have moved to a neighborhood where they don't know anyone, or to
a dangerous neighborhood, making device time perhaps a safer option for these
kids than outdoor play, where the risks are unknown.

Half of kids under eight watch TV or play video games in the hour before
bedtime, and most who have cell phones sleep with them. More than half (52
percent) check those cell phones in the middle of the night, a habit that contributes to sleep deprivation.[10] Among teens, screen time is even higher: 91 percent
go online every day, and a quarter say they are online "constantly."[11] Although
some argue that digital media is facilitating creativity for kids, studies have found
that digital devices are mostly used for passive entertainment, like watching
videos or listening to music (41 percent). Common Sense Media talked about
this passive entertainment and how it can lead to long gaps in conversation with
those around them; here, they talk about one of their interviewees, a fifteen-
year-old girl:

Videos—short or long—often lend themselves to relatively quiet consumption so that viewers do not miss anything. For example, our interview with one 15-year-old participant was marked by frequent gaps in verbal interaction while she showed the researcher previews for her favorite TV shows or funny videos on YouTube. In contrast, social-networking apps such as Instagram and Snapchat can be attended to and then looked away from, allowing more social interaction in a face-to-face context. Yet these same apps, unlike videos, are always "on" and can pull youth from a conversation at any time. This same participant, for instance, checked her phone continually throughout the interview, never pausing for more than three or four seconds and often shifting topics abruptly due to distraction.[12]

This passive, distracted attention is the norm rather than the exception for most kids. As it turns out, only 3 percent are actively creating something online, like making digital art, composing music, writing, or programming.[13] Nearly half of eighteen-to-twenty-nine-year-old digital natives use their phones to avoid other people, a rate three times higher than older users; this trend is something that starts in childhood now, with the high rate of smartphone ownership among kids.[14] Cell phones can lead to distractibility and unfocused attention to social interactions around them, possibly contributing to social deficits later on. Recent research has found that those iGen kids (also known as Gen Z, who are approximately ages six to twenty-four at the time of writing, 2019) who are coming into college now are more socially awkward and timid when it comes to social interactions. This can be attributed to their low levels of experience with face-to-face relationships compared to older generations, due to their high levels of interaction through devices.[15] I had a conversation with a sorority house mom recently. She said the girls don't know how to have conversations and quickly run out of things to say; she said there's then an awkward silence, so they pick up their cell phones and start texting someone else to break the awkwardness. Each week on Monday night, they all gather for a formal dinner. "Do they talk to you at dinner?" I asked. "No," she replied, "I just eat my dinner and look around the room." She lives with these girls, and they don't speak with her.

This lack of sociability is just one example of how kids' behaviors are beginning to change because they're growing up digital. Analog leisure activities that used to be routine for parents and grandparents when they were kids now seem quaint and antiquated. An ad for Nature's Valley snack bars highlights the differences in play between the generations. It begins by asking grandparents and parents what they did for fun as kids. "So, we'd go blueberry picking, for instance," one grandmother says with a twinkle in her eye. A grandfather recounts a funny story of being out on a river, fishing. Discovering a bear watching him, he quickly hatches a plan to throw fish out of his basket at the bear as he runs for safety, so the bear would be too full to eat him. A mother remembers the huge backyard forts they used to build outside to play in. With a warm smile, she reminisces, "It was really wonderful." Next it's the kids' turn. There was no remembering of forts or fishing or picking berries on idyllic summer days. In fact, there was no mention of analog activities at all. Kids' play has moved indoors: The boys talk about playing video games, and the girls mention texting or emailing, sometimes for three to five hours a day. One boy excitedly talked about binge-watching twenty-three hours of a TV series in just four days. The ad culminates with the producers showing a tape of one of these interviews to the boy's father and grandfather. Seeing "their boy" on the iPad, their faces glow with love and pride. But as soon as they hear what he had to say, their faces turn to concern. The boy, about seven, says that when he plays video games, "I forget I'm in a house, I have parents, I have a sister, I have a dog. When I'm in the video game, I just get completely lost." Even more worrisome, the girl following him says, "I would die without my tablet."[16]

Clearly, play has become virtualized. In the early days of the internet, online users would to talk about activities being "IRL," meaning "in real life," as opposed to online. Kids today make no such distinction. For them, digital life *is* real life. Their digital experiences are beginning to reshape their real-life experiences. My friend Amanda posted on Facebook about how she took her son and another boy to the park one day; she was shocked to learn that their Minecraft play online had reshaped their view of the real world; digital and reality for kids growing up digital have blurred. She said:

> My son, Weston, age 7, at the park yesterday, said, "Mom, some kids that play Minecraft think the grass was placed here in green cubes," after his friend Hunter asked him what kind of inventory they'd used to make this playground. When your kids think the ground was put down by a guy in a video game named, "Steve" by placing blocks that are called grass we have a problem.

Friends that kids meet or play games with online are viewed as real friends, just as real as those in their classrooms at school. Since they grew up immersed in an online world, for them, online is an equally valid space as face-to-face. In fact, they prefer it. For them, it's not mobile first; it's mobile only, and they'd rather text than talk, and rather email than call.[17] They prefer a digital interface mediating their interactions. I experienced this recently with a teenaged dog walker I'd booked through the Wag! dog-walking app. At the appointed hour, when no one showed up to walk the dogs, I checked the app and found a text saying, "I'm here." "Where?" I replied, "Downstairs?" "No, outside your door!" he texted back. I opened the door, and there, to my surprise, stood Bentson, a lanky, green-and-black-haired teenager with a nose ring and a goofy smile. He had texted rather than knocked, since knocking is apparently just too analog. This desire for a digital interface to mediate interactions is common. Globally, the majority of teens and young adults (65 percent) say they text more than talk in person on any given day. In the United States, it's even higher: three-quarters of teens and Millennials text more than talk. Many are now using Snapchat to do so.[18] A mother I spoke with on Facebook Messenger told me about her teen's use:

> In one year's time, I noticed my teen daughter and her high school friends gravitated toward messaging one another in Snapchat rather than texting. Literally, texts are so last year. Their texting is occasional, for sending house addresses or sharing photos. They use Snapchat hundreds of times a day for individual and group messages. Plus, they are slaves to their list of nightly streaks habit. [Streaks are counts of how many days the teens have messaged each other. It's a way to gamify it and encourage them to keep using.] Instagram? They tend to have two accounts: a "main" with about a thousand followers or more and a "private" with about 100 close, trustworthy friends. On the main, they post once a week or less, usually with a calculated, stylized selfie, group pic, or vacation photo. Instagram messaging is rare. On the private account, posts are a few times a week with pictures or memes that are silly, ironic, or not-for-parents-or-teachers to see types of posts—displaying behavior kids would get grounded for, which is probably what's being shared over at their Snapchat, too. Whoever makes an app for parents to trace Snapchat messages will be rich! Rich, I tell ya! Snapchat is the bane of every parent of a teen I know. Yet, Snapchat is what teens prefer to communicate the good, the bad, and the ugly.[19]

One reason Snapchat is so popular is that the messages disappear after they're seen, so they don't remain for the prying eyes of parents or other authority figures to see. One couple recently found out that their daughter had gone beyond a mere disappearing message app. She actually acquired a "burner phone," a prepaid phone separate from her regular family phone plan, to keep her calls and texts private. The phone was locked, and she refused to tell her parents the password. She's ten.

This intervention of smartphones mediating our relationships at one level or another has left us, as MIT psychologist Sherry Turkle puts it, "alone together."[20] Many adults fail to understand just how vital connectivity has become to kids. Teens and young adults would rather lose their wallet or purse, or go home without house keys, than lose their cell phone.[21] Because of this growing dependency on devices, some psychologists have suggested that they are addictive.[22] Pinterest, Facebook, Twitter, Instagram, and Snapchat all present users a vast array of imagery, films, and text, ranging from boring to novel or exciting; this serves as something that psychologist's call "random reinforcers" of behavior. It's the same process that goes on when you pull the lever on the flashing slot machine—and keep on pulling it.[23] Random reinforcement—where sometimes you win, sometimes you lose—is the most powerful behavioral reinforcer there is. It's no surprise, then, that it's baked into all of the major social media apps to keep users coming back for more. Parents are also getting sucked into the same addictive vortex, compulsively using devices when they're with their kids, leaving kids hungering—and perhaps acting out—to get their attention. In one study, 38 percent of kids said they felt unimportant when their parents were with them, staring at devices; even sadder, 28 percent of the parents agreed with them.[24]

Smartphones and tablets are inadvertently starting kids from infancy on a path of digital immersion: devices now are the new pacifiers. One in four parents says they use such devices to lull their kids to sleep. Twenty percent of one-year olds have their own tablet device.[25] Parents routinely hand phones or tablet devices over to pacify kids on buses or in waiting rooms, restaurants, or other public places. Returning home from a business trip recently at LAX, I saw a kid in a stroller in the baggage-claim area, frowning, brows furrowed, screaming and kicking his feet, right arm jutting out in angry demand, chanting, "Give me my phone! GIVE ME MY PHONE!" over and over again. His demands grew louder and more insistent, like an addict withdrawing from heroin and in need of a hit. The father, embarrassed by the scene, capitulated. The boy quickly snatched the phone out of his father's hand, his face relaxing as the dopamine washed over his brain, eyes opening wide to take in the screen. He'd won, and he knew it. And he would keep winning. One mother of a ten-year-old son posted in a private group for mommies on Facebook, "I seriously hate my son's iPad. I hate the attitude he has because of it. I hate how obsessed he is with it. I hate how much attitude and s— he gives me when he's not allowed to play on it. I hate how it's the most important thing to him. I hate how everything else is secondary to it. I HATE HOW IMPORTANT it is to him. He just got the damn thing less than a year ago and it's seriously become the center of his universe. And please don't try to tell me to just take it away from him or teach him moderation or make it sound like you have the solution [because] I have tried everything and no matter which way I go I'm the bad guy when it comes to this thing and he makes sure I feel like it." Given the addictive nature of these devices, addiction rehab counselor Mandy Saligari has suggested that giving phones to kids is "like giving them a bottle of wine or a gram of coke."[26] Two-thirds of the patients she sees for digital addiction now are between the ages of sixteen and twenty, a "dramatic increase" from ten years ago. Some are as young as thirteen. Clinical psychologist Dr. Kelly Flanagan suggests that parents should take away their kids' devices from time to time as a form of "digital detox" to promote family togetherness, but he warns that if they do, there will be consequences. He says, "First, they'll begin to spasm and screech, as if possessed by a demon. What do I mean by that? Well, picture a demon possession. Got it? That's what it will look like. There will be a significant amount of overlap with how an addict responds when you take away their crack. That's not coincidence. They're addicted and you're taking away their crack."[27] Then, he says, "They will hate you."

After handing kids the device, oftentimes parents don't monitor what it is the kids are watching. "Family-friendly" channels like YouTube Kids have become popular with parents as a go-to kid-friendly space for on-demand, quick entertainment. Knowing this, channels like it have become "open season" in terms of advertising to kids, or worse. If parents were to see what their kids are actually viewing sometimes, it might make their skin crawl. A series of bad actors ranging from copyright infringers to out-and-out tormentors of children have infiltrated YouTube Kids (a common channel parents use to entertain their children), twisting it for their own financial or even nefarious gains. One popular genre to exploit is nursery-rhyme videos. Little Baby Bum, which shows sleeping bunnies coupled with nursery rhymes, is the seventh most popular channel on YouTube, with over 16 million subscribers and 13 billion views. The finger-family song is another popular video that teaches kids the names of the fingers. It has garnered almost a billion views. "Dark" content creators are taking the comfort and assurance of these and other well-known brands like Peppa Pig or Doc McStuffins, and twisting them to create knock-off videos that at first glance appear to be the real deal, yet they quickly turn dark or disturbing.[28] Mommy blogger Laura June described her three-year-old daughter's foray into this faux children's video territory, where she stumbled upon fake Doc McStuffins videos. In them, she says:

> Kids wet the bed and scream at their parents. It's loud. Everyone cries. . . . On faux *McStuffins*, people break legs. Bones get exposed. It's terrifying. One video opens with a man injecting a pumpkin with a hypodermic needle, which somehow results in Doc and her buddies becoming zombies.[29]

As soon as June realized what her daughter was seeing, she quickly took the iPad away. Parents choose branded videos like Doc McStuffins and Peppa Pig precisely because they trust them as safe and wholesome content for kids. But with knock-off cartoons made to look exactly like the beloved characters, few parents even notice the difference when one of these darker videos pops up on the screen. Other videos targeting children exploit popular search-engine terms, cobbling together child-targeted oft-used search words into strange, almost-unintelligible titles like, "Learn Colors, Surprise Eggs 3D Cartoons for Children Videos for Kids." These counterfeits are seeking kids' views to generate revenue from YouTube traffic. Yet even more disturbing are the videos that take these counterfeits to another level. Created by bad actors of unknown origin, these videos serve up questionable content like "PAW Patrol Babies Pretend to Die Suicide by Annabelle Hypnotized Ghost Pranks," where popular Nickelodeon characters commit suicide in various different ways.[30] Other videos feature inappropriately sexualized themes, including strip clubs or Spider Man in sexual situations with Disney Princesses, including urinating on *Frozen*'s Elsa.[31] Perhaps most disturbing are the sexualized "play doctor" videos in which their thumbnail images show gigantic syringes pressing on children's nude buttocks, with some starring adult "doctors" whose faces are painted like Heath Ledger's characterization of the deranged Joker in *The Dark Knight*. Their titles are also search-engine-optimized into nonsensical mash-ups like, "PlayDoh butt Doctor Syringe Injection Learning Colors with Finger Family Nursery Rhymes," hoping to lure those seeking innocent videos into seeing these instead.[32] Many of these "injection" videos, and others with similar sexualized content, seem to be emanating from Russia. Clearly the content of the videos themselves is troubling, but the kind of audience these videos may attract and expose children to in the comments section is also disturbing; and one cannot ignore the threat of these videos possibly serving as "grooming" devices to lure children to sexual predators.[33]

LIVING IN THE NOW

Aside from potential exposure to troubling content, or the addictive nature of the devices themselves, there are other impacts of growing up digital. Fast-moving social media and digital technologies are reshaping values, beliefs, and behaviors such that the present is valued over history, and youth is prized over experience. In the fast-spinning digital environment, the importance of history, and a certain sentimentality or nostalgia toward the past, seems to be waning, leaving younger users living in a kind of eternal now. Capturing everyday life on cameras was common for proud parents by the time the Baby Boomers were born, but life certainly wasn't documented on a daily or even hourly basis like it is now. Rolls of film cost money to develop then and took time to view. It wasn't until after the introduction of the first camera phone by Sanyo in 2002, and later the iPhone in 2007, that photos could be both processed and posted online or texted instantaneously, virtually for free.[34] Now, many, if not most, kids' and teens' entire lives are documented and posted for an always-on audience in constant search of fresh content. This kind of pressure to post is amplified on kids' preferred platform, Snapchat, where users' histories literally disappear, and they are rewarded for serial posting, called streaks. There, you're only as good as your last snap. As one young digital entrepreneur in a private conversation on Facebook put it:

> Every generation finds it a problem to tolerate their elders as they slip into senility.... This generation, with its access to global Internet fact and collaboration is set to be the most disruptive generational transition ever. We have the Millennials with technology that provides them with 21st-century insights and AI-backed knowledge being admonished by parents who are educated at an 18th-century level and sometimes operate at a stone-age level trying to control the outcome. It's not going to happen and the elders will lose this every time. Best to show the older generation that is still learning how to adapt to this rapidly changing technology and leave those who wish to live in the 18th-century do so in isolation ... like Mennonites do now.

Mark Zuckerberg of Facebook expressed a similar sentiment in a speech for a class of budding entrepreneurs at Stanford (and later apologized for it after receiving blowback). There, he said:

I want to stress the importance of being young and technical. . . . Young people are just smarter. Why are most chess masters under 30? I don't know. . . . Young people just have simpler lives. We may not own a car. We may not have family.[35]

In a digital environment, living in the now has become the norm. Tech journalist Steven Meloan recounted an incident of this type with his teenaged son, Tyler. Driving home from work one night in the Sonoma Valley, Steven saw a strange, lighted object hovering over the high school: a possible UFO, but more likely a drone high up in the sky.[36] He quickly drove home and got his son, jokingly telling him, "They've arrived! Get in the car!" Together they quickly drove back to the school. In his excitement about the "close encounter," Steven had forgotten to plug in his cell phone, so he asked his son to take videos of "the UFO." After the adventure, Steven later reminded his son, "Be sure and forward me that video," to which Tyler replied, "I can't—I Snapped it, then erased it." Steven expressed his disappointment to me, saying, "I was kind of pissed, because I hadn't taken video of my own." His son had already moved on to the next Snappable event. He was over it.

This kind of "Snap and forget" behavior that Steven Meloan experienced with his son has larger implications than simply lost "UFO" footage, when extrapolated to the larger societal level. Speaking about the loss of historical continuity at the Getty Center in Los Angeles, Disney's chief of research, Danny Hillis, said that "Historians will look back on this era and see a period of very little information. A 'digital gap' will span from the beginning of the widespread use of the computer until the time we eventually solve this problem."[37] Looking back in a digital environment is increasingly difficult due to "link rot," a term coined to describe the links that become permanently dead online over time. Studies have found that half to 75 percent of links are dead ten years after an article's publication. Given link rot, you can't look back even if you wanted to.[38] This emphasis on the present has even changed some teens' views of the past: For some, looking at the past *too* closely, reviewing someone else's old posts on Instagram, for example, is viewed as creepy, like a kind of cyber-stalking. Snapchat is the third most popular app among teens and young adults aged eighteen to twenty-four.[39] There, since all of the snaps disappear, there is no looking back, no history. The main problem with this emphasis on the eternal now is that *perspective* depends on the ability to look back, since it is sometimes only in hindsight, with the passing of time, that the significance of something is revealed. In digital culture, things have become so transient, so ephemeral, they're often gone before this significance can come to light. A perfect example is the Bill Clinton and Monica Lewinsky affair of 1995. When the story broke, a news photographer who had been following Clinton thought there was something vaguely familiar about Monica, so he asked an assistant to sort through thousands of negatives to look for her. They finally dug up shots from an obscure rally that happened about a year earlier at the Washington, DC, Sheraton Hotel. At the time, photographer Dirck Halstead, who took the photo in 1996, was still analog, using film in an era when almost everyone else had gone digital. As a result, he was the only one who still had the negatives from that seemingly inconsequential night. He soon made a small fortune on them, as his negatives contained the explosive picture of Bill Clinton kissing Monica Lewinski at the crowded fundraiser, the significance of which was not to be revealed until nearly two years later. The famous shot eventually made the cover of *Time* magazine.[40]

To kids living in the now, the past is over and the future, along with its consequences, often seem distant or nonexistent. This, combined with teens' lowered capacity for self-regulation and their susceptibility to peer pressure, means having a smartphone and the ability to transmit anything at any time can become a recipe for disaster. In seeking popularity online, the banal or the mundane doesn't cut it. What stands out is the unique, the extreme, the over-the-top. Images go viral now of "roof toppers," teens (usually males) perched precariously atop a single girder at the very pinnacle of a skyscraper, as do videos of death-defying jumps off cliffs in "wingsuits," showing young people "flying" at up to 150 miles per hour.[41] These flights have led to thirty-one deaths in the last couple of years alone. Still others "train surf" atop the roofs of moving trains or perform equally dangerous acts of derring-do.[42] Even something as banal as babysitting has been amped up for online broadcast and consumption: A video went viral of a teenaged babysitter putting her crying charge into a refrigerator and shutting the door, while her friend filmed it.[43] She says "bye" and laughs; the terrified screams of the infant emanate from inside the darkened, closed fridge. She and her friend then posted the video to Snapchat. Other equally shocking, attention-seeking videos have been posted or live-streamed on Facebook, like the live Instagram stream of eighteen-year-old Obdulia Sanchez, which shows her crashing her car in California while live-streaming. The accident left her fourteen-year-old sister dead and another girl seriously injured when they were ejected from the back seat. Throughout the crash, Sanchez never stops streaming. Exiting the crashed car, she lifts her younger sister up, then drops her. The girl's lifeless body rolls away from the camera like a limp rag doll. Without missing a beat, the intoxicated Sanchez looks right back into the camera and says, "I know I'm going to prison—I killed my sister, but I don't care. . . . Imma hold it down."[44] Living in the now and seeking attention online blinds some young people to the consequences of their actions. The two teenagers who allegedly Snapchatted the crying baby in the fridge were arrested and charged with child endangerment, assault, and battery with a dangerous weapon, and they were arraigned the same day in juvenile court.[45] Sanchez, who killed her sister and injured another young girl in a car crash while live-streaming, was arrested for manslaughter. She was sentenced to six years and four months in prison.[46] In a later interview, she said she often live-streamed on Instagram while driving, saying, "Trust me, it's like a reflex," she said.[47] "Everybody does it. Everybody does. They take Snapchats. Why not? People take video of them in cars, like, all the time. And I'm only 18—we're still young." Still young, living in the eternal now, where there is no past, no future, and no perceived consequences.

DIGITAL DATING: TEENAGE WASTELAND

Living in the eternal now negates the "pull factor" of the future. Having goals in mind, such as those of the American Dream of earlier generations, acts as a kind of North Star, pulling people forward into the future. Without that pull factor, there is no endgame—everything is about the now, about "experience." With the pull factor of the proverbial American Dream diminished, there's no rush to the initial steps of that dream, such as getting into a relationship that may lead to marriage. Previous generations of teens typically either had a girlfriend or a boyfriend in high school. Around World War II, the average age of marriage was twenty for women and twenty-two for men, with many marrying their high-school sweethearts after the war. Compare that to now, when 64 percent of US teens have never even been in a relationship.[48] Now, traditional dating is rare. Instead, teens "talk to" someone (or multiple someones) via text, Snapchat, Facetime, or Skype. "Talking to" is followed by "hanging out with," often in groups, which may or may not lead to an exclusive relationship. Raul, a tech executive I interviewed, told me his teenage niece is "talking to" five guys at once; no one is committed, though one of the guys she was talking to stumbled across the niece's profile on Tinder and got upset (ironically, since he must've been swiping, too, to see it!). Raul's college-age nephew recently took a girl with him on a birthday trip to Cuba. Though they're sexually active, he says they're not dating. Perhaps ironically, fewer teens are having actual sex now compared to 1998, so, in some ways, digital foreplay seems to be taking the place of actual physical sexuality.[49] Rather than actual sex, around a third of teens say they've sent sexually explicit photos to someone via text-messaging (referred to as "sexting"). Although teens and kids may seem more sophisticated in some ways, sexting and other questionable activities done through text or online abide in ways that physical acts of sexuality do not. Alan Silberberg, an expert on cyber-security and cyber-bullying, reminds us that, "Their brains are still those of kids, and they do not understand the short- and long-term ramifications of their digital lives yet."[50] Some sexual photos sent by teens privately to people they are talking to, for example, have ended up shared publicly in group texts or posted online as "revenge porn" after a budding teen romance has soured. This can have tragic results, as it led several young girls to kill themselves out of shame. One study in the United States found that 51 percent of teen girls faced with the humiliation of revenge porn—and the bullying that often goes with it—have considered suicide.[51]

There are still other unintended consequences of kids being "always on" that have begun to emerge, with implications for their relationships. Most of the social platforms now—group texts, Snapchat, Instagram, and others—are location-driven. Apple phones have "Find My Friends"; Facebook shows people's locations when they post; dating apps like Grindr and Tinder have built-in location-based services; Match.com recently added a Craigslist-style "missed connections" feature, which shows users' profiles of other daters nearby; Insta-gram integrates users' locations into posts; and Snapchat offers geofilters that highlight one's location at local concerts or sports venues.[52] These "geosocial" technologies render teens' every move visible for monitoring, judgment, and dissection, sometimes by romantic hopefuls, heartbroken exes, or even cyber-stalkers. Jeremy, a seventeen-year-old boy who is cute and in a band attracted the attention of a girl who soon began monitoring his every move this way. His father, Michael, recounted the story:

> There's a girl from Jeremy's crowd who has become almost like a cyber-stalker. He's known her for a number of years, originally via one of the guys from his band. But she used to be part of a much bigger crowd of friends, and now almost everyone is out of the picture but Jeremy. This girl comes from sort of a troubled family, where she has a lot of friction with her parents, but they seem to have a fair amount of money. She is the antithesis of Jeremy, who is very

motivated and self-directed, and has all kinds of personal projects in the arts—
music, film etc. He is also fine to spend time by himself—hiking, listening to
music, watching movies, etc. This girl is the kind of person who can't stand to
be alone or not doing something, and she has no personal interests or hobbies.
She went one year to Cal State Fullerton, but apparently all but flunked out.
Now, her parents have put her and a roommate up in an apartment in Los
Angeles. He says she endlessly texts him, communicates on social media, etc.
He's not at all interested in her romantically, but I think she is with him. He's
tried in a nice way to basically say that he's "not that into her," but it hasn't
taken. He says he will regularly put this girl off for some suggested activity, but
then he has to very carefully watch what he does online, because then she will
bust him—"I thought you said you were busy working on a paper? I saw that
you liked Jenny's post on Instagram." Or—"I saw that you read my text, so why
didn't you respond?" Or, things having to do with Snapchat, where there are
location features that can potentially bust you for saying you were home when
you weren't. He says that it's really gotten stalker-like, where he has to think
through anything that he does online, in terms of whether she might be aware
of it, and then what he's told her he was doing, versus whether online activity
might contradict that. He says it's incredibly stressful, and increasingly [it]
makes him want to limit what he does/says online.[53]

Cybersecurity expert Silberberg says that this kind of online stalking can
become "a precursor to actual stalking and/or a socially engineered attack ...
the watcher learns so much, they can launch cyber bullying attacks by having
the info."[54] Some teens try to combat this by creating private Instagram accounts
and limiting those who can see their posts to a close group of friends, or they
create fake accounts for public consumption, which they call "Finstas." This
does not prevent someone with access to a private account from screenshotting
and sharing the info publicly, nor does it protect emotionally vulnerable teens
from the guilt, shame, or embarrassment—or even fear—of someone physically
stalking them or cyber-stalking or bullying them. Michael's son, Jeremy, said to
him, "Imagine if I was a woman, and there was some dangerous ex-boyfriend
stalking me." He actually started limiting his postings as a result of this girl's
activities, fearing they could escalate.

YOU ARE VALID

Teenagers have one main psychological task to master, and that is to establish their identity, often through a painful process of trial and error, trying on different identities until they find the one that fits. Now, digital devices have become an integral part of that process, as the indie film *Eighth Grade* explores in excruciating detail, chronicling the coming of age of an awkward teenage girl who makes YouTube videos and posts cute filtered pics on Instagram, trying desperately to fit in and be cool. With only a handful of followers, she never quite makes it.[55] Media analyst Marshall McLuhan's work presages the kinds of struggles that teens are facing now in our media-immersed society. He said that the medium we grow up within shapes both our process of becoming as well as changes the contours of whom we become. This is because particular communications media promote certain values and ways of being over others, which changes from one historical epoch to another. Having died in 1980, McLuhan missed our current digital era completely, including the massively accelerated pace of information and the enchantment consumers have with digital devices. During his time, computers were room-sized contraptions run by punch cards, usually housed in universities, at large corporations, or on military bases. The personal computer didn't appear until 1975, and only then as a do-it-yourself kit for geeky tinkerers to assemble. The first mass-market personal computer, the Apple Macintosh, wasn't available until 1984, four years after McLuhan died, and the internet didn't gain widespread popularity until nearly ten years later.[56] Though internet-enabled Nokia smartphones came out in 1999, it wasn't until the iPhone and apps in 2007 that smartphones really took off. Now, kids are growing up with these devices, which reshapes who they are and who they are becoming.

Such early-age connectivity means that the online arena is one of the factors shaping kids' identity and sense of self from their earliest days. Now, instead of playing in the neighborhood, they can go online to seek their identities and find their own tribe or "community of interest." They could become one of Lady Gaga's fans, whom she nicknamed "Little Monsters"; followers of a YouTuber celebrity; or part of a group based on a particular interest or hobby, like cosplay, where people dress up like their favorite anime characters.[57] My friend's kid, Ricky, is seventeen years old and small for his age, yet he has always been mature way beyond his years, easily carrying his end of the conversation with other adults at social gatherings, even at a very young age. He's active in theater and attends a high school for the arts with other kids who are artsy and perhaps a bit "different" from the norm. Ricky's goal is to become an on-air sports analyst. To pursue his interest and hone his skills, he takes part in online sports discussions—with adults. The men and women in the forums he debates with have no idea they are interacting with a high-school kid. Online, kids like Ricky who are precocious or gifted, or with interests that differ from those of their peers, can find their place; online, they can continue to grow and develop their interests, aptitudes, and self-image at their own pace.

Gender is another long-standing social structure from which teens and kids are increasingly untethering. Gender (e.g., masculinity, femininity, etc.) often shapes our social interactions as an ingrained and taken-for-granted aspect of our lives. Kids are gendered from the moment of birth, when the doctor (or midwife, and so on.) announces "It's a boy!" or "It's a girl!" The pink or blue hat is put on to signal gender to others, and off we go. Prior generations coming of age in the United States were presented with a fairly narrow spectrum of possibilities for their gendered selves. Boys were taught to be masculine "tough guys," displaying behaviors indicating that they were physically strong, ambitious, and aggressive. Girls were taught to be feminine—crossing their legs when seated and being quiet, nurturing, caretaking, and "nice." Our expectations around gender color how we see others and how we treat them. In the 1950s, men and women were confined to a relatively tight and rigid set of social roles and expectations linked to gender. Women were taught from a young age to expect to grow up to be teachers, nurses, secretaries, or housewives; achieving marriage and motherhood was synonymous with the achievement of femininity. Men were taught to be husbands and breadwinners, taking a largely hands-off approach to nurturing children or being emotionally present. Emotions were for girls, they were told, as "big boys don't cry." These expectations started young, shaped in part by children's play and toys (playing with dolls or "playing house" versus playing with trucks and soldiers, for example). Sanctions for breaking these gender norms, particularly for boys, could be swift and strong, and they came from parents, teachers, coaches, and even peers themselves.[58]

The digital age has opened up a myriad of new possibilities for "doing gender" for kids and teens, adding many "degrees of freedom" within which they can construct their identities well outside the traditional binary masculine/feminine categories. Twenty percent of Millennials identify as something other than strictly straight and cisgender (someone whose gender is in line with the sex they were assigned at birth), compared to 7 percent of Boomers.[59]

Now, rather than being a relatively stable and reliable part of one's identity, one's gender can even fluctuate day to day. Some kids have taken to wearing a pink or blue bracelet to indicate to their friends how they'd like to be identified that day (e.g., as "he" or "she"). Other nonbinary gender labels are emerging: young people are asking to be referred to as "they" or "them," rather than as "he" and "him" or "she" and "her." Some, like rapper Angel Haze (who recently changed their name to Roes) even identify as "agender," or genderless; Haze prefers the pronouns "they/ them," and they do not identify as a woman, but rather as "an experience."[60] Identity doesn't simply relate to an individual—rather, identity also exists in relationship, between people, helping to choreograph the subtle social dance we do when interacting with one another. Certainly these new forms of identify can send unclear or confusing signals, stretching one's ability to even comprehend—how does one identify as an "experience," for example? It certainly renders social relations more complex (though not unnavigable) while reshaping not only individual identities but also our relationships.

Other kids are turning to social media to find their tribe and where they may fit in, as a way to seek and (hopefully) find identity. Kids and young adults who are non-gender-conforming or lesbian, gay, bisexual, transgender, or queer/ questioning (LGBTQ+) are increasingly turning to online spaces. These spaces range from YouTube to websites like 7 Cups to dating sites for teens. One study of LGBTQ+ teens found that these kids spend five hours a day online, an average of forty-five minutes per day longer than their non-LGBTQ+ peers. The majority (60 percent) of LGBTQ+ teens say that their online friends are more supportive than their friends "in real life."[61] Tumblr is one of the spaces they're looking to for support when struggling with sexuality or gender identity. One high-school teen described the support she found there, saying, "I've been on [Tumblr] for a few years, and I think it was the single most important thing in allowing me to accept myself. Seeing other LGBT teens who were actually happy with themselves and their identity caused me to realize that I could actually do [the same]. It was also on Tumblr that I first came across terms like 'bisexual' and 'non-binary,' which was fundamental in shaping my identity."[62] Some bloggers on Tumblr present in traditionally masculine or feminine ways, but others are "nonbinary"—neither masculine or feminine, while still others are some combination of both, or neither. "Cis" or "cisgender" are those who identify with the sex they were born with. "Genderqueer" refers to those who are nonconforming in terms of their identity (i.e., outside the traditional masculine and feminine). Specific subcategories of genderqueer include "transgender" (those who feel their gender is different than the one assigned to their birth sex), or "gender fluid"—meaning they express themselves sometimes as male and sometimes as a female.[63] A myriad of other terms can also be found on Tumblr to name one's gender identity, including: "agender," "demi-boy," "demi-girl," "pangender," "demi-guy," and "genderflux." Bloggers on the site are given their choice of pronouns with which to self-identify. One I saw chose "All Pronouns." A survey of gender categories on Tumblr has counted more than sixty, with bloggers there using hashtags to denote their identity.[64] Facebook gives its users somewhere between fifty-eight and seventy-one gender labels with which to self-identify, as well as a custom "fill in the blank" one for people who want to add still other options.[65]

Some families have trouble accepting kids who are different, particularly when it comes to sexual identity, which in some cases can run up against strongly held religious beliefs. Some kids who come out to parents or friends are rejected, which drives feelings of alienation, depression, and hopelessness. For these kids, finding their tribe while searching for identity is important, possibly even critical. Being different is hard—kids who are or gay, for example, have a much higher suicide rate than straight kids. According to the Centers for Disease Prevention and Control, nearly a third (29 percent) of LGBTQ+ youth had attempted suicide at least once in the prior year, compared to only 6 percent of heterosexual youth.[66] Being transgender is also a risk factor. Validation is a key component of these kids' self-acceptance. On Tumblr, over and over, I saw bloggers saying or hashtagging "You Are Valid," meaning whatever journey of self-exploration and identity you are on, it is okay. *You* are valid. Fifteen-year-old Paz (who uses all pronouns) writes on his/her blog on Tumblr:

> hey yeah so like if you're bisexual or pansexual or nonbinary or any other gender/sexuality that gets a lot of flack for "not being queer enough" or "not being real" then i hope you know that you're super valid and it takes a lot of courage to go through the day being your genuine self despite being attacked for it.[67]

Another Tumblr blogger, Jessica, also normalized the search for identity, reassuring kids on Tumblr by saying: "It's okay to be questioning. It's okay to not know your sexuality. You're not invading lgbt people's space. You are not asking for attention. You're not 'pretending.' It's okay."[68] A kid who may face rejection, experience self-doubt, and question themselves and their own self and identity can look to bloggers like Paz or Jessica to receive the validation they are seeking.

"You're super valid." It's exactly the kind of empathy kids are looking for, validation that they may have a hard time finding at home or at their own schools, and these few words may make all the difference. Finding community and like-minded others online can give nonconformist youths a sense that they are not alone. That in and of itself may serve as the lifeline they need, as they grow surer of themselves and find and solidify who they are and whom they want to be.

EXTERNALITY AND CHASING LIKES

There is more to be said about the topic of validation. Kids' posting behavior is driven by the external validation of others—that is, likes, shares, comments, and subscriptions or follows. As such, teens and kids are becoming more externally driven than ever before, motivated to chase likes, shares, and attention. Being a popular YouTuber has captured kids' imaginations: When asked what they wanted to be when they grow up, kids of prior generations said they wanted to be ballerinas, doctors, nurses, or firemen. Now, 75 percent of today's kids say they want to be YouTubers or Vloggers (i.e., video bloggers).[69]

Vloggers are reinforced for their digital antics by an additional external driver—money. Ryan is one of these. He's a cute, rambunctious little boy, with big, dark eyes, a ready smile, a sturdy body, and a mop of chocolate-brown hair. "Open your eyes!" his mother says from off camera in one video posted on YouTube. Ryan opens his eyes and spots the giant egg; breaking out into a "spontaneous" grin, he jumps up and down, and overexcitedly exclaims, "WOW! It's so BIG!" Though a typical kid in many ways, Ryan is atypical in another: He probably makes more money than you do. At the age of five, he has the number one channel on YouTube, raking in an estimated $25 million a year for videos like the "Giant Egg Surprise."[70] Ryan garners a whopping 645.2 million video views a *month* with his YouTube channel Ryan Toys Review, only slightly trailing the 646.2 million views of popstar Justin Bieber. His schoolteacher mother has quit her job to make the videos full-time. Some of Ryan's videos are an embarrassment of over-the-top conspicuous consumption. In one, he opens over a hundred brand-new toys at a go. One wonders: What do you do for an encore when you're five, and every week is Christmas on steroids? One can only imagine what the long-term consequences might be for these young YouTubers, given the tragic life outcomes of some child actors of the television era, who peaked early and fizzled out before reaching adulthood.[71]

Jake Paul is the older version of Ryan. Tall, athletically built, with a square jaw and messy, spiked blond hair, he has the all-American good looks of the captain of the local high-school football team. He is the leader of "Team 10," a YouTube crew extremely popular with young teens and tweens. Their daily video logs (or "vlogs") can garner 12 million views. The official Team 10 rap video, "It's Everyday Bro," has almost 163 million views. Many of their videos feature pranks of various kinds. In one called "Homemade Backyard Water Slide," a Team 10 boy lights his jeans on fire, then skateboards off a homemade wooden waterslide into the pool. "Wooooo!!" Jake yells into the camera as he strides back into the house, "What a way to start the morning! Sometimes you've just got to light yourself on fire!" It reminded me of the famous line in *Apocalypse Now*, "I love the smell of napalm in the morning!"[72] The similarity to *Apocalypse Now* isn't coincidental; the neighbors describe the Team 10 house as a war zone. In one interview, Jake described his young fans, for whom the house has become a kind of Mecca, saying, "They are yelling at the neighbors; they're in the street; they're chanting my name and taking up parking."[73] Fed up, the neighbors filed a class-action lawsuit after a furniture fire in the backyard sent flames up higher than the building, and toxic fumes from the burning plastic wafted into their homes.[74] Videos like the ones made by Team 10 are the ways many kids are choosing to express themselves and socialize now. They are used to alleviate boredom, channel creativity, and (hopefully) garner popularity. They are teen cultural capital; it's how they show they're "cool" in a world all their own, a world often outside adult supervision. Many adults have no idea who the current band of YouTube stars even are, yet some, like PewDiePie or Lilly Singh, command tens of millions of followers and rake in tens of millions of dollars a year.[75]

In *Lord of the Flies* fashion, viral "challenges" sweep through this world like wildfire, enveloping kids along the way and encouraging them to one-up each other in videos capturing increasingly outlandish behavior. Hashtagging is the way to latch onto the latest viral craze. It all began rather harmlessly with the Ice Bucket Challenge in 2014, where kids and adults dumped ice water over their heads as a way to call attention to and raise money for the neurological disease ALS. Later, the Harlem Shake challenged groups of friends, family members, college students in dorms, and even the army and navy (possibly hoping to recruit young viewers) to dance up a storm in weird costumes and goofy props, set to the relentless trap beat by DJ Baauer.[76] The Mannequin Challenge followed, with kids posting videos of themselves in mannequin-like frozen poses. Started by a group of high-school kids, the craze took off, involving everyone from sports fans in gigantic stadiums to celebrities like Paul McCartney, the beat of Rae Sremmurd's "Black Beatles" thrumming in the background.[77] These challenges were done with a sense of humor and innocent fun, as people weighed in with their own unique versions.

Viral videos are the digital version of "social proof," where behaviors are repeated in copycat fashion and encouraged by media propagation.[78] Social proof gives credence to behaviors, that this is what others are doing, and it spreads them like a virus, even promoting behaviors that are dangerous or potentially fatal. Online, with the sheer quantity of people and information, social proof is amplified as viral videos cause the most unique behaviors to stand out, thus making them more likely to be shared, commented on, or repeated. Even negative attention is still attention, and that attention can serve to reinforce destructive behaviors. One particularly vivid example is the Fire Challenge. In one such YouTube video, an athletic-looking teen pours what looks like rubbing alcohol back and forth over his chest while standing in a shower. With the entire front of his torso coated with the substance and a big grin, his girlfriend hands him a small lighter. Looking down, the lighter about stomach level, he flicks the ignition and instantly goes up in flames, diving out of the frame, while shouting "OH NO!" The girl filming screams and begins shouting "Get in the WATER!!" He runs back in the tub, as the woman hysterically shouts "Take it OFF!" apparently thinking his shorts are on fire and that would help somehow. As the fire alarm starts to sound, the teen rolls on the ground, feet seemingly on fire, and the video cuts out. "Shower Fire Challenge Gone Wrong" has so far attracted nearly 90,000 views.[79] The human impulse to view these kinds of scenes is not specific to digital natives: in the VCR era, people used to go to seedy video stores to rent videos like *Faces of Death* to view such horrifying or gruesome content. Now, it's just one click away on a kid's cell phone.

Other dangerous challenges have emerged. The Salt and Ice Challenge, where kids place salt and then ice on their arms and legs to instigate a kind of hypothermic reaction, causing freezer burns and ugly red welts to swell up on their arms and legs. A search of these videos on YouTube yields results including "Salt and Ice on My Balls," "Salt and Ice Challenge Fail" and "Salt and Ice Challenge Warning—Blood."[80] A Lip Challenge was spawned by girls (along with a few boys) trying to emulate Kylie Jenner's full lips by sucking on various items ranging from plastic "devices" to the lids of spray-paint cans to frozen champagne glasses, in an attempt to swell up their lips. The results for some kids was physical injury, ranging from abrasions to bruised lips to a lip sliced in half.[81]

The challenge only came to an end after Kylie Jenner admitted to getting lip-enhancing cosmetic surgery.[82] The latest #ShiggyChallenge, inspired by Drake's song #InMyFeelings, has teens jumping out of moving cars and dancing on the streets, with at least one doing so on a freeway.[83] Similar to the case the earlier-mentioned flying suit and roof-topping videos, copycatting these dangerous challenge videos can lead to serious injury or even death. In one example, an eleven-year-old boy accidently hanged himself while imitating one of these viral videos called "Suicide by Hanging Prank on Mom" that he saw on YouTube. As of August 2018, it has garnered over half a million views and who knows how many copycats.[84] Since kids lack the brain development that can limit their ability to understand the consequences of their actions, these kinds of videos can pose a serious threat to their health and safety.

To be sure, kids have always done dumb things, but the desire to stand out and be cool in the crowded milieu of social media, where different, exaggerated, or over-the-top stunts stand out, spurred on by the social proof of likes and viral shares, has driven some to extremes. Given the churn rate of social media, which creates a high level of social noise, today's viral video becomes yesterday's news in a matter of days, rendering last week's doers this week's has-beens or never-weres. One has to continue to raise the bar and raise the stakes to stay relevant online.

UNINTENTIONALLY EXPOSED

All this connectivity has bred an unintended consequence kids rarely consider. Teens and adolescents documenting everything now opens up not only them-selves but also their families to security risks that the adults would never have exposed themselves to intentionally. What goes online can stay online (barring the link rot discussed earlier). That stupid act that used to be done in private is now public and indelibly etched into the digital record, which can follow the young person for the rest of his or her life. Cybersecurity expert Alan Silberberg discussed this issue with me over lunch recently. As the former White House technology director, he is acutely aware of the need for cybersecurity. He told me the story of a recent client of his who is extremely wealthy but also extremely private. The man, whom I'll call "Mr. Warbucks," has no social media accounts—no Facebook, no Twitter account, and no websites that focus on him. He keeps a very low digital profile. A search for him on Google a couple of years ago would have revealed almost nothing. The man enjoys the finer things in life and has several homes around the world, each filled with beautiful art, furniture, and antiques, yet you'll never see these things on Instagram or Facebook. Folks like Mr. Warbucks realize it's a security risk to be too flashy. Throughout the years, he's been able to maintain a high level of discretion—until now.

When Alan did a recent analysis of Mr. Warbucks's online presence, pictures popped up of his private jet, his house in the Grenadines, and the multi-million-dollar Marc Chagall painting in his living room. The photos are geotagged, so people can find the city, the street, and even the address where the treasured items are located—and potentially steal them. Now, the most private of spaces, the wealth, the items secured quietly away for so many years are out there on the internet for all to see, courtesy of none other than Mr. Warbucks's seventeen-year-old grandson, whom I will call Jason. When confronted, Jason shrugged it off, saying, "I'm just documenting my life." But by doing so, kids like Jason are unintentionally exposing their father's, mother's, grandparents', siblings', and potentially even their employer's locations, and other specific information online for which they could be targeted. Most kids have no idea they are even creating risk. The army is struggling with this now, having experienced problems with young soldiers revealing the locations of top-secret military bases through geotagged photos posted on Facebook.[85]

Parents have inadvertently set the stage for this "document everything" mentality. Security firm AVG found that 81 percent of children under age two already have some kind of digital profile, with images of them posted online by their parents. The CEO of AVG, J. R. Smith, has said that, "Our research shows that the trend is increasing for a child's digital birth to coincide with and in many cases pre-date their real birth date."[86] One study found that as of 2010, a quarter of babies had sonogram photos posted of themselves online before they had even been born. Kids are growing up digital, so documenting everything as they grow becomes second nature.

Another growing crime uses children's photos culled from social-media postings. Called "digital kidnapping," individuals or companies steal children's photos from the internet without their parents' permission and repost them across the internet, using "fake accounts" for advertising purposes, fraud, or even worse. Infants' and children's photos have been used with the hashtag #RP—to roleplay on Instagram as a baby or child, some with sexualized themes. Some kids or teens are doing this themselves, creating fictional accounts on Instagram, "playing" online by pretending to be the sister of a famous band member or using hashtags like #dirtyrp, #sexrp, or #lewdrp to connect with and role-play sexualized scenarios and engage in pornographic discussions with strangers.[87] This digital footprint, including the role play—complete with the kid's pictures—can later come up in a search of these hashtags.

Kids' behavior online can inadvertently harm them later, when they apply for internships, jobs, or even college. Over a third of university admissions counselors now search social media, and in over 35 percent of checks, they discover information that harmed the prospective student's application.[88] In hiring situations, three-fourths of companies look at applicants' online reputations as a part of their vetting process, and at least 51 percent have rejected candidates based on what they've found online. The top reason a candidate is rejected is that he or she posted provocative or inappropriate photographs or information, and second is information about them drinking or using drugs. That party shot on Instagram of you passed out on the ground, surrounded by discarded red cups, could come back to haunt you one day. I've had students tell me they've even lost college internships at big companies as a result of these kinds of posts that they've made on their social media accounts.

To be fair, not all of these issues are the fault of the kids alone. They are, rather, the result of a confluence of factors, including kids' digital connectivity and a particular kind of overprotective parenting and other factors that emerged out of the 1980s. That's when the faces of missing children started appearing on the backs of milk cartons.[89] That, along with the 1983 movie *Adam*, which was seen by millions, about the child abduction of Adam Walsh, followed by Adam's father, John, creating the program *America's Most Wanted*, which spotlighted child predation and helped create an inordinate fear of strangers. As a result, kids' lives have become increasingly structured and surveilled. Scheduling "play dates" for busy working parents meant parents became increasingly involved in children's play. Playing alone outside became increasingly verboten. Unlike prior generations, walking or biking to and from school alone now is rare. Instead, kids are accompanied to the school bus stop by parents, who stand close by them until they are "safely" loaded onto the bus, or they are driven directly to school. In some towns, a kid walking alone to the bus stop is even against the law. In this culture of fear, keeping kids indoors, on devices may have seemed "safer."[90] Yet by raising kids without analog experiences in the world, oversurveilling them, and keeping them from any challenges to be overcome have inadvertently kept kids from the very life lessons that youngsters of earlier generations learned routinely through exploration, discovery, and trial and error outside. Falling down and skinning your knees meant you learned not to pop wheelies on your bike or roller skate a certain way. Wandering far from home meant you had to find your way back, navigating while avoiding cars, errant dogs, or other obstacles. With devices added to the mix as a way to be "safe," kids' lived experiences have become increasingly virtualized. While parents think the kids are safer indoors, in fact, the online world contains addictive qualities that keep kids logged into it, while simultaneously serving up comparative and competitive aspects that fuel their anxiety levels, isolation, and potential for depression. What's missing for these kids is the feedback mechanisms of the learning processes through analog experience. Though the indoor way to play is one that can be monitored, it precludes kids from developing the sort of resilience and self-determination that come from outdoor exploration and self-determined play. Without it, many kids are unable to develop a sense of competence and mastery critical for the development of self-esteem. The goal of the teenage years is a transition to adulthood. The substitution of the digital for the analog has left kids floundering as they try to transition into the world as competent, self-reliant adults. Many are struggling or failing in that venture. Colleges are now seeing a lack of resilience and the highest levels of mental illness among the student population in thirty years; one in five college students is suffering from anxiety or depression, which are now the top two reasons driving students to seek counseling.[91] Devices and mediated socializing can paradoxically serve as a crutch, impeding young people from getting to know one another and exacerbating isolation and loneliness. A Facebook post shared with me by a girlfriend of mine sheds light on this experience. Newly minted freshman Hanna said:

> There's definitely a tendency for us to focus communications online with most gratification centers being immediately accessible digitally (dumb YouTube videos, distracting content etc.). These devices snag me badly. This has led to a lot of isolation from what I've witnessed while at school in particular.

Another friend of mine recounted a story about isolation caused by devices on college campuses involving his son, Ryan, who had recently started junior college. He said:

> Ryan has started his first semester at the local junior college this week. Even as plugged-in as he and his friends are, when the teacher for a 3-hour evening class gave them a break, he figured that people would wander outside and maybe chat, and get to know one another. Instead, everyone just stayed in their seats, got out their phones, and proceeded to do solitary social media.[92]

The girlfriend who sent the comment from freshman Hanna ended her text conversation with me in bewilderment, saying, "Hanna's a talkative and friendly person. Its stunning."[93] Hanna ended up posting that she should be more active in other people's lives, then in a moment of self-doubt, asked, "Do people [even] WANT me to be more present in their lives?" It's a good question. Unmediated interactions seem to be on the wane.

IMAGINARY FRIENDS

Growing up, kids have often had imaginary friends over the years. Pretend play like this helps inspire creativity and can help kids get through stressful times. Kids today are now growing up with imaginary friends that live as voices on computers—virtual entities named Google and Alexa—whom they can call upon for information or to do things like play their favorite song. One enterprising little six-year-old even asked her "friend" Alexa to order $350 of toys she wanted on Amazon and had them shipped to the house. Imagine her parents' shock when the gigantic pile of boxes arrived.[94] An estimated 60.5 million people in the United States—a little less than a fifth of the population—will use one of these digital assistants at least once a month, and about half a million will do so on a speaker-based device like Amazon Echo or Google Home.[95] As digital technologies mature and become more sophisticated, these kinds of entities will become smarter and will increasingly mimic humans, passing the Turing Test with ease (i.e., we won't be able to determine whether they are human). In 2014, a thirteen-year-old "boy" by the name of Eugene Goostman fooled a third of investigators at the Royal Society of London into thinking he was real, and not the supercomputer that he really was.[96] This was a milestone in merging the perception of reality and representation (i.e., map and territory) between human and machine.

In the future, digital agents will take the form of online computer-generated-image (CGI) humanoids that mimic humans convincingly, or even three-dimensional robots embedded with artificial intelligence that may serve as nannies, as caretakers, or in other service roles. Children growing up with these kinds of intelligent agents will communicate with them and perhaps even see them as just another "person," interacting with them much as they do with family members, friends, or even the family dog. Even now, when it comes to artificially intelligent devices, there is a blurring of boundaries between what is real and what is not for children. Rachel Metz, the technology editor for the *MIT Review*, asked her four-year-old niece if Alexa was a real person. The child's answer was that "Alexa is 'a kind of robot' who lives in her house, and robots aren't people."[97] But she did anthropomorphize that "robot," adding that she does think Alexa has feelings, happy and sad. A study from the MIT Media Lab of children ages three to ten who were interacting with voice-controlled digital agents like Alexa or Google Home found that kids generally find these agents both friendly and trustworthy.[98] Amazon has even released a kid's version of the popular digital assistant.[99]

As these kinds of digital assistants become more sophisticated, it will become more difficult—especially for children—to tell them apart from a "real" person. Many were surprised in the spring of 2018 when popular Instagram influencer Lil Miquela announced that she is really a computer-generated image, not a human. By then, she had already garnered over a million followers on Instagram and had been hired as a brand ambassador for brands popular with youths, like Supreme. More established brands, like Prada and Chanel, have also hired Miquela as a brand ambassador, in an attempt to build a relationship with a younger audience.[100] In recent years, technology and humans have coalesced in the music industry, as computers are increasingly used to "tune" voices and synthesize musical instruments. This week, that transition was taken even further, as Lil Miquela dropped her first single, titled "Hate Me."[101] Interestingly, it is being promoted on social media and offline in the exact same way that a new song by a real human singer is promoted. A billboard went up in Times Square for "Hate Me"—and nowhere on it is there an indication that this is not a real person. Lil Miquela is being marketed to kids as if she is real. The song is, of course, heavy on electronic music and Auto-Tune. It turns out, AI agents like Lil Miquela and robots may exert influence on kids just like other people do. For instance, although adults are largely impervious to being influenced by robots to give the wrong answers to questions, kids, unfortunately, are not as immune. In the Asch conformity studies (which we examined earlier, in chapter 3, where participants compared lines and were pressured to say the wrong answer, based on the group around them) performed with children aged seven and nine years, researchers found that kids were more likely to give the same responses as the robots, even if they were obviously incorrect; this indicated that the children were clearly pressured by roboticized social influence.[102] The implications of this influence are unsettling because kids may increasingly be persuaded by virtual agents like Lil Miquela, and, in the future, by robots; their behaviors may be influenced in yet unforeseen ways.

For parents and others concerned about the impact of all of this digital immersion, striking the right balance between kids and their devices is difficult. Some try to meet kids where they are with their love of devices, to encourage more positive behaviors. Psychologist Dana Klisanin is one of these. She is using kids' immersion in devices and virtual worlds to combat things like cyberbullying and to encourage prosocial behavior. She has developed the Cyberhero League, a version of "serious games" (games that aim to teach new values or behaviors), or what she calls "augmented imaginary play" to create an alternative "myth" to the cyberbully: that of the cyberhero. Her goals are to use gaming to teach kids a sense of empowerment, environmental stewardship, and social responsibility. Kids can earn actual money to donate to environmental and other causes through both physical activity and playing games. There is a battle now between the designers of apps and games like Instagram, Snapchat, and Fortnite (who intentionally make their apps and games engaging, "sticky," and addictive) and parents who are trying to avoid raising kids who are digital addicts. Parents, psychologists, and school administrators are looking for ways to deal with the proliferation of devices and the ills wrought by them in a variety of ways. Apps like Star Chart, which identifies the constellations in the stars, or PlantSnap, which identifies plants in the wild from a cell phone picture, will hopefully encourage kids to become more physically active, even if that play is a hybrid between digital and analog, rather than spending hours binge-watching TV shows or gaming in their rooms all day. Apps like unGlue are being developed as a way to both teach kids to manage their time spent on devices and encourage physical movement.[103]

Although kids might not like it, keeping an eye on their online activities is smart. Some parents do it by insisting on knowing their kids' passwords. Others restrict access to Snapchat until after their kids reach a certain age. Still others place limits on the use of the devices themselves, insisting they be used only in "public" areas of the house rather than in bedrooms. Some take the devices away at night to charge them in the parents' bedroom. Child psychologist Dr. Stephanie W. Marcy of the Children's Hospital of Los Angeles and clinical associate professor of pediatrics at USC suggests limiting kids' screen time after school to one hour a day, with parents co-watching and co-engaging. Otherwise, it's virtually impossible to limit what kids see on sites and apps like YouTube.[104] As one parent pointed out to me, your kid can start watching one of the branded cartoons, like Peppa Pig, but with auto-loading, YouTube can suddenly serve up troubling content automatically. Limiting screen time, not allowing kids to sleep with their phones, and utilizing positive-behavior-reinforcing apps like unGlue may help parents get a hold of their kids' screen addiction, but these must be implemented at the outset. Marcy said in recent talk that, "It becomes much harder, once kids have the phones, to pull back the reins."[105]

Clearly, digital immersion is reshaping children's behaviors. Like behaviors, kids' brains are also malleable and can be shaped in different ways, depending on the stimulation and input they are given. Given this "brain plasticity," we must ask ourselves, What is all of this digital connectivity doing to kids' brains—and to ours?

CHAPTER 5

YOUR BRAIN ON DIGITAL

"Rabbit's clever," said Pooh thoughtfully.
"Yes," said Piglet, "Rabbit's clever."
"And he has Brain."
"Yes," said Piglet, "Rabbit has Brain."
There was a long silence.
"I suppose," said Pooh, "that that's why he never under-
stands anything."
                    —A. A. Milne, *Winnie-the-Pooh*, 1926

JANUARY 14, 1967. GOLDEN GATE PARK, SAN FRANCISCO

The orgiastic, animalistic cry of Grace Slick's powerful voice singing "Somebody to Love" cuts through the air of Gold Gate Park, thick with the sickeningly sweet perfume of pot, patchouli, and sweat on this beautiful, sunny day. This song would become the anthem of what came to be known as the "Summer of Love" of 1967. Hippies float by with a glazed look in their eyes and soft smiles. A girl wearing a sheer white caftan is lifted up on a guy's shoulders above the crowd, backlit by the sunshine behind her, her figure visible through the fabric, and a woozy smile on her face. Timothy Leary, the LSD-using countercultural icon and Harvard professor approaches the microphone. Wearing a white, Indian-style linen sarong with the sleeves rolled up, loose pants, and flowers tucked over each ear, accentuating his greying hair, he stands, surveys the crowd for a long moment, then raises his hands like a preacher giving his followers the benediction. He utters the phrase that would reverberate for years to come, enunciating slowly: "Turn on . . . tune in . . . drop out."

In the 1960s, experimenting with drugs to "optimize" the brain was a key part of the counterculture movement. Tom Wolfe's widely read *Electric Kool-Aid Acid Test* documented the acid-fueled voyage of Ken Kesey and the Merry Pranksters in their psychedelic bus "Furthur." Their "Acid Test" LSD party flyers, which would paper every town they landed in, said, "Can you pass the acid test?"[1] By the 1980s, the '60s party was over as a new conservatism fell over the country in the Reagan era. Drug use became a pivotal issue, championed by First Lady Nancy Reagan. The story goes that her "Just Say No" campaign was inspired by her visit to an Oakland, California, middle school. A little girl there raised her hand and asked, "Mrs. Reagan, what do you do if somebody offers you drugs?" and she replied, "Well, you just say no!"[2] The "Just Say No" campaign was created, and was soon championed by the Kiwanis Club, which put up two thousand billboards nationwide, featuring Mrs. Reagan and her "Just Say No" slogan. The Girl Scouts and Boy Scouts of America got involved, introducing their versions of "Just Say No" merit badges. The Partnership for a Drug-Free America came out with its own slogan: "This is your brain on drugs." The "fried egg" was supposed to represent the negative impact on your brain from using drugs (see figure 5).

The campaign quickly became comedy fodder for many late-night comedians.[3] None of these efforts resulted in any substantive reduction in drug use and, in fact, both the medical and recreational use of marijuana is now being legalized in many states. Drugs are still a feature at many concerts, but rather than natural "herb," they're often lab-synthesized, like Ecstasy, ketamine, AK-47 24 Karat Gold, 5F-AMB, PX-2, MDMB-CHMINACA, and a raft of other synthesized cannabinoids, including K2 and Spice, substances which can be 80 times as potent as marijuana.[4] Rather than having full bands onstage, entertainment has gone digital, with DJs like Skrillex, Deadmau5, Steve Aoki, or Alison Wonderland appearing alone on stage with only a laptop or mixing board; behind them are gigantic, video-game-like 3-D projections, like Excision's giant robotized cat, which bops its head to the high-energy beats, and shoots flames out of its mouth before transforming into a robot.[5]

LSD has come back into fashion lately in the form of recreational or attempted mind-optimizing "microdosing," which entails ingesting small doses of the psychedelic drug. It is gaining popularity among the tech set in a movement called "biohacking."[6] Online documentation of trips takes place on sites like PsychonautWiki, a Reddit discussion board on microdosing that now has over 23,000 users.[7] LSD and many other drugs were sold on the dark web, on sites like the Silk Road. Founded in 2011, the Silk Road was the first known

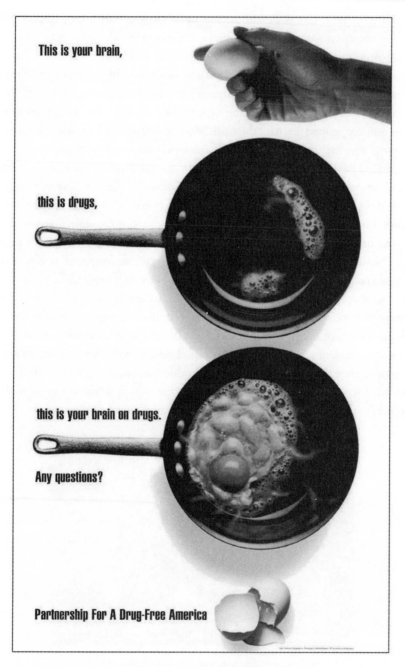

Figure 5. Partnership for a Drug-Free America, 1987.

dark-net market. Using a combination of TOR (the dark web), Bitcoin (for anonymous payments), and PGP (encryption for privacy), it established itself as the central marketplace for buyers seeking drugs and other contraband, before it was shut down. It's owner, Ross Ulbricht (who went by the nickname Dread Pirate Roberts), received a life sentence for money laundering and trafficking narcotics.[8] Still, buying and selling drugs on the dark web continues, as other sites quickly popped up to fill the void. Wikis about psychedelics are maintained by users who include lists of dark websites where one can find them.

Mind-bending psychedelics may seem a natural draw for those who spend a lot of time online, where imagery, music, and life itself is already enhanced, tuned, amped up, and more intense than real life itself. It may be then that the "brain on drugs" concept was merely ahead of its time, addressing the wrong target. "This is your brain on digital" may have been a more apropos and, indeed, truer head-line. New brain research has emerged that suggests that long-term and particu-larly dense use of digital media (i.e., long hours every day) may indeed be "frying" brains, or at least rewiring them. From infancy, babies' brains are "tuned in" to a steady diet of digital media. A third of infants under one year old are using smart-phones or tablets before they can walk or talk. One in seven is using them for at least an hour a day.[9] Forty-two percent of children aged a few months to eight years now have their own tablet device.[10] Products are emerging to facilitate digital connectivity, like the Fisher-Price Apptivity seat, which comes complete with a holder for the iPad, to feed babies a steady stream of digital content.[11]

Figure 6. The Fisher-Price Newborn-to-Toddler Apptivity Seat. (Fisher-Price/Mattel.)

The full impact of baby gear with holders for iPads and other similar devices—like the Apptivity seat or baby-toilet-seat potty trainers—on developing brains remains to be seen, yet studies are beginning to hint at the consequences. They are revealing some undesirable impacts in terms of both the structure and the functioning of brains of heavy users of digital devices. Parents are implicated in this, of course, as they increasingly turn to these screens as a kind of digital pacifier. A search of YouTube for "baby with iPad" now yields thousands of videos. One in particular, titled, "A Magazine Is an iPad That Does Not' Work" has garnered almost 5 million views.[12] In it, the baby, who cannot speak yet, swipes, pinches, opens, and closes apps and games like a pro. In the second scene, the baby's father trades the iPad for a magazine. The baby regards the image for a moment and then begins to swipe and pinch the paper page, activities and movements that are common when using an iPad but are clearly ineffective for handling and reading a magazine. The father runs a commentary across the screen that says, "To her, the magazine is an iPad that doesn't work." The baby finally gets frustrated when the magazine doesn't "react" and then reaches out, fussing. The father hands her the iPad. The baby immediately starts opening programs. Her face relaxes, and she smiles while staring wide-eyed at the screen.

I've shown videos like this during my keynote addresses to tech audiences. Typically, the audience begins to laugh, murmur, and smile as they process what they've just seen. The final comment on the YouTube video then rolls across the screen, "Steve Jobs has re-coded her operating system." This statement itself is surprising enough to cause one to pause and think about the implications. But then I say to the audience, "Think about it: This baby—and the thousands of others in similar 'baby with iPad' videos—has learned digital skills before it's learned to talk." A hush falls over the crowd. Serious faces then, as they try to more deeply process the video. What at first seemed a light, comedic look at the "digital generation" at work, upon closer inspection, becomes something else. What exactly *are* the implications of this ostensibly benign video? What does it mean that children are acquiring digital skills *before* acquiring language? Could it be that growing up digital might, in fact, be rewiring their operating systems, forever altering the brains of an entire generation?

Research is beginning to emerge indicating that early exposure to digital media is, in fact, altering brains. The American Academy of Pediatrics is concerned enough that it has called for a limit on exposure to digital media by this age group, citing multiple studies that identify numerous deleterious effects of a constant mental diet of digital media, including negative impacts on sleep, attention, and learning.[13] The AAP suggests no digital media for infants under eighteen months, other than video-chatting, and a limit of one hour per day of high-quality programming for children ages two to five—and that's only if they are co-viewed with a parent.[14]

FORT GREENE, BROOKLYN, NEW YORK

Sitting outside the corner French café in Fort Greene, Brooklyn, on a sunny, easygoing spring day, Nina and I sat talking about this idea of younger folks being hyperconnected to digital devices. Out of curiosity, we begin watching the passersby, to see how many of them were staring at cell phones or wearing headphones of some kind. Nina, my Airbnb host, is an event planner and stylist in New York City. Stylish and model thin, her mocha skin and beautiful, high cheekbones hint at her Somalian background. Today she's wearing her hair pulled back in a neat bun and sporting bright-red matte lipstick, with big, round, dark sunglasses that hide her eyes. Last night she ran the after-party for the Met Ball, and everyone from Rihanna to Madonna was there. It'd been a long night for her. Passersby smile and nod as they walk by. Nina is a well-known figure in this neighborhood, having been here for seventeen years. Brooklyn is hip now, particularly neighborhoods like DUMBO (short for Down Under the Manhattan Bridge Overpass) and Williamsburg to the north. Nina was one of the first "urban pioneers" in Fort Greene, when it was still rough around the edges, and she knows everyone. She lives in a lovely, historic brownstone. Her boyfriend is a musician currently on tour in Europe; they're talking about getting an apartment together in Barcelona. Nina's dream is to become a digital nomad, traveling as a style blogger and curating items for the home, from Bali to India, while writing and video-blogging (vlogging) her travels.

An elderly lady with bags of groceries smiles and waves at Nina as she shuffles by. Groups of kids pass us as well, on break from the school across the street. The majority grip a cell phone in their hands. Most are walking in the now-familiar head-bowed position: a physiological and behavioral change that has taken less than ten years for a generation to adopt. Many wear earbuds. One boy sports a pair of blindingly bright-green Beats by Dre headphones. Even while walking in groups, most are staring at their phones. One girl with earbuds in her ears is singing loudly, completely oblivious to the fact that she is inappropriately loud, almost embarrassingly so. Nina took off her glasses and, setting them on the table, told me about a *New York Times* article she'd read on how so many Millennials are multitasking. I casually remarked that one has to think about what that's doing to everyone's brains. Nina suddenly sat bolt upright, her mouth falling open and eyes wide in big circles. She placed both hands flat on the table as if to brace herself and exclaimed, "This reminds me of something that happened to me recently!"

She began telling me how she'd been on a trip to India, where she noticed that the colors were all very bright. She'd taken a lot of photos to upload to Facebook. Before she did, however, she used a filter to enhance the colors even more, to make her trip look even more fabulous than it was. After spending a couple of weeks looking at these enhanced photos, she said she came home, and it was if her brain got used to seeing those falsely bright colors. Looking around, her stylish apartment seemed a dull disappointment. She told her boyfriend, "I don't know. Everything just looks kind of dingy compared to India." Her brain had gotten used to seeing the over-the-top reds, the bright sunflower yellows, intense cornflower blues, and pure golds that she had actually created with her cell phone camera. Her photos of the trip were much brighter and purer than the real things she had documented in India. Somehow, looking at these punched-up photos, her brain had recalibrated, readjusting itself to her virtual world. The bright colors became what she expected to see. The digital had overtaken the real. After a couple weeks of this intensified color, she'd tuned in, turned on, and dropped out of the real world, as Timothy Leary had imagined, only this time not with LSD, but with digital technologies.

Nina said that after a few days, she woke up one morning and opened the windows wide. The sun shone in brightly, and as she looked around and felt more satisfied; things didn't look quite so gray and sad to her anymore. Her brain had once again recalibrated, this time to "real life." Nina's experiences make me wonder, What really *is* the effect of all of this digital immersion, especially among young people who spend hours a day staring at digital screens or, even more disconcerting, for those who begin digital immersion as babies?

Many people now use filters on Instagram and other social media sites to "bump up" the colors in their photos—to make them brighter and more fantastical than the actual image photographed, like Nina's photos of India. It turns out, people prefer these unreal photos: Studies have found that the enhanced photos garner more likes from Facebook friends and others with whom they are shared. For kids growing up digitally immersed, their brains may, in fact, begin to crave these kinds of digitally enhanced images, which also garner more likes on social media, driving a vicious cycle of posting even more enhanced images. A UCLA study on teens and brain activity looked at teens aged thirteen to eighteen undergoing an fMRI while viewing photos on Instagram; the fMRI is a form of brain imaging that shows brain activity by analyzing blood flow.[15] Researchers found that when the teens were looking at photos with more "likes," their brains showed more activity, particularly in the "reward centers," with the most notable activation in the neural regions tied to social cognition, imitation, and attention. What this means is that "likes" on social media prime kids' brains to want to imitate what "the group" most likes, to be a part of the group, in an effort to get more attention and likes from others themselves. Likes online serve as a form of "social proof" that then attracts more likes. Kids in the study were more likely to say they preferred photos that had many "likes" compared with photos that had few, indicating that virtual peer endorsement can create a snowball effect for posting even more enhanced photos. Perhaps even more troubling is the fact that this peer endorsement can extend to photos that depict risky behaviors—like the "roof-topping" selfies on skyscrapers or other dangerous places, and other behaviors that teens view as "rebellious" (such as drinking, smoking, or doing drugs), as well as dangerous viral-video "challenges."[16] In the competitive atmosphere of social media, regular photos won't cut it anymore, as they don't garner as many likes. Normal colors aren't enough anymore; hence the popularity of filters on Instagram and Snapchat, especially those that make life even more fantastical, that blend the real and the digital by turning users into adorable bunnies or perfected beauties with glowing crowns of flowers in their hair. Given this context to compete with, "real" reality is often just too bland. As the likes pour in, they serve as behavioral reinforcers to continue to enhance photos. Nina's experience that "ordinary life" is just too bland may increasingly be the experience of young people immersed in social media channels. Filters that "enhance" users' faces are also driving an increasing number of users into the offices of plastic surgeons, in an effort to get the face they imagine in their mind—the one they see "filtered" on Snapchat and Instagram—to match the face they have. Surgeons are calling this disorder "Snapchat dysphoria."[17]

Digital natives' brains are being rewired in other ways as well. Neuropsychiatrists completing MRI studies of digital natives' brains are finding they have altered neural networks that make them less capable of focusing their attention and listening. They also crave instant gratification and are weaker at abstract thinking and planning.[18] Digital natives have been found to thinker shallowly, which is characterized by rapid attention shifting and reduced thinking about what they are taking in. Their alleged improved "multitasking ability" is really a myth; switching from program to program and focusing attention between their analog surroundings and the online world is actually leading to diminished concentration and the loss of the ability to ignore irrelevant stimuli.[19] Being hyperconnected to devices is also resulting in a notable underdevelopment in the frontal lobes and executive region of their brains, which are areas that control judgment and decision-making ability.[20] The brain, when it is always-on and on devices, is in a constant state of "partial attention," leaving it in a state of constant stress. There is no down time, no quiet time to reflect or to contemplate and make thoughtful decisions—all of which depend on our full attention and time. In this constantly stressed state, the brains of digital natives turn to adrenaline and cortisol—stress hormones—to boost energy levels. This cacophony of near-constant overstimulation affects the areas of the brain linked to deep thinking and contemplation, over time impeding the ability to be creative, as the constant noise of visual and auditory stimulation drowns out the ability to concentrate.[21] This can lead to burnout and depression. How can we better care for our brains after prolonged use of these devices? One way suggested by Harvard cognitive researcher Sara C. Mednick is a simple twenty-to-thirty-minute nap. She found that even a short nap like this can help the brain to refresh after long periods of digital activity, with a sixty-minute nap being even better.[22]

RECODING OUR OPERATING SYSTEMS

Other changes in the brain are happening as a result of our transition from an analog to a digital culture. Digitally immersed kids and adults are now keyboarding as opposed to writing things out by hand. As a result, cursive writing is going the way of the dinosaurs in schools, and people's handwriting is decompensating. Hand writing was actually one of the first things to go in the late 1990s and early 2000s, as fewer and fewer people actually put pen to paper to write things down. I gave a talk at Carnegie Hall in New York for the Lexus Dealers Board of Directors Summit. On my panel were executives from Google and Facebook. As we took our places, preparing to be introduced, I looked at my cell phone and spied an ugly black blotch of ink on the smooth silver case. "My pen exploded on the plane," I confessed to the panelists. "What's a pen?" the fellow from Google quipped. He didn't actually say that, but that's what I told the audience he said, several minutes later, as I launched into my talk. What he actually said was that he never uses a pen anymore, except to sign checks in restaurants. I told my mentor, Don Paul, the former chief technology officer of

Chevron, this story. He then recounted an incident he'd experienced where he'd gone into a bank to send some money to a relative. At the teller window, he had written his relative's information on a piece of paper and handed it to the teller. She looked it over briefly, then handed it back to him, saying, "I can't read cursive writing." "There we go! We're done!" Don said to me, exaggeratedly throwing his hands in the air.[23] Like this teller, young people educated in the United States today will no longer be able to read someone's handwriting. I mentioned this to a student, saying that he and others won't be able to read historical documents written in cursive, to which he replied, "I don't need to read cursive; those kinds of documents will be scanned and uploaded to the internet." Soon, these kids will probably need a Google Translate option for cursive writing.

Cursive writing is a practiced analog skill that links the brain to the fine motor skills in the hands. Mastering it takes time, patience, and practice. Kids were originally taught penmanship in school to prepare them for jobs when they grew up. Penmanship meant mastering cursive writing in a particular style, which then varied from individual to individual in terms of the formation of the various letters. In the early days of the United States, professional penmen hand-wrote important documents, like the Constitution of the United States, which was written by penman Jacob Shallus over the course of two days.[24] From 1850 until 1925, children were taught the Spencerian method, an elaborately articulated style developed by George Spencer that became the de facto style for business correspondence well into the twentieth century.[25] At the time, having beautiful penmanship was thought to be an important skill. Now, one study found that the average adult hasn't written anything down by hand in forty-one days; one in three hasn't written anything by hand in the last six months.[26] In the United States, putting pen to paper is so rare these days that teaching cursive writing has been dropped from the core curriculum in all fifty states; it has been replaced, since 2013, by lessons in digital keyboarding.[27] Why is this important? It's important because keyboarding and writing call on different cognitive and physical skills, which result in different implications in terms of the neural pathways developed in the brain. These neuropathways may impact later learning, recall, and other related skills. Cursive writing involves many varied skills that must be mastered, such as holding the pen correctly, feeling the paper, making the correct letter shapes, and spending the time and patience it takes to learn the skill of writing in this style. Not to mention the fact that cursive writing is indelible, that is, not easily erased, a fact that made writing with care and thought all the more important. Contrast this with using the "delete" key on a keyboard or the spell check in an email or on a word processor. While this may seem like a simple shift in tool use, or perhaps a nostalgic yearning for the beautifully crafted penmanship of days gone by, it is much more than that. Research from the fields of neuroscience, biopsychology, and evolutionary biology have demonstrated that "our use of hands for purposive manipulation of tools plays a constitutive role in learning and cognitive development and may even be a significant building block in language development."[28] Writing has always incorporated technology of some kind—whether it be a craft person's stylus, pen, crayon, or other writing implement—yet typing requires a very different set of cognitive processing skills and physical movements than writing by hand. Indeed, recent thinking on the matter has pointed out that perception and motor action are closely connected and are reciprocally dependent, an idea psychologists and philosophers of mind call "embodied cognition."[29] Embodied cognition recognizes that perception and learning are not simply the work of the brain, rather, they occur via the real time interplay of task-specific resources distributed across the brain, body, and environment.[30] Early mastery of fine motor skills are a significant predictor of later academic achievement in reading and mathematics, as are other sensory motor (action) skills, giving support to this notion of body-brain-environment integration in learning.[31]

Claire Bustarret, an expert on handwritten medieval manuscripts, has studied the differences between writing by hand and typing on a keyboard. She says that typing requires a single tap of a key in the right place, a place that is invariable; writing by hand, however, allows a lot more latitude in terms of creating the shapes, positioning them on the page, as well as a myriad of other small variations between the shape and spacing of the letters, the height of the letters, the relationship of the lines of writing to the lines on the page, and various other fine details and small variations from writer to writer. This isn't merely some kind of academic navel-gazing; it turns out that writing may, in fact, shape our ability to read and to recognize letters *later*, as there seems to be a kind of "bodily memory" that encodes recognition of letters.[32]

Subsequent studies seem to bear this out. In a French study of seventy-six children, half were taught letters by handwriting them, while the other half learned from a computer screen.[33] When asked to recognize various letters later, the group who learned via handwriting performed better than the computer group. The study was repeated with adults, teaching them characters from a foreign alphabet, with the same results.

Gunther Kress, a professor of semiotics (the study of signs and symbols) and education at the University of London has explored the shift in teaching methodologies, from textbook to digital. He notes that writing is increasingly being displaced by the image in teaching. He has talked about the impacts of this, saying, "The combined effects on writing of the dominance of the mode of image and of the medium of screen will produce deep changes in the forms and functions of writing. This in turn will have profound effects on human, cognitive/affective, cultural and bodily engagement with the world, and on forms and shapes of knowledge."[34] Kress calls this move of semiotic materials from one mode to another (i.e., from the written word to a digital image) "transduction." Transduction is significant because it changes meaning, in that various media have different affordances (i.e., qualities or properties) that can lead to differing social effects. The question then becomes what meanings and interpretations are sanctioned in the learning process, and whether the active, or agentive, work of learners is recognized. In the educational realm, where multiple meanings exist, the role of teacher and learner also changes. Some schools are already experimenting with these changing roles in the form of the "flipped classroom"— where students watch or listen to the lecture *outside* of class (rather than doing homework), then come prepared to discuss the concepts and ideas and make new meanings and interpretations of their own with the teacher or professor facilitating. The flipped classroom makes students active participants in meaning making and learning, rather than simply passive recipients of a teacher's lecture. Sociologists Faye Wachs and Juliana Fuqua and their colleagues experimented with a flipped classroom in an engineering course for Dan Nissenson at Cal Poly Pomona. They found that this kind of new pedagogy resulted in lowered dropout rates, while increasing students' engagement with and understanding of the material.[35] For digital natives, then, an active, participatory approach to learning may yield better results than the traditional, more passive approach (e.g., lecturing).

Participatory learning may also mean participating in learning using the body. Although many argue that we've been through and adapted to technological changes before, during the industrial era—when agrarian workers moved from work on the farm to work in industrial factory settings—one could argue that then, the learning mechanisms remained the same (e.g., turning a faucet with their hand on the farm would be the same as turning a wheel on a factory machine). The feedback mechanism didn't change: The factory worker adapted by learning this new world of work through similar mechanisms of embodied learning and feedback. The difference now is that digital technologies and keyboarding have disaggregated the body from the learning process, thereby changing the feedback mechanisms for learning and going against hundreds of thousands of years of human evolution in terms of connecting physicality, the brain, learning, and memory. Educators and parents would be wise to reconsider the use of analog rather than digital or simulated learning, including through hand-writing, to develop young people's brains and maximize their learning, reconnecting mind and body for a cohesive feedback loop of embodied cognition.

THE SOUND OF SILENCE

Hands-on learning used to figure prominently in compulsory education after the rise of the industrial era, particularly in "trade" classes like woodshop, metal shop, auto shop, and physical education. Music education also figured prominently in many elementary, middle, and high schools. School bands received a real boost in America after World War I, when veterans, returning from the war and trained to play in service bands, accepted teaching positions as music instructors in schools. The turn of the century brought with it a veritable explosion in the number of professional bands, some with as many as a hundred members. One estimate put the number of these bands at ten thousand.[36] By the 1920s, with the rise in popularity of professional and community bands, the quality of the players dropped as more bands formed to meet the public demand. But as the quality of musicians dropped, so did their pay; the changing tastes of audiences toward jazz and the introduction of the automobile caused many of these local bands to break up. Emil Holz, a former school music teacher turned University of Michigan music professor talked about the time:

> These thousands of bands provided music for parades, civic ceremonials, concerts, and dances. As the popularity of Sousa and the other great bandleaders increased, a host of imitators appeared. The intense competition that developed led to price-cutting and charlatanism. As quality deteriorated the attraction of the town or park band waned. By 1920 many had succumbed under the simultaneous attacks of jazz, the automobile, the moving picture, and the phonograph. The great concert bands ceased touring and village bandstands stood deserted.[37]

Instrument sellers sought new markets for their instruments and looked to the schools for new customers. A series of state and national contests ensued, which sparked a boost of interest that encouraged band directors in schools to work hard to establish a competitive band.

Music was first introduced into schools in the United States in the 1830s, in part because of its role in religion, because it was thought to instill "happiness, contentment, cheerfulness, and tranquility," while exercising the lungs of those with wind instruments and those who joined choirs.[38] Learning to play an instrument in harmony with others was also thought to encourage passivity, orderliness, and discipline, while providing a spiritual and moral foundation for youth, qualities thought essential for industrial-era workers.[39] Kids now often skip the time-consuming, tedious, and often-frustrating task of learning an instrument; instead, they turn to "instant gratification" computer programs like GarageBand, Guitar Hero, or other musical-creation programs. In some ways, "real" versus "fake" instruments seem to make no difference. One Guitar Hero instruction webpage shows pictures and has text on how to "play" the Guitar Hero controller "guitar." Kids are told there, "You will then see colored circles moving down the screen. Match up the colors with the targets and hold that fret button. When the color passes over the target, strum! Voila! You've hit a note!"[40] There are five buttons on the frets, which kids push down to play a "note." The website tells the kids that "Guitar Hero controllers are just like real guitars, especially in the way they are played"—except they're not. On YouTube, videos show "experts" playing Guitar Hero controller guitars along with the videos. In one featuring the group Queen's "Bohemian Rhapsody," the "guitar" plays along with notes that are actually played in the song by a piano.[41]

One of the impacts of these kinds of digital variants to music making is lessened interest learning to play analog instruments, and a resultant decrease in musical-instrument sales across the country. Piano stores are shuttering their doors as kids' attention spans wane. One piano dealer is Mr. Jim Foster. He has sold pianos in the Midwest for over thirty years. Mr. Foster is closing his doors as the last holdout in the Iowa/Illinois Quad Cities area after all his competitors folded. He says, "Computer technology has just changed everything about what kids are interested in. People are interested in things that don't take much effort, so the idea of sitting and playing an hour a day to learn piano is not what kids want to do."[42] Many adults who play piano had their first introduction to playing in school. In recent years, public schools nationwide have been suffering from budget cuts; often first to go are classes in the arts. According to one report aptly named "The Sound of Silence," music classes and teachers declined dramatically between 1999 and 2000 and again during the 2003–2004 academic year, while the California public-school-student population meanwhile increased by nearly 6 percent. Students involved in music education there declined by 50 percent, the largest of any academic subject area. The number of music teachers declined by almost 27 percent, equating to 1,053 teachers. California is not the only state to do away with music courses. Funds have been cut for music and the arts in 80 percent of schools since 2008, particularly in high-needs areas.[43] This problem extends all the way to the top of the music market. Steinway Pianos—a company founded in 1853 in Manhattan, and the makers of the finest in grand pianos—is now in acquisition talks with the Chinese.[44]

Students devoid of music education are being impacted in unforeseen ways. Music has been an integral part of the human experience. It can be found in every culture, past and present. It plays an important part in our bonding together, and it is laden with shared cultural meanings. Think of the nostalgia evoked by Christmas carols, or think of when "Here Comes the Bride" is played at a wedding, and the guests rise to their feet, with tears in their eyes, as the beaming bride enters; or think of the time you may have heard the soulful sound of bagpipes playing or someone singing "Amazing Grace" as a loved one is quietly laid to rest. Couples often have "their song," which played at some pivotal moment in their relationship. Music is the soundtrack of our lives, both as individuals and as a culture. It is there to mark our milestones: birthdays, weddings, religious events, and holidays. It makes us laugh or cry; it causes us to swell with pride and patriotism at our national anthem; and it evokes feelings of religious piety and faith, joy or love. Music has been with us since the Stone Age. In 2008, a flute carved out of bone was discovered in the Hohle Fels cave west of Ulm, Germany. Dating back at least 35,000 years, it showed that the sweet sounds of the flute wafted on the breeze prior to the invention of written language.[45] Making music touches our emotions, but it also calls on a variety of motor, sensory, and perceptual skills, including memory and higher-order cognitive (thinking) and perceptual skills.

Musical training in childhood leads to long-lasting effects, even into older adulthood, by integrating multiple parts of the brain and its functions. Dr. Christopher Steele from the Max Planck Institute for Human Cognitive and Brain Sciences and his colleagues explored the connection between brain development and early musical training. He has said that this is easily quantifiable, meaning that it is easy to identify who did versus who did not have early musical training. When Dr. Steele and his colleagues compared the brain structures of musical versus nonmusical groups, the findings were surprising. The impacts on the brains of the two groups went far beyond musical aptitude. Dr. Steele's studies found that learning a musical instrument before age seven deepens the connections between the right and left hemispheres of the brain, resulting in both motor skills and brain structure that are long-lasting. The researchers suggest that this kind of cross-brain connectivity serves as a kind of "scaffolding" upon which later experiences can be built, which can expand one's ability for problem solving and cognition.[46] Though some researchers had suggested there is a "Mozart effect" whereby children merely listening to music makes them smarter (a foundation of the "Baby Einstein" CDs)—efforts to replicate these findings in more recent studies was unsuccessful. Later researchers found that there was a kind of pseudo-Mozart effect—but it was when young children actively participated, not when they simply sat back and listened, that the impacts were seen, and those impacts were long-lasting, including gains in reading, mathematical, verbal, and spatial abilities.[47] Another long-term study found that as little as two years of music training had the effect of changing "both the structure of the brain's white matter, which carries signals through the brain, and gray matter, which contains most of the brain's neurons that are active in processing information. Music instruction also boosts engagement of brain networks that are responsible for decision-making and the ability to focus attention and inhibit impulses."[48] Music training accelerates maturity in areas of the brain responsible for sound processing, language development, speech perception, and reading skills.[49] A long-term study of both teens with high and low socioeconomic status found that those with higher involvement in the arts in school (including music) were more likely to take a calculus class, more likely to graduate high school, and three times more likely to get a bachelor's degree in college, when compared to teens with a lower socioeconomic status and without access to an arts-rich environment.[50] Students who participate in school band or orchestra have the lowest levels of current and lifelong use of alcohol, tobacco, and illicit drugs among any group in our society. According to the College Board, among college-bound high-school seniors in 2012, those who participated in music scored an average of 31 points above average on the SAT in reading, 23 points above average in math, and 31 points above average in writing.[51]

The benefits of a music education can last long after early education has ended. A study by Travis White-Schwoch and his team of neuroscientists at Northwestern University found that older adults who took music lessons at a young age process the sounds of speech faster than those who did not, even if they haven't picked up an instrument in forty years. Music education in childhood permanently alters the structures of the brain, which can have long-lasting positive effects, including staving off age-related declines in cognitive and neural function.[52] Music making has other nonmusical benefits beyond its positive influence on cognitive functioning. On a personal level, music making helps integrate our thinking and emotions and regulates our well-being. On a societal level, music builds social cohesion and facilitates shared social meanings. Tapping buttons on an electronic "guitar" controller is not the same as creating music, either alone or together in a group, and it does not offer these kinds of long-lasting cognitive benefits.

If the digital world were entirely beneficial to one's growth and development, it would stand to reason that tech entrepreneurs would be among the first to teach their kids digital skills, in an effort to enhance their brains. There is perhaps no single person more associated with technology than Steve Jobs of Apple. Yet, early on, he realized the potentially detrimental effects of digital devices on kids. Two years after the iPad launched, a reporter said to him, "Your kids must love it!" to which he replied, "Actually we don't allow the iPad in the home. We think it's too dangerous for them in effect."[53] Likewise, Bill Gates limited his daughter's screen time after she developed an unhealthy attachment to a video game.[54] The children of elite tech titans in Silicon Valley who attend school at private institutions like the Waldorf School of the Peninsula are also learning tech-free. The school's philosophy statement on technology states:

> Today's children spend far less time than earlier generations engaging with other children, caring adults, and nature. The lure of electronic entertainment in our media-infused society influences the emotional and physical development of children and adolescents on many levels, and can detract from their capacity to create a meaningful connection with others and the world around them.[55]

At Waldorf Schools, the arts (including music making and "eurythmia" or rhythmic movement) are emphasized and, perhaps surprisingly, no screens are to be found anywhere. The curriculum of the Waldorf School, an elite private school with 160 locations across the country, emphasizes the arts and physicality, painting, rhythmic movement and dance, and music, including both choral and instrumental music. This kind of education comes at a price, though:

tuition runs over $24,000 a year just for elementary school.[56] Education is decid-edly analog, physical, and experiential. Waldorf Schools draw on brain research to support its low-tech approach to children's education:

> Brain research tells us that media exposure can result in changes in the actual nerve network in the brain. This can affect such things as eye tracking (a nec-essary skill for successful reading), neurotransmitter levels, and how readily students receive the imaginative pictures that are foundational for learning. Media exposure can also negatively affect the health of children's peer interac-tion and play.[57]

It is interesting to note that the lower the socioeconomic status of the family, the more time kids spend looking at screens; and the higher the socioeconomic status, even in schools, the less time children spend with digital screens. Also, minority youth—blacks, Latinos, and Asians aged eight to eighteen years old—consume more hours of media per day than white kids do; for example, African American teens use an average of over eleven hours of media daily, compared with almost nine hours among Latinos and eight and a half among whites. The long-term outcomes, even into later adulthood, will be interesting to see over time.[58]

THE NO LATENCY LIFE

Attention spans seem to be another casualty among kids growing up in this digital era. In social media and texting, there is a constant bombardment of information, requiring rapid-fire attention shifting through multiple texts, snaps, videos, and other stimuli. Many apps are designed to be addictive and reinforce this behavior, hijacking people's minds through things like gamifica-tion, showing a leaderboard, for example, of how many snaps your friends have sent to pressure you to keep pace.[59] Mobile phones are omnipresent, vying for kids' attention even in the classroom. A 2012 survey by Pew Internet found that 87 percent of teachers think that technology is creating an easily distracted generation with short attention spans. Sixty-four percent said that phones "do more to distract students than to help them academically."[60] One study at six different universities found that students use their phones an average of eleven times during the hour and a half or so they are in a class lecture.[61] Other studies found that having the device in the class not only is distracting to the student herself but also breaks the concentration of the students seated around her. In fact, student outcomes of those who are texting in class are poor; they frequently do worse on tests, take poorer-quality notes, and retain less of the material that is taught to them.[62]

Digital connectivity is changing the mental perceptions of digital natives in other ways as well. It is reshaping their notion of time, particularly in terms of expectations around the pace of life and the pace of change. Digital culture is a dynamic (some would say frenetic) environment that depends on a constant churn of posts, texts, tweets, and snaps. The heaviest users check their phones literally hundreds or even thousands of times a day. The average teen aged thirteen to seventeen sends 3,300 text messages a month.[63] Texting among teens is so popular now that is has become their favorite method of communicating, overtaking the frequency of every other common form of interaction with their friends, including cell phone conversations, social media, or face-to-face meetings.[64] They're nimble multitaskers, quickly shifting from Spotify or their iTunes playlist to Snapchat, to a chat app, to Instagram, to a text message, then back around again. This kind of roving attention and surface-level focus, never focusing too deeply on one particular thing for too long, has become the norm. Eventually, these young folks will comprise the workforce of the future, and will perhaps find it difficult there to achieve what author Cal Newport has called deep work—focusing without distraction on a cognitively demanding task.[65]

This distractibility and lack of focus is, of course, flowing out to other areas of their lives. Having become accustomed to this accelerated environment, young people have grown impatient, with no tolerance for waiting, even for the time it takes for a video or website to load, or what's called "latency time." As such, there's a growing demand for a no-latency life. The average time they'll wait for a video to load before giving up is a mere two seconds.[66]

Tech writer Steven Meloan experienced this firsthand with his teenaged son, Tyler. Like many Boomer parents, he longed to introduce his son to the music and films he remembers enjoying as a kid. One film he wanted to revisit was *2001: A Space Odyssey,* which seemed very futuristic and edgy at its debut in 1979. As the film began, son Tyler sat, head bowed, texting with his friends. Steven had to keep nudging him to alert him that something important was about to happen on the screen. After about fifteen minutes of this, Steven asked Tyler how he liked the film, at which point his son replied, "It's been, like, eleven minutes and there are still apes." It was at that moment Steven realized that what seemed gripping and interesting when he was younger now appeared plodding and pedantic, and sometimes downright silly, when viewed in this new context. Based on this and other similar experiences with Tyler, Steven mused on the pace-of-life differences that are amplified when consuming cultural content together, saying:

> It's funny about the movie thing and teens. It's been a real wake-up experience for me. Many films that I remember fondly from the '70s and '80s now seem corny, dated, amateurish, or even unintentionally funny when watched with Tyler. The intervening years have brought such sophistication and edginess to drama and shows like SNL have brought so much satire of things once taken seriously, a lot of it no longer works. I'll try to get him to watch things with me (that I may not have seen in ages and would like to revisit), and after 30 seconds of a trailer, he'll look at me with eyes like ... "Really?" A few years back, my brother and I got him to watch the original *Ocean's 11* with us—with Dean Martin, Sinatra, Sammy Davis, etc. As Tyler pointed out, the "ordinary world" setup for the film (before the adventure even begins) went on for 30 minutes (as with the *2001: A Space Odyssey* apes). And the acting was often really bad.[67]

For Steven and his son, Tyler, their mismatched pace-of-life expectations has rendered movie-watching together a bit of a burdensome annoyance, rather than a pleasurable leisure activity shared by father and son. "Don't care how, I want it now" could be the mantra for digital natives, as their expectations built within the digital environment are beginning to impact their expectations of the pacing of the world around them.

The changing pace of life and the shortening of attention spans has also meant that television, once the center of entertainment in homes across America, is falling out of favor with younger generations. Having to wait for scheduled broadcasts just isn't appealing. Fourteen-to-seventeen-year-olds are abandoning TV at the rate of 33 percent for movies and television shows and 26 percent for sporting events.[68] Even the stalwart NFL is fast losing viewers, and fewer people are showing up at stadiums to watch games (although there are other contributors to this as well, including the concern about concussion rates, the politicizing of the game through kneeling players during the national anthem, etc.). One teen said he doesn't watch TV at all anymore "because it's not interactive." Many younger viewers prefer to stream their videos from YouTube, Hulu, and other sites, where it's on demand and where they can also chat and give feedback on what they are seeing. Live-streaming video apps like Periscope or Facebook Live let them create content themselves or take part in conversations the moment the content is streaming. Using devices while watching video streams on another screen is also increasingly common. Globally, 74 percent of fourteen-to-seventeen-year-olds use multiple screens, most often a combination of a television and a smartphone, while viewing shows or movies. In North America, 59 percent use a laptop for simultaneous viewing, while 42 percent use a smartphone.[69] Using multiple devices has become so common now that many kids want to text or check Snapchat or Instagram or other apps while in movie theaters (contrary to the short "silence your phones" film that is now shown by the theater management at the beginning of every movie); this is frustrating to older moviegoers who feel assaulted by the bright glow of screens lighting up throughout the film. Movie-going used to be the main form of visual entertainment in the early part of the twentieth century, and people would typically go to the theater every week. Now, people are only buying movie tickets an average of four to five times a year. Younger viewers (aged eighteen to twenty-four) are abandoning movie theaters faster than any other group. Ticket sales haven't been this low since before the 1920s. To digital natives, it seems that attending a movie at a particular time, spending the money and time to do so, and having to put away their devices for two or more hours just isn't appealing.[70]

While many are concerned about the impacts of digital technologies and the multitasking they encourage, others see the rapid attention shifting and quicker pace of information gathering developing in younger digital natives as adaptive to the changing times. Microsoft researcher danah boyd is one of these. An expert on children, teens, and technology, she has said:

> Brains are being rewired—any shift in stimulus results in a rewiring. . . . The techniques and mechanisms to engage in rapid-fire attention shifting will be extremely useful for the creative class whose job it is to integrate ideas; they relish opportunities to have stimuli that allow them to see things differently.[71]

Rewiring of brains via digital devices may indeed be adaptive to certain job types in the future, yet the waning of music education, physical education, and even outdoor play is ushering in with it a series of unforeseen and unintended consequences for children. Angela Hanscom, an occupational therapist and author of *Barefoot and Balanced*, reports that as a result of less outdoor play, kids now have underdeveloped vestibular systems (the bodily systems that control balance and spatial orientation). This leads to an insufficient sense of balance and a decreased sense of their own bodies and space.[72] As a result, children are now tumbling out of their desks at school, running into each other more often, and are clumsier than children of previous generations. When playing games together, they often don't know their own strength and push each other with more force, an action that is bound to cause hurt feelings or initiate fights. New York City public schools have experienced a 30 percent increase in the number of students who are referred to occupational therapy in the past four years. Other cities are experiencing similar increases: Chicago is up 20 percent, and Los Angeles is up 30 percent within the past five years.[73]

BLURRING MAP AND TERRITORY ONLINE

As younger people spend more and more time online, the boundaries between online and offline life are beginning to blur. As mentioned in a prior chapter, in the early days of the internet, people used to distinguish their online activities from "IRL" ones, which stood for "in real life," offline. Now, the perception of what is real is changing, fundamentally changing the nature of "reality," as well as our understanding of perception and the brain. Gregory Bateson, the well-known communications scholar quoted in an earlier chapter, recalled philosopher and scientist Alfred Korzybski's idea that "the map is not the territory" and applied it in the context of human relationships. Bateson meant that the communication about relationships is not the same as the actual relationship itself, that is, a representation of something is not the thing itself.[74] Within digital technologies, map and territory are blurring. For younger users, reality and online life have merged, rendering them almost indistinguishable from one another. Digital social networks are now both map and territory, containing both one's network of friends, family, and associates and the representation of self and others. This is similar to the old days of cartoons, where children would sometimes hit each other with hammers and such things, thinking that their playmate's head would just pop back into shape like it did on TV.

In the 1990s, when America Online was all the rage, map and territory were still easily distinguishable. People used nicknames or "handles" in early online settings, demarcating their identity online from off. Some created completely false identities in fanciful role-playing worlds. Accessing online worlds meant dialing up with a modem via a telephone line. It was slow and expensive, as users sometimes paid for access by the minute. Some spent long hours a day connected to these virtual worlds, chatting or playing games with others; for most, the time spent in front of the screen was limited because the computer was connected to the wall, the cost was high, and the speed was slow. Now, with mobile devices, the cord has been cut. Being untethered from the wall, combined with the advent of social networks like Facebook, where users provide their real names, map and territory have coalesced. People now build up large social followings based on their real online personas. Many younger users aspire to become "influencers" or internet celebrities. The digital realm is now not a reflection of some other "IRL" reality; rather, it has become a reality of its own. Someone can now have a host of friends online that one never encounters face-to-face, yet whom they interact with on a daily basis. This is the digital version of a popular decades-old interaction known as "pen-pals," which were people who lived far away from each other but used letters and photos to communicate and get to know one another.

THE VIRTUAL MIRROR

Digital technologies are also impacting digital natives' brains and psyches in another way, in terms of the development of their self-image. The developmental task teens are faced with is the critical stage of *becoming*, a stage that developmental psychologist Erik Erickson has called identity versus role confusion, as was discussed earlier. Again, their main developmental task at this stage is to solidify their identity before moving on to adulthood. Erickson has said that part of this identity is constructed through the reflections of ourselves we receive back from others. Mirrors have been used as a metaphor to evoke this notion of a reflected self. Mirrors first came into being in Venice, Italy, in the 1500s, when Cristallo, a crystal-like glass with an ultra-clear finish, was developed. When a silver amalgam of tin and mercury was applied to the back of the Cristallo glass, for the first time, people could see an accurate reflection of themselves. These beautiful, gold-framed mirrors quickly became sought-after luxury items among royals, who eagerly paid hundreds to thousands of dollars for a single one.[75] By the mid-1600s, the cost of mirrors had decreased with the arrival of cheaper knockoffs from France. Wealthy merchants rushed out to buy them, to emulate the style of their wealthy lords. These mirrors soon drove a surge in portraiture, as wealthy patrons wanted to capture more-permanent renditions of their images for others to see, dressed in their best clothes and often in luxurious settings, showing off their accumulated wealth, prosperity, and "good life" to others.[76] Since the existence of the earliest mirrors, which consisted of pools of water held in dark vessels, they have been used by writers to signal narcissism, beginning with the ancient Greek myth of Narcissus. In the original story, Narcissus wastes away while gazing at his own image in a meadow pool. The mirror appeared again in the 1812 fairytale *Snow White*. The Evil Queen, a female narcissist, demands that her magical mirror answer her question, "Who is the fairest of all?" The story hints at aging, fading beauty, and the diminishing value of aging women on the marriage market. As such, rival beauties must be eliminated. Mirrors make an appearance again in the psychoanalytic theory of Jacques Lacan. He described a "mirror stage" of psychological development in which an external image of the body triggers reflected back to the infant through the mother or primary caregiver helps create one's internal self-image. Lacan viewed the mirror stage as critical for the formation of the "I" for people.[77] Sociologist Charles Horton Cooley in 1902 later used the mirror to describe the development of one's self-image through the reflected appraisal of others, a process he called "the looking glass self."[78]

Today, the mirror still plays a vital role in the construction of self for kids and teens who are in the process of learning who they are in the world, but it has now moved from analog to digital, with digital devices and social media acting as a virtual mirror. This virtual mirror differs from earlier mirror technologies in one fundamental way: rather than reflecting back an accurate image, it acts as a funhouse mirror, reflecting back a distorted image of self and others. John Brunner, in his 1968 science fiction novel *Stand on Zanzibar*, foreshadows this kind of virtual mirror when he wrote about an "advanced TV" that would allow people to insert themselves into the frame and go on various adventures around the world. He called these people "Mr. & Mrs. Everywhere."[79] The adventures of Mr. and Mrs. Everywhere were designed to evoke jealousy and envy in their viewers, very similar to those portraits of wealthy merchants after the invention of the mirror in Venice. Social technologies have now caught up to Brunner's sci-fi fantasy, enabling the real Mr. and Mrs. Everywhere. Online, people can present a highly curated "idealized self," and lifestyle, that can far exceed—or bear no resemblance whatsoever to—face-to-face reality. Many present highly curated, "exciting" lives on sites like Instagram and Facebook to boost social status and approval. Photos can be easily taken and retaken to achieve the desired effect, with filters applied to make people and scenes appear even more perfect and fantastical than they are. Many online pics emphasize sexualized body parts—exposed "six-pack" abs, muscles, and well-barbered haircuts for guys; round butts, full lips, and breasts for gals—which serve as style role models. Some celebrities with huge social followings, like Kylie Jenner, have gotten plastic surgery to present even more exaggerated or perfected images, driving a "cosmetic gaze," which fuels a multi-billion-dollar plastic-surgery industry.[80] Like Mr. and Mrs. Everywhere, some pics are shot in exotic locales, for instance, photobombing the *Mona Lisa* at the Louvre in Paris, or posting selfies that have dramatic religious shrines such as the Taj Mahal or the Wat Chalong temple in Phuket, Thailand, looming up in the background. Others emphasize status aboard private jets with expensive champagnes or wines, dining on gourmet food, or showing a display of newly purchased Louis Vuitton handbags or the latest in athletic footwear. Still others feature beautiful "models" on yachts or at poolside parties in Vegas, on the playa at Burning Man, or stage-side at Coachella. To be the most fabulous of all and capture the most unique shots, some take huge risks. Some 259 people have been killed around the world while taking selfies; some tumbled off cliffs (including Machu Picchu in Peru and the Grand Canyon); others crashed their cars; some have even been hit by trains while trying to get a great photo opportunity.[81] One young man even shot himself in the head while showing off a gun, which led the media to coin the term "death by selfie."[82] The US National Parks Service has issued a warning for people not to take bear selfies, after a spate of selfies with black bears cropped up on social media.[83] And one teen girl suffered online backlash after she posted a smiling selfie at the Auschwitz concentration camp.[84]

The warped image reflected back to people from curated social media is in part due to the frequent use of filters and other photo-altering apps to enhance their shots and physical appearance even further. "Internet celebrity" is something many younger people aspire to; many post frequent photos, snaps, and videos in the hope of attaining the maximum number of likes, reposts, shares, and follows. Many young men and women check their Twitter, Facebook, Instagram, and other feeds multiple—sometimes hundreds or even thousands of—times a day, hoping for positive feedback. In this competitive environment, normal pics don't cut it anymore. Amateurs are using some of the same tools professionals use to enhance or "tune" their photos—to even their skin tone, add makeup, remove blemishes, whiten teeth, broaden a smile, boost bust size, or shave off a few pounds. To achieve this, they use sophisticated programs like Photoshop or simple apps on smartphones like Facetune and Perfect365.[85] This sets the stage for an unequal, distorted "gaze" that can become internalized and cause (unfounded) distress in the viewer. Living in an analog world, one is keenly aware of one's own or others' flawed and imperfect "real" self, "warts and all." Comparing one's real-life imperfections to the online others' idealized, "tuned," and perfected images, and their over-the-top, fabulous, curated lives, will ultimately end in failure, since the "other" they're comparing themselves to doesn't really exist. Exacerbating this issue is the fact that the pool of peers teens can now compare themselves to has greatly expanded. That pool includes celebrities (whose images may have been altered or whose bodies may have been surgically enhanced), as well as a global collection of potentially attractive others. The "competition," as it were, for young people has never been more intense. Not surprisingly, many teens feel they can't measure up.[86]

At the same time, the unraveling of the social fabric, which used to support young people, has eroded. The combination of thinking they are "free" of obligations like a relationship, career, or home, and the intensification of social comparison to standards they can never achieve because of the virtual-mirror effect can yield other, darker effects. Rather than simply "traveling light through life" in search of the next experience, there is a negative impact of all of this on digital natives' mental health. As described earlier, Émile Durkheim's examination of suicide found a correlation between the social and individual acts of suicide, in that one's connection to the social fabric of life has a direct impact on one's mental health. He concluded that a large driver of mental illness was a lack of connection to one's community, in other words, that one was untethered. Durkheim called this "excessive individuation," a new version of what can be seen among those growing up digital.[87] Being untethered, combined with social media competition and the use of dating apps like Tinder, which reward or punish users based on attractiveness, can drive negative feelings about the self. Studies have found that using apps like Tinder can lead to lowered levels of satisfaction with users' faces and bodies, as well as a lowered sense of self-worth when compared to those who don't use these apps.[88] Researcher Jessica Strubel, an assistant professor in the Department of Merchandising and Digital Retailing at the University of North Texas, has said that, "people who are on Tinder after a while may begin to feel depersonalized and disposable in their social interactions, develop heightened awareness and criticism of their looks and bodies and believe that there is always something better around the corner."[89] Another study published in the *American Journal of Epidemiology* found that the more time one spends on Facebook, looking at pictures and stories of other people's curated and optimized lives, the more deleterious effect it has on one's mental health.[90] Following 5,208 people over two years, the study found that using Facebook is tightly linked to compromised social, physical, and psychological health. For each statistical step away from average in liking, sharing, or posting updates, users experienced a 5–8 percent increase in likelihood that they would experience mental-health problems in the future. Still other studies have found that using social media increases feelings of isolation, anxiety, and inadequacy.[91] Ironically, it is the most vulnerable kids, those who are lonely in the first place, who are the ones most likely to use the internet to seek connection, which paradoxically leaves them even lonelier.[92] In this sense, social media feeds on the socially vulnerable. Not surprisingly, hyperconnectivity seems to correlate also with an increase in issues like depression and anxiety, which we're seeing now among young adults. A survey conducted by the Association for University and College Counseling Center Directors and published in 2016 found a sharp uptick in mental health issues among college students, with 44 percent of their clients having severe psychological problems; this represents a marked increase from 16 percent in 2000.[93] Many are calling this "a growing crisis," as college mental-health facilities are overwhelmed by the demand and are unable to meet the needs of the students. One in twelve college students has made a suicide plan; 60 percent say they've felt lonely; and almost 50 percent have felt hopeless in the past year. Sixty-two percent of college students say they experience "overwhelming anxiety." Compare that to the pre-digital era numbers of just 18 percent in 1982.[94]

Many young people are turning to antidepressant medications to treat their symptoms of depression and the anxiety. Currently, more than one in ten Americans aged twelve and older in the United States takes an antidepressant.[95] The trouble is that these medications are not very effective and can actually *increase* thoughts of suicide and the chance of a suicidal attempt or completion, particularly among younger people. The National Institute of Mental Health has said that "mild depression tends to improve on placebo so that the difference between antidepressant use and placebo effect is very small, or at times, absent."[96] In this case, the side effects can far outweigh the benefits of these medications, if a sugar pill or some other nonmedical intervention—like exercise or talk therapy—works just as well.

THE EMPATHY GAP

Growing up staring at screens is impacting another area of psychological development, and that is digital natives' emotional intelligence, or what employers now refer to frequently as their "soft skills." Termed "EQ," emotional quotient, or emotional intelligence, these soft skills have been shown to be more important in adult success than have one's grade point average, test scores, or even IQ. EQ includes the ability to read and understand one's own emotions and the emotions of others; the ability to delay gratification; the ability to understand one's own emotions and the emotions of others; and the ability to feel and display empathy for others.[97] Empathy, a cornerstone of EQ, is defined as the ability to "put oneself in another person's shoes." A story in the news out of Cocoa, Florida, in the summer of 2017 illustrated the developing empathy gap among digital natives. Five teenage boys, aged fourteen to sixteen, watched as a man, Jamel Dunn, who was aged thirty-two and the father of two boys, waded out into the water of a nearby fenced-in pond; when he got outside his depth, he struggled to stay afloat and called out for help. Dunn was disabled and walked with a cane. Instead of calling for help, the teens whipped out their cell phones and began filming, which, sadly, is the reaction to many tragic incidents these days. The boys jeered and laughed as the man slowly drowned. One of the teens can be heard on the film shouting, "Get out the water, yo." Another shouted, "Ain't nobody fixin' to help you, you dumb b*&^%—you shouldn't have gone in there." The boys then laugh. As Mr. Dunn's head dipped underwater for the last time, one of the boys said: "Oh, he just died." The cell phone video taken by the teens was two and a half minutes long and was posted to Facebook. Not one of the five called 911 or anyone else for help during the event or afterwards.[98] Mr. Dunn's body was not found until five days later, when it was seen floating near the edge of the pond. The teens were not charged with a crime for failing to help.[99]

Videos like this seem to put the empathy gap on public display, particularly among younger users, who seem to routinely both produce and consume violent imagery. Videos of brutal schoolyard fights are popular, and many have gone viral. One such video of a fight between two teenage boys in New Jersey that was broken up by a third party has been viewed more than 20 million times and was even shared by basketball great LeBron James (in acknowledging the person who stopped the fight).[100] Nowadays, instead of not intervening during emergencies or taking a passive role, bystanders whip out their phones to film, and rather than taking an active role to provide aid, sometimes they even live-stream to Facebook, Instagram, or Snapchat.

Empathy is important, as it is a key ingredient of prosocial, or helpful, behavior to others. It is also key to the development of an internal moral compass, our internalized notion of right and wrong. As such, empathy plays an important role in the development of well-adjusted adults. It has been known for some time that part of the development of empathy—reading people's nonverbal expressions of emotion—has been more developed in females than in males, likely because as females grow up, they have more experience and spend more time gazing at the faces of others; in contrast, males tend to look more at things.[101] Now, however, since both sexes are staring more at screens than at people's faces (often starting in infancy), their ability to both read the emotions of others and to develop empathy for them—and potentially the ability to understand and express their own emotions—may be compromised. This is critical because emotional intelligence—of which empathy is a component—has been shown to be more important to later career success than IQ, grades in school, or performance on standardized tests.[102]

TOOLS 'R' US?

Lastly, devices are changing our brains because we offload many of our cognitive processes to our devices. Just as telescopes greatly expand our ability to see, cognitive technologies—like the computers in our pockets—extend the scope and power of cognition, our ability to think and process information. We're using our cell phones and digital assistants, like Alexa, Google Home, or Siri, to do things that we used to do routinely with our brains. For example, people used to remember phone numbers of family members and friends, but now everything is stored in the cell phone. There are implications to this. For example, recently there was a story in the *New Yorker* detailing how a girl's car had broken down, and she'd called her old boyfriend (much to the chagrin of her new boyfriend) for help. When asked by her upset boyfriend why she'd called the ex and not him, she replied that it was the only number she could remember. Other activities, like doing math in our heads, have been supplanted by the cell phone's tools, like its calculator, calendar, and mapping apps. In fact, apps like Apple Pay and other payment devices on our phones will soon make using cash—and figuring out how to count back change—a lost art. A friend of mine, Barry Caplan, recently went to a fast-food restaurant and encountered problems with the cashier when he tried to pay:

Cashier: that's $6.05
Me: Here's twenty
Cashier hits buttons on screen
Me: I might have the change
Digs in pocket

Me: here's a dime
Cashier:
Cashier:
Cashier:
Cashier:
Cashier:
Me: you owe me 14.05
Cashier: ok.[103]

Neuropsychological researchers who analyze our use of digital devices are beginning to consider the impacts of offloading our cognitive work to these tools. Psychologist Itiel E. Dror, of Southampton University in the United Kingdom, asked: "What about a modern child, who has never bothered to memorize the multiplication tables, as you did, because a computer is always at hand? The only way he ever retrieves 7×9 is to key it in and read off the product. He blindly consults his computer when you blindly consult your memory: What's the difference?"[104] Are the cognitive skills of memorization and calculation in our heads, for example, no longer needed in this time of distributed cognition, where our devices work with us to do the heavy lifting? Henry Wilmer, a psychologist from Temple University, sees cognitive offloading as negative, saying that "involvement with these devices may have a negative and lasting impact on users' ability to think, remember, pay attention, and regulate emotion."[105]

Using our devices to do our cognitive work is all well and good—until it's not. We're creating a series of dependencies on devices that is fine as long as those devices are up and running; but the minute they're not, due to either power outages or connectivity issues, a de-skilling effect takes place such that young people, who are dependent on these devices, are unable to complete tasks, including transactions, mathematics, or even finding their way using a paper map; the latter of which is a skill that three-fourths those under age twenty-five no longer possess.[106] Over time, such de-skilling will envelop a wider and wider swath of tasks and skills—driving, for example. As cars and other objects become embedded with their own autonomous intelligences within the widening scope of the Internet of Things, it will leave people (who depend on their devices to augment their cognitive functions and who do not have the analog experience and skills to "do it themselves") unable to function outside of a fully wired environment. Humans then will become fully augmented, virtual cyborgs—half human, half machine—in the modern world.

People's attachment to digital technologies is blurring the boundaries between digital and analog so much that many are beginning to leave the analog world behind, choosing instead to spend more and more time engaging with people, entertainment, and information only in virtual worlds. The majority of adults and most children spend all of their time indoors now; only a few are spending any time outdoors in nature.[107] All of this makes us wonder, what impact is untethering from nature having on our bodies and minds, as nature becomes virtualized and we lose touch with embodied experiences of the sublime?

CHAPTER 6

UNTETHERED FROM NATURE

Allons! whoever you are come travel with me!
    Traveling with me, you find what never tires.
    The earth never tires;
    The earth is rude, silent, incomprehensible at first—Nature
is rude and incomprehensible at first;
    Be not discouraged—keep on—there are divine things, well
envelop'd;
    I swear to you there are divine things more beautiful than
words can tell.

                            —Walt Whitman, "Song of the Open Road,"
                                            Leaves of Grass, 1900

"THE McRIB IS BACK!"

For many Americans, the mere thought of the elusive, juicy, BBQ-sauce-laden McRib elicits feelings of excitement and pure joy. There's even a McRib locator app that helps rabid fans find the elusive sandwich; some travel hundreds of miles to savor the tangy goodness.[1] A funny episode of *The Osbournes*, a reality show starring rocker Ozzy Osbourne and his family, featured the McRib. In it, Ozzy's wife, Sharon, and the kids drive to the local McDonald's. Upon pulling up to the menu, son Jack gasps and breathlessly proclaims, "The McRib is back! I'm so excited!" Sister Kelly derisively responds, "You're getting excited over the *McRib*?? . . . The f—ing *McRib*!?"[2] Jack's excitement is apparently shared by many: Late-night talk show host Stephen Colbert has said the McRib is "the only fast food sandwich I know with a cult following."[3] One fellow on Reddit described his wife's obsession with the McRib, saying:

I like the McRib well enough, but my wife takes it to a whole new level. The first day they have them again, she calls the local McD's and pre-orders 2 or 3 dozen, for pick-up the second or third day. (They have to plan a chunk of time for this.) When I get them home, she'll eat one or two, then put all the rest in the freezer (carefully wrapped) and dole them out to herself for maybe 6–8 weeks. Last year when I drove over to pick them up, the staff all lined up behind the counter and gave me an ovation.[4]

Talk-show host Colbert may have put his finger on the key to the McRib's popularity when he said: "As much as I love ribs—there's one part that I hate. The ribs."[5] The McRib is a kind of re-assembled frankenfood, or what the industry calls a "restructured meat product." It starts out as a low-quality mix of ground pork tripe, heart, and scalded stomach, which is then bound together and molded into a fake slab of ribs before being slathered with enough tart and tangy BBQ sauce to disguise its true color and form.[6] A "before" photo online shows a dull-grey slab of rib-shaped meat, its color vaguely reminiscent of the Formica flooring in the typical junior high school cafeteria.[7] The original McRib contained some seventy ingredients, including azodicarbonamide, a flour-bleaching agent also used to put the "bounce" in yoga mats or the spring in the step of gym shoes.[8] McDonald's and other restaurants quietly removed this ingredient after social-media blogger Vani Hari, known as the "Food Babe," started a signature drive to pressure Subway to remove the "yoga mat chemical" from its bread.[9]

Another fast-food item that has generated a lot of excitement is the KFC Double Down. The Double Down consists of bacon, cheese, and the special Colonel's sauce, sandwiched between two pieces of fried chicken in lieu of a bun. KFC sold ten million of these little cholesterol bombs the first week of their release in 2010.[10] The Double Down became comedy fodder for Stephen Colbert, who said, "It's like an edible Hieronymus Bosch painting wrapped in a paper straitjacket."[11] At 540 calories, the Double Down is almost a "diet" food, compared to Wendy's Triple Baconator burger, which packs a walloping 1,350 calories between its buns, almost 70 percent of the daily recommended calories for an adult woman; add to that large fries and a Coke, and you're over the daily recommended calories in just one meal.[12] Such highly processed, lab-created foods like the McRib and the Double Down are examples of our how far away we've moved from simple, natural, whole foods. Given the popularity of these and other similar highly processed food products, one could argue that we've traded nature for convenience.

Food is an important indicator of our relationship to nature, since historically it's been our direct connection to the natural world. Yet, in recent years, the industrial application of technology to food has increasingly distanced us from that world. Fast-food chains came along in the mid-twentieth century, as a way to tame the messy business of food preparation.[13] Fast food is now created and perfected in labs, as scientists develop food flavors, textures, and so on for the cheapest possible cost. Wendy's lab, called 90°, is situated right next to a college campus in Ohio, an intentional move, as Millennials are now their key demographic.[14] Fast-food restaurants themselves provide a lab-like setting that is denaturalized, "sterile," and clean. The final food product is usually devoid of any hint that it hails from the natural world, having been processed, reconstituted, and reshaped into consistent and reliable sizes, shapes, colors, and tastes. In this way, food becomes a mass-produced, uniform "product." Prior to the industrial era, such over-processing was not a common practice (other than techniques like canning, drying, or salting for preservation). At that time, the United States was largely agrarian. Young people then not only would have known where their food came from but also would have lent a hand in its production, from gathering eggs from the chickens; to milking the cows; to tilling the fields with oxen or mules; to picking vegetables, fruits, or nuts at harvest time. Compare this lifestyle to the children of today who, for the most part, not only don't have a hand in the production of their own food but also don't have any knowledge at all about the "farm to table" aspect of the food they eat. Since the 1800s, county fairs and 4-H organizations have been a way for farmers, ranchers, and kids to show off their best farming efforts—often for prizes. They would show anything ranging from produce to fresh-baked pies to animals they'd raised, like cows, pigs, or sheep. A friend of mine recently went to the Los Angeles County Fair, where he saw a little urban kid of about seven years old point to one of the goats on display and say to his mother, "Is that a deer?" My friend said to me, "I was heartbroken."

But we needn't just look to the past to see how disconnected Americans are from their whole, natural foods. One can simply look overseas to contrast our national fast-food mentality with a country that places a high value on whole foods and quality ingredients: France. There, on any given day, one can find multiple farmers' markets presenting a huge array of colorful, farm-fresh produce, meats, and freshly caught fish. Lining the streets of Paris and other cities and towns are specialty shops, each devoted to a particular ingredient: the butcher selling fresh meat, the seafood monger with an array of fresh fish and shellfish, and little shops devoted to selling beautiful, handcrafted cheeses; honey; or fresh, warm baguettes and beautiful pastries that line the window. There is a long history of this: Patisserie Montorgueil, for example, a bakery in the Montorgueil neighborhood, has been in continuous operation since before the United States was a country. In Lyon one can find the famous Les Halles de Lyon Paul Bocuse, a food hall named after "Chef of the Century" Paul Bocuse. Les Halles in New York City, where Anthony Bourdain became the executive chef, was named after this place. I can easily see why chefs are inspired by it: Stall after stall offer up nature's bounty. Walking through the gigantic fresh market, I came upon foods that most typical supermarkets in the States never carry: a pig's head smiled at me from the case; the bodies of chickens were displayed with their heads; an entire rabbit, fur and all, and other animals, were displayed with their full bodies intact. Live lobsters and crabs sat in aquariums, next to rows of shiny, red whole fish.[15] In another area were great trays of glazed tropical fruits wrapped in bright-yellow cellophane; a variety of olives; small goat cheeses gently wrapped in chestnut leaves and tied with rough twine. Finally, the desserts: Scores of individual pastries were lined up neatly in cases, some topped with whole glazed strawberries or fresh raspberries with a dusting of powdered sugar, or blackberries or blueberries; others were finished with a tiny leaf of 24-carat edible gold. Everywhere I looked—nature, in abundance. There is an integrity to the food here. The restaurants inside the hall maintain this same integrity in their food preparation: From steaming beef bones cut in half to reveal the rich, juicy marrow inside, served with crusty, fresh-baked bread, to escargot in their shells and the lush oysters on the half shell, displayed on a bed of ice. None of the food at Les Halles was disguised as something else; there were no chicken nuggets shaped like dinosaurs to be found. French foods at these markets are as honest as they can be. The honey is raw; the eggs, unwashed. This is in stark contrast to the United States (as well as Japan, Australia, and Scandinavia), where eggs are processed before they go to market. Eggs are shampooed with a soap-and-water solution for "hygiene"—allegedly to avoid salmonella, and for aesthetics, to produce a "clean" egg. Yet this practice actually renders the eggs more susceptible to spoiling, since the natural protective glaze is washed away during this very unnatural process. This is why American eggs must be refrigerated, whereas eggs from almost every other country in the world not only can be stored at room temperature but often are, sitting out on shelves right next to the bread.

Adherence to traditional food production like that found at Les Halles is becoming rare in the United States. Although there are weekly farmers' markets in some American cities, the array of fresh foods available on any given day is limited when compared to Europe. Consumers in the States really have to work to seek out fresh, whole foods, and it usually costs more when they do find them. Whole Foods is one store that offers shoppers an array of fresh produce, meat, seafood, and baked goods. Shoppers jokingly refer to it as "Whole Paycheck" because its goods are expensive, putting them out of the range of many. Amazon's recent acquisition of the company has helped address this problem somewhat, but analysts say the chain still hasn't shed its whole-paycheck, high-cost problem. According to Morgan Stanley, a basket of sixty items at Whole Foods, including fresh and processed goods, costs $195, a sum that is roughly 40 to 45 percent higher than the same groceries at a conventional store.[16] Inner-city neighborhoods have been called "food deserts" for their lack of access to whole, natural foods and their abundance of highly processed, highly advertised and marketed prepared foods.[17] Even in gentrifying Downtown Los Angeles, fresh food can be hard to find: I went to six different small grocers one night in search of fresh vegetables for dinner and was surprised at how difficult it was to buy something fresh. Of the six grocers I went to, only one had a single head of semi-wilted lettuce. Some carried no fresh food at all. For many inner-city neighborhoods, this is the norm. The "walkability factor" to access fresh food has a direct impact on weight and health: In Los Angeles, a longer distance to a grocery store was associated with higher body weight; those who traveled more than 1.75 miles to a supermarket weighed 0.8 BMI units more (the equivalent of about 5 pounds more for a 5'5" person).[18] In California, obesity was 20 percent higher for those living in the least healthy food desert areas. In Indianapolis, researchers estimate that adding a new grocery store to a high-poverty neighborhood results in a three-pound weight decrease, while eliminating a fast-food restaurant in a neighborhood dense with them (defined as six or more fast-food restaurants per square kilometer) translates into a one-pound decrease in body weight for local residents.

Fast food has become a staple in the American diet. Even though the majority of Americans know that "junk food" isn't healthy for them, they generally don't care—the appeal of brands like McDonald's Happy Meal and the tasty salt, fat, and sugar in the cheap meals outweigh the health concerns.[19] Trips to McDonald's and similar fast-food restaurants have increased from a "treat" enjoyed occasionally in the 1950s and '60s to a weekly or even daily staple for many. The National Center for Health Statistics found that more than 37 percent of adults—or more than one in three—consume fast food on any given day.[20] Fast

188 LEFT TO THEIR OWN DEVICES

food is more popular with younger eaters, and its consumption decreases with age: Almost half (44.9 percent) of those aged 20–39 reported eating fast food on any given day, compared with 37.7 percent of those aged 40–59, and only 24 percent of those aged 60 and over.

Fast food and prepared meals are the most popular with younger diners. Almost 60 percent of eighteen-to-twenty-nine-year-olds in the United States eat fast food during any given week.[21] One reason is that Millennials have grown up with a "convenience" mind-set. For them, cooking from scratch is rare; they are the least likely group to cook from scratch at home when compared to older generations. Of all the age groups, Millennials are the most likely to eat out or buy prepared meals at stores like Trader Joe's. Despite the fact that 80 percent of Millennials claim to want to know where their food is grown, on average, they spend less than twenty minutes preparing meals, just about enough time to warm something up.[22] I can attest to this general lack of cooking skills from first-hand experience; as a faculty in residence for several years at an apartment dorm at the University of Southern California, I lived with the students. Students would try to warm up leftover pizza in their ovens—in the box. The resulting fires necessitated full evacuations from the building, sometimes at two in the morning or later, during which time we'd stand in the cold for about 45 minutes until the building was cleared by the fire department. Another time, a student turned on the broiler, which was filled with plastic food containers. You can imagine how that turned out. Another evacuation.

One of the keys to fast food's success is its marketing. It is a driving force even more powerful than having a conveniently located fast-food joint in the neighborhood. Early marketing efforts by companies like McDonald's targeted children, and their efforts paid off; by 1971, 96 percent of American kids could identify the McDonald's mascot, Ronald McDonald—the same number that could identify Santa Claus.[23] By 1977, the proportion of American food dollars spent on food outside of the home had risen to over 35 percent, up ten percentage points from 1954.[24] By the late 1990s, it had reached almost half (47 percent). These trends have continued to escalate; spending on fast food in the United States has risen from $187 billion in 2004 to $290.2 billion in 2017.[25] Americans now eat fast food at least once a week, while a third of kids eat it on any given day.[26] Young adults in the eighteen-to-twenty-four-year-old group are the most likely to eat out three or more times a week for dinner, and 72 percent eat out at least once a week.[27]

Perhaps surprisingly, contrary to accepted "common knowledge," low-income people are not the top consumers of fast food. Those earning $75,000 a year are actually those who most often eat fast food weekly, when compared to lower-income groups.[28] So it seems the driver for fast food's popularity isn't the cost—it's the time and convenience. Undoubtedly, it takes time to shop and cook food from scratch. With the majority of people—both men and women—working outside the home now, fast food is a convenience after a long day at work. Many kids of working parents are growing up on Chicken McNuggets and other similar salty and fatty items. Some won't eat anything else. One in three children between the ages of two and eleven eat at least one fast-food menu item a day. By age twelve, it becomes one in two.[29] Again, marketing and advertising is the main driver behind the success of fast food; every dollar of advertising money spent directly drives up demand for processed and fast foods. Not surprisingly, all of this fast-food consumption is linked to obesity in kids. Every increase of one fast-food meal per week is linked to an increase in body mass index (BMI) by 0.8 kg (although BMI alone may not spell ill health, as it fails to account for muscle mass versus fat, for example).[30]

Studies have found that many Millennials don't know how cook something as simple as fried eggs or spaghetti with meatballs.[31] A study by Porch, a company that connects home owners with home-repair professionals, found that only a third of Millennials can poach an egg (compared to 61 percent of Baby Boomers), half know how to roast a chicken (compared to 80 percent of Baby Boomers), and only 32 percent can make an apple pie from scratch. The one cooking skill where Millennials beat out other generations was making chocolate-chip cookies from ready-made dough.[32] Part of this move away from home cooking is due to waning role models, since each generation has cooked at home less frequently than the one before. This trend is exacerbated by the elimination of home-economics courses in schools, which used to be mandatory for students.[33] A US Department of Agriculture study in 2014 found that the total budget spent for the least convenient foods—unprocessed ingredients—had fallen to less than a quarter of household spending, and that the most convenient foods, purchased at fast-food and "fast-casual" or other sit-down restaurants, make up half of people's household food budget.[34]

Fast food is one of the indicators that we've come untethered from nature. These days, many younger folks spend little, if any, time outdoors, and a significant proportion of unhealthy eating patterns are linked to a sedentary lifestyle associated with indoor life and screen time. Twenty percent of high-school students in a national study said they watch TV and other devices more than five hours a day, including playing video games.[35] Those same kids also drink more sugar-sweetened beverages, get inadequate physical activity, and suffer from sleep deprivation, all of which are known risk factors for obesity. This connection between screen time and obesity doesn't stop with childhood: Studies that followed children from birth found that TV viewing in childhood predicts obesity risk well into adulthood and midlife, a finding that will surely extend to the extensive use of digital devices prevalent in kids' lives today.[36] Naturalist John Muir presaged this untethered world we find ourselves in today, a world populated by digital natives, wearing earbuds and staring at screens. He said, "Most people are on the world, not in it—[they] have no conscious sympathy or relationship to anything about them—undiffused, separate, and rigidly alone like marbles of polished stone, touching but separate."[37] Being humans who are touching but separate, "alone together," and detached from our surroundings has contributed to some of the negative health outcomes (whether mental, emotional, or physical) that are now beginning to show up in increasing numbers, including escalating anxiety and depression. John Muir considered the connection to nature absolutely essential, saying: "Everybody needs beauty as well as bread, places to play in and pray in, where nature may heal and give strength to body and soul alike."[38] As an example, he describes the rejuvenating effects of nature for anxious city dwellers, whom he considered over-civilized:

> Thousands of tired, nerve-shaken, over-civilized people are beginning to find out that going to the mountains is going home; that wildness is a necessity; and that mountain parks and reservations are useful not only as fountains of timber and irrigating rivers, but as fountains of life. Awakening from the stupefying effects of the vice of over-industry and the deadly apathy of luxury, they are trying as best they can to mix and enrich their own little ongoings with those of Nature, and to get rid of rust and disease.[39]

Muir was right about the health benefits of nature: A study out of Harvard University's T. H. Chan School of Public Health of 108,630 women over eight years found that women who lived in the greenest surroundings had a 12 percent lower mortality rate compared to those who lived in areas that were less green.[40] Also, women in greener areas had a 34 percent lower death rate due to respiratory issues, and a 13 percent lower cancer death rate. The researchers concluded that the results were due to physical benefits of living close to nature; they also said that those surrounded by nature are less likely to be depressed, as well as less likely to be exposed to noise, pollution, chemicals, and extreme heat. As we consider a way forward, looking to find solutions, this may be a very good time to rethink our hyper-attachment to technologies and our untethering from nature, since fellowship with each other and communing with nature yield important benefits for mind, body, and spirit.[41]

What's missing now is the experience of "the sublime." The sublime made its first appearance in Greek philosophy in the first century. At that time, it was used to mean the grandeur of thought that a writer could convey to his reader, as a way to lift the reader outside of himself. Later the sublime was expanded to mean the experience of the grandeur of nature that allows people to transcend their everyday life, through experiencing something larger than themselves. In the 1690s, three English writers expanded the notion of the sublime: John Dennis, Lord Shaftesbury, and Joseph Addison. Each had separately experienced the peril and grandeur of the Swiss Alps, and those experiences had changed them. They described the sublime as nature evoking a feeling of awe, sometimes mixed with fear or even terror. As English Romantic poet Lord Byron wrote:

> I live not in myself, but I become
> Portion of that around me; and to me,
> High mountains are a feeling, but the hum
> Of human cities torture: I can see
> Nothing to loathe in nature, save to be
> A link reluctant in a fleshly chain,
> Class'd among creatures, when the soul can flee,
> And with the sky, the peak, the heaving plain
> Of ocean, or the stars, mingle, and not in vain.[42]

The essential qualities of the sublime are boundlessness and infiniteness. The sublime evokes feelings of unity and completeness. Byron encapsulates this with, "I live not in myself, but I become / Portion of that around me." The sublime evokes the sense of something greater in life than ourselves. Many of the world's most illustrious writers and artists advocated experiences of the sublime, including nineteenth-century transcendentalists Henry David Thoreau and Ralph Waldo Emerson; poets Walt Whitman, Emily Dickinson, Henry Wadsworth Longfellow, and Robert Frost; and artists ranging from Claude Monet to Georgia O'Keeffe to plein air painters around the world. Some of the most recognizable paintings in the world were inspired by nature, including Vincent van Gogh's *Starry Night* and Monet's *Water Lilies*.

One genre of the sublime in the arts is the pastoral. First popular in Renaissance writings, the pastoral is a way of connecting the dots between life, art, and nature, through an idealized depiction of simple country life. It occurs in three-parts that come full circle—first, a flight or exile from the city; second, a retreat to a rural setting; then, third, a return to city life, after being changed or renewed. William Shakespeare's *As You Like It*, *The Winter's Tale*, and *The Tempest* all use the pastoral convention. It allowed his characters to take leave of their normal constraints by retreating to a place where the ordinary rules of urban living no longer applied. This "taking leave" of the constraints of civilization facilitates the experience of "aha" moments," of finding new insights, and of interacting with both nature and society.[43]

Pastorals found their way into the work of many great composers as well, as they sought to translate the sights and sounds of nature into musical scores. Notable among them was Austrian composer Gustav Mahler. He worked lakeside in a small cabin he had built on the edge of a meadow in Steinbach on the Attersee, just outside Vienna and within view of the majestic Austrian Alps. There, he could hear the water and the sounds of nature all around him. It was in this little cabin that he composed the sunny and extroverted Symphony no. 3. His assistant and lifelong supporter, conductor Bruno Walter, stopped by for a visit one day. Mahler played for him the new symphony on his piano. Walter wrote about it, "I was overwhelmed to feel in his playing the same creative fervor and exaltation which had given birth to the work itself. His entire being seemed to breathe a mysterious affinity with the forces of nature. I saw him as Pan."[44] Mahler's little cabin still sits undisturbed by the lake to this day, his piano still there, serving as a small memorial to the great composer and his work. It is surrounded now, perhaps somewhat ignominiously, by a trailer park.

Perhaps no one was more inspired by experiences of the sublime than renowned composer Ludwig van Beethoven. Though he had moved to Vienna from Germany to study composition under Joseph Haydn, like Mahler, he would often go to the countryside to compose. For someone for whom sound was so critical, it was particularly tragic when Beethoven became stricken with hearing loss at age twenty-six. By forty-six years old, he was completely deaf. Though the reason for his deafness was unknown at the time, doctors now believe it was the result of lead poisoning from a particular wine he used to enjoy, which had been fortified with lead to improve the flavor.[45] Because of his growing deafness, Beethoven had to rely on remembrances of the subtle sounds of nature he had heard along his long walks outdoors. His Symphony no. 6 in F Major, op. 68, known as the *Pas-*

toral Symphony, or Recollections of Country Life, paints a nuanced and joyful aural picture of springtime. In it, Beethoven suggests the sound of a babbling brook, the tempest of a passing storm, the happiness and simplicity of a shepherd's song after the much-needed rain, and a covey of songbirds whom he said, "composed along with him," which ended up as "a nightingale in the flutes, a quail in the oboes and a cuckoo in the clarinets."[46] The pastoral symphony later became the soundtrack for the beloved animated Disney classic *Fantasia*. In the film, fanciful woodland creatures like fauns, centaurs, and cupids flirt and frolic to the music in a fantasy woodland scene. The Latin root for sublime means "uplifted, high, or exalted."[47] Both the sublime and artists' interpretation of it can have that effect on us. Work still needs to be done, though, to spark digital natives' interest and to provide opportunities for them to reconnect with nature. One hip brand may have found a way to reach them and spark that interest: In August 2018, Vans, a brand popular with skaters, surfers, and teens in general, signed a deal with the Van Gogh Museum to feature Van Gogh's art drawn from nature on a limited-edition line of shoes, T-shirts, and jackets. Now, Van Gogh's sunflowers, almond blossoms, and a skull have found their way onto the clothing of a new generation of people who will be able to appreciate his version of the pastoral. The collection sold out within days.[48]

AMERICA'S BEST IDEA

The national parks were developed so everyone could enjoy pastoral moments and the sublime. Writer and conservationist Wallas Stegner called the national parks "the best idea we ever had."[49] Michael T. Reynolds, the National Park Service acting director in 2017 (and now superintendent of Yosemite National Park), described how the parks transcend place, that instead: "Our national parks embody the idea of the American Dream. Parks are created and protected by dreamers who saw the value of preserving these special places that are tangible reminders of our country's rich history."[50]

Naturalist John Muir was one such dreamer. Award-winning documentarian Ken Burns said about him, "As we got to know him . . . he ascended to the pantheon of the highest individuals in our country; I'm talking about the level of Abraham Lincoln, and Martin Luther King, Thomas Jefferson, and Elizabeth Cady Stanton, Jackie Robinson—people who have had a transformational effect on who we are."[51] As a wilderness explorer, Muir is perhaps best known for his adventures along California's scenic Sierra Nevada. He thought of nature as a tonic: "Climb the mountains and get their good tidings. Nature's peace will flow into you as sunshine flows into trees. The winds will blow their own freshness into you, and the storms their energy, while cares will drop off like autumn leaves."[52]

Muir's eloquent words inspired President Theodore Roosevelt to invent the National Park Service. During his tenure (1901–1909), Roosevelt designated five new national parks, eighteen national monuments, four national game refuges, fifty-one bird sanctuaries, and over 100 million acres of national forest. Muir himself contributed to the creation of Yosemite, Sequoia, Mount Rainier, the Petrified Forest, and the Grand Canyon National Parks. At their inception, travel was slow and the parks were far removed from the most populated cities, so visits were mostly made by the affluent. After World War II, park visitation was given a lift by the establishment of the National Highway System. In the postwar years, newfound affluence combined with freshly built unscarred highways, a boom in car purchases, and a "boom" of children, drove many families to seek respite and relaxation in the parks.

By the 1960s, this boom began to reverse, as views on nature and the parks as places for rest and rejuvenation changed. Hippies ushered in an eco movement, inspired by Rachel Carson's bestseller *Silent Spring*. The book was based on a letter to the editor of the *Boston Herald* by Carson's friend Olga Owens Huckins. She described the death of birds around her house after the aerial spraying of DDT to kill mosquitos.[53] The 1960s eco movement resulted in a shift in thinking about the national parks, from places to visit and enjoy, to fragile ecosystems needing to be conserved and preserved. Some parks moved to limit visitation as a result.

This change in thinking regarding park visitors contributed to a gradual drop in rates of national park visitation over the years; this combined with the gas crisis of the 1970s and the later financial crisis, which made visiting them difficult. With fewer people taking respite from the cities in nature, away went its calming effects, leaving many with a lack of experience outdoors and a growing unease about the wild. Wireless carrier T-Mobile joked about this in one of its recent ads: a couple is shown lying next to one another in a tent, surrounded by the sounds of nature. An orchestra of crickets wells up; you hear a bird's call and the distinctive "who-who" of an owl as the camera zooms in on the couple's faces. "We did it!" the wife says, in a forced cheery tone. Her husband grins and chimes in, "We're campers!" She replies, "It's so nice to get out of the city." They lie together in awkward silence for a moment, then the husband suddenly blurts out, "It's so . . . quiet." The wife quickly replies, "Is it too quiet?" He responds, "It's awful." The wife quickly pulls out her phone and locates a YouTube video called

"Relaxing City Noises"; she presses play, and out comes the familiar sounds of city traffic and honking horns. In the next shot, both are dead asleep. It's funny because it's true: People aren't going out into nature anymore. The average American now spends 93 percent of his or her life indoors.[54] Children too are living an indoor life: they spend half the amount of time outside as the adults who were questioned in the study self-reported about their own childhood years.[55]

Many people are growing afraid of nature due to their lack of experience in it. This is particularly true for younger adults, urban and suburban residents, and minorities.[56] This demographic disparity maps directly onto younger folks, who are more likely to be urban and nonwhite. In a *National Geographic* piece titled "Can the Selfie Generation Unplug and Get into Parks?" National Park Service director Jonathan Jarvis described this fear; he recounts a situation in which a beautiful photograph of a national park was shown to inner-city kids, and their reaction surprised him. Instead of awe, Jarvis said,

> It looked scary to them. Empty. Forbidding. Not welcoming. They said, "Where are all the people?" We had the same experience when we brought a group of students from Los Angeles to Death Valley. They wouldn't get out of the van. The quiet, the pure darkness, unnerved them and threatened them.[57]

Millennials are the most racially and ethnically diverse of any age group, yet national-park visitation doesn't reflect their diversity. In Yellowstone in 2016, 83 percent of the visitors were white, 11 percent were Asian, 2 percent were American Indian, and only 1 percent were black.[58] In other parks, like Cuyahoga Valley, outside of Cleveland, 94 percent of visitors were white.[59] In her book *Black Faces, White Spaces*, Berkeley social scientist Carolyn Finney discusses the racial disparity both in the national parks and within the larger environmental movement. She points out that people of color are usually not represented in conservation groups and activities, and that they are usually missing from depictions in visual media for the outdoors, leading to a lack of role models. Finney gives the example of a *Vanity Fair* "Green Issue," which highlighted well-known eco-activists, environmental organizations, and celebrities who are proactive in combating climate change; of the twenty-eight pages of photos and bios that followed, only two were African American, and one was African.[60] A study by sociologist Derek Martin that reviewed outdoor magazines found what he calls a "racialized outdoor identity," which is almost always strong, young, and white.[61] In the over four thousand images in magazines he examined from 1984 to 2000, including from *Time, Outside*, and *Ebony*, the majority of the models used in outdoor ads were white. Black models were mainly shown in urban or suburban environments, leading him to conclude that the low participation of African Americans in outdoor leisure activities might be linked to a lack of visual role models in popular culture. A comedic video that pokes fun at this issue went viral on social media; in "A Black Hiker," actor Blair Underwood is out for an afternoon hike in the local mountains. White hikers who encounter him on the trail express shock and surprise. In a tone reminiscent of old nature shows, he says to a white, middle-aged couple, "Prickly pears . . . they're edible." In awe, the wife responds, "You *know* that?" The video goes on to show others who are shocked at seeing the lone black hiker out on the trail. One man who commented on the video said, "I have experienced nearly every scene in the clip, as a male, black hiker."[62] Recognizing this issue, journalist Timothy Egan wrote in a story for *National Geographic*, "At a time when nearly one in four Americans is under the age of 18 and half the babies born are racial or ethnic minorities . . . most park visitors are older and white."[63] This could threaten the existence of the national parks in the long run; as Park Director Jarvis put it, "If we were a business, we'd be out of business in the long term."[64]

More time in nature could be a tonic for our nation's current mental-health crisis. Anxiety, depression, and suicide are all up among young people, and few know why. Many don't seem to be connecting the dots between these growing mental-health struggles and the increasing time spent staring at glowing screens, which keeps them indoors and out of nature's calm. Yet, as found by studies questioning this issue, there is a direct connection between screen time and higher rates of anxiety and depression.[65] Those suffering from anxiety and depression don't seem to understand why they are suffering, and then they continue to pursue the very thing that is negatively driving their mental health, even experiencing withdrawal-type symptoms when their smartphones are taken away.[66] Fueled by this addictive quality of devices and social media, they become locked in a self-reinforcing cycle: feeling anxious and depressed often results in self-isolation and increased use of digital devices, which causes more anxiety and depression, and so on. Removing the rejuvenating effects of nature by isolating oneself indoors inadvertently removes the possible corrective to this vicious cycle.

The national parks have been one place prior generations went to seek rest and relaxation from the city. Yet digital natives who have grown up indoors are not adopting this practice, therefore having no experience with the natural sublime. Reading media reports, one would get the idea that people are stampeding to the parks. Headlines trumpet that visitation rates for national parks is skyrocketing. And that is true—if you count "visits" and not "visitors." Statistics are a funny thing; we've come to count on them to tell us the objective "truth" of a matter, yet they can be presented in a way that's misleading. There's a wonderful little book called *How to Lie with Statistics*, which shows us how data can be manipulated to skew the impression given by the numbers.[67] For example, we might see an ad that says, "2 out of 3 dentists recommend this toothpaste," which means one thing when three thousand dentists are surveyed, and something completely different when it's only three. Something similar is going on with the National Park Service numbers; although total *visitation* may be at an all-time high, visitation has actually *declined* on a per-capita basis (i.e., when counted as the number of *visitors*). Shortly after the parks were established, visits per capita (i.e., per person) grew at a relatively constant annual rate of 3.7 percent from 1929 to 1941.[68] After World War I, growth continued at an average annual rate of 2.2 percent from 1945 to 1960. Since then, per-capita visits have grown more slowly: From 1979 to 1990, it went down to 1.1 percent per year; and from 1990 to 2000, it declined even further, to an average rate of 0.1 percent per year. From 2000 to 2009, the growth rate was negative, at −0.9 percent per year. As of 2014, per-capita visits average about 21.6 visits per 100 people in the United States, which is down from a peak of 25.8 visits per 100 people in 1995. Overall, according to the National Park Service Public Use Statistics Office, the total drop in visits between 1987 and 2006 was 14.6 million, or a 5.1 percent decrease from a peak of 287.2 million. The visitation "bump" in 2016 and 2017 to record levels did indeed happen (based on "visits"). But what this means is that a certain small *subset* of people are going to multiple parks or perhaps the same park multiple *times*. But who are these exuberant frequent visitors? It turns out, they're not digital natives. As Jonathan Jarvis, director of the National Park Service, put it, "Young people are more separated from the natural world than perhaps any generation before them. There are times when it seems as if the national parks have never been more passé than in the age of the smartphone. The national parks risk obsolescence in the eyes of an increasingly diverse and distracted demographic."[69]

Younger and more diverse visitors simply aren't showing up. A look at the data on visitors to the top three national parks, Yosemite, Yellowstone, and the Smoky Mountains, reveals that most visitors are both white and older, between the ages of thirty-five and sixty-four. The median age is forty-three, meaning that half the visitors are middle-aged or older. The average age of visitors to Denali

Park is fifty-seven. In Yellowstone, its fifty-four. In the past decade, the number of visitors under the age of fifteen has fallen by half.[70] Only 14 percent of visitors are Millennials aged nineteen to thirty-five. In some parks, that number drops as low as 5 percent, making Millennials the least represented age cohort in the national parks. Until the youngest generation's arrival, many children grew up having intimate contact with nature. One critical reason for starting nature experiences at a young age is that it leads to a lifetime of conservation behaviors. The more *personal* children's experiences with nature are, the more environmentally concerned and active they are likely to become as adults.[71] Yet, clearly, younger folks are simply not getting these experiences. In 2016, for example, 91 percent of visitor groups to Yellowstone contained two or more people, yet the majority (60 percent) of these groups contained no children at all.[72]

Another way to look at this is through the lens of time. The most visited national park in America is the Great Smoky Mountains National Park, within an hour's drive of Gatlinburg, Tennessee, or Asheville, North Carolina. The average stay there is less than seven and a half hours, about the length of an all-day hike. Most visitors aren't hiking, though. Instead, they're driving through the park on Newfound Gap Road, stopping along the way at the two main visitor centers and several park overlooks to take pictures; after this, "visitors" feel that they've "done" the park from the safety of their vehicles, and call it a day.[73] What is their actual time spent in nature? One could argue zero. Unfortunately, this kind of drive-through nature visitation is becoming the norm. More than 9.2 million people camped in the national parks in 1998.[74] This number dropped to 8.54 million in 2003; to 7.99 million in 2008; and finally to 7.91 million in 2013. A 2010 study found that out of 392 national parks, only eighteen had visitors who stayed more than a day.[75] Only six of the 392 parks had visitors who stayed for more than two days. These tend to be the more remote parks that require a boat or plane to reach, like Isle Royale National Park in Michigan or the Yukon–Charley Rivers National Preserve in Alaska. This makes sense; after going to that much trouble to get there, you want to stay for longer than a photo op.

THE FOUNTAIN OF LIFE

All of this raises the question: Do we really *need* nature experiences for our mental and physical health? It turns out, we do. Modern psychological research literature lends support to the notion that writers, composers, and artists have believed intuitively over the years—that time spent in nature reinvigorates the spirit and calms our soul. Some psychologists have suggested that communing with nature has restorative effects on the brain, since being outdoors allows our minds to wander, giving them a break from the everyday grind of life and its information overload. Neuroscientist David Strayer has said, "You let the prefrontal cortex rest, and all of a sudden these flashes of insight come to you. [Time spent in nature] supports creativity, positive well-being, [and] reductions in stress. There are all kinds of reasons why it's helpful."[76] Nature activates a different kind of attention, one that is softer and less focused, allowing the brain to rest. Psychologist William James described two types of attention that are activated in different settings, *directed* and *indirected*. Directed attention is the kind we use to navigate the city on a daily basis to avoid running into people, or to stop at a crosswalk for a red light to avoid getting hit by a car. Indirected attention refers to the effortless, "soft fascinations" that nature affords us: It is the attention we spend to witness the clouds floating slowly by, above us in the sky; the leaves rustling overhead; or a bird singing. Soft fascination is watching the hypnotic beauty of softly falling snow in the winter. These kinds of experiences rest and replenish our brains. Environmental psychologist Stephen Kaplan calls this "attention-restoration theory." He says that the directed attention called upon every day to navigate a busy city environment—and the kind we now use to stare at devices—leads to mental fatigue.[77] Cognitive psychologist Strayer says forays into nature without this constant, focused attention alters the prefrontal cortex, which is the brain's command center. This allows it to dial down and rest, like resting an overused muscle.[78] A stroll in the park, a walk on the beach, or a hike in the mountains can act as a reset button for the brain, allowing one to relax by not having to be always "on," focusing on the demands of the city. The kind of easy looking back and forth, taking in one's natural surroundings, was the inspiration for EMDR, or eye movement desensitization and reprocessing, a therapy used with success for those suffering from trauma and PTSD. Its pioneer, Francine Shapiro, was inspired to create it after a walk in a park, when she felt noticeably better afterward. She had noticed that her eyes moved back and forth in indirect attention as she walked, and then she artificially re-created this movement in her therapy method.[79] The subsequent research on the success of EMDR should suggest that forays into nature would calm stressed-out or anxious city dwellers, or calm traumatized individuals, in a similar manner. In fact, doctors in the United Kingdom are beginning to prescribe forays into nature for just this purpose.[80]

The impacts of time in nature on one's health are being studied, and the results are positive. Environmental psychologists Rachel and Steven Kaplan of the University of Michigan have researched the effects of nature on people's relationships and health. Their conclusion, after reviewing hundreds of studies on the topic, revealed many benefits from forays into nature, which they summarized as follows:

> The immediate outcomes include enjoyment, relaxation, and lowered stress levels. In addition, physical wellbeing is affected by such contacts. People with access to nearby natural settings have been found to be healthier than other individuals. The longer term, indirect impacts also include increased levels of satisfaction with one's home, one's job and with life in general.[81]

Despite these benefits, the message about the rejuvenating effects of nature seem to be falling on deaf ears, particularly among today's parents and youth. Characterizing this change, the American Wildlife Foundation has said that, "childhood has moved indoors."[82] This shift to an indoor childhood has accelerated in the past decade, with huge declines in spontaneous outdoor activities like bike riding, swimming, and hiking. According to the Centers for Disease Control and Prevention (CDC), only 6 percent of children ages nine to thirteen now play outdoors unsupervised in a typical week. This difference in outdoor play is showing up on their bodies. Outdoor play can be a full-body activity and workout; the muscles used for climbing trees and running around a playground are different from those used to swipe and scroll. Among children aged six to eleven years, only 7 percent were obese in 1980, compared with 18 percent in 2016.[83] Twenty percent of teens are now obese.[84] In fact, the average child now spends less time outdoors than the average prison inmate.[85] One in five spent no time at all outdoors on the average day, leading the British Heart Foundation Report to conclude that just one in ten of the "iPad generation" of toddlers is active enough to even be healthy.[86] Parents say that kids spend three times as much time on electronic devices as they do playing outside.[87] The Nature Conservancy wanted to find out why. The answers ranged from physical discomfort, with concerns about bugs and heat mentioned (36 percent); a lack of transportation to get to a natural area was another barrier (28 percent), as well as a lack of a nature area near the home (26 percent).[88] An additional 17 percent simply weren't interested. Obesity turns out to be another important factor, with almost half of the overweight kids (based on standardized BMI, or body mass index) preferring to spend time playing indoors;

in contrast, only 26 percent of children whose BMI falls within what is considered the "normal" range wanted to play indoors. In this sense, obesity becomes a vicious cycle: Those kids who would benefit the most from outdoor activities are the least likely to pursue them, preferring to stay at home, staring at screens, which leads to a cycle of more unhealthy eating, more soda drinking, and more obesity.[89] Nature is particularly impactful for children with Attention Deficit Hyperactivity Disorder (ADHD): studies show that those who took a twenty-minute walk in a green park tended to be calmer than those who walked in a downtown urban center.[90] Two hundred years ago, most children spent their days in fields, farms, or the wilds of nature. Yet now, childhood is increasingly urbanized and nature is something more likely to be watched on screens than experienced directly. Richard Louv, author of *Last Child in the Woods*, says children are suffering from what he calls "nature deficit disorder," the impacts of which are diminished use of the senses, attention difficulties, and higher rates of physical and emotional illnesses.[91] Children's wandering outdoors unsupervised has declined by 90 percent since the 1970s. Parents contribute to this because they increasingly view playing outside as dangerous. For instance, Angela Hanscom, a New England–based pediatric occupational therapist, recounts the day she and a group of third-graders visited a nature center with a few chaperones. Once they were out in the woods, the kids became very quiet and began to build a teepee out of sticks. Suddenly, one of the chaperones began to sound the alarm:

> "Put the sticks DOWN!" I looked over to see a chaperone running frantically towards the children. "Danger! Danger!" she screamed. Momentarily astonished by the sudden state of perceived emergency, I finally found my voice. "It's okay," I yelled over to her. "I said they could use the sticks as long as they respect each other's personal space." Speechless, the chaperone frowned, turned and walked to a group of nearby chaperones.[92]

Alienation from nature among children can be fueled by these kinds of irrational fears by parents and teachers. A United Kingdom–based National Study on Children and the Outdoors summarized these fears, which include: (1) concerns about the danger from traffic; (2) the issue of health and safety, and an obsession with trying to achieve a "zero-risk" world; (3) parental fears of "stranger danger"; and (4) the negative attitudes of some parenting gurus, who regard children's natural play as something to be stopped rather than encouraged, to protect them from harm. An unintended consequence of these shared fears is that they set the stage for a continuing loss of the natural environment, and its continued exploitation and destruction—since positive views of nature have been linked to regular contact with nature in early childhood, which the children of today simply are not getting.[93] Given our current challenges related to clean water and air, pollution, climate change, and declining animal and insect diversity, this is a problem. We will need those who care about nature to step up as good stewards of the environment to address these issues.

Yet even if kids and teens wanted to go out in nature, their opportunities for doing so in an organized fashion are waning. The Boy or Girl Scouts had been providing these opportunities for generations. Founded in 1902 by British Lieutenant-General the Baron Robert Baden-Powell, the Boy Scouts taught boys survival skills in the wilderness while emphasizing spiritual and leadership development. The Scouts instilled a value of nature conservation in the boys by providing for them direct experiences with nature recreation (via hiking and camping); teaching them natural history; and communicating to them an ethos of protecting nature, including through such practices as "leave no trace" when camping.[94] At their peak, the Boy Scouts swelled to over 25 million members, who enjoyed learning to camp, hike, light a fire, and engage in other outdoor pursuits while earning merit badges. Boys could rise through the ranks of Cub Scouts, Webelos, Boy Scouts, and, finally, for the top 4 percent, all the way to the coveted Eagle Scout rank. Early merit badges included outdoor skills handy on a farm, such as beekeeping, dairying, and blacksmithing.[95] Given the wane of rural living due to industrialization and urbanization (i.e., the move to cities), these badges were discontinued in the 1990s. Other analog, physical skills relevant to an industrial workforce (like machinery and masonry) were also discontinued, replaced by indoor-focused, digital-era badges like those for robotics, inventing, and digital technology.[96] The number of Scouts has dwindled in recent years, from 3.35 million in 2010 to only 2.34 million in 2016. Membership in the Girl Scouts is also down, dropping 30 percent from a peak of more than 3.8 million in 2003.[97]

Many middle-aged and older Americans have expressed sadness that younger people aren't growing up with these experiences like they did. Dr. Stephen R. Kellert, a professor at the Yale University School of Forestry and Environmental Studies, interviewed older adults in focus groups to better understand and foster Americans' relationship with nature. He summed up their thoughts on the topic, as follows:

Middle- and older-aged adults expressed deep concern that American society in general and younger generations in particular are disconnected from nature. In particular, older adults were concerned that younger generations are overly reliant on electronic media, unaware of how the natural world works, and unacquainted with the simple enjoyment of being outdoors.[98]

Kellert identified five main reasons for this emerging interest and effort gap. These are: (1) the places where people live, work, and go to school generally discourage contact with the natural world; (2) there are competing priorities of time, attention, and money that prevent contact with nature from becoming routine; (3) there is declining direct dependence on the natural world for livelihoods and subsistence, which allows Americans to orient their lives toward other interests and activities; (4) new technologies like smartphones and video games distract and captivate us, diminishing our desire for the slower-paced experiences in nature; and, finally, (5) there are shifting expectations about what "good" contact in nature ought to be, meaning that adults are generally satisfied with the relatively little time they spend outdoors in nature.[99] Although most of these fears aren't intimately tied to devices themselves (like the fear that your child will be hit by a car if he walks down the street with his eyes constantly focused on his smartphone), all of the fears are implicated in driving childhood indoors, toward device play and screen watching as supposedly "safe" alternatives to being outdoors. Unfortunately, being indoors and online provides only an *imagined* cocoon of safety. This kind of childhood can actually be limiting or dangerous on its own—indirectly, due to the health and obesity factors outlined earlier, and more directly, as social media and digital communications present their own set of mental-health challenges to kids, teens, and adults.

INSTANATURE, OR THE MEDIATED SUBLIME

Unlike their parents or grandparents, when digital natives *do* go out into nature, their devices go with them, mediating and reshaping their experiences. A new study from KOA Campgrounds found that 93 percent of campers bring their digital devices along while camping.[100] Photographing nature is, of course, is not new, and indeed it can be an artistic way to capture the sublime. Ansel Adams is perhaps best known of the photographers capturing the sublime of nature. He began photographing in Yosemite National Park as a child, using the Kodak No. 1

Brownie Box camera his parents bought for him. In 1941, Adams was hired by the Department of the Interior to photograph the national parks. The resulting dramatic black-and-white photographs of Half Dome in Yosemite and other natural wonders remain some of the most iconic photos ever taken.[101] Nowadays, what's changed is that smartphones are more than just a camera: the addition of internet connectivity and social media change the behavioral drivers when out in nature, which can reshape people's experience and alter their connection to it, as they become driven by the external reinforcement of like, shares, and comments. The experience becomes all about getting the best (and, increasingly, most extreme or unique) shot for Instagram or other social sites, then posting those images (often filtered) on social media. Driven by these external forces, 44 percent of Millennials say that Wi-Fi will determine how long they will camp. They are (probably unsurprisingly) the group most likely to post on social media while camping, while simultaneously saying that technology is distracting while in nature.[102] Smartphones change the nature experience by creating a mediated, focused experience rather than the restorative, diffused attention of wandering and discovery, which is the part of natural experiences that is most restful to the brain and, by extension, to the body and spirit. Pulling out a smartphone also encourages "task creep," that is, engaging in other activities, like texting, checking messages or social media, sending email, or watching videos, which further distances the person from the diffuse experience of nature.

Digital natives have the reputation for being more environmentally conscious and "greener" than other age groups—and, indeed, they see themselves that way.[103] Some students even choose their college now based upon its stated eco-friendly and environmental policies and practices, including energy conservation or renewable energy generation, recycling programs, and so on.[104] A majority (72 percent) of iGen teens and young adults of aged 15–23 are willing to pay more for green products, as are three out of four Millennials.[105] Millennials also say that a green work environment is important to them. Yet, in spite of all their green values, it turns out that their positive *attitudes* toward sustainability don't align with their *behaviors*. A nationwide survey found that although 69 percent of Millennials expressed genuine interest in the environment, they tended lack personal involvement in actual green-related activities.[106] They report fewer sustainable behaviors than do older age groups (e.g., recycling, conserving water, and adjusting the thermostat).[107] A study that analyzed forty years of data from 9.2 million high-school seniors found that environmental actions haven't kept pace with pro-green attitudes. Three times as many Millennials as

Baby Boomers said they made no personal effort to help the environment. Only 20 percent of Millennials indicated that they were actively involved in environmental cleanup, compared to a third of Baby Boomers. Psychologist Jean Twenge concluded from her research that—driven by social media—digital natives are less interested in community-mindedness and are focused more on money, image, and fame.[108] This concern with image and fame reshapes their forays into nature (when they do go), as we shall see.

Bringing internet-enabled devices along into nature is more than a simply a distraction from the experience: the drive to post on social media has had the unintended consequence of harming or even destroying nature itself. Those seeking external validation, seeking likes, comments, and shares via the most unique or over-the-top photos on social media, have inadvertently or even intentionally destroyed wildlife and natural formations to obtain those flashy shots. Here are just a few examples:

> In Buenos Aires, two tiny franciscana dolphins were pulled out of the ocean and paraded around so tourists could get a closer look at them.[109] Tourists in a great mob passed the dolphins around and even held one under the water for a time, taking selfies with the mammals until one died.
>
> In the Yunnan Animal Park in China, a peacock died after tourists picked him up to get a few close-up photos, holding him too tightly and plucking out some of his feathers.[110] A second bird died three days later; tourists were shown abusing it while grinning at their cameras. Park officials say the birds were "shocked to death." This park is approximately 6 kilometers wide and allows visitors to walk among the (non-threatening) animals. The sheer size prohibits park attendants from monitoring every visitor at all times.
>
> A tourist in Southern China viciously grabbed a seagull.[111] After grabbing it by its wings, she posed for a selfie, pretending to take a bite out of the bird.
>
> In Macedonia, a tourist killed a swan by dragging it out of Lake Ohrid in order to take a photo with it.[112] In the photos, the frightened bird is shown struggling to get away. After shooting the selfie, the woman abandoned the bird on the sand, where other people continued to take photos of it with their smartphones.
>
> In Palm Beach, Florida, a young man was videotaped pulling a bull shark out of the water by the tail and gripping it hard around the head to take selfies with it.[113]

In Guanacaste, Costa Rica, a large group of tourists disrupted the breeding
pattern of sea turtles by trying to take photos with them as they came
ashore to lay their eggs.[114] The tourists were petting them, taking selfies,
and standing on their nests. Several of the turtles turned back to the
sea, alarmed and unable to lay their eggs at all as a result.

These are just a sampling of a few cases that made it into the media. Imagine
what might be the actual tally of such incidents that have never come to light.

Rangers in Lake Tahoe, Yellowstone, and other parks had to warn visitors
to stop trying to take selfies around bears. Since 2014, the incidence of wildlife
selfies has shot up 294 percent. When animals become the objects of fascination
for unique selfies, they become objectified "things," rather than living beings,
which can lead to their mistreatment. A vivid and tragic example is a viral video
out of Florida, in which three young men laugh and point as a shark struggles
to survive while being dragged by the tail at high speed behind their speedboat.
One of the men points and laughs at the tortured shark that is bouncing off
the boat's wake, saying "It looks almost dead." They uploaded the video to Instagram. Then they were charged with two felony counts of aggravated animal
cruelty and illegal method of take. An earlier video of them showing something
similar was also discovered. Upon seeing the shark-dragging video, Miami fish-
erman Mark Quintano said, "I've been shark fishing for 50 years, and I've never
seen a disrespect for an animal my entire career that was that evil."[115] Charges
were dropped against one of the four men in the boat, but felony charges have
been filed against the other three for aggravated animal cruelty.[116] Over 40
percent of wildlife selfies are what experts call "bad wildlife photos"—pictures
or videos of people hugging or holding wildlife, or inappropriately interacting
with the animals in other ways. Some opportunists seeking tourist dollars have
turned to *providing* these animals for untethered tourists who are in search of
animal selfies. These creatures are often kept in barren cages or unsanitary conditions, with many showing signs of illness or neglect, including lacerations or
open wounds. Some are beaten into submission by their owners before they are
trotted out for the photos.[117] In Manaus, Brazil, 94 percent of tourist excursions advertise the ability to touch or hold wild animals.[118] A study of Instagram found that direct contact with wild animals for photo opportunities was
offered in 94 percent of excursions at six different locations, and that official
tour guides actively encouraged this type of activity 77 percent of the time.[119]
The majority of animals offered up (61 percent) are species that have been clas-

sified as needing protection by the Convention on the Trade of Endangered Species (CITES); another 21 percent have been classified as "threatened." Ever since the widespread distribution of personal cameras, tourists have regularly taken photos as mementoes from their trips, but now, tourists who are driven by a desire for social media attention are actually destroying natural structures and harming or killing animals.

Seeking fame on social media has also lead to the desecration or destruction of natural formations, purportedly in the name of "art." In urban centers, street art has been a way some "outsiders"—the disenfranchised, and those outside the typical money and power structures of society—have gained attention. It has led to acclaim for some, like talented artists Shepard Fairey and Banksy. A single Banksy piece has been auctioned for almost $2 million. Instagrammer Casey Nocket (aka @theofficialcreepytings) tried to follow in Banksy's footsteps, using the rocks of natural parks as her canvas. She made her way with paint and smartphone camera through nine national parks, defacing all the way. Her amateurish acrylic paintings of women's heads turned up on the sides of rock formations in Yosemite National Park, Death Valley National Park, and Joshua Tree National Park, all in California; Colorado National Monument and Rocky Mountain National Park, in Colorado; Crater Lake National Park, in Oregon; and Zion National Park and Canyonlands National Park, in Utah. Her paintings caused an uproar among both park rangers and other hikers alike.[120] After her posts on Instagram triggered an outcry online, she took to Tumblr to defend her actions, saying that "if [B]anksy did it u'd have a hardon"; her statement appeared along with the hashtag #betterthanbanksy.[121] She has since been banned from the national parks, and she was sentenced to two years' probation and two hundred hours of community service, plus a fine for her defacements, the removal of which may cause permanent damage. In another case, two former Boy Scout leaders destroyed a rock formation in Utah's Goblin Valley State Park that was millions of years old; they videotaped their destruction of it for social media while high-fiving, singing, and laughing.[122] Later, they uploaded the video to Facebook. The men faced charges and ended up paying thousands of dollars in restitution.[123] Of course, such a fee is paltry when compared to the impact of their actions and the damage done to the structure.

Other nature photos and videos that were driven by attention and approval seeking on social media have led to injuries or even death to the visitors themselves. In Yellowstone, a forty-three-year-old mother and her daughter tried to take a selfie with a bison, which promptly charged them.[124] The woman was the third to be injured while attempting to do so. Others engage in extreme sports in nature, using GoPro cameras to create videos for social media. For example, BASE jumpers, who are usually young men, will record themselves wearing "wing suits" and jumping off the sides of mountains to soar up to 150 miles per hour; sadly, the deaths of at least thirty-five persons have resulted, and one even streamed his own death on Facebook Live. With videos of the exciting flights readily available on YouTube, former navy pilot and BASE jumper Richard Webb said that "right now, wingsuit BASE jumping is, globally, the hottest thing going for the impressionable, 18-to-35-year-old single-male demographic."[125] In another incident in Yosemite, two siblings, a brother and sister named Colin and Sable Scott, hiked 225 feet off the marked trail to "hot pot," or take a dip in one of the hot natural mineral-water pools. As his sister filmed their activities, Colin slipped and fell into the pool; tragically, he was boiled to death in the scalding water, and the acidity dissolved his body. The only evidence that was left of his presence were his previously discarded flip-flops, and the video his sister had recorded.[126] Unfortunately, given YouTube, Facebook, and other social media, these kinds of videos often go viral, tempting others to take similar chances. Perhaps seeking thrills like this is understandable, though, given the context of a "no risk" childhood bereft of adventures due to the overprotection of parents, schools, and others who limit young people's access to dangerous or thrilling adventures.

FAKE NATURE

The main takeaway here overall is: Nature makes us happy. Perhaps we are wired that way. Perhaps on some genetic level, we respond to nature since the majority of our time on Earth over some 200,000 or so years was spent in a close relationship with nature. Perhaps in response to some inner "call of the wild," an increasing number of people are trying to bring nature into their lives. Some are doing it through essential oils and diffusers that bring into their lives relaxing scents like lavender, healing scents like eucalyptus, or invigorating scents like peppermint. Others are using digital devices to evoke nature. I have to admit to being one of those. "Hey Google, play the sounds of the forest," I told my digital assistant the other night. Like many city dwellers, I sometimes turn to my new Google Home Mini to help me sleep. "Okay, here's the sounds of the forest," it replied. I lay there in the darkness of my loft, in the middle of Downtown Los Angeles, not a tree, shrub, flower—or any other living thing—in sight. As I was listening to the gentle sounds of nature on a recording to help calm my racing mind, I suddenly realized that this kind of simulated experience of nature is the closest many people will ever come to engaging in a natural experience now. Digital natives are increasingly turning to simulated experiences of nature like this, in an attempt to bring its calming and transcendent aspects into their lives. Los Angeles–based artist Jennifer Steinkamp has done this with her art. Through her work in 3-D digital animation, she evokes elements of nature, including flowers, vines, butterflies, swirling leaves, and swaying tree branches. Her piece *Judy Crook* was designed to be projected on the wall of whatever gallery is showing it, integrating it with the local architecture. This piece shows a tree in hypnotic undulation, as if blown about by a breeze. The digitally created tree slowly fluctuates between the four seasons—first full, with bright-green leaves, it quickly turns bright red and orange, then the leaves gracefully fall away, revealing the barren branches of winter. The tree is on a continuous loop, so the cycle of nature never ends. Steinkamp refers to her work as "fake nature." She talks about the ephemerality of it, saying, "I like that world, non-reality putting itself into reality and transforming reality. If the power goes out, it doesn't exist anymore."[127] Another example of fake nature is cropping up in on treadmills that provide simulated "hikes," with scenes of nature rolling along on a screen. Workout maven Jillian Michaels hawks one of these on TV: It not only inclines but also features videos so you can "work out wherever you want," walking or running with a trainer along Point Dume, Malibu; along the streets of Venice, Italy; or up a hillside in Hawaii or Santorini.[128] Except you're not. Other videos, available on YouTube, featuring natural scenes captured for digital devices range from crackling fires to thunderstorms, rainforests, bubbling springs, or gentle rain. All of these clips sit at the ready, waiting to help you relax or put you to sleep.

Fake nature is increasingly being integrated into self-health and wellness videos and apps, which promise to deliver up nature at the touch of a button. Some of the nature videos mentioned above are accompanied by the gentle voice of a hypnotherapist who provides sleep hypnosis for reducing anxiety or depression.[129] Sales of mindfulness and wellness apps are up: The top ten mindfulness and wellness app companies made 170 percent more revenue worldwide in the first quarter of 2018 than they did in the whole of 2017.[130] The wellness category of apps is growing, given anxiety-prone Millennials and their affinity for self-care, accounting for $27 million in worldwide sales in the first quarter of 2018 alone. Just two apps racked up much of these sales; Calm and runner-up

Headspace claimed 90 percent of the revenue of the top ten apps, worldwide, in this category.[131] Calm grossed $13.5 million worldwide. Some universities are creating their own nature-evoking apps, in an attempt to stave off the crushing mental-health issues faced by their students. The University of Southern California is one of these; it has developed the Mindful USC app. Mindfulness is the practice of being present in the moment rather than stressing or ruminating about events in the future or past. It has been described as "paying attention, in a particular way, on purpose, in the present moment, and intentionally."[132] The Mindful USC app alerts students to mindfulness events at the university and provides guided meditations, which include some titled "Manage Difficult Emotions," "Calm Down When You're Overwhelmed," and "SoundScapes that Connect You with Nature and Help You Calm Down."[133] Despite the increasing popularity of these apps among stressed-out digital natives, studies are sparse as to their effectiveness. I tried the Mindful USC app—and, I have to admit, I did feel more relaxed after the seven-minute meditation. It asked me to envision a stream, with my thoughts floating away on it on leaves. But I couldn't help but think, I've not only seen streams but also had analog experiences with them. I used to go away to camp up in the mountains of Forest Home in Southern California. I remember picking raspberries off the bushes nearby, then putting my hands in the running stream to rinse them off, so I could eat them. I can still remember the juicy, ripe berries and the ice-cold stream. When told to "think of a river" to float my cares away, I can evoke these visceral memories. Yet, I have to wonder, how does this work for digital natives who have no such analog experiences? Many have no embodied, kinesthetic memories of a river to draw from. Will these kinds of apps work for them, given that those with a nature deficit must evoke a totally imagined, disembodied nature they saw on a screen? Is pretending to remember a river the same as the kinetic memory of one?

Few studies focused on the efficacy of these apps exist at this point. One that does examined 560 mindfulness apps, using a 1-to-5 scale to rate app quality and user satisfaction (1-Inadequate, 2-Poor, 3-Acceptable, 4-Good, and 5-Excellent).[134] The Headspace app came away with the highest overall rating, a 4.0 out of 5; it was followed by Smiling Mind, at 3.7. Calm was not one of the apps rated in the study. One critique that could be leveled is that these apps provide a relatively surface experience of nature at best, leaving behind the body and the senses of smell and touch during the experience. The Calm app is addressing this by launching Calm Sleep Mist, an aromatherapy "sleep spray" to provide what it calls a "multi-sensory sleep solution, combining scent and sound."[135] Further studies that look at generational differences in effectiveness of these kinds of nature-based apps or videos (e.g., whether digital natives find more solace in them than Boomers, etc.) will be interesting to see.

RECONNECTING WITH NATURE

So how do we reconnect with nature? Our technologies seem to have widened the nature/culture gap such that many are now completely devoid of nature experiences, their only connection being to "fake nature"—like the crackling Yule log that can be streamed on YouTube to their smart TV screen. How do we calm our anxieties and reduce the depression that is running so rampant in young people these days? Reconnecting our digital lives with nature will mean rebalancing our priorities. It will require a willingness to perhaps set aside our devices for a period of time. Naturalist Richard Louv has provided us a road map for solving what he identifies as nature deficit disorder, but the journey will be difficult. Getting youth on the road is the first step. The National Park Service is trying to do so by using a "reach them where they're at" approach to get digital natives excited about nature and to encourage park visitation. It has launched the biggest advertising campaign in its history, focusing much of the effort on social media. A "visual culture" ranger, "Spokesranger" (as he calls himself) named Michael Liang, was hired as part of this outreach. I had the pleasure of meeting him at USC at the *Los Angeles Times* Festival of Books. He's the perfect guy to curate the visual imagery of the parks, and he is hoping to lure digital natives in that way. In a magazine interview, he said:

> Essentially, I get to help inspire people to care about the national parks through visual media. I went to art school, and I like to use publications, photography, video, and social media to help connect visitors to the national parks.[136]

Being gay and Asian, Ranger Liang is particularly sensitive to the lack of diversity in the promotional materials for the national parks. He's also working on an inclusive public-relations and visual-culture campaign, in an effort to attract a more diverse population of visitors:

> We recognize that sometimes, some people who we want to come to the National Park Service don't necessarily see themselves represented in our mar-

keting and our media. . . . I'm personally very conscious of that, making sure that we have people of color, people of different backgrounds, [and] LGBT people represented in our photographs on our websites and our publications. We try to help welcome all to our national parks, because it's a federally funded agency and everyone deserves to have a national park that resonates with them.

The park service's Instagram account, @nationalparkservice, is attractive, containing beautiful and fascinating imagery of the parks. It shows pictures of young people having fun with the rangers. In 2015, the National Park Service rolled out a social media campaign with the hashtag #FindYourPark, in concert with the one-hundredth anniversary of the park service. The parks have also launched a Go Digital campaign, encouraging users to use the hashtag #NationalParks, in an effort to remain relevant to connected digital natives.

Alexis Dickerson is another who is "fighting the good fight" to get natural experiences to our nation's youth. Dickerson, who is an African American environmentalist and a Millennial, works with an environmental group concerned with waterways and pollution on the East Coast. She is the co-president of the DC Environmental Education Consortium. Her work is focused on instilling environmental literacy in both children and adults, to get them interested in and excited about nature and its conservation. She works within the context of the Chesapeake Bay Watershed Agreement, signed in 2014 by Pennsylvania, Virginia, Maryland, Delaware, and the District of Columbia. A watershed is an area of land that feeds all of the water running under it and draining off of it into a body of water. The Chesapeake Bay Watershed impacts about 18 million people across six states. Five of these states have come together with the promise that every student of theirs will graduate with one outdoor experience learning project in elementary, middle, and high school.[137] Their approach is interdisciplinary and focuses on a real-world context. Alexis takes kids out on sailboats for experiential learning. She takes teachers out for nature-learning experiences, hoping to change their feelings about nature and encourage behaviors that support stewardship and conservation. She is working to develop systemic thinkers and sees students who understand the relationship between human and natural systems as the future. She views nature as a continuum between civilization and the wild and tries to impart that idea to the kids and others she works with. She said to me about her work:

The whole world that we have constructed comes from nature. All the parts and pieces, synthesized or not. What could be more important than understanding that? What have we, as humans, created that has stood the test of time with more engineering precision and efficiency than nature? So, that's what I do. I try to understand the elegant designs of nature, which are endlessly awe-inspiring. Then I try to teach others how to convey the same, and hopefully be similarly moved and inspired in the process.[138]

Dickerson says her goal is to get kids interested in nature again—the goal is not to "create little hippies" but to train the next generation to recognize problems, and to see themselves as capable of solving them."[139]

Another "reach them where they're at" effort targets underserved communities in the Los Angeles area. LA Ranger Troca is a portable park-visitor experience in a truck, sponsored by the National Park Service. Rangers drive the truck to schools in the Los Angeles area, to bring nature to the students, with the hope of piquing their interest in visiting a national park. LA Ranger Troca has its own Instagram account, @larangertroca, showing smiling kids and families; lots of bright art; and interesting natural items, like furs, animal skulls, and feathers, which the kids get to interact with while the park rangers supervise. The truck delivers pop-up installations that are interactive, ranging from a ping-pong photosynthesis bucket game to campfire programs using a solar-powered "fire." Another program, called Every Kid in a Park, targets fourth-graders, trying to sow the seeds of a love of nature and conservation early, to help shape positive behaviors and attitudes for a lifetime. The goal of this program is to provide an opportunity for each and every student across the country to experience the national parks in person— for free. Each kid in fourth grade is given a free pass to the parks, which they can use over the course of their entire fourth-grade year.[140]

National Park Service officials have also been considering wiring the parks for better digital connectivity. They have been discussing a $34 million fiber-optic line, which would stretch from Grand Teton National Park into Yellowstone in Wyoming. The line would dramatically improve connectivity for mobile devices. Critic of this idea Jeff Ruch, executive director of PEER (Public Employees for Environmental Responsibility), opposes these efforts, saying that "the National Park Service will not find its institutional relevance on the Internet. Our national parks risk their unique role by striving to become just another consumer-driven entertainment provider."[141] He may be swimming against the tide here, pitted against younger potential park goers who desire a digital interface. Whether the parks should be a place to unplug or whether they should be wired remains a heated debate.

KOA Campgrounds is also trying to promote forays into nature via visual culture. Its webpage highlights the social media accounts of young campers, RVers, and other Instagrammers who are creating beautiful, enticing imagery from their adventures on the road. One of the featured accounts is @moon-mountainlife. On the KOA site, an attractive couple is pictured smiling at each other in a small tent, with a baby sleeping softly between them. The orange tent flaps are drawn back, perfectly framing a view of the craggy, snow-covered mountains outside. From the picture, theirs looks like a dream life. The site described the couple, Jacob and Natasha Moon, saying:

> New parents Jacob and Natasha Moon take their baby girl on advanced backpacking adventures and document it all on @moonmountainlife. At two months old Zoey went on her first backpacking trip to the breathtaking Moraine Lake in Canada. The family often swaps a crib for a baby tent, stroller for a baby carrier and PJs for a snowsuit onesie. Pitching a tent as they hike, testing the waters in a raft or relaxing in a hammock with glacial mountain peaks as backdrop, this is a family to follow on Instagram.[142]

For stressed-out city dwellers, this may sound pretty idyllic. Another Instagram account featuring young couples pursuing an active outdoor lifestyle is the DIYers (do-it-yourself-ers) @this_little_adventure. Their Instagram account shows an amazing makeover of an old motor home, which they transformed into a comfortable, modern, small apartment on wheels. Their remodel became the focus of an IKEA inspiration shoot for living in small spaces. Other accounts, like @campingcollective, show awe-inspiring views from their tents, ranging from redwood forests to the dramatic red-rock formations of the Arizona's Monument Valley to exotic-looking tree tents by @Tentsile, which are shown hanging like brightly colored beetles in the trees. Tentsile's Instagram account has nearly 190,000 followers to date. Tentsile markets its tents and hammocks with the tagline "adventure travel." Perhaps this experiential focus, in other words, a focus on the adventure of it all and the fun you can have with friends or a partner—as opposed to traditional shots of the "things" you can see out in nature—is a better approach to attracting younger, social potential campers.

These efforts seem to be yielding some positive results. A study last year by KOA Campgrounds of 2,903 people in the United States and Canada found a six-percentage-point increase in Millennial campers since 2015. Of the campers, 39 percent said they camped in a cabin, so perhaps this is more "glamping" (short for "glamorous" camping, involving more comfortable amenities) than actual camping. Still, it shows that Millennials are starting to get out there. A third of Millennials camped with their Boomer or older parents, suggesting that perhaps their parents are instigating these trips in an effort to instill their love of nature into the next generation. The children of Boomers on these trips say they like that their parents can relax. Echoing the results of the National Park Service's studies, the KOA results indicated that just over half (51 percent) of the new campers were white,[143] so the lack of diversity among those participating in outdoor leisure is still something that needs to be addressed.

Although Millennials aren't camping as much in the national parks, studies have found they are doing so at music festivals like the Bonnaroo Music and Arts Festival in Tennessee; Burning Man, which takes on the playa of the Nevada desert; the Coachella Valley Music and Arts Festival, in Palm Desert, California; or at one of the many other EDM (electronic dance music) festivals worldwide. As such, Millennials haven't developed the interest in outdoor brands like REI, which mainly targets wealthier Baby Boomers who are more likely to camp in the traditional way. A master's thesis out of the Department of Geography and Environmental Studies at the University of Boulder sheds some light on some of the reasons behind the decline in interest among Millennials in camping in our national parks.[144] The study surveyed 216 college students and yielded some interesting results. In particular, there were several notable answers to the open-ended question, "In your opinion, what would attract a more diverse visitor demographic—meaning one that is more representative of the U.S. population as a whole—to our national parks?" The majority of the respondents completing this question suggested ideas for more amusement, in one form or another. Their responses included:

Better cell phone service, Wi-Fi, using Pokémon Go.
Field days, tours, maybe some small amusement park
More amusement, i.e.: horseback riding, concerts, food trucks, etc.
Better souvenirs?[145]

Another response addressed the diversity issue as follows:

Many minorities have histories of exclusion from these places and/or have negative associations with places away from cities and structured environments. It [the national parks] is an unknown to many minorities. One main way would be to somehow get people of different ethnic backgrounds to work in these places to help open the door for visitors of different ethnicities to visit.

Some suggested new uses of mobile technology:

They should make an app where you can learn about all of the different parks, with like daily fun facts or [a] "park of the week" or something, since everyone uses their phones more than anything.

Or more advertising:

More Advertising, Make Nature "more mainstream."

Perhaps the most cynical of the answers was this one:

I honestly don't think that the problem resides in our parks. In order to change the diversity of the people who [go to] our parks we would need to change the mindset of the community as a whole. But as we know that isn't fathomable. So your only other option would be taking the nature out of national parks. People are different these days [and] they don't care about nature or appreciate its beauty as our society has been brainwashed and dumbed down by technology and other material possessions.

From these answers, it would seem that the National Parks Service and other nature-based agencies are facing an uphill battle.

A 2014 study by the Outdoor Gear Industry Association found that rather than camping in the national parks, Millennials and those younger are enjoying other kinds of outdoor activities.[146] These activities center around sports and include running, skateboarding, outdoor yoga, surfing, kiteboarding, stand-up paddleboarding, or snowboarding. Digital natives are more driven to participate in activities they can engage in with friends or family, rather than by themselves. Millennials currently make up 38 percent of the outdoor consumer market. To attract younger camping consumers, outdoor brand the North Face has partnered with Hipcamp, an online travel service focused on camping experiences, to create a series of campouts that featured live music. In 2016, they released a new tent that includes an oversized cooking shelter and superwide sleeping bags, or, as Andy Coutant, product director for the North Face, put it, an outdoorsy "party house" for festival goers.[147] Millennial tech executive and surfer Luke Kilpatrick captured this desire for nature plus community involvement, saying, "I'm a surfer and scuba diver, the ocean is my nature and I love being in it, on it or under it. Many digital natives surf and dive, as it allows both community and disconnection from the digital."[148] Tesla recently came out with a limited-edition bright-red and matte-black custom surfboard this past year, in collaboration with Lost Surfboards by Mayhem. The board were shaped by Matt "Mayhem" Biolos, surfboard shaper for World Surf League Championship athletes. The surfboard was meant to appeal to the tech-surf crowd, and even though it sold for $1,500, the entire lot of two hundred sold out in a single day.[149] Tech entrepreneur and investor Bill Tai and professional kitesurfer Susie Mai have been tapping into this love of active outdoor ocean sports, hosting a series of "Mai Tai" kitesurfing camps/venture-capital events around the world— at locations ranging from Long Island to Maui to Richard Branson's Necker Island—where aspiring tech entrepreneurs can network, kiteboard, and seek funding for their start-ups.[150] Recently, Bill Tai and his team have launched a new venture called ACTAI Global, to unite the community of athletes, conservationists, technologists, artists, and innovators. Its fundraisers include partnerships with Ocean Elders and Lonely Whale to support ocean conservation; and its events include both a kiteboarding trip to Necker Island for the Xtreme Tech Challenge finals and a blockchain summit in Morocco.[151]

REBALANCING NATURE AND CULTURE

Bill Tai's combination of technology innovation and nature conservation, merged with athletics and outdoor experiences in beautiful locales, represents some of the best efforts taken to rebalance nature and culture. Others who aren't getting out in nature in a physical sense are finding ways to integrate nature back into their lives via nature-evoking self-help apps, the aforementioned "experience nature" YouTube calming videos and hiking videos on treadmills in the gym, and the work of digital artists like Jennifer Steinkamp and others, whose depictions of "fake nature" are blurring the nature/culture divide. For many urban dwellers, fake nature may be all they've got. Whether such contrived natural experiences and apps can bring about the same sense of calm as forays into actual nature remains to be seen, particularly as digital experiences become more immersive. The trouble is, that hike in the woods activates other senses: the relaxing feeling of the warmth of the sun on your skin, the sound of crunching leaves underfoot, the feel of the breeze caressing your cheek, or the smell of flowers, plants, moss, and more. These digital versions of nature are unable to accurately mimic many of the experiences that are afforded to you in the wild: The startle evoked by an unexpected bird suddenly flying up out of the brush. The feeling of the cool water of a stream on your hands; the refreshing taste as you take a sip. The sweet aroma of that fresh berry picked ripe from the bush. That splash of the water as you run into the ocean. Exploration, discovery, the elements of surprise and delight, and the beauty of a waterfall just over the next ridge, that wave that sucked you under, or even the fear of heights after you've climbed up to get a closer look are all part of the experience. None of these sensations and experiences are available on the Google Home Mini or on a treadmill near you. Tactility and the body are largely written out of the experience apps and videos, leaving behind a veneer of the senses. Real nature activates *all* the senses. The other thing is, as artist Steinkamp put it earlier, if the power goes out, fake nature is gone. Its transience certainly can be a drawback for those who are counting on their devices for their peace of mind.

But, it should be noted, these apps and devices can be useful tools—when used appropriately—to try to find, cultivate, or maintain that much-sought-after peace of mind. Perhaps one way to attempt achieving a rebalancing of nature and culture is by using apps like Mappiness. A 2.0 version is due out soon. The idea behind this app is that it uses people's digital devices to track their behaviors in real time—such as socializing with friends, working, sleeping, and spending time outdoors—and then it maps those activities onto people's self-reported happiness levels.[152] By tracking the natural ups and downs in your happiness over the course of time and across activities, you can get a better sense of which things make you happy, and which lower your happiness. Perhaps seeing firsthand how time spent outdoors impacts you personally might get you to increase your time spent in nature, for your own happiness and health. Again, it comes down to whether and how such digital devices and tools are implemented.

There are still other approaches to rebalancing nature and culture on the horizon. Leigh Gallagher, in his book *The End of the Suburbs: Where the American Dream Is Moving*, writes that the "old" American Dream of the house in the suburbs is losing its appeal for younger Americans, as they move to cities in search of the many urban amenities that appeal to those who are increasingly living single.[153] Urban planners and policy makers are beginning to address this need for "green" to enhance mental and physical health, by designing it back into both urban and suburban environments. Greening urban spaces via green walls or rooftops, or by designing entirely new sustainable and green cities using a New Urbanism or Green Cities model, are among the efforts being made to address the nature deficit; in this framework, towns and cities are designed around walkability and offer plenty of landscaping and green spaces.[154] The World Health Organization has also identified urban green spaces as one of its core health and sustainable development goals.[155] It has identified positive environmental outcomes of having green spaces like parks, woods, and natural meadows in cities, as refuges from noise, a way to cool the temperatures of the cities, and a place where trees can produce more oxygen. The WHO identifies some of the human benefits, such as having safe routes for walking or cycling, as well as places for exercise and recreation.

Talking about the issues of nature deficit disorder and devices, writer Paul Boutin recounted an example that brought the issue into clear focus: Back in Maine when he was a kid in the 1960s, the worst punishment you could get was "you're grounded," meaning you couldn't go outside and play.[156] Now, for his nine- and eleven-year-old nephews growing up there, "going outside" isn't a desire that can be withheld; for them, the worst punishment is "no PlayStation." The kids instantly snap into line when faced with that threat. It shows the shift in both values and behaviors that has taken place from his generation to now, the key difference being the incorporation of digital technologies. So—where do we go from here? What concrete steps can we take to balance the time spent on devices, to rebalance ourselves and bring us back to mental and physical health? As we have seen, modern science now confirms what artists and composers like Mahler, writers like Thoreau, and naturalists like Muir knew instinctively: nature is a tonic for the stresses of urban life, stresses that are amplified through our hyperconnectivity to digital devices. As such, we need to make a conscious effort to move closer to nature, to connect back with ourselves, while calming the mind and healing the body. Teens themselves are beginning to realize that they're spending too much time on devices: Half now say they're trying to curtail their time online.[157] This may be the perfect opportunity to intervene with outings in nature to replace some of that screen time. The good news is unlike other attempts at health-seeking, like expensive fitness gadgets or boutique gyms, time in nature is often cheap in comparison. Scheduling green time may be a way to make sure it gets onto the calendars of our busy lives. Another way to rebalance is to start consciously eating more natural, whole foods. Some efforts are already underway in this regard, which are steps in the right direction. One of these is the meal kits that are being shipped right to people's homes: They contain fresh ingredients that are already chopped and assembled by companies like Blue Apron, Plated, and HelloFresh. Meal kits like these feature a variety of recipes and encourage people to cook at home, using whole foods and pre-measured and portions, reducing waste. The kits are gaining in popularity; sales of them were up 67 percent in 2018.[158] Though they do seem to be catching on, particularly among more affluent consumers, companies like Blue Apron are struggling with profitability and retaining subscribers, as more than half of subscribers fall off after six months, and three-quarters do so within a year.[159] One company, Chef'd, already went belly up in 2018. One reason for the steep drop off in subscribers may be that the kits are designed for couples or families; with more Millennials living single, perhaps a single option needs to be worked out, though that may not be profitable. Alternatively, I've heard folks say they end up with too many leftovers, and that's why they quit their subscriptions. Perhaps meal-kit makers could encourage subscribers to freeze the leftovers, and provide them with easy ideas for making new meals later on using them. Teaching cooking skills in school again would also help a move toward whole, fresh foods, by bringing back home economics and life-skills classes in high school and college—and making them mandatory. Other countertrends are emerging that address our growing sedentary, indoor lifestyle, like the "no device hikes" for city dwellers in LA that are cropping up on Meetup.com. Device-free hikes encourage communing with nature and friends old and new while affording time away from the pressure to post on social media for a while. Perhaps most amenable to these kinds of trends will be the iGen generation, many of whom are teens or college aged now. They are already health conscious and are driving a movement toward eating a plant-based and dairy-free diet. Many of them actively seek out fresh, cruelty-free, and fair-trade ingredients in their foods.[160] They're also the generation most likely to seek out recipes online and try them out, and they're taking an interest in yoga, meditation, and mindfulness (i.e., quiet time away from devices, using apps like Mindful USC, discussed before). As such, this group of kids may be ripe for forays into nature, to extend their health habits already well underway. But we need an infrastructure to get them there; we need more individuals—including parents and teachers, as well as organizations—to provide kids, teens, and young adults the opportunities to connect with nature in positive ways. The National Wildlife Federation is trying provide structure: It is pushing a "Green Hour" campaign, to get adults to commit to an hour a day of outdoor play time with kids.[161] It is also working on service learning projects and gardening for youth, particularly for those in underserved communities, in an effort to get kids outdoors and away from their devices for a while. LifeSail in Marina del Rey, California, is another organization trying to get urban kids out in nature: It is not only getting them out on the water and teaching them to sail but also teaching them how to build their own boats, thereby providing them valuable life skills while developing a sense of competency and self-determination along the way.[162] As we know, changing habits can be hard, and these new forays into nature may initially be met with opposition: Comedian David Baddiel turned to social media to post a picture of his son, Ezra, out in nature, with a caption indicating that Ezra was "hypnotised and overawed as ever by the beauty of nature."[163] Meanwhile, the accompanying photo showed his son, head bent, staring at a screen, screening out the nature around him. Other parents have followed suit, trying to find some humor in the situation when their kids are totally oblivious to their surroundings. The best course of action, of course, will be to set clear ground rules for device use ahead of venturing into nature, and to be good role models for kids by being present with them, not taking calls, texting, checking email, or posting on social media oneself. Doing it together gives families and friends the opportunity to reconnect; after a while, everyone may actually feel a sense of unexpected relief to be free of device pressure for a bit.

Meanwhile, some digital natives are quietly returning to nature on their own terms: They are untethering from traditional workplace and are using their connected devices to work remotely from anywhere. Some, like Instagrammer @this_little_adventure, are converting vans into cool, rolling apartments, so they can live as digital nomads, adventuring and exploring. Could this be the shape of untethered life in the future—the synthesis of nature and culture as digital natives work "on the road," reconnecting to nature via mobility of both their devices and their homes?

CHAPTER 7

THE UNTETHERED WORKER

People are finding that, because of the way the machines are
changing the world, more and more of their old values don't
apply anymore. People have no choice but to become second-rate
machines themselves, or wards of the machines.
                                    —Kurt Vonnegut, *Player Piano*, 1952

L iz Bryant's Instagram account is filled with colorful, cheery photos of her adventures outdoors. A photo she used to use as her profile pic conveys a sense of casual ease; in it, she's sitting atop a countertop inside her customized Mercedes Sprinter van, sporting a wide, sunny smile, with her long legs stretching the width of the van. The doors behind her are flung open wide to catch a breeze and the sunset. Her long blond hair, tanned skin, and toned physique mark her as the typical Millennial California surfer girl, a style she adopted from her hometown of San Diego that belies her Midwestern roots. In her debut YouTube video, she introduces her tricked-out van, saying, "This is my Mercedes Sprinter van, Wild, because I'm born wild and sprinting free."[1] Liz left behind a seven-year career as a full-time television newscaster for NBC News in San Diego to pursue van life full-time. Her van "Wild," is both mobile office and home. In another video, she talks about how and why she made this transition from what she calls "normal life":

> I hiked the Pacific Crest Trail in 2015, and it took me about five months to get from Mexico to the Washington border. After that, I went back to normal life, reporting at NBC San Diego as a reporter that you would see on the five and six o'clock news. Within six months of leaving the trail and going back to my career, I thought to myself, "What are you doing? You just learned all about what adventure is and about what living life is and being out in nature."

I started looking at van life on Instagram. I came across it and then for the next year and a half researched it every single day. Finally, I just said, "I'm not researching this anymore. I'm doing it." I bought a 2016 (brand new at that time) Mercedes Sprinter, and I just said [to myself] "There's always a back-up plan, so just do it." And I did it and I've never looked back.[2]

Liz is one of the new faces of a growing trend of untethered workers who are unhooking from the traditional office nine-to-five and "sprinting free," in all sorts of new and interesting ways. Liz's Instagram account and YouTube channel, "Wild by the Mile," paints a bright, optimistic picture of the digital-nomad lifestyle. Sitting cross-legged and looking zen on the hood of her vehicle, with a mountain range behind her; showing off her toned abs in a bikini, while showering out behind the van; or sporting a hip, white straw fedora and wind-blown hair, while gazing out on lakes, mountains, or beaches—the version of Liz you see in her photos gives the impression this life is but a dream. Some still question, though, whether her life in Wild was borne more out of financial necessity than wanderlust—a charge she vehemently denies:

> Another comment I hear is that "you must [be doing] this to avoid rent or paying property tax; you don't want to pay high rent in San Diego." That's actually not true—I chose van life because I am restless, and I want to see the world, not because I'm trying to pinch pennies.[3]

For work when she's not paddleboarding, swimming, or hiking, Liz shoots and edits freelance videos for clients in the medical sector. She's also working on building a following to monetize her channels on social media. This is her new American Dream.

She is not the only one pursing the dream in a different way. Amy Groesbeck is another untethered worker—in this case, her job is a side hustle. An elementary-school teacher by day, Amy has built up an impressive following of tens of thousands of teachers, parents, and the simply curious on Instagram, with her Pinterest-worthy bulletin boards, creative classroom art assignments, and amazing organizational skills. Businesses like Michaels, Oriental Trading Company, and Scholastic Corporation pay Amy, and other Instagram teacher/influencers like her, to tout their products to other teachers via their social media accounts.[4] Groesbeck makes additional money from an online "store" on Teachers Pay Teachers, a website where teachers can buy and sell lesson plans and other teaching materials from other teachers. There, Amy sells lesson plans and ideas for bulletin boards and classroom organization to teachers who want to emulate her style. She's doing really well: While earning $50,000 a year as a teacher, Amy puts in about six hours a day after school, working on her Instagram account and her store, which together bring in a whopping additional $200,000 a year. Amy talks about the significant impact the extra income has had on her family:

> I'm a single mom, and it's because of Teachers Pay Teachers that I've been able to buy my own home, buy my own vehicle, fund vacations for my family. I would never have been able to do it just teaching alone.[5]

Though, granted, Amy is making a lot of money—she's also devoting a lot of time to doing so. Because of this, one could question how much time she actually has left after two jobs to devote to her family, and the "fun" vacations and other activities she's now able to afford for them. Being untethered comes with a cost.

"Virtualized teaching" like Amy, providing lessons plans and mentoring to other teachers, is not the only arena being digitally transformed by the internet: work in the arena of sports is another. Over the years, scores of little boys have dreamed of growing up to become professional athletes. Girls are having that dream too now, since their opportunities for careers in professional athletics have expanded. For the boys, their dream has often been focused on a career in football, basketball, or baseball in the big leagues, playing for the NFL, NBA, or MLB. Though boys may begin to play football as early as age nine or so and play clear through college, few make it to the big leagues: Only 2 percent of NCAA college players are ever drafted to play for an NFL team; and for basketball players, that number is even smaller (less than 1 percent, in fact), since there are only about 360 active NBA players altogether, making them the cream of crop of pro athletes.[6] For those few who do make it, their careers are short-lived, lasting on average just over three years.[7] Although the salaries are high (the average salary for an NFL player is $2.1 million USD as of 2018), the physical injuries accumulated during school or professional tackle football can last a lifetime.[8] Of the 111 brains donated by deceased former NFL athletes, 99 percent showed indications of chronic traumatic encephalopathy (CTE), a kind of brain damage resulting from repeated blunt-impact trauma to the head.[9]

Parents of aspiring athletes are beginning to understand the unintended costs of a pro football career, and the lifelong damage that can occur as a result of concussions and other injuries sustained on the field; half now say they would discourage their child from pursuing the sport of football.[10] In part because of these concerns, the NFL is experiencing a drop in both viewership and in-person game attendance. Though the reasons for this decline are likely complex, some mix of concern about injuries to the players combined with anger toward them for protesting during the national anthem, along with an increase in "cord cutters"—that is, those who are unhooking from TV and watching content exclusively online. Half of Millennials and Gen Xers don't watch any TV at all anymore.[11] Instead, the digital native's version of sports entertainment is coming from games like League of Legends and Fortnite. Professional and amateur video gamers can play on Twitch, a gaming website where they play in front of and interact with a live virtual audience.[12] Comments are shown in a small box on the bottom of the screen, so fans can communicate directly with the gamer. As the Twitch banner says, "Don't just watch, join in. . . . With chat built into every stream, you don't just watch on Twitch, you're a part of the show."[13] The lack of interactivity of television and the rigidity of preprogrammed shows are two other factors contributing to why TV, and in particular the NFL, is falling out of favor with younger viewers. Instead of attending traditional sporting events, stadium-goers are flocking to eSports competitions. Stadiums are now being filled with tens of thousands of screaming fans who come to watch their favorite gamers play electronic games live. Now, 162 million people frequently watch eSports, and another 131 million say they watch occasionally.[14] The League of Legends World Championship in 2017 drew more than 80 million viewers. By comparison, the Super Bowl attracted 103.4 million viewers in 2018, a 7 percent drop from 2017. Over $93 million in prize money has been awarded to the winners of big virtual games.[15] Seventy-one colleges so far are fielding eSports teams, including Menlo College and Miami University, with some even offering scholarships to recruit the best players.[16] In fact, gaming scholarships rose 480 percent since 2017, prompting author and technologist John Koetsier to ask if eSports scholarships are the new football scholarships.[17] Fortnite, released in 2017, is the most popular eSports game right now, with over 140 million downloads and a monthly revenue of $318 million.[18] The free game matches one hundred players at a time, in a "battle royal" format where players compete to be the last one standing. Though the game is free to play, it generates revenue by selling customizations for players' characters, like special "skins" or dance moves. Viewers watched an incredible 574 million hours of Fortnite on Twitch in a single month in 2018.[19] Talks are underway now to include eSports like Fortnite in the Paris 2024 Summer Olympics, and they are already a medaled event in the 2022 Winter Olympics in Asia.[20]

Twenty-six-year-old blue-haired gamer Tyler Blevins is the most popular Fortnite player in the world. He goes by the online alias "Ninja" and is a professional eSports gamer. Tyler streams six days a week, for ten to twelve hours a day or more, and can fill large stadiums with fans willing to pay to watch him play live in tournaments with sports celebrities and others, like his recent bout with EDM DJ Marshmello.[21] In March 2018, Tyler made history when he reached 100,000 subscribers on his Twitch channel. He was also the first video gamer to be featured on the cover of ESPN. In an interview with them, he was asked when he realized he could make a living through gaming; he said:

> I think I was twenty years old when I was making enough money to stop going to college, and then I quit my job. . . . And once I started making really good money, that's when I was like, alright, that's when I can just kind of put everything aside and focus on the streaming.[22]

By "really good money," Tyler means an estimated $500,000 a month, largely made in his bedroom, from tips, subscriptions, and sponsorship deals, including one with Red Bull.[23] Tyler's popularity and follower count soared after his match with Drake, who had "DMed" (direct-messaged) him on Instagram to ask for a game, thereby boosting Tyler's crossover celebrity status between gaming and popular culture.[24] The match drew 628,000 viewers, breaking the record for the most viewed eSport live-stream.[25] Catching on to the opportunity for their kids to make big money, some parents are hiring Fortnite tutors for their kids to up their game, much like prior generations of parents might have hired a physical trainer to coach their aspiring football players. eSports, with its big-money prizes and global audience, is now poised to match, if not exceed or even replace, more traditional sporting entertainment among younger audiences, opening up an entirely new arena of untethered work for motivated digital competitors.

THE PLATFORM ECONOMY, PATCHWORK CAREERS, AND THE END OF RETIREMENT

Digital connectivity is also enabling other new ways of working. With wages stagnant and a rising cost of living, people are increasingly doing "side hustles" through the gig and sharing economies to help make ends meet, particularly in cities that are expensive to live in, like Los Angeles, San Francisco, and New York. The gig economy refers to a part-time job that is typically short-term or freelance in nature, while the sharing economy includes everything from renting a spare room on Airbnb, to driving passengers for Lyft or Uber, to doing handyman tasks for TaskRabbit or delivering food for Postmates. There are now an estimated 150 million gig workers in the United States and Western Europe, with knowledge-intensive work and creative jobs being the fastest-growing sectors.[26]

I've tried out many of these platforms myself, and have had multiple Uber drivers tell me that they are just putting in a few extra hours before or after work. "Task rabbits" who have come over to lend a hand with everything from building shelves to hanging pictures, have typically held day jobs or have said they were launching tech start-ups on the side. Even teaching, done by PhD-level lecturers, at colleges or universities has become a gig: 70 percent of university jobs are now part-time. Tenure, or a "job for life" seems to be going the way of the dinosaurs. A young woman I met at a paid focus group for professors hosted by an academic book publisher (another gig) told me she was teaching at five different universities, and she's not getting benefits from any of them. The typical full-time professor would normally teach two or three courses in a term and make twice as much as she did. Unsurprisingly, she's starting to burn out and is looking for ways to start her own private school. In Los Angeles, people like her are known as a "freeway flyers"—professors who drive like bats out of hell from one college to another on the city's wide maze of freeways, trying to get to their next class in time. Another common gig includes hosting travelers in one's home via Airbnb; some people with small apartments are even share their own bedroom or one-room studio with complete strangers to earn a few extra bucks. Some people are going so far as to rent out a tent in their backyards. Eighth-grade teacher Jennifer Bankston and her husband are Airbnb hosts. Together, they earn a combined $4,000 a month as teachers in Los Angeles (where the median house price is almost $675,000). The Bankstons make an additional $2,000 to $4,000 a month by renting out the guesthouse on their property. Jennifer says she responds to inquiries from Airbnb travelers during her school lunch break. It turns out, one in ten Airbnb hosts is a teacher.[27] With more professor jobs becoming gigs themselves with the demise of tenure, or a "job for life," we will surely see more teachers and professors—many with master's or even doctoral degrees—turning to the gig and sharing economy to make ends meet.

Like schoolteacher Amy Groesbeck and the Bankstons, many digital natives are patching together an income from a variety of gigs, juggling a day or night job with driving for Uber, putting together IKEA furniture for the busy or the mechanically challenged, or dog-walking through the Wag! app, caretaking for adults or children through Care.com, renting rooms to traveling nomads via Airbnb or VRBO, or providing a myriad of other consulting, delivery, or other services to keep a roof over their heads or gas in the tanks of their live-in vans. Jon Yongfook is one of these. "Screw it, let's just leave," he decided one day, after working a stable job for two years as the head of Digital Product & Design at Aviva.[28] A serial tech entrepreneur and a violinist, Jon sold his start-up Pitchpigeon (an automation platform for tech press releases) to a US marketing firm for a six-figure sum. Yongfook has been on the road for five years now, following in the footsteps of his hero, Anthony Bourdain. His *No Reservations* lifestyle is captured in his sumptuous Instagram photos (@yongfook). Clearly a "foodie," he fills his feed with glorious pictures of the food he encounters on his travels, like the photo he took in Spain of four bright-orange shrimp simmering in aromatic garlic and olive oil on a heavy cast-iron pan; or another, in Malaysia, of a feast of rice drenched in curry, alongside cucumber raita, fried cabbage, and fried fish and squid, all artistically arranged on a bed of banana leaves. In the Moroccan town of Chefchaouen, Jon staged his own "kind of blue" moment; with a heavy, wood, Majorelle Blue door behind him, he posed wearing shorts, shoes, and a shirt in three different shades of blue. As he put it in the caption, "Ahh Chefchaouen, a magical place where even the crappiest of photographers can get mad likes on IG [Instagram]."[29] Jon supports himself through a patchwork of consulting gigs, tech start-ups (he only half-jokingly threatened to create a start-up a month in 2018), and a book he wrote on growth hacking, the latter of which he crowdfunded on the self-publishing platform Publishizer. One month after the book's launch, he had already raised $12,775 in presales.[30]

Although these examples of digital nomads who have untethered from traditional, stable, full-time careers may seem like outliers, they are actually the early pioneers of a new trend that will become more common over time, as the platform economy reshapes the nature of both work and the workplace, while also reshaping workers' relationships to them. Platforms like Airbnb, Publishizer, Uber, TaskRabbit, Care.com, and others are transforming business in this way. As a whole, this has resulted in both quantitative and qualitative changes, untethering workers from the place of work itself, while shortening the duration of the contracted work between employers and employees—from decades to perhaps hours or even minutes—as visualized in the chart 3.

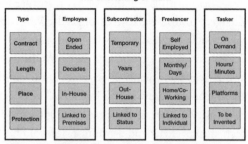

The Shortening of Work

Type	Employee	Subcontractor	Freelancer	Tasker
Contract	Open Ended	Temporary	Self Employed	On Demand
Length	Decades	Years	Monthly/ Days	Hours/ Minutes
Place	In-House	Out-House	Home/Co-Working	Platforms
Protection	Linked to Premises	Linked to Status	Linked to Individual	To be Invented

Adapted from Malone, T. W. The Future of Work: How the New Order of Business Will Shape Your Organization, Your Management Style, and Your Life. Boston, MA: Harvard Business School Press, 2004.

Chart 3. The Shortening of Work. (Adapted from Thomas Malone, *The Future of Work: How the New Order of Business Will Shape Your Organization, Your Management Style, and Your Life* [Boston, MA: Harvard Business School Press, 2004].)

Digital platforms are reshaping the workplace from being a *place* where employees go to work to being a thing you *do* in a new "platform economy." Types of platforms range from sites like Publishizer for authors; TaskRabbit for handy DIYers; Amazon Mechanical Turk for those performing digital piece-work; or asset-"sharing" sites like Airbnb, Uber, or Lyft.[31] The latter platforms typically don't own the assets that are shared. Instead, they act as intermediaries between buyer and seller/renter, and charge a fee for helping facilitate the transaction. Upwork and Fiverr are two examples of gig-work platforms. Upwork has over 12 million registered freelancers and 5 million clients, racking up a $1 billion in annual sales.[32] Each site offers a range of freelance jobs, including search engine optimization; graphic or website design; and selling "likes," follows, and reviews on sites like Amazon. Airbnb is expanding its gig game, from renting homes or rooms, to creating a platform for freelancers to offer curated "experiences" for hire—such as local neighborhood walks, wine tastings, a "Laugh Your Way through the Louvre" tour in Paris, or your own personal photographer in Barcelona or Tokyo; there's even a class in London to "Learn the Tricks of Taxidermy."[33] The Eatwith platform gives amateur or even professional chefs a chance to host delicious homemade meals in their homes for diners at home or abroad. Diners can choose from a Greek feast with a 180-degree view of Athens, to a luxurious dinner aboard a houseboat in Amsterdam, or even a meal prepared by a winner of the popular TV cooking show *Master Chef* in Nashville, Houston, Hollywood, Florida, and other locations.[34] Even blue-collar work is being disrupted by the shift from workplace to work platform. For example, tech start-up Convoy raised $185 million for its digital platform that allows long-haul truckers to connect with shippers who need loads shipped across country—it's kind of like the Uber for freight loads.[35] As venture capitalist and cofounder of LinkedIn Reid Hoffman put it, "Automation is happening in transportation today, it's just not in the way you think. Convoy is helping truck drivers run their own business and experience the American Dream."[36] This kind of app will untether truckers who own their own rigs from specific companies, allowing them to gig as often and as long as they like. The app is free to use for truckers, as the clients pay the fees for the service. The opportunities for platforms to emerge that facilitate transactions for buyers and sellers from a variety of sectors will continue to grow. For the platform developers, it's a way to get into business without the initial capital investment in analog goods; for sellers, it's a way to offer their assets for use or their goods for sale without the expense of a storefront, marketing, and so on, lowering the barrier to entry and offering more ways for sellers to capitalize on their assets, be they physical or skills-based.

The emergence of the platform economy means that lifetime careers like those known to Baby Boomers are going the way of the dodo, as more and more jobs become "giggified," that is, rendered part-time or contract work, and employees become taskers. The freelance workforce is growing three times faster than the US workforce overall since 2014; remote work is up 115 percent since 2015.[37] One in five workers now has a job that is a gig, part-time, or temporary.[38] Within a decade, that number is likely to grow to half.[39] Among younger workers, it has already reached that level (49 percent), as more and more take advantage of the widening availability of Wi-Fi in coffeehouses, libraries, and coworking spaces to work untethered.[40] Freelancing is growing so rapidly, in fact, that if current growth rates continue, it will become the dominant form of work by 2027.[41] Digital connectivity combined with cheap airfares and cheap places to stay via hostels, CouchSurfing, Airbnb, and a growing array of co-living and coworking spaces has made working while traveling the world a real possibility. Perhaps not surprisingly, a majority of digital natives now *want* this kind of flexibility built into their work: A 2017 study by Bank of America and Merrill Lynch found that 59 percent of Millennials say they're worried about finding a career path that will support the lifestyle they've envisioned for themselves, and that they're likely to job-hop if a career doesn't offer that possibility.[42] In fact, many are now "ghosting" their employers, disappearing without a trace, just like they do their expendable dates from Tinder, as they search for the next best thing.[43] Using these platforms, digital natives are hacking the American Dream, using it to have the freedom to work remotely and with flexible hours, both of which are a big part of their new dream.

Coworking spaces like WeWork and coworking/co-living spaces like Outsite are beginning to show up as a growing infrastructure to support these digital nomads. At any one of Outsite's global co-living spaces, you just show up with your duffle bag of clothes and your electronics, and you're moved in. Designed to be "Millennial friendly," co-living houses offer free perks ranging from coffee to printing, to an instant network of friends and community, facilitated by free beer at happy hour and people there who function very much like what folks in university housing call residential advisors, or RAs. These "hosts" are tasked with planning outings, dinners, talks, and other get-togethers for residents, to keep them interested and engaged. WeWork is another digital-nomad infrastructure that is rapidly expanding. Its offices look and feel more like a hip coffee shop than a corporate cubicle; their atmosphere, and free coffee, Wi-Fi, and snacks, have proven a winning formula. With coworking offices in the Los Angeles area, San Francisco, and New York, WeWork was looking to expand its footprint in Manhattan, and was in negotiation with the Durst Organization to take over an additional 200,000 square feet of One World Trade Center—which would have made WeWork the borough's largest tenant—but the deal fell through.[44] The company has been on an aggressive real-estate-acquisition campaign, having already leased 25,000 square feet of additional space in Manhattan's West Village; 70,000 square feet in the Plaza District; and 258,344 square feet in Midtown Manhattan.[45] Clearly, WeWork is going all in on the bet that untethering is the future of work.

Although the "free" in *freelancing* seems attractive, judging from the brightly colored Instagram accounts of various digital nomads, the downside lies in its instability. Gigs come with no job or income stability, no benefits, and no health insurance. With a higher number of younger workers gigging, an untethered freelance work opportunity often means unsteady work, with the majority of workers (63 percent) dipping into their savings every month to stay afloat, compared with only 28 percent of non-freelancers.[46] Most Millennials (66 percent[47]) have zero savings available to dip into, which has spawned an enlarging opportunistic (some even say predatory) "payday loan" sector. This network of payday-loan-and-pawnshops are there to pick up the slack for those living paycheck to paycheck, by typically charging annual interest rates of 400 percent or more for their short-term loans. Millennials and Gen Xers (the generation just ahead of Millennials, now aged approximately 40–54 years) are the most likely to use these payday loan shops; over half of Millennials in a recent study said they've considered it.[48] Seeing opportunity, some banks are also getting into the game: US Bank is one of these, offering short-term loans of $100 to $1,000, payable in three monthly installments. The cost for these loans is 70.65 percent annually, or 5.88 percent a month; although these rates are high, they are, at least, significantly less than those offered by the cash-advance stores.[49]

In addition to financially running short, Millennials are finding that the duration of jobs themselves is shortening. Job tenure is measured in days or even hours now, rather than decades. In the recent past, college students have often been told to expect to reinvent themselves several times, and that they'll have three or four "careers" across the span of their lifetimes. LinkedIn crunched the numbers, looking back over the past twenty years: Millennials had, in fact, changed jobs three to four times, but this churn was much quicker than a lifetime—this happened during their first ten years out of college. In comparison, Gen Xers changed jobs twice.[50] With the emergence of the platform economy and untethered work, this job churn rate will rise, as more and more full-time work is automated and the remainder is broken down into part-time, gig, or contract jobs. Now, instead of three or four sequential "careers," digital natives entering the workforce can expect to have a patchwork career, cobbling together multiple gigs simultaneously, rather than sequentially, into some semblance of a job, sans benefits. In the platform economy, there are no guarantees—work is "at will"—and jobs can evaporate at any time.[51] The recent closure of Telltale Games in the San Francisco Bay Area is a good example. Two hundred and fifty game developers unexpectedly lost their jobs when Telltale suddenly shuttered its doors. Some were brought on board as recently as the week before the closure; all were giggers without any safety net to catch their fall. Emily Grace Buck was one of the designers at Telltale. She was also the design and story lead on *The Walking Dead: The Final Season* and is perhaps best known for her work on the *Batman* series. On Twitter, she tweeted about her experience at Telltale, saying:

> To clarify some questions people have been asking (and keep in mind I am NOT a company rep)
>
> • We did not get any kind of severance
> • Our healthcare only lasts for one more week

- Many former employees were contract & can't get unemployment
- Due to the insanely high cost of living in the Bay Area relative to pay-scale, many of my (unbelievably skilled and talented!!!) colleagues were living paycheck to paycheck and do not know what they are going to do to make ends meet this month
- There are people who started at Telltale as recently as a week ago.
- Some of those people have children.
- At least one of them relocated cross country
- A lot of the Telltale devs have families & children. And now they don't have a paycheck. Not even a severance paycheck.[52]

Game developer Brandon Cebenka also summed up his experience of the Telltale closure on Twitter, saying:

I got laid off at Telltale. None of my sleepless nights or long hours on weekends trying to ship a game on time got me severance today. Don't work overtime unless you're paid for it, y'all. Protect your health. Companies don't care about you.[53]

Unfortunately, as jobs become more ephemeral rather than the decades-long careers enjoyed by many of the Silent and Boomer Generations, employees become a replaceable resource. Digital connectivity also means that some labor can be outsourced to cheaper labor overseas, further undermining US workers' stability and driving them toward labor participation in an untethered economy of sharing and freelancing.

Freelancing and the freedom that comes with it does bring some benefits. These include such attributes as the freedom to determine one's own schedule, to travel, to write a book, to make a film, or to "sprint free" as an artist or a rock star. Some untethered workers dream of becoming the next Mark Zuckerberg, coding that next unicorn start-up beachside. Yet this kind of freedom comes with a cost, a cost paid forward into their future. Increasingly, freelancing, or a patchwork career, will become less of a choice and more the norm as automation pushes more workers out of the workforce. As these two trends converge—automation, and freelancing by choice where "at will" employment is offered as the sole pos-sibility—it may well spell the end of retirement, meaning untethered workers will have to continue working well past retirement age. Rather than sitting in a rocking chair, watching the sun set, untethered retirement may be refashioned into something resembling Amazon's growing seasonal workforce. Beckoning to RV and van-life dwellers, Amazon's website breathlessly announces, "Your next RV adventure starts here!"[54] As it turns out, the "adventure" the company is offering isn't your typical hike into the Grand Canyon or raft down the Snake River. Instead, it consists of a free campsite and a chance to walk up to twenty miles a day stuffing, moving, and shipping boxes in an Amazon warehouse in the exotic locales of Hebron, Kentucky; Murfreesboro, Tennessee; or Whitestown, Indiana—for minimum wage and no healthcare benefits. This new itinerant workforce is emerging to support the digerati's "I don't care how; I want it now" mentality, where goods are expected on their doorstep in smiling brown boxes the following day, if not within hours. Although Amazon's warehouses are fully automated, with robots doing the work, Amazon is recruiting aggressively for a contingent workforce it calls its "Camperforce" to step in and help out during the holiday crush. Setting up tables at popular RV spots like Yellowstone National Park and RV parks in Arizona where many go to winter, recruiters give away swag with the Camperforce logo, which features an RV sporting Amazon's signature smile. There's even a new term for this kind of van-life itinerant work: "workamping." Chuck and Barb Stout are two Camperforcers; retirees, they live in a mobile home that they use to rotate between Amazon locations, working seasonally to restock, fulfill orders, and do other physical work. After losing all their money during the 2008 financial crisis, their "golden years" are sandwiched in between packing boxes for the delight of online shoppers. Keeping a sense of humor about the whole thing, Barb refers to this chapter of their lives as "Barb and Chuck's Great Adventure."[55]

Like the Stouts, younger "technomad" couple Chris Dunphy and Cherie Ve Ard have also been full-time workampers since 2006.[56] They thought they'd give Camperforce a try, as a supplement to their "on the road" freelance income doing technical and marketing strategy online. They split their time between a classic-looking 1961 stainless-steel-clad bus, which they gutted and renovated, and a forty-foot Bayliner motor yacht. Working Amazon's Camperforce, Chris and Cherie made $11 an hour, or a little over $5,500 for the holiday season, which helped pay their expenses into March of the following year. The work sounded physically demanding, even for younger workers who are in good shape. After the experience, Cherie created a list of items she would recommend to other workampers before they set out on their own Amazon "adventure." Her list hints at the physicality of the job; it included "supportive shoes and insoles for all the walking and standing," "extra shirts and underwear" (for when there's no time to get to the Laundromat), and, lastly "a big bottle of Advil."[57]

Cherie described the grinding physicality of the work on the Camperforce, which sometimes left her in tears:

> The work is very physically demanding. Chris and I both are in pretty good shape, and there were days we'd come home in tears of pain ... and we were assigned to what is considered the "easy" job—Sortable Singles (packing single order items into single boxes). The first week or so, we were both living on Advil to keep swelling down. I ended up in Amazon's "Amcare" Center once for extreme pain in my wrist and arms due to swelling and abrasion from the boxes. I had to call in sick one day simply because my feet were too swollen to fit in my shoes. Some of the positions required 15–20 miles a day of walking. We were some of the younger workampers there[;] most [were] of a more traditional retirement age—I've gained new hope that in 30 years I may still have the energy to take on a gig like this again.[58]

In a way, the Camperforce is a manifestation of what Kurt Vonnegut envisioned would be the result of workplace automation in his dystopic yet prescient 1952 novel, *Player Piano*. In it, automation is central; the only people still employed were those who existed solely to support the machines. The Camperforce, as described by Cherie, could have been a page pulled right out of the novel, with her human frailties—like having to call in sick because her feet were too swollen to work—showing how in the automated workplace, humans are rendered second-rate machines.

Some potential Camperforcers may balk at the next of Chris and Cherie's revelations: Adding to the physical demands of the job, overtime became mandatory after Black Friday. Cherie explained that she and other Camperforce workampers were pressured to work increasingly long days or would be laid off; Amazon devised a disincentive system to keep workers on track. Cherie described it, saying:

> Immediately following Thanksgiving, everyone was on "scheduled" overtime of five 11-hour shifts a week. Scheduled overtime means, it's mandatory—and you will start racking up "points" if you miss a shift. Accumulate enough points, and you'll be let go.[59]

Gigging in jobs like these, "supporting the machines" for minimum wage, may be the new "look" of retirement, eroding the American Dream of the "golden years" of retirement, which was once a taken-for-granted aspect of the long-term careers of earlier generations.

Harvard University professor Jonathan Zittrain, cofounder of the Berkman Center for Internet and Society, while addressing an audience of digerati at SXSW (the hip tech/music/film festivals held each year in Austin, Texas), talked about how emerging digital platforms are changing the nature of work. He used the Mechanical Turk as his example. The Mechanical Turk dates back to an automaton built by engineer Wolfgang von Kempelen in 1770 to impress Empress Maria Theresa of Austria. It was designed to look like a man in a turban; an "automaton," he excelled at chess, winning most of the games he (or it) played. However, the Mechanical Turk was actually an elaborate illusion; in reality, a flesh-and-blood man sat concealed inside the box, playing the games against his (or its) opponents.[60] Amazon named its digital task platform, Amazon Mechanical Turk, after this invention. Its Turk is a crowdsourced platform through which people or businesses can hire others to complete tasks ranging from survey completion to color matching. Amazon Mechanical Turk echoes the same "man in the box" phenomenon of the original eighteenth-century machine. What at first glance looks like mechanized (i.e., computerized) labor is actually performed by a whole host of "men in boxes" around the globe, often for pennies, doing tasks called "HITs" (human intelligence tasks) that are hard to automate.[61] Current tasks include such activities as "draw boxes around car components in images, e.g., trunk, bonnet, front wheel, etc." (likely for identifying image log-ins) or "transcribe up to 35 seconds of media into text." The "reward" for completing each of these tasks ranges from five to twenty cents. To make $15.00, California's current minimum wage, one would have to transcribe three hundred "35 seconds of media" clips in one hour.

Zittrain argues that such computerized, crowdsourced work platforms like Amazon Mechanical Turk amount to digital sweatshops.[62] Far from "freeing" workers to lead exciting digital-nomad lifestyles like working beachside in Bali, freelancer "exchanges" like Amazon Mechanical Turk, Upwork, Fiverr, and others like them have begun a race to the bottom. Using these platforms, a graphic designer in Portland or Seattle in the United States competes for work alongside someone who might live in, say, Bangladesh, where the cost of living is much lower. Facebook is hiring workers in the Philippines to "clean" data, which means reviewing "flagged" or reported inappropriate content.[63] Workers there have a quota of 25,000 images a day, and the cleaners make $1 an hour. The global nature of digital connectivity has created a buyer's marketplace for IT work, graphic design, website creation, and other digital skills, lowering the cost that people expect to pay for it (e.g., "Just go to Fiverr—you can get a logo done for $10"). In some cases, the buyer gets a good deal; in many cases, though, the work is slapdash and the quality suffers. As is often the case, you get what you pay for.

Change may be in the wind for untethered workers, though. As a way to rebalance the playing field, in 2018, Airbnb CEO Brian Chesky sent a letter to the US Securities and Exchange Commission, asking the SEC to reconsider its regulations regarding shareholder eligibility. To date, shares can be held only by investors or employees of a company. At this point, gig workers or people working in the sharing economy (like Airbnb hosts) are ineligible to receive a stake in the company, or others like it, in the form of stock options. In his letter, Chesky wrote that Airbnb wants to recognize the changing nature of work and the workforce, arguing that an update to the SEC rules is necessary. He says, "[It] is necessary to reflect the evolving nature of how individuals earn income" and that the changes would spur entrepreneurship and support business start-ups.[64] A shift like this would benefit gig workers when their companies decide to go public. There is talk of Airbnb possibly going public in 2019.[65] Allowing those who share their assets in companies like Airbnb to have a stake in the larger company could be a game changer for gig workers; and it could open the door to tokenization and the development of a blockchain sharing economy, which will be discussed later.

THE UNTETHERED WORKPLACE

Even for those who are pursuing a more traditional career path, digital connectivity and devices are transforming the workplace. Given the high rate of mobile-device ownership now, and the increasingly ubiquitous Wi-Fi in coffee shops, libraries, coworking spaces, and at home, untethered workers are beginning to see remote or flexible work as a "right:" three-fifths of college students and young employees in their twenties believe they should have the right to work remotely—from the corner Blue Bottle coffeehouse, from home, or even from Bali—and 77 percent would take a pay cut to do so.[66] Whether or not it's actually true, a quarter of college students and young workers think they are more productive when working from home.[67] This attitudinal sea change is spreading to older workers. As digital natives begin to question the "traditional" ways of completing tasks at work, other, older workers are beginning to catch on to the idea of working remotely as well; in other words, untethering is spreading among generations. Ninety-three percent of workers believe that they're not productive in the office.[68] Interestingly, their reasons for wanting to work remotely were tied to concerns about health: 78 percent of people said that having a flexible job would allow them to be healthier (eat better, exercise more, etc.), and 86 percent said that they'd be less stressed.

Companies are struggling to develop the proper response to the untethering of the workforce. Their responses to worker's changing expectations and desires have varied, as management tries to figure out the appropriate way to retain their talent while maintaining productivity and the bottom line. IBM is one of these. At first, it was a pioneer of remote work, with 40 percent of its 386,000 employees in 173 countries working remotely by the year 2009.[69] In a surprising turnabout, IBM CEO Ginni Rometty reversed this policy in 2017, calling for workers to return to the office, to work shoulder to shoulder again with their colleagues, or face being fired. The move was made in an effort to improve collaboration and to accelerate the pace of work. Best Buy, Aetna, Yahoo!, and others have followed in IBM's footsteps, reversing their policies on remote work.[70] Others have taken the opposite approach: Billion-dollar tech start-up Automattic (the company that owns WordPress) made it an option to work remotely from home or a local coffee shop or coworking space, even offering Starbucks gift cards to sweeten the deal and keep the productivity-enhancing caffeine flowing. After the policy change, on any given day, only about five Automattic employees would show up to work in the gorgeous, newly remodeled 14,250-square-foot space, which works out to about 2,850 square feet of room per employee.[71] The company decided to sell off its beautiful corporate office in the San Francisco Bay Area and go fully unte-thered, embracing the remote-working trend in a way much different from the "shoulder to shoulder" approach of the above-mentioned companies.

"Always-on" digital natives bring other challenges to traditional work-places, with their changing values around connectivity. A Cisco Systems study found that a "bring your own device" policy and the ability to stay connected while working is a more important factor than salary to Millennials.[72] Sixty-five percent of college students and young professionals also believe that their cor-porate devices should be available for them to use on social media, and four out of five want to choose their own device for their jobs. Social media connectivity has become so important that two-thirds of college students will ask about social media policies during a job interview. The majority (56 percent) won't accept a job from a company that bans social media at work, and 66 percent believe that they should be able to connect whenever they want to; many will connect anyway, regardless of company policy. I've seen some workers do so by using a fake name on social media accounts, so their employer won't know they're on Facebook during work hours, for example, going against company policy by doing so. Connectivity and access to social media is of particular concern to companies and organizations for which cybersecurity is a high priority, including the military. As mentioned above, some have banned the use of social media at work altogether; but, especially given the aging workforce in some fields, the ban leaves these organizations with a real conundrum. They want (and need) digital natives to replace aging retirees as workers, but they are also concerned about the security and loss of productivity that potentially come with this desire for constant connectivity.

Remote work clearly has advantages for the worker. It's nice to be able to work in your pajamas, at the hours during which you might be most "on"; early birds can work the morning shift, and night owls can get their work done at night, when they feel most productive. Yet the problem with working untethered becomes the relationships, or the lack thereof. Some have suggested that remote work, where colleagues aren't face-to-face, dehumanizes people. Project-management and collaboration apps like Slack and Trello facilitate remote work by enabling easier team communication in a chat-based environment. Yet written communication, like chatting or texting, is prone to misinterpretation because it lacks the nuance and added information carried by the inclusion of nonverbal cues, such as tone of voice, inflection, facial expressions, and other body language. Ugly "flame wars" have been known to flare up in work chats as tempers boil over well beyond what they would in face-to-face interactions. Texts or chats also come laden with the assumption of an instantaneous reply. Remote programmer Martin De Wulf describes how using Slack to work remotely has led to constant interruptions of his perceived work "flow" and productivity:

> When working remotely as a developer, the chat (usually Slack or HipChat) quickly becomes your lifeline to the company: that is the way most people will try to contact you. And to me, being responsive on the chat accomplishes the same as being on time at work in an office: it gives an image of reliability. It also implies that if you do not really want to give the impression that you are taking a lot of breaks, you might find yourself checking your notifications a lot . . . [Whereas,] if people had seen you working the whole morning . . . you would not feel the need to be so responsive. I actually often realized that other colleagues working remotely were criticized because they were not answering very

quickly on the chat. A part of the problem is that on a chat, people do not see you physically, so they cannot really estimate if you are at a good moment to be interrupted. So, you are interrupted a lot, and if you are a bit like me, you feel forced to answer quickly. So, you interrupt your work a lot. And in case you do not know it: interruptions are loathed by programmers, since it is really bad for their productivity as it breaks their focus.[73]

It can be harder to maintain team cohesion and manage those working outside the traditional office setting when employees are working remotely. Relationships take some face-to-face time to build both trust and unity; and without it, resentments can fester and anxieties can grow. A study of 1,100 remote workers conducted by VitalSmarts, a firm that provides corporate training, found that if you're out of sight, you're out of mind: Reduced or absent face-to-face time can lead to an erosion of trust. Those working remotely are more likely to report that they fear that people are talking behind their backs, that others will make changes to projects without filling them in, that people will "clique up" and lobby against them, or that colleagues won't fight for their priorities.[74] And they may be right. Without the face-to-face connectivity garnered from working shoulder to shoulder, intimacy and trust may suffer, and the resulting lack of loyalty may lead to these very unintended consequences in an unfortunate game of self-fulfilling prophecy. One way to help coalesce remote teams is to consider bringing back the body and nonverbal communication via video meetings and conferences on Zoom, Skype, or similar apps. In addition, the study authors suggest frequent and consistent check-ins; the communication of clear expectations and objectives; and maintaining an "open door" availability policy among managers via IM, Slack, Skype, email, phone, or text; VitalSmarts determined that these factors will help foster and maintain closer relationships with remote workers.[75]

THE RISE OF THE FAKE WORKFORCE

As digital technologies continue to get smarter and become embedded in more "things" and processes, the future of work for humans is rendered uncertain. Amusements such as eSports will most certainly continue to grow, providing new opportunities for both gig work and ecommerce, even as traditional jobs begin to wane or morph under the pressure of artificial intelligence (AI) and automation. There is no doubt that AI and automation will play a major disruptive role in the workplace; but the impacts are subject to some debate, with two main schools of thought emerging: The first I call the *Replacement Model*, which states that these technologies will *replace* human workers as they reach the point at which AI outperforms humans, which some have called the Singularity; the second I call the *Augmentation Model*, which more optimistically sees AI and automation as *augmenting* human capabilities, automating boring, repetitive duties, and freeing humans to focus on higher-functioning creative or strategic tasks in the workplace. Some in the replacement camp think we are heading toward a dystopic future of rampant joblessness like the one portrayed in the Steven Spielberg's film *Ready Player One*, based on the novel by Ernest Cline, in which we're all left amusing ourselves to death in virtual-reality (VR) headsets, playing video games and escaping to virtual "Gardens of Eden," as envisioned by game developers. Like nature on steroids. The second camp has a more utopian vision for humans as we relate to machines, where AI "augments" what people do at work, such as the case of the surgeon or doctor who may access remote specialists or information to better serve his rural patients. Historically, technologists have been inspired to create the fanciful technologies and worlds they read about or see in science fiction, envisioned by authors and screenwriters like Ray Bradbury, Gene Roddenberry, and others. Vonnegut was one of these, and perhaps among the first to imagine the unintended consequences of a world run by machines. At the time of his book *Player Piano*'s publication, Steve Jobs, Bill Gates, and Mark Zuckerberg were mere twinkles in their parents' eyes. Vonnegut envisioned a world very much like the one we may be heading toward, and, in some cases, are already in—a world where automation has taken over and has divided the nation into high- and low-IQ groups (now, Vonnegut's IQ stands in for level of education). In the novel, only the high-IQ group, the engineers and managers, still have jobs. Lower-IQ workers have become the detritus of automation, residing "across the river," where they live lives devoid of any meaning or purpose, their jobs replaced by the machines. At least for some, Vonnegut's vision is beginning to come true. A report by McKinsey & Company has indicated that by 2030, as many as 800 million workers worldwide, and a third of workers in the United States, could be replaced by robots or automation.[76] The employees at risk of being outed by automation are not simply the factory workers of old, many of whom have already fallen victim to replacement by automation. Now, automation via artificial intelligence is reaching up the job food chain to replace even white-collar workers. Surgeon Shafi Amed, from the Royal London Hospital and cofounder of virtual and augmented reality firm

Medical Realities, believes that artificially intelligent robots will absolutely replace surgeons in the coming years.[77] IBM's AI phenom, Watson, has shown that it can outperform human doctors when diagnosing rare forms of cancer.[78] Watson is able to screen cancer patients faster for clinical trials, meaning that more patients can be seen per hour, thereby cutting costs and increasing profits for shareholders. For rural hospitals or clinics that lack access to medical specialties, Watson or similar AIs may allow local doctors to diagnose and reach better solutions on how to treat their patients, particularly for difficult or non-routine cases. Further, hardware like smart glasses such as Google Glass may combine with AI to allow surgeons to gather needed information "on the fly," particularly if they run into surprises or difficulties in middle of performing surgery, and particularly for surgical training.[79]

Lawyers are another group subject to being replaced by AI as well. Twitch cofounder Justin Kan recently raised $65 million for his start-up Atrium, with the aim of replacing lawyers with virtualized AI. Kan told TechCrunch reporter Josh Constine that he's "pretty stoked about that."[80] Another group that is being incrementally replaced is accountants: IBM's Watson has teamed up with tax preparer H&R Block to offer AI-assisted tax preparation, indicating that it's not only factory workers, surgeons, and lawyers whose jobs are at risk of obsolescence with the advent of more advanced AI and automation; it can reach across entire industries, top to bottom.[81]

AIs are slowly yet methodically wiping out entire classifications of jobs, from simple order-taking at McDonald's to investment trading on Wall Street. National chains like Panera and McDonald's are installing touch-screen self-order kiosks in its restaurants. Discussing this, app developer Lance Mayfield said to me in a private Facebook conversation that "it's cool and sad to have McDonald's employees show customers how to use the kiosk which means they are helping to eliminate their own job."[82] In this sense, the McDonald's workers are like the humans in *Player Piano*, ultimately serving the machines that are rendering them irrelevant. Domino's Pizza has introduced Zero Click, an app in which the customer does nothing other than open an app to place an order. Once the app is opened, a ten-second kitchen timer appears. Do nothing but watch it count down to zero, and *bam*, your preexisting favorite pizza order is automatically placed and on its way to your door.[83] Given these instances of digital automation, there will be less need for order takers, for bussers cleaning tables, for waiters and waitresses in restaurants, and, eventually, even for cooks or bartenders, as those making the food and drinks are being automated away, too. We're already seeing the beginning of this; Royal Caribbean Cruises has introduced robot bartenders to shake, stir, and serve cocktails to its guests:

> First unveiled on *Quantum of the Seas* in 2014, four ships—*Harmony of the Seas*, *Quantum of the Seas*, *Anthem of the Seas*, and *Ovation of the Seas*—now feature the popular Bionic Bar. Manning the bar are two robots; each one has its own name (on *Anthem of the Seas* they're called "Shaken" and "Stirred," and onboard *Harmony of the Seas* are "Mix" and "Mingle"). Engineered in Italy, these special robots can muddle, stir, shake and strain all types of drinks; the cocktail combinations are endless, with 30 spirits and 21 mixers from which to choose.[84]

These robot bartenders are so fast, they can create two specially mixed cocktails a minute, or one thousand cocktails a day, far exceeding the productivity of any human bartender. They don't do as well, however, when trying to perform such human tasks as providing a listening ear and acting as a counselor, confessional, or coach to troubled patrons.

As with the bartending robots, the problem becomes this: the pace of technological diffusion is accelerating such that at some point, the average person won't be able to keep up. The advances in machine learning, deep learning, artificial intelligence, robotics, and other types of automation are happening very quickly, and largely without regard to the human consequences, which those in the tech sector may be blind to until joblessness has passed a critical tipping point. The world of work is changing as we move from an analog industrial model toward a global, decentralized, highly automated digital world in which "the robots" can outperform us both physically and mentally. Figuring out how we prepare for the changing workplace of the future is a major challenge. Baby Boomer and former model Tom Stillwell works to restore homes. In a public Facebook group for former residents of Newport Beach, Stillwell talked about how, as a kid, his Silent Generation father prepared him for an analog workplace:

> I always did chores for my Dad, but one thing stuck with me my entire life from one job. Dad told me I could sweep out the garage for fifty cents, maybe a dollar. When I finished I showed him and he pointed out all that I had missed and said, "Let me show you the right way." He then proceeded to show me a simple yet completely effective way to sweep the floor. Used it the rest of my life and taught it to more than a few young men who worked with me 30 years in the building trades. Dad's admonishment that day, "If you know how to sweep a floor, a man has a reason to hire you."[85]

For prior generations, such hands-on skills as sweeping a floor might well have gotten someone hired. During the Industrial Revolution, decent-paying jobs in factories could be held by people with lower skills and little to no education. Yet now, those jobs have largely dried up, having been offshored to countries with cheaper labor, like China, Bangladesh, India, and others. Factory work itself has been transformed by the digital revolution, and it now requires a more educated worker, thereby creating a barrier for entry to the under-educated and the unskilled. While US manufacturing is producing 40 percent more goods per year, they've cut workers by about a third.[86] The skills gap may be widening: Judy Marks, the CEO of Siemens USA, has said that there are now more computers on the manufacturing floor than machine tools and other types of equipment.[87] Workers now need advanced skills, working to troubleshoot computerized systems or working with data-driven interfaces to industrial processes, all of which require higher education and specialized training. The Bureau of Labor Statistics shows that in the ten years ending in 2009, factories shed workers, erasing almost all the gains of the previous seventy years; roughly one out of every three manufacturing jobs now—about 6 million in total—has disappeared. Yet many potential workers can't even pass the basic literacy tests required to run the advanced machinery common on the floors of factories these days: When German company Siemens Energy opened a gas-turbine-production plant in Charlotte, North Carolina, ten thousand people showed up at a job fair for eight hundred positions. But fewer than 15 percent of the applicants were able to pass the reading, writing, and math tests, which were geared toward a ninth-grade education. The recently retired CEO of Siemens USA put it bluntly: "There are no jobs for high school graduates at Siemens today."[88] Siemens is just one of many companies where this is an employment reality. Since only 29 percent of Millennials have a college degree, this spells trouble for those seeking jobs in a world where even manufacturing jobs may soon require a master's degree.[89] For many, this will also mean taking on a load of crippling student loan debt, which can bury them for years. The trade-off between getting educated and going into debt is a gamble, as some may not make enough to meet the student-loan payments.

With the rapid march of automation on our heels, we may be facing an "end-of-jobs problem"—and a resurgence against that—as inevitabilities on the horizon. The Vonnegut novel *Player Piano* envisions the kinds of counterforces we may be able to expect to rise up against the oppressive forces of technology. The protagonist, Dr. Paul Proteus, stages his own quiet resistance to the meaninglessness of life left over after the rise of the machines. He buys a farm, with the return to nature and the land painted as humankind's salvation. Others in the story join forces to create a social movement against the increasingly dehumanizing system, a group Vonnegut calls the Ghost Shirt Society. This was a nod to the Lakota Native Americans, who were perhaps among the first to resist the rise of culture and technology in the United States. They made and wore "ghost shirts" and performed a ritual dance in an effort to protect themselves against the white man's bullets, aiming to make the intruders disappear while rendering their bullets harmless.[90] The US government felt that the dance was dangerous, since it was acting as a unifying force among disparate tribal groups and a catalyst for resistance among the Plains peoples—a unity that could threaten US expansion. The government outlawed the Ghost Dance and sent the cavalry to break up Native American gatherings, with full authority to use whatever means necessary. The end result was the massacre of some three hundred Sioux men, women, and children at a place called Wounded Knee, South Dakota, the ghost shirts unable to stave off the technology of guns used against them. Today, a surprise coalition of some of Silicon Valley's biggest technologists and innovators comprise a Ghost Shirt Society for our time. Technologists including Elon Musk, tech accelerator Sam Altman, and Y Combinator cofounder Jessica Livingston; investors Peter Thiel and Reid Hoffman; video-game developer Gabe Newell; and Skype founder Jaan Tallin have banded together to form OpenAI, a group intent on helping to invent a safe and ethical AI future. Elon Musk is of the mind that, left unchecked, AI will pose a threat to people, as power falls into the hands of fewer and fewer companies. He told his staff that there may be as little as a 10 percent chance of making AI safe.[91] In 2017, he warned that the United Nations needed to act in order to avoid a killer-robots arms race. Despite being vocal in his concerns about the future of AI and humans, Elon Musk quit the board of OpenAI in early 2018, citing potential conflict of interest, as his company Tesla delves deeper into AI.

Some have suggested that the remedy to automation and the end-of-jobs problem is to offer people a universal basic income (UBI). Technological utopians see UBI as a way to "free" people from the burdens of work, enabling them to "self-actualize"—as artists, thinkers, ballerinas—or to become whatever their heart truly desires. Some think it will enable more creative entrepreneurship to emerge. But not everyone is cut out to be an entrepreneur; many enjoy the confines of a simple, nine-to-five existence that they can leave behind at the end of the day. Others find reward in the jobs they do, such as nurses who comfort a child going into surgery or are there for a mother who has just delivered her first child. Some revel in these kinds of tasks and loathe the idea of changing their professions to the administrative side of the workplace. Still others may already be self-actualized. Take long-haul truckers, for example. Their median yearly wage is $73,000, meaning half make more than that.[92] If their jobs are replaced by automated, self-driving trucks, it is hard to imagine what five-figure-income job may emerge to replace them. A friend of mine called his trucker cousin in the Midwest to ask his view of the coming self-driving trucks. His cousin's answer, as recounted to me, was: "They're gonna have a hard time driving those trucks when we shoot the tires off of them. And we own all the guns. And we know how to use 'em."

Clearly, the pitchforks could come out if enough people are deprived of their livelihoods. Also, if people lack income due to unemployment or a dearth of jobs, how will they afford the goods and services that the economy does create? In an attempt to turn down the flame on any possible backlash to the automation ahead, some Silicon Valley firms have been among the first to launch small pilot studies to see if the idea of a UBI may be a viable alternative to a jobless horizon. One of these is start-up accelerator Y Combinator, the company that launched firms such as Dropbox, Airbnb, Reddit, DoorDash and others.[93] As of 2017, some seven additional pilot tests of UBI are underway in Finland, Kenya, the Netherlands, Ontario, Scotland, Uganda, and the United States, to explore their impact.[94] In Finland, two thousand people were randomly chosen to participate, from a pool of individuals who were between the ages of twenty-five and fifty-eight and were receiving unemployment benefits. Participation in the basic income program was mandatory for those selected; participants were not pressed to seek employment and were told the UBI would persist even if they found employment. The two thousand participants are receiving about US$590 per month (to give you an idea of how far this income will go: the average salary in Finland is US$2,580.24, and the average city apartment is US$835.00[95]). The province of Ontario, Canada, has set up a UBI experiment in three locations.[96] Four thousand participants will be chosen from a pool of low-income adults between the ages of eighteen and sixty-four years who have lived in one of the three test locations for at least one year. Each participant will receive approximately US $13,649.57 per year for singles and US $19,305.26 per year for couples. The results of this study will be made public in 2020. In the United States, Y Combinator's founder Sam Altman is pursuing a privately funded basic income experiment. As currently planned, it will use a sample of between two thousand and three thousand individuals from two states, who are between the ages of twenty-one and thirty-five, with household incomes below the median in their area. A group of at least one thousand will receive US$1,000 per month for three years, and a subset will receive the payments for an additional two years. The payments will be given unconditionally and irrespective of income (among those below the median for the area). The remainder of the sample will be used as a control group (meaning they won't receive the UBI, so the researchers can compare the outcomes of the two groups). A pre-pilot has been launched in Oakland. Though these pilot studies of the impacts of UBI will reveal insights, their brevity and containment to a small sample will likely not reveal some of the other, unintended consequences of providing basic income.

While providing basic income may address part of the end-of-work problem, namely, the economic aspect, it does not address other very important (perhaps critically so) social and psychological functions that jobs provide. "Idle hands are the devil's workshop" is a phrase that can be traced all the way back to biblical days. The folks who wrote that line knew all too well that work provides much more than a way to make a living: it addresses boredom or the ennui of having absolutely nothing to do. Sociologist Pierre Bourdieu discusses how work is much more than a paycheck, a point that is usually absent from current discussions of the end-of-work problems and universal basic income. He says:

> In the absence of regular employment, a person lacks not only a place in which to work and the receipt of regular income but also a coherent organization of the present—that is, a system of concrete expectations and goals. Regular employment provides the anchor for the spatial and temporal aspects of daily life. It determines where you are going to be and when you are going to be there. In the absence of regular employment, life, including family life, becomes less coherent. Persistent unemployment and irregular employment hinder rational planning in daily life, a necessary condition of adaptation to an industrial economy.[97]

Current plans for UBI don't begin to address these kinds of non-economic impacts of the end of work. People need a sense of meaning and purpose to bring coherency to their lives, something a comprehensive UBI program would need to consider.

Overall, the key to keeping up with the pace of change lies in the education and retraining of workers. In Sweden, a nation known for its solid social safety net, workers aren't worried about the relentless march of automation taking their jobs, as they know the combination of strong unions and a social safety net will ensure that they are trained for other jobs. As the Swedish minister for employment and integration, Ylva Johansson, put it, "The jobs disappear, and then we train people for new jobs. We won't protect jobs. But we will protect workers."[98] Germany is another country that is committed to addressing the ever-evolving need for more highly trained workers: It has committed a significant budget to its apprentice program, where young people get hands-on experience in one of Germany's many manufacturing plants. Upon completion, they attain the title of "meister"—an achievement that is announced in the local paper and celebrated. In the United States, vocational and trade programs like this have often been stigmatized, and a college degree is thought to be the path to a solid career and future.[99] Yet many in the tech sector and in manufacturing have said they can't find enough workers in the trades or construction area, so high-paying jobs go wanting. Other countries and companies need to take note of Sweden's and Germany's approaches, in order to stay economically viable and to ensure the availability of needed workers in the fast-churning world of digital disruption.

THE UNTETHERED ECONOMY

Digital natives' values have undergone a sea change compared with earlier Boomers, which is impacting how they view work and determine what they want to buy and support. This shift is even causing them to question the structure of capitalism, banking, commerce, and the nature of work itself. A study of consumers' ranking of brands, comparing the values of Millennials to Boomers, sheds light on these generational changes. Enso, a creative impact agency that seeks to make people's lives better, has created the World Value Index, which measures how Americans are inspired by brand's missions. It asks survey takers whether or not a brand's mission aligns with what they care about as consumers. The results are eye-opening regarding brands that have historically been held in high esteem for their social-good approach. One of these is Paul Newman's charitable company, Newman's Own, whose ranking fell from number 7 among Boomers to number 81 among eighteen-to-thirty-four-year-olds, as Newman's star fades for younger buyers.[100] Amazon landed in the top 10, showing that convenience is king, and that digital mediation is important to digital natives. Web and tech companies like Twitter, Snapchat, PayPal, Spotify, Uber, and Kickstarter were also among the most important to Millennial consumers, along with customizable brands like Starbucks and Chipotle. Also highlighting this generational gap were the rankings of companies that produce physical products, like Starbucks (ranked 111 by Boomers but 25 by Millennials), the Honest Company, Chipotle, and H&M (ranked 142 by Gen Xers but 69 by Millennials). The brands that were the biggest movers for Millennials, compared to the general population, were those companies that not only are both digitally connected and customizable but also are perceived as offering the most value outside of making money. These include Fitbit, Chipotle, Uber, Starbucks, Twitter, and Etsy. Also notable in addition to the changing of brand perceptions is the fact that people's trust in businesses has eroded. Fifty-nine percent of people surveyed said they don't trust business leaders to do what's right. At the same time, 68 percent of Millennials agreed that "creating change in the world is a personal goal of mine that I actively pursue," compared to only 42 percent of Boomers who agreed with this statement.

In response to these trends, some people are beginning to dream of new ways of doing business. Umair Haque of Havas Media Labs is one of these. Responding to the rising dissatisfaction with the current way of doing business, he has suggested a paradigm shift for business, from economics to eudaimonics, saying: "Social media has great *economics*: Facebook and Twitter and so on maximize incomes and earn fortunes. But its *eudaimonics* are profoundly unsuccessful: it makes people unhappy, unfulfilled, and more distant—and it's a vector for misinformation and mistrust that's eating away at the fabric of democracy."[101] Haque hopes to create a new economy that maximizes well-being; his stated goal is for people to "live and breathe lives genuinely well lived naturally, effortlessly, genuinely, and transformatively." As Haque points out, eudaimonia isn't a new idea, but our digital culture tends not to value old things; as he puts it, "we discard old ideas like last year's iPhone."[102] Clearly, his vision of a new economy transcends economics and considers happiness and well-being in ways that are quantifiable, such that companies can set target goals and be held accountable.

Others see blockchain and cryptocurrencies as the way forward toward a healthier and more just, equitable, and sustainable world. At the recent launch of EOS Lynx (a digital cryptocurrency "wallet" for the everyday consumer) in Santa Monica, an area becoming known as "Blockchain Beach" for its density of blockchain start-ups, the excitement about this emerging tech sector was palpable.[103] One young man said to me, "We're creating an entirely new world!" Brock Pierce is one of these crypto-utopianists: Inspired by the sharing economy of Burning Man, former child actor Pierce and his merry band of tech developers, clean tech entrepreneurs, and other hangers-on want to create a new American Dream in Puerto Rico.

In 2017, Puerto Rico was hit by Hurricane Maria, which left the island devastated and without power—in some areas for months. Nearly three thousand people died in the wake of the storm.[104] The National Oceanic and Atmospheric Association (NOAA) has estimated the damage at more than $90 billion, making it the third costliest hurricane to hit the United States.[105] With aid slow in coming, resident Christine Nueves described the feelings of disillusionment about America many felt post Hurricane Maria, when their dreams and reality failed to align:

> The story that we've been passing from generation to generation is [that] America is gonna protect us . . . it's gonna provide . . . it's going to . . . when it matters . . . they can defend us. And then when it mattered, they couldn't get people here. I think it was a great moment of just a story collapsing. And that's important and very powerful because that's a story we've been holding on to for generations.[106]

For some, this devastation represented an opportunity—not only to rebuild, but to help Puerto Rico rise like a phoenix from the ashes, into something new and even better than it was before.

Brock Pierce is one of these dreamers. He originally built his wealth in the video-game space, selling virtual goods for real cash.[107] Later, he made a fortune as an early investor in cryptocurrency. He is now the chairman of the Bitcoin Foundation; cofounder of one of the first blockchain venture funds, Blockchain Capital; and an early investor in some of the biggest coins and tokens, including EOS and Tether. He now plans to give away the whole of his estimated $1 billion fortune during his lifetime; some of that will go toward rebuilding hurricane-devastated Puerto Rico.[108] Meanwhile, he's living life as an untethered digital nomad, living out of a suitcase between Santa Monica, Ibiza, Puerto Rico, and Burning Man. In an effort to understand Pierce's vision, Neil Strauss, who is the author of the bestselling book on players, called *The Game*, and a journalist for *Rolling Stone*, tagged along with him on a trip to Puerto Rico. He described him as a kind of Robin Hood with a Burning Man aesthetic:

> In nearly 10 full days together, I rarely saw him sleep in a bed or eat a full meal. He crashed on random couches, in the back seats of cars, on tables at bars. He gave away necklaces, bracelets, food, money, time, tequila, you name it.[109]

Strauss' observations were confirmed by a friend of mine who recently stayed with Pierce in Ibiza and recounted a similar story, saying that Pierce offered up his own bed so my friend could stay with his girlfriend. When my friend felt guilty at the thought of taking him up on the offer and instead went to a hotel, Pierce gave his bed to someone else. Brock Pierce and others in a loosely organized gang of techno-utopists in the blockchain and cryptocurrency ecosystem see themselves as harbingers of a new world, where they are rewriting the rules. Calling their rebuild "Puerto Crypto," their aim is to establish Puerto Rico as a "crypto-utopia," reshaping it as an innovation hub and site for their own brand of digital-nomadic beachfront living. The idea is to rebuild the island in Robin Hood fashion, using cryptocurrency and money saved from IRS tax incentives to "rob from the rich" and give to the poor.

But what are cryptocurrencies (which include EOS, Tether, and Bitcoin) and blockchain? Touched off in 2009 by a white paper on Bitcoin that was written by the mysterious Satoshi Nakamoto (a pseudonym for a person or group of persons still unknown), cryptocurrencies are seen as a democratizing force because they disconnect currency from the central control of banks and the nation-state. As such, they hold the potential to create a new "crowdsourced" global economy that transcends national bounds. The blockchain is basically a distributed ledger system with no central control: Everyone on the blockchain has a copy of the ledger. The goal is to reach consensus on every transaction, rendering fraudulent transactions more difficult and negating the need for centralized control via a central overseeing organization, or what's been referred to as an "Oracle." This is referred to as "mining." Mining cryptocurrency has become one of the new "jobs" emerging out of the crypto scene. Many cryptocurrency miners have made small fortunes by mining Bitcoin, Ethereum, Monero, or other so-called "alt coins," which now number in the thousands (although lately the Bitcoin bubble has burst a bit, as prices have retreated). Miners help reach consensus on the distributed blockchain ledger by solving mathematical problems, which is referred to as a "proof of work," in which they verify transactions (or "blocks"). The first miner to solve the problem is rewarded in cryptocurrency (or coins) for doing this work, and the verified transaction (the block) is then stored on the blockchain. Miners compete with each other to solve these mathematical "puzzles." Those with faster "rigs" with more computational power can get to the answer more quickly and thus have an edge on those with slower rigs. The mining reward is 12.5 bitcoins per block; it halves every 210,000 blocks, or about once every four years. By January 2018, 80 percent of the entire 21 million available bitcoins had already been mined. Miners also earn a transaction fee for their efforts, which varies.[110] There is also "proof of stake," in which the more coins a person has, the odds increase that he will be the creator of the next new block, based on the amount of his wealth or "stake." Dash and NEO are two proof-of-stake cryptocurrencies.[111] In proof of stake, those with the most "stake" will confirm the transaction and reap a transaction fee as their reward. Since there is no block reward, these "miners" are referred to as "forgers."

Blockchain technology creates an immutable record, affording users the ability to trace the provenance of any item or transaction. Enterprises and governments are beginning to develop their own blockchain use cases and strategy. The use cases can include everything from medical health records to tracing the provenance of goods, data, or identity. The CEO of retailer Overstock announced a partnership with a Peruvian firm to use blockchain technology for a global property registry. For example, EverLedger is using the blockchain to trace the provenance of diamonds: The digital record contains dozens of attributes for each diamond, including the color, carat, and certificate number, which can be inscribed by laser on the crown or girdle of the stone. Using a laser scanner, one can instantly determine the provenance of any stone, thereby avoiding fakes and "blood diamonds."[112] Some blockchain start-ups are even taking on previously disruptive digital platforms, "sharing the wealth" via tokenization of assets; Bee Token is one of these tokens, linked to the Beenest home-sharing platform. This start-up is working on setting up a decentralized home-sharing market to compete with Airbnb; it aims to offer lower fees for home sharers and is backed by a smart contract system that will automatically process payments between visitor and host. Tokens like the Bee Token can then be bought and sold on an exchange or traded for US dollars or other currencies. The blockchain can be used to facilitate micropayments, for example, paying independent musicians for snippets of their music used in YouTube clips or other videos. Homeowners can also use a blockchain microgrid—a small-scale, local energy grid—to sell excess energy to one another in a peer-to-peer energy market like Power Ledger or Omega Grid; in this sense, green energy production becomes a form of "gigging" by selling the power generated from home solar panels or wind turbines to others.

New currencies built atop blockchains, called cryptocurrencies, like Bitcoin, Ether, Ripple, and others, are setting the stage for a new digital, global financial market. Start-up companies are beginning to rethink their funding strategy, essentially crowdfunding their start-up costs via an Initial Coin Offering, or ICO, rather than pursuing traditional venture funding. Using an ICO, they issue tokens for some use on their blockchain, as opposed to going the traditional venture-capital route. For those who are statistically less likely to be funded by traditional means, an ICO can boost their chances of securing financing. Take women, for example: of the $59.6 billion in venture capital invested in 2016, only $1.46 billion of it went to woman founders, or just under 2.5 percent of all venture funding. Despite this lack of funding for companies run by women, research shows that having women in leadership positions, both in upper management roles and on advisory boards, actually boosts the bottom line. A global study by research firm MSCI found that companies with female leadership generated a return on equity of 10.1 percent per year, whereas those without any females in leadership positions returned only 7.4 percent.[113] Companies lacking board diversity also tend to suffer from more governance-related controversies than female-run businesses, which poses a troublesome problem particularly for male-dominated technology companies, given many recent gender-diversity and related controversies in Silicon Valley companies.[114] The blockchain can open up opportunities for nontraditional businesses founders—that is, businesses run by women and others—giving them a shot at funding to which they might not have had access otherwise. One of these founders is Geo Star, a female Millennial who is a blockchain and crypto entrepreneur. She sees blockchain as a way to usher in a new type of economy and world. Though her plans for an "Atmosphere Ecosystem" are complex, multifaceted, and ambitious, her foundational value is to help usher in a new economic system built upon blockchain technology and a cryptocurrency called KARMA:

> With the miracle of being introduced to a whole new world of opportunity, I have been working my ass off with some of the most powerful people on the face of this planet, creating new Economic Ecosystems of Subscription for the world to turn to as the current models crumble beneath the weight of their own inefficiency and corruption (which is happening now—and will increase more rapidly than anyone thinks). In less than a few months, I went from having 6 dollars in my pocket to having over 6 figures in my online wallet that continued to grow. With that first large blast of income, I spearheaded the acquisition and regeneration of GENESIS—the first property entered into PORTAL, the global property/community matrix for the world's most influential people to gather, co-create, cross-pollinate, evolve, and inspire! Genesis is a sacred land located in the mystical Redwoods of the Santa Cruz Mountains, where us New World Servers (people who have ACTUALLY dedicated their lives to the betterment of the whole of humanity) come together and CREATE

the future we wish to exist in. Understanding that the Atmosphere Ecosystem has MANY moving parts, while also recognizing the increasing importance of focusing on a Universal Basic Income token and needing a way to move past transactionality, while tracking value within the Portal community, I prioritized dialing in on KARMA, the world's first Universal Scaling Asset token (moving beyond UBI, [universal basic income] because we need more than an income in a jobless economy to be a thriving species). Karma is attached to ALL of the value entered into the Atmosphere Ecosystem (including Land, Crypto Returns, Investments, and all other forms of Income), giving every token holder fractalized ownership of the greater whole![115]

Geo's ambitious plan for a new blockchain economy that emphasizes fairness, creativity, and the notion of a better way of living is one of many emerging out of this new space. Geo is looking to expand her vision even further and is currently scouting Los Angeles for a location for a new music studio and blockchain-based music label called Blockchain Records.[116]

The blockchain represents the digital manifestation of coming untethered. It is a paradigmatic shift that both embodies and facilitates the emerging values and physical changes of digital nomadism, disaggregation, and the decentralization of work and the workforce. Having grown up in a world during a recession, where trust in banks as institutions and the government to regulate them fell, crypto folks are rethinking the traditional economy. Their vision is to create a "new world" society—based on a different core value proposition. Blockchain is untethered at its core. The crypto community envisions business that is communal, connected—and micro-compensated, for things like contributions of knowledge online, which to date has often been shared for free, then monetized by platforms like Facebook without compensation to the authors. SENSE coin, created by Sensay, is one example of this kind of monetizing; its aim is to put "your brain on the blockchain," by compensating people for their knowledge, shared with others on an as-needed basis, with the touch of an app.[117] Blockchain and cryptocurrencies may turn out to be the largest social experiment since the 1960s. Many Boomers look back on the 1960s as the "good old days," when things like Woodstock; antiwar protest marches; the civil rights, gay rights, and women's rights movements; and the use of marijuana and other mind-altering drugs brought them together for unforgettable communal experiences. Bonding rituals emerged, such as passing the joint so everyone could take a "toke." The similarity between then and now is that Boomers felt like they were making a difference in the world, that they were a part of something bigger than themselves. With all of the social fragmentation going on now as a result of untethering, where people are increasingly atomized rather than a part of established community groups (like joining churches or having long-term careers), and where social media or gaming stands in as a kind of virtualized community, sometimes actual community gets lost. We are increasingly becoming, as MIT psychologist Sherry Turkle put it, "alone together."[118] Digital natives never knew life before digital technology, so many don't know the difference between "IRL" (i.e., in real life) community and virtual community. Soon, no one will.

Blockchain as an untethered economy is the digital native's attempt to reclaim and monetize these kinds of communal experiences again. Blockchains and cryptocurrency start-ups are aiming to build a digital infrastructure and digital economy that spans the boundaries of nation-state and goes global, in an attempt to respond to the growing untethered workforce. The idea is that digital nomads can receive payments for global services quickly and easily when they work outside the bounds of any particular country. The blockchain can also allow new things to be built for the common good, like a global 911 emergency system on mobile phones, which is the focus of blockchain start-up Guardian Circle. Their Guardian Tokens will be used to compensate citizen rescuers who respond in the case of an emergency, like an off-duty EMT or doctor, for example.[119] Though blockchain technologies are still in the pioneering phase of development, their real value will be revealed as applications like Bee Token, Guardian Token, and others like them organize and monetize work and the sharing of physical and virtual assets, potentially providing new income streams for those who are untethering from the traditional workforce by choice or by force.

Though there has been a recent bear market in the cryptocurrency space, large companies like IBM, Amazon, SAP, and Oracle are betting on it for the future; all are developing blockchain-as-a-service platforms.[120] Amazon will manage blockchains for corporate clients, built atop the Hyperledger Fabric blockchain, using Ethereum to create distributed apps. Likewise, IBM is developing a blockchain solution for enterprise clients, also using the Hyperledger Fabric as the foundation for its platform. Although Los Angeles has been an early mover in this space with its "Blockchain Beach," New York is aiming to become a hub of innovation in the blockchain arena: New York City's Economic Development Corporation is opening a blockchain center as a way to promote awareness and education for business professionals in the uses and applications of blockchain technology. Workspaces like New York's BuroHQ are also cropping up to provide office and meeting space, and to facilitate building community for investors and blockchain start-ups.[121] On the consumer side, the blockchain can align with digital natives' desire for buying local and sourcing their goods. As mentioned above, blockchain allows for increased transparency into the sourcing of goods. This is particularly important for Millennials, since 73 percent of them surveyed have indicated that the environment and sustainability are important factors in terms of their purchasing decisions.[122] The blockchain can also align with Millennials' concern that food be grown locally, and that products like coffee, food, and other items be non-GMO and ethically sourced. The ability for consumers to track from supplier to coffee shop, or "farm to table," for example, will also support small and local businesses, as small-business owners can make their supply change more transparent to customers who want to buy ethically. Blockchain can also help businesses "green the supply chain" by making their efforts to conserve energy, water, and other resources transparent to consumers; in this way, businesses can add distinction to their products and services by appealing to customers' green sensibilities. In that sense, the blockchain can be seen as the digital manifestation of the shifting values and mind-set of the emerging Untethered Society, as we transition toward a global, disaggregated, yet connected world.

Clearly, these seismic shifts in the digital transformation of work and the workplace have global implications, as those who are working gig and freelance jobs as they seek their own version of an "adventure" lifestyle or work/life balance look for cheaper places to live. Some, as we have seen, are choosing to live in refurbished vans or motor homes. Car companies like Honda, Volvo, and others are seizing this opportunity; they are reimagining cars and vans as mobile live/work spaces, seeing in this the future of the automotive industry, especially when these vehicles become self-driving and autonomous.[123] If this trend of vehicle living/freelance working continues to escalate, infrastructure to support such untethered workers may emerge. Right now, many van dwellers park illegally at night, on city streets or in vacant parking lots. In the future, developers may convert city garages into overnight parking lots that offer van or RV dwellers the amenities of modern city apartments, including showers; gyms; and perhaps rooftop BBQs, pools or Jacuzzis, and, of course, plenty of places to charge devices and electric vehicles—as well as fast Wi-Fi. This kind of nomadic living/working arrangement may become the untethered home of the future.

Resilience will be critical in coping with the instability that comes with working untethered; someone following this lifestyle must have the ability to "bounce back" from a setback such as an unexpected layoff or a sudden drop in income when a client doesn't pay, the start-up doesn't find funding, or work hours are suddenly cut back. In the platform economy, the half-life of jobs will continue to grow shorter as an ever-widening swath of full-time jobs becomes contract, gig, or temporary. The willingness and ability to shape-shift—to reinvent oneself to keep up—will be key. The capacity to transfer skills to new areas and to be flexible in terms of time and task switching will be pivotal to adapting to the platform economy and increasingly to untethered work. Life-long learning, and the acquisition of chunks of knowledge and new skills via certifications or digital badges that can be displayed digitally, like on one's LinkedIn profile (as opposed to attaining an entirely new degree), will help ensure that workers' skills stay fresh and relevant within the ever-changing tide of digital transformation. Managing the anxiety that will come with this high-churn digital working world will also be critical. Of course, planning a savings account for emergencies and retirement would also be a good practice, perhaps framed as "long-term self-care" for untethered workers.

As we are seeing, with the movement toward the digitation of everything, experiences mediated by a digital device are becoming the norm. French philosopher Jean-Francois Lyotard discussed the postmodern condition we now find ourselves in and predicted way back during the digital era's inception in 1979 that, as we enter the digital era, any knowledge that cannot be translated into computer language will be abandoned.[124] Increasingly, history seems to be proving him right. Yet we ourselves are not digital; we are still embodied creatures who have evolved over many thousands of years to take in information and—indeed, to take pleasure from—sensual experiences. But now, digital experiences are increasingly disembodied, shaving off only a thin veneer of embodied experience. What happens to the body in this environment, and to embodied experiences like tactility, in an era that prefers the digital? Is ours a post-body, post-human phase, as we drive toward automation, robotics, and virtualization? Or will we become cyborgs, hacking our bodies such that we become half human and half machine, fitted with neural nets so we can always be on? While digital life races forward, what happens to our analog lives as we untether from the body?

CHAPTER 8

UNTETHERED FROM THE BODY

"For God's sake, let us be men
not monkeys minding machines
or sitting with our tails curled
while the machine amuses us, the radio or film or gramophone.
Monkeys with a bland grin on our faces."
—D. H. Lawrence, "Let Us Be Men"

NEW YORK CITY, UPPER EAST SIDE. THE RECTORY

Franklin sat in the kitchen, seemingly wedged between a glass-doored cabinet filled with an incongruous medley of curios and a small kitchen table. Among the items in the cabinet were a tiny midcentury modern house model, a small American flag, an In-N-Out Burger sign, and a little 1960s reindeer ornament. Somehow it all worked. The room blazed with a symphony of color: the small, round dining table was covered with a gay French Provincial yellow-and-white floral-print tablecloth. On his desk, a thick, hand-knotted Persian rug. Franklin's assemblage art in frames salvaged from local thrift shops circled the wall in front of him. He apologized for his garb: he was wearing his version of pajamas—a black t-shirt and flannel pajama bottoms topped by a two-toned red, shiny, silk Chinese robe. He had on the eyeglasses favored by architects like himself—navy blue, owlish modern frames with a slight horn on the rims—through which he peered at the page in front of him. His six-foot-three-inch frame was hunched over a black-and-silver vintage Olivetti typewriter he'd found in the basement of the church downstairs. Puccini's *"O mio babbino caro"* blared loudly from a small speaker above his head. "It helps with the dyslexia," he said. "Keeps the mind focused.... Is that too loud?" I indicated it wasn't, and he hunched over again and leaned closer to the page, squinting slightly as he tapped gingerly with two fingers on the keyboard. *Clack, clack, clack*—there's no autocorrect on these devices. "I'm getting faster at this!" he said with a chuckle. There was a pleasing little *ding* at the end of each sentence; he'd then push a lever to move the carriage over for the next line—*ding, zzzzrp, clack!*—each time he came to the margin of the page. In a couple of minutes, he pulled the half sheet of cream paper out of the machine and, looking pleased, folded it carefully in thirds on the table. He then placed it in an envelope, licked the flap, and sealed it. He turned the envelope over, then startled me with a loud *BANG*. The words "Franklin Vagnone—Twisted Preservation Consulting" now glowed on the white envelope in blood-red stamp ink. With the precision of a scientist conducting an experiment, he carefully lined up a stamp with a painting of a pink skater girl on the upper right corner of the envelope.

Franklin is not only a historic preservationist but also a painter and found-object sculptor, fashioning items he finds at local thrift stores or flea markets into wonderful contemporary art. Though his interest is in historic preservation, which usually comes with a "don't touch" mentality, he takes a tactile approach to his work, such as having fabrics people can touch and furniture they can sit on in the historic homes he curates, with tactility forming an integral part of the visitors' experience. Franklin inspected his creation; It seemingly met with his approval. He then reached over and set it neatly in front of the other three envelopes that were finished and ready to go. I said that I love the fact that he's using a handmade note to thank these various people, one they can see and feel in their hands, as opposed to an email. He looked up at me over the top of the navy-blue glasses, with his warm brown eyes, and said, "It's all about tactility."

It *is* all about tactility. Tactility—our sense of touch—is a core component of what makes us fully human. Our fingers, toes, skin, and extremities are not separated from our surroundings; they instead serve as a kind of "antennae," continually taking in information, that shapes our behaviors and actions in response. Tactility is one of the central ways we experience the world. If we think about our bodies as part of a *system*, we can think of tactility and our environment as forming a closed loop between our bodies and the world around us. Scientists distinguish between two particular "phases" of information processing in this loop between body and environment. The first is the taking in of information, the *sensing*. In the case of touch, we do this via our fingertips or other body parts interacting with our environment; the information about that interaction is then transmitted from the nervous system to the brain in a process called "tactile sensation." The second step is the actual *processing* of that information: our brains interpret what it means and what we are to *do* about it as a result. This second phase is referred to as "tactile processing." For example, say you touch a burner on a hot stove; your brain will process the finger's sense of the heat first, then it decides on a reaction—in this case, you yank your hand back off the stove. Humans use their hands and fingers to actively sense their world, stroking a surface to detect texture, tracing edges to judge a shape, pressing on something to determine its hardness, and so on.[1] Our experience of the world really is all about the tactility.

Media theorist Marshall McLuhan discussed how technologies extend our bodies and our senses, creating new possibilities. In *The Gutenberg Galaxy*, he wrote:

> It would seem that the extension of one or another of our senses by mechanical means [such as the wheel as an extension of the foot; the book, of the eye; the telephone, of the ear], can act as a sort of twist for the kaleidoscope of the entire sensorium [sensory system]. A new combination or ratio of the existing components occurs, and a new mosaic of possible forms presents itself.[2]

The digital era has diminished our sense of touch as a receiver of information, in a world where everything becomes mediated by a device. The difference between technologies then and now is that previous technologies remained analog. A foot walking still touched the ground and moved the human forward; likewise, a wheel abstracted the circular gate of a human foot and its movement, and, touching the ground, moved us forward more quickly. The telephone amplified our voices across space so they could be heard by someone on the end of the line through a receiver pressed to the ear. The television allowed a moving image of our bodies and our voices to be broadcast across space and time. Now, the digital environment may amplify our thoughts and our voices—yet the movement away from the analog leaves the body behind. Although television broadcast bodies, they were the bodies of the few—paid—"stars" and newsmen and women who were amplified out to the many. Now, with "everyone a broadcaster," and with the method of both production and amplification of ourselves a portable, mobile device that goes with us everywhere, and that has become the preferred mode of communication among digital natives, digital signifies a paradigm shift. It represents more than a "new mosaic of possible forms," as McLuhan suggested. Instead, in the digital era, the body and tactility are largely left behind, and the feedback loop between us and our world is significantly changed or broken, compared with that of earlier, analog technologies emanating from the introduction of the printing press or the Industrial Revolution.

Our digital devices and, in particular, virtual reality, are acting as a "new combination" or new twist for our senses, yet our brains—evolved in an analog world—may still function "as if" a virtual event were real. I recently took a delegation of German manufacturers to TiltShift, a company in Los Angeles that creates immersive, 3-D, and virtual reality/augmented reality content. There, with headsets on, they were transported to a virtual beach in Tahiti, where they laughed and played with a beach ball. On the other side of the room, a three-dimensional spaceman floated above their heads. Peals of laughter and shrieks of surprise and joy rang out around the room, as the group of German Baby Boomers tried virtual reality for the first time. One of the demos involved a virtual car: wearing a headset, you could open the door, look in, and manipulate different finishes for the exterior paint and trim (e.g., change the color of the leather seats or dashboard, etc.). The 3-D virtual car was created from actual design data for the physical car. Essentially, the car looked like a real car parked in front of you on the showroom floor, and you could play with it and customize it to your exact specifications. The experience is so convincing that Max, the fellow showing the visitors the demo, warned the visitors to be careful, as he's seen people try to sit down in the virtual car, and then fall to the floor. In VR, the tactile-processing side of the brain begin to interpret the virtual car's visual information as if it were real, directing the body to "sit in that seat" as if it were a physical thing. In a sense, VR presents what looks like physical data, and the brain begins to process it, and the reactions to it, as such.

Younger people who are spending more time in simulated virtual environments may not make the distinction between real and virtual at all. A poll of one thousand thirteen-to-eighteen-year-olds found that 22 percent of the boys and 18 percent of the girls believed that they had never had a real-life adventure; yet a third of the boys claimed that most of the adventures they had had were through gaming and virtual experiences.[3] A quarter believed that an online adventure is just as satisfying as one in real life, and one in five said that their most memorable experiences have been during a video game. This goes to show how key experiences in younger people's lives now take place in (disembodied) virtual worlds.

Haptics is the science of virtual touch. In virtual reality, it includes modeling features like shape, texture, and density so users can "feel" simulated objects.[4]

Yet outside VR, with the average smartphone, haptics, or that sense of touch, is fairly limited. We "press" so-called buttons that are merely digital images on a screen. We swipe, we tap, we pinch—and these kinds of gestures cause the computer to execute various commands. Our phone may vibrate to indicate an incoming call or message. Yet the range of tactility itself—what we can actually *feel* with our fingertips and hands—is limited. Smartphones and tablet devices are still basically "black mirrors" with an invariant surface that is devoid of rich textural experiences, a thin veneer of the vast range of tactile experiences we are capable of experiencing.

Because of our high level of adoption and daily use of these devices, some have suggested that tactility and the physical will be subsumed by the digital. A classic example is the ebook. With the emergence of ebooks and e-readers like the Kindle, many wondered if they spelled the end of paper books.[5] It turns out, to the surprise of many, that has not been the case. At first, ebook sales at out-performed paper book sales on Amazon; yet now, with changes in pricing and the novelty of ebooks wearing off, people are turning back to paper books in droves. Michael Tamblyn, chief executive of Kobo, maker of e-readers and ebooks for book retailers such as WHSmith, Waterstones, and others, has said, "When we first started the business, there was an expectation we would see 50% print/digital within five years [from 2012]. Instead, the ebook market has been plateauing in the 25–30% range."[6] Price certainly is one factor: as ebook prices have risen, and a paperback or even a hardcover book can be purchased for the same price. Yet, for many, price isn't the only factor, or even the deciding factor. Instead, it is *tactility*—and the *pleasure* one takes in a physical book—that is the main reason many prefer a paper book. Science writer Brian Keim, in his *Wired* article titled "Why the Smart Reading Devices of the Future May Be—Paper," describes it this way:

> Paper books were supposed to be dead by now. For years, information theorists, marketers, and early adopters have told us their demise was imminent. IKEA even redesigned a bookshelf to hold something other than books. Yet in a world of screen ubiquity, many people still prefer to do their serious reading on paper. Count me among them. When I need to read deeply—when I want to lose myself in a story or an intellectual journey, when focus and comprehension are paramount—I still turn to paper. Something just feels fundamentally richer about reading on it. And researchers are starting to think there's something to this feeling.[7]

Tactility, and the sensuality tied to touch, is one of the fundamental pleasures of being human, and some are lamenting its reduction in the digital era. One of these is Donavan Freberg, photographer and son of famous New York satirist and advertising creative Stan Freberg. He says:

> I actually think this is the #1 thing lacking from today's world. Pleasure. We all have these tiny, mini-dopamine hits of "likes" and "shares" but where is the actual pleasure? The dirty, gritty, delicious, raw and real pleasure? It's all becoming a virtual, sanitized, dull, substitute. Like a dystopian sci-fi novel that we are all starring in, playing to an empty house of virtual guests.[8]

Like Brandon Keim's notion of "this feeling" tied to paper books, Donavan is putting his finger on something that seems to be getting lost in the digitization of everything, and that something is the body. Two hundred thousand or so years of sensory adaptation by humans isn't going to disappear within the ten or so short years since the invention of the iPhone. Tactility is ingrained in our DNA. Yet we increasingly try to control, shape, and discipline the body through our technologies.[9] Part of this has to do with the forces of civilization as we've evolved from nomadic hunter-gatherers to more stable forms of existence in cities. For modern city dwellers, controlling the body and bodily functions enables us to coexist in such close quarters together over long periods of time. Yet our animalistic instincts are never fully tamed; they persist, sometimes to be expressed in covert and markedly uncivilized ways.

CIVILIZING THE BODY

Walking or driving through the city, one encounters row upon row of tents, punctuated by makeshift blue-tarp shelters and piles of garbage and stacks of boxes; huddles of men squat or sit on the ground. One man leans over a fire hydrant and pours a cup of water over his head for a makeshift shower. The air hangs heavy with the stench of urine and feces, the source of the Hepatitis A outbreak beginning to rage across this and other city centers in Southern California. Were this a tribal hunter-gatherer society, one would expect to see tents and people huddled outside and perhaps bodily excrements somewhere nearby; but this is Los Angeles, where, on any given night, somewhere north of 52,000 men, women, and children live on the streets, sleeping in tents, in cars, on sidewalks, and in emergency shelters like the Midnight Mission.[10] Some wander along, schizophrenic, muttering to themselves or screaming at passersby or at no one in particular; others lie half hidden within the indentations of buildings along the sidewalk, drifting in and out of a haze of heroin, their heads lolling lazily on their necks. Most are dirty; their clothes, ill-fitting or torn; hair, matted or chopped off or even pulled out—some wear no clothes at all. These bodies are thought uncivilized, and they are treated as such: residents and business owners discuss ways to clothe, house, feed, and get medical and psychiatric care to them. Or how to get them out of sight. Many of the homeless have been offered shelter and have turned it down, preferring instead to live a lifestyle free of society's expectations and constraints, modern-day Bedouins, free to up and move at any time to new, seemingly better locations. In some cities, less than 1 percent agree to go to shelters when offered. "I don't trust no shelters," a homeless woman named Sarah in New York said.[11] "Stuff happens there all the time." Facebook groups for Downtown LA are filled with local residents complaining about the homeless defecating on the sidewalks, loitering in front of businesses, drumming late into the night outside their expensive apartments, and sometimes becoming violent. Some contractors are apparently constructing bridges between their buildings, to allow the luxury residents the ability to traverse the street while avoiding their homeless neighbors below, marking a physical separation between civilized and uncivilized bodies.[12]

Cities, and civilizations in general, have served to hide, control, and regulate bodies and bodily functions, through laws, regulations, and social norms, reshaping our sensory experience of the world. Part of civilization is the development and codification of bodies of knowledge, psychiatry being one of these. The *Diagnostic and Statistical Manual of Mental Disorders* is one example of a body of knowledge that controls and regulates bodies.[13] The *DSM* was first developed by the American Psychiatric Association in 1952.[14] Now its fifth iteration, the *DSM-5*, categorizes the ever expanding and contracting list of mental disorders, and is used by psychiatrists, psychologists, and other counselors to standardize diagnostic criteria for patients. In it, not bathing or caring for the body are potential symptoms of a mental disorder, which lands one into an involuntary commitment in a mental hospital; in California, someone who is considered "unable to care for the self" or "gravely disabled" is subject to what is referred to as a "5150 hold" for seventy-two hours.

Cities themselves are technologies, or, more accurately, technological systems, that reshape and regulate bodies as well. In 1912, sociologist Georg

Simmel explored the ways that cities have reshaped our senses. As people migrated from farms to cities, he found that the emphasis on the different senses had changed:

> Social life in the large city as compared with the towns shows a great preponderance of occasions to *see* rather than to *hear* people. One explanation lies in the fact that the person in the town is acquainted with nearly all the people he meets. With these he exchanges a word or a glance, and their countenance represents to him not merely the visible but indeed the entire personality. Another reason of special significance is the development of public means of transportation. Before the appearance of omnibuses, railroads, and street cars in the nineteenth century, men were not in a situation where for periods of minutes or hours they could or must look at each other without talking to one another. Modern social life increases in ever growing degree the role of mere visual impression.[15]

What this shows us is that technologies can reshape not only *where* we live but also *how*, and that our environment changes our embodied experience of the world.

These kinds of civilizing factors can be traced back to our earliest days of dwelling in towns. During the Middle Ages, norms about our embodied lives began to be codified in books and in emerging social norms, as we had to figure out ways to live in harmony in close proximity to one another. Books were written then on etiquette, and social norms emerged around the body and bodily functions, which changed how people comported themselves. Sociologist Norbert Elias explored this notion in the early 1900s at the British Museum, where he researched the etymology of words like *civilization* and *civilized*, which led him all the way back to early medieval and Renaissance manuscripts. Elias's studies took place during the dawn of the industrial era, when the move from rural to urban centers was in full swing. Through his historical research, Elias noted that the carnal side of human affairs having to do with the body—including things like eating, elimination, sexuality, and violence—had all been drastically transformed during and since the Middle Ages. The "civilizing processes" of urbanization resulted in these kinds of bodily acts becoming increasingly controlled in public or moved "behind the scenes," as thresholds of shame and revulsion steadily rose, along with social controls against vulgar bodily displays. During this same time, noted psychotherapist Sigmund Freud was hard at work on his psychoanalytic theory, which was influenced by the emerging field of physics. Freud described the ultimate "goal" as taming or civilizing the body and its unabashed seeking of pleasure (i.e., "the pleasure principle"), saying we should instead channel these drives into prosocial pursuits, thereby allowing the super-ego's[16] (i.e., the conscious "judging" part of our mind) ultimate triumph over the id (i.e., the immature, pleasure-seeking part). Those who do not successfully traverse the stages of psychosocial development, moving through fixations with the body's various erogenous zones, or pleasure centers—the oral, the anal, and, finally, the genital—became candidates ripe for the development of neuroses, hysteria, and other mental ailments. In his essay "'Civilizing' Sexual Morality and Modern Nervous Illness," Freud theorized that the civilizing forces that aim to control the body—particularly the sexual drives via cultural mores—can lead to repression, the outcome of which is neurosis. Freud believed that without an outlet for drives that are pleasurable for the body, other "substitute pleasures" would develop. In his view, bodily instincts, like the sexual drive, in and of themselves don't cause problems; it is when these instincts interact with the outside world, with its social norms and its expectation of *repression* of instincts, that mental illness ensues.[17]

After Freud, the civilizing processes around the body changed; after the destruction of World War II, postmodern and post-structural sociologists and philosophers in France took up the mantle to think about a society they saw vastly changing before them. These philosophers thought about the impact of civilizing processes on the body in the emerging age of television. French philosopher Michel Foucault's influential book on the regulation of the body, *Discipline and Punish*,[18] and sociologist Jean Baudrillard's analysis of television and "the spectacle" helped people better understand how civilizing forces had been transformed from the print era through the electronic era of television. In the electronic era, in Baudrillard's view, technology replaces capital (i.e., manufacturing and production of things) as images; information and "signs" replace the production of goods. This shift brought with it a propensity toward simulation and simulacra, a movement on a continuum that shifts from the real toward a *representation* of the real and onward still further, toward something that never had any "real" referent at all outside of television—something he calls a simulacra. Baudrillard refers to the simulacra as something that is always already reproduced. He uses as an example tract homes, where there is no original, or the endless replication of 1980s workout videos. In his view, television images, and in particular, television news, doesn't just reflect reality but actually creates it, shaping audiences and their views along the way.[19] Baudrillard identified four phases of the image as it moves toward simulacra, where there is no reference point in reality; they are as follows:

(1) It is the reflection of a basic reality.
(2) It masks and perverts a basic reality.
(3) It masks the absence of a basic reality.
(4) It bears no relation to any reality whatever; it is its own pure simulacrum.[20]

In Baudrillard's view, the map is not only not the territory but instead it actually *precedes* the territory. In this view, television supports particular ideological views of self and behavior that serve as civilizing forces. In Baudrillard's *Illusion of the End*, he discusses how the boundaries between what is *real* and what is simulated begin to blur. As he put it:

> Right at the very heart of news, history threatens to disappear. At the heart of hi-fi, music threatens to disappear. At the heart of experimentation, the object of science threatens to disappear. At the heart of pornography, sexuality threatens to disappear. Everywhere we find the same stereophonic effect, the same effect of absolute proximity to the real, the same effect of simulation.[21]

Baudrillard's work was in response to the television era, the beginning of our movement toward what he called the hyperreal, where everything is always already reproduced and there is no longer any original remaining. For example, capital is one thing our society has been tethered to, and it, too, has been separated from its physical nature (e.g., via the cryptocurrencies discussed previously). Within a classical capitalist society, capital and relations of labor provide the structure for social relations. Yet today, in the society of the digital era, as everything becomes virtualized—including the economy—simulation is increasingly the norm. Consequently, our social relations are structured by simulations, signs (like brands), and codes. The current rise in urbanization has entailed a need for stricter social codes. When this intensification of civilizing factors is coupled with virtualization and simulation (via the mass adoption of digital technologies), the body itself threatens to disappear. This means that in a virtualized world, the body increasingly has no referent in reality.

Before we explore this idea of a body without a real-life referent, we must first analyze the systems that caused this disconnect, including the shifting of populations from rural and suburban areas to city centers. Since the industrial era, urbanization has intensified, as the population moved to seek jobs, opportunities, and the amenities available within cities. In 1960, one-third of the population lived in urban areas; now, according to the United Nations, globally, the percentage of urban dwellers is at 55 percent of the population, and this number is projected to grow to 68 percent by 2050.[22] Digital technologies and social media have also expanded exponentially, as more and more socialization takes place over digital networks. Digitization coupled with urbanization has meant that this emphasis on the visual (which we've historically seen as an outcome of urban living, as explored by Simmel) has amplified while the emphasis on tactility and the body has diminished. Online, our growing emphasis on the visual has expanded as connection speed and bandwidth have increased, shortening the "latency" or wait time to download a picture or a video. This has meant that pictures and videos can now be uploaded and viewed almost instantaneously. Everything from dating apps like Tinder to visually intensive social media like Instagram, Snapchat, or Facebook, to YouTube and texting apps serves to expand our digitized visual culture exponentially. They augment people's desire and ability to "see" one another, even providing peaks behind the curtain, or "backstage," into people's private lives in a way not possible before.

Another civilizing force that is amplifying as we move from an analog culture to a digital one is around what Baudrillard termed "the disgusting." Baudrillard discussed how the civilizing forces of society intensified in cities, where bodily functions and other "uncivilized behaviors," like sexuality and violence, were socially proscribed, relegated to what he calls "the disgusting." In the television era, the disgusting was packaged up and sold back to us in the form of violent news coverage, reality TV, and tabloid talk shows like *Maury* and *The Steve Wilkos Show*—the latter of which routinely featured out-of-control guests fighting and acting out on stage, in episodes like "Is My Mother Sleeping with the Man I Love?" These kinds of programs serve as outlets for our baser instincts—as Freud predicted we would need, well before the advent of television—including violence and sexual behaviors, that is, embodied behaviors that "polite society" does not approved of, a manifestation of Baudrillard's "the disgusting."[23]

Baudrillard died prior to the advent of the digital era, so he did not live to see its impacts. But in a world where instincts of the body are increasingly controlled, and life increasingly digitized, his notion of "the disgusting" has been amplified. During the early television era, broadcasts of "the disgusting" were constrained by Federal Communications Commission (FCC) regulations, which limited the kinds of sexual or violent content one could air across broadcast airwaves. Over time, television and cable networks were able to loosen these strictures, yet hardcore sexual and violent content remained verboten. As time goes on, though, recent televised depictions are increasingly hard-core and pornographic, as cable programs vie to compete with digital content. Social media, the internet, and the dark web have allowed for the propagation of disgusting content, opening the floodgates to the expression of hardcore expressions of violence and sexuality. Videos of schoolyard or after-school fights have become popular, and extreme violence has become a recurring theme in video games and pornography. A vast array of rude and disgusting behaviors are readily available for viewing online, from zit popping on YouTube to live-streamed videos of murders and suicides that have cropped up on Facebook Live. In one case, popular YouTuber Logan Paul, the younger brother of Team 10's Jake Paul (Team 10 being the über-popular YouTube crew of content creators followed by millions of teens and tweens), uploaded a video for his 15 million (mostly underage) subscribers showing him "accidently" coming across the corpse of a suicide victim in Aokigahara, Japan's infamous "Suicide Forest."[24] In the video, he calls the body "it" and makes jokes about it. The video was seen by almost 6.5 million viewers before it was taken down by Paul himself in response to protests that flared up by upset viewers. Logan Paul was following the trend of creating increasingly extreme content to garner attention in the noisy world of social media.

"The disgusting" in terms of sexuality is also readily available online—much of it for free—in the form of pornographic materials. The infamous "2 Girls, 1 Cup" video went viral for its absolutely debased content of (apparently) eating feces.[25] Sexuality has become interactive, with simulated bodies available for purchase in the form of virtual and robotic "dolls" with which people are able to act out fantasies that many real women might find distasteful. While such virtualized women cannot be psychologically and physically harmed in the same way as humans would be, their availability online can create tastes that may extend to real women and girls in the offline world. In this way, digital networks facilitate "the disgusting," for instance, in the form of the sex trafficking, with victims that include girls and boys (often from countries like the Philippines), who are made available for online sex tourists on live webcam streams or via child porn on the dark web.[26]

Given the lack of physical proximity and the relative anonymity offered by the internet, the difficulty of controlling content when no one is in charge and the network spans national borders, and the ability to virtualize "the disgusting," perhaps its amplification online was inevitable. It has proven a vexing issue—both for lawmakers and for parents trying to shield their children from disgusting content, particularly when it's so easily accessed on their connected smartphone.

BODY LANGUAGE IN A DISEMBODIED WORLD

The erasure of bodies in a digitized world has also led to other surprising or unexpected impacts offline. Growing up gazing at screens from an early age has impacts real bodies as communication vehicles. Communicating through devices necessarily means spending less time looking at faces, which leads to a deficit in being able to "read people." Reading people is the subtle but important "soft skill" of being able to detect what's *not* being said or, in other words, what's not being said verbally—by looking at and properly interpreting the nonverbal signals of the other person's (or people's) body language. Some have suggested more than 90 percent of communication is nonverbal.[27] Being able to read people, and to understand one's own emotions and emotional expressions, are aspects of what's been called "emotional intelligence."[28] In a piece he wrote for the *Wall Street Journal*, English professor Mark Bauerlein talks about some of the changes he's noticed in this regard in his classrooms at college, saying that younger generations who grew up digital are "all thumbs" when it comes to reading the nonverbal signals of others:

> We live in a culture where young people—outfitted with iPhone and laptop and devoting hours every evening from age 10 onward to messaging of one kind and another—are ever less likely to develop the "silent fluency" that comes from face-to-face interaction. It is a skill that we all must learn, in actual social settings, from people (often older) who are adept in the idiom. As text-centered messaging increases, such occasions diminish. The digital natives improve their adroitness at the keyboard, but when it comes to their capacity to "read" the behavior of others, they are all thumbs.[29]

Young folks now "are all thumbs" when it comes to reading the behavior of others because they are simply getting less practice at it. Studies have found that among teens, online interaction greatly reduces face-to-face social interaction.[30]

Face-to-face time drops by almost thirty minutes for every hour a person spends on a computer.[31] On average, the more time spent on the internet, the less time spent with friends, family, and colleagues in person.[32] Studies have also found a connection between the increased use of technology for communication and poor social skills among college students, and also an increase in social anxiety.[33]

Communicating in a mediated way also means a lessened need for *making* emotion faces. As I was preparing to teach a class one day at the University of Southern California, I overheard a conversation between two girls: "How's your internship going?" one asked. "It's fine," the other replied. "The only thing is— they talked to me the other day. . . . Apparently, I'm not giving them the kind of emotional responses they're expecting. So I figured out a way around it: I just envision a delicious pizza, and then they see the face they're expecting to see." To me, this conversation says it all when it comes to nonverbal communication in face-to-face encounters of many digital natives. Nowadays, emojis are used as a kind of "prosthetic emotion" that stands in for the physical in digital environments. Emojis are a visual shorthand for the smiles, laughter, tears, and other emotion faces previously displayed physically, in person. As a result, digital natives have less need for—and thus less experience with—*making* emotion faces of their own. As my student above showed, she *manufactured* a face to suit what she thought her boss wanted to see, her own analog version of a prosthetic emotion. Like Dr. Bauerlein, I've also noticed a marked lack of emotion faces in students in recent years, compared to, say, ten years ago, and other professors I know have noted the same. Professors look to their students' facial feedback as a way to gauge levels of interest and understanding. Now, instead of a laugh, we see a neutral face; instead of the glow of understanding, we're met with a neutral face. This lack of facial feedback has unintended consequences: First, physically smiling results in a kind of positive feedback to the brain that can actually boost mood; research has found that the brain interprets one's smile to mean "I'm happy," so the pleasure centers in the brain are then activated, lifting one's actual mood to meet that thought.[34] Smiling also results in lowered levels of stress. So the bottom line is, as digital natives are making less physical emotion faces— particularly happy, smiling ones—their brains are not getting the emotional "lift," and thus they may be muting their own potential for a positive mood. A second unintended consequence is that shy kids may use mediated communication as an emotional crutch, as way to avoid face-to-face contact, which itself becomes a self-reinforcing feedback loop. Research has found that shy teens— those who, when interacting with others face-to-face, experience social anxiety, blush, or stammer in conversations—actually spend *more* time online, and thus have even less practice in face-to-face communication skills.[35] The device thus becomes a way for them to avoid interactions "in real life," hence they don't get better at communicating in person, a skill set that can only be learned through experience. The end result is decreasing emotional intelligence among digital natives, being "all thumbs" at reading the emotions of others (as Professor Bauerlein noted), or failing to emote themselves. They simply need more practice with speaking face-to-face without a device mediating the conversation, since conversation is both an art and a skill.

Why is all of this important? Because emotional intelligence (EQ)—the ability to read others' nonverbal emotional expressions through body language, and the ability to understand one's own emotions—has been found to be a key factor in success. A long-term study of the career trajectories of graduates found that social and emotional abilities were four times more important than IQ in determining professional success and prestige.[36] Areas of the brain having to do with executive functions (i.e., capacities that allow people to control and coordinate thoughts and behavior) and social cognitive skills (e.g., the ability to discern another's emotions) are developed during adolescence; thus, teens who are spending much more time staring at screens (compared to earlier generations) are not only not developing these areas to the same extent but also, in fact, may have difficulty "catching up" later, since the "window" for establishing this area of the brain may have been missed.[37] The research suggests that long-term excessive electronic exposure can have severe consequences to the development of nonverbal communication skills, empathy, and interpersonal relations. Those who spend more time staring at screens—particularly playing violent video games—may even "turn off" the switch to empathy in their brains.[38] This lack of empathy may lead to actual violence to physical bodies, or to a lack of helping behaviors in a crisis, as we've seen in earlier chapters. Neuroscience researchers have suggested that violent computer games may reduce reactivity of the frontal brain areas, and they say that the long-term effects resemble the patterns of those prone to violence.[39] One study found that just ten minutes of violent video-game play was enough to reduce helping behavior right after game play, since it desensitized the gamers to the pain or suffering of others.[40] Another found a similar lowering of empathy and concluded that chronic exposure to violent video games also lowers the levels at which frequent game players notice the emotion faces of others, as they tend to "overlook" others' pained expressions.[41] The researchers concluded that these frequent players simply became "numb" to the expressed emotions of others. People who claim that video gaming is "just a game" may be overlooking some of the potential negative outcomes of violent video games on the emotional and cognitive development of young people who play them, and the impacts on their ability to read the emotion faces of others—impacts that may negatively impact their future path to adulthood.

Another important aspect of embodied communication is the development of trust, which is the cornerstone of all relationships, be they business or personal. Trust has traditionally been built through the subtle dance of reading nonverbal signs during face-to-face encounters. Upon a first meeting, we look for that "firm handshake," unwavering eye contact, or a friendly smile—all of which are examples of what sociologist Erving Goffman calls the "sign activity" of the other person.[42] Goffman identified two kinds of sign activity: the "expression given" and the "expression given off." The expression given involves verbal communication (i.e., what people *say*). The expression given off is expressed through such things as clothing, appearance, sex, age, racial characteristics, size, looks, posture, speech patterns, bodily gestures, and so on. Goffman's model is dramaturgical, that is, he sees life like a play: he calls people "actors," and the activities of a person that are designed to influence another, a "performance." Through a positive verbal and nonverbal interaction, we create a favorable first impression of someone during our initial encounter, or performance—an impression that lasts. A weak handshake, a lack of eye contact, or being "shifty eyed" can create an impression of being a person who is less competent or not trustworthy.[43] There is also a moral aspect to every performance, that is, we assume that the actor is who he says he is. For example, if a person comes into your room at the hospital and he is wearing a white coat and stethoscope, you assume that he is a doctor and not someone *posing* as a doctor. People are, however, aware that others may be trying to present a favorable image of themselves, such as trying to put their best foot forward. To form impressions, people divide an actor's performance into two parts: the verbal language, which is relatively easy for the actor to manipulate, and the nonverbal signs given off. These signs provide a glimpse into the actor's possible hidden motives, background, veracity, and so on, and they are often given more weight than the verbal messages. People tend to believe that signs given off are less intentional and thus less controllable by the actor; therefore, the signs given off may reveal "hidden" information that the actor is not volunteering.

The signs given off are hidden in most digital communication, and, as discussed previously, digital natives have less experience both giving and giving off signs in person, since much of their communication is mediated. The lack of eye contact and diminished ability to "signal" emotional responses, which are common among digital natives, may be disconcerting to others, particularly older individuals. Even habitual behaviors like attending to text messages and checking alerts on phones during meetings or dates can send out (perhaps unintentional) nonverbal signals of a lack of interest, a lack of respect, or boredom—particularly to older people who came of age in a face-to-face world and are used to different communication norms. Beyond causing interpersonal difficulties, the repercussions of this tendency among digital natives can extend into their future career paths. Some have even suggested that the diminished ability to read and send nonverbal cues makes digital natives perhaps ill-suited for high-trust professions that involve the establishment of face-to-face relationships.[44] Also, not having bodies present online can erode trust in another way, by allowing bad actors to step in and manipulate people for their own selfish or nefarious gains. "Catfishing" is the perfect example of this, and the case of Army Colonel Kassem Saleh is one of the most egregious:

Fifty women gathered in June 2003 at a television news conference to announce that they had all been duped by a man they had met online: US Army Col. Kassem Saleh, a military officer whom each had met via an online dating site, had been wooing all fifty women simultaneously, even going so far as to propose to many of them, despite the fact that he was already married to another woman. At least two of the unwitting women had already bought wedding gowns before discovering the ruse. One woman called Colonel Saleh's email love letters "intoxicating," and another said they were "more romantic than the works of poets William Butler Yeats or Robert Browning." Saleh allegedly wrote to one of his many mistresses, "You are my world, my life, my love and my universe."[45]

Online communication can facilitate deceptive communication and predatory relationships, as mentioned in another chapter, since people aren't as easily able to "fact-check" identities against face-to-face interactions with them. People can (and do) create entirely fake online personae designed to "lure" others into relationships, sometimes purely for the attention, but often as a way to con people out of large sums of money, which is referred to as "catfishing." Typically tipped off by women's "single" status on Facebook, con men approach women (though sometimes men are the targets) by posing as strapping young men who are interested in a relationship. (Often, they pose as military men posted in the Middle East, which would explain their lack of ability to meet in person.) Once the victim is on the hook, requests for increasingly large sums of money ensue. Sarah, a forty-six-year-old woman, met a catfish who was going by the name of Chris Olsen on an online dating service. Over seventeen months, she sent him over $1.4 million from her inheritance to accounts in Africa via Western Union.[46] Manti Te'o, a standout senior football player at Notre Dame University, became another unwitting victim of catfishing. In 2013, he had a bright future ahead of him in the NFL, until he became embroiled in controversy when it was revealed that the woman he was dating online was actually a male acquaintance who had fallen in love with him and had concealed his true identity.[47] Te'o's involvement romantically with a man caused reputational damage, as the media labeled it a hoax he must've been in on, causing an uproar among fans and the media.[48] He entered the NFL combine under a cloud of doubt and scrutiny from recruiters; every one of them asked him about what had happened. Afterward, he fell from projected first-round draft pick to the mid-second round, decreasing his salary and signing bonus by at least half while also losing a guaranteed contract. His story underscores how the inability to identify the person one is talking to online due to a lack of physical proximity can open the door to a disastrous combination of projection and deception, ultimately leading to disappointment, heartbreak, and potentially substantial financial loss for unwitting victims.

Some catfish go online to deceive others as a ploy for attention, like the perpetrator in Manti Te'o's case. Yet now, the lure of love is being used as bait to hook lonely hearts on places like Facebook, in an effort to con targets out of money, sometimes to the tune of tens of thousands of dollars. As noted earlier, catfish often pose as army men stationed overseas, a fact that is somewhat difficult to confirm, since face-to-face "dates" are rendered impossible by the distance. This has turned out to be a successful ploy for organized crime rings, some of which are located in parts of Africa. Having been used as a pawn in this con game, General John F. Campbell felt compelled to post a disclaimer on his Facebook account after more than seven hundred fake online profiles that purported to be him were discovered, having been created by online scammers. "I am happily married and my wife Ann is very much alive and my children do not need money for any medical procedures," Campbell wrote.[49] "I will NEVER ask you to send money. . . . I DO NOT use any dating sites, Skype, Google Plus, Yahoo! Messenger, or any other account," he continued. A lack of face-to-face communication to confirm people's identities can lure the lonely and the lovelorn into catfishing schemes, which are a kind of predatory relationship.

Given the complexities of modern urban life and the immersion in digital technologies, others are untethering from embodied relationships for other reasons, seeking to strike up relationships not with others online but with digital boyfriends or girlfriends. In Japan, nearly 70 percent of unmarried men and 60 percent of unmarried women aren't in relationships. Some are turning to virtual partners to fill the gap. Similar to the movie *Her*, in which untethered and slightly melancholic city dweller Theodore Twombly falls in love with his operating system, games like LovePlus, played on the pocket-sized Nintendo DS, provide young male users with virtual girlfriends. The women can be programmed to suit the desires of their real-life partners. The young men go out on "dates" with their Rinkos (one of three choices in the game), and some profess their love—at least one has even "married" Nene, his virtual Love Plus companion.[50] Players can take pictures with their "girlfriends," which can be posted on Facebook or other social media sites. LovePlus is spreading: An English-language version has attracted players now in the United States and other countries.[51]

Others are untethering from face-to-face relationships altogether, preferring digital company instead, if any at all. In Japan, an entire subset of adolescent males are completely severing ties with any embodied communication at all, even with their families, preferring to stay in their room and play video games, listen to music, or engage in other digital activities. This has become so commonplace that the Japanese have a name for it: *hikikomori*, which literally translates to "pulling inward, being confined."[52] The mothers of these boys leave ramen or other food for them outside their doors; in some cases, the parents haven't seen the boys in years.[53] Some estimate the number of hikikomori at between 700,000 and a million. Most are depressed or anxious, and an estimated half have been violent toward their parents. As Japan continues to "disembody," its population has dropped by a million in the past three years alone, reaching the lowest level in 118 years and prompting economists to call this a "demographic time bomb."[54] This time bomb has serious ramifications for Japan's future because, as older members "age out" of certain roles and need to be replaced, young people don't or won't step up to fill vacated roles in society—at work, in the government, as parents, and as active community members upon whom societies depend to continue functioning properly.[55]

One reason the hikikomori are able to stay in their rooms for years on end is because they are getting some level of social needs met via virtual connectivity with others—in video games, for example. As more of social life becomes virtualized in this way, it will become harder and harder to tell real bodies from fake. Perhaps in the future, kids who grew up with virtualized bodies (e.g., socializing in video games or in other virtual environments) won't make a distinction between real and fake at all. As was discussed at length in an earlier chapter, it was recently revealed that a popular social media influencer who had amassed 1.2 million Instagram followers wasn't a real person. Cathy Hackl, coauthor of *Marketing New Realities*—which deals with using augmented and virtual reality for marketing—writes:

> Let me introduce you to Lil Miquela: The stylish, 19-year-old model from Downey, Calif., leads an enviable, carefree lifestyle—skateboarding with friends, visiting New York for fashion shoots and attending the Coachella music festival, among other fun activities. With her 1.2 million Instagram followers, Lil Miquela has become an influencer, working for brands such as Prada, Diesel and Moncler. But as Lil Miquela's fans learned in April (and as other people had previously suspected), she is not real. She's a CGI—computer-generated image—created by a Los Angeles–based computer-software firm. (*Wired* magazine described the revelation as "postmodern performance art.") Lil Miquela is a high-profile example of the emerging phenomena of CGI influencers and their close cousin, the "digital human."[56]

Like automated factory workers, CGI social media influencers are the perfect employees: They never take a break, never go on strike, never leave for another studio or producer, and never OD on opioids. They are pure profit machines. Computer-generated social media influencers like Lil Miquela are projected to become a $2 billion industry by the year 2020.[57] Not having the physical constraints of actual bodies, CGI bodies can be optimized, tweaked, and perfected—and exaggerated in proportion—to meet young digital natives' desire for the more extreme online. These bodies can be shaped in particular, unique ways to call attention to brands in a noisy digital world. With tastes for bodies being driven by the cartoonish imagery of virtual bodies in video games, these "digital humans," avatars who mimic us but are actually hyperreal simulacra of ourselves, pose many new ethical and other questions, including whether an AI agent like Lil Miquela (and others, as they become even more sophisticated and harder to identify) should have to reveal to consumers their "fake human" status. As touched upon earlier, the blending of real and fake bodies online—and the filtering and tweaking of images of real bodies to make them unreal, using Snapchat and other such apps—is also having an impact, particularly on real bodies, as plastic surgeons are seeing a surge in the number of young women coming to their offices with an interest in getting facial plastic surgery to look more like their filtered photos.[58] One can wonder what other effects fake bodies will have on real bodies, and what body modifications young folks will seek out in the future as they try to bring their analog bodies more in line with the fantastical bodies they see and increasingly spend time with online, in virtualized settings.

DIGITAL IMPACTS ON ANALOG BODIES

"I'm not a man! I'm not a beast! I'm about as shapeless as the man in the moon!" shouted Quasimodo, perhaps the world's most well-known "hunchback," at the beautiful Esmeralda, who was played by the newly discovered Maureen O'Hara in the 1939 film *The Hunchback of Notre Dame.*[59] The medical term for Quasimodo's back deformity, sometimes also referred to as a "dowager's hump," is kyphosis, a condition stemming from injury or other degenerative diseases like arthritis. Now, young folks are beginning to show up in doctor's offices with a new form of "hunchback." Eighty-four percent of teens now complain of back problems from being slumped over their phones. Spine surgeon Dr. Kenneth Hansraj has said that although our heads weigh between ten and twelve pounds, as we angle them downward to look at our phones, the effective weight on our necks increases—from twenty-seven pounds at a fifteen-degree angle, to about sixty pounds at a sixty-degree angle—resulting in a condition some have (half-jokingly) termed "text neck."[60] Tendinitis is also flaring up among those who use the phone a lot for activities like texting. The latter condition is an inflammation of the tendons that can cause pain in the hands and wrist. Other repetitive-movement-type injuries, such as carpal tunnel syndrome, are also beginning to show up among those who are frequent texters.[61]

The expansion of time spent with digital devices has been problematic for physical bodies in other ways. For example, kids used to ride their bikes to school and around the neighborhood to play. Now that is not such a common pastime. In fact, one shocked mother noted on a child-rearing blog that kids who were eight-to-twelve-years-old still had training wheels on their bikes. When she asked the other mothers why, the answers included: "Kids aren't riding bikes around the neighborhood anymore, so [they] don't have the same motivation to learn to ride."[62] Others referenced their own fears about their children's safety: One mentioned that they had a playdate to ride bicycles around on a tennis court. Less bike riding and outdoor play means less gripping handlebars. Kids are also not doing other gripping activities outdoors, such as mowing the lawn. As a result, younger adults are now showing a marked decrease in grip strength in their hands when compared to earlier generations. In a study of Americans aged twenty to thirty-four, occupational therapists found that men younger than thirty have significantly weaker hand grips than their counterparts did in 1985.[63] The same was true of women aged twenty to twenty-four. In 1985, men aged twenty to twenty-four had an average right-handed grip of 121 pounds and left-handed grip of 105 pounds. Today, men in that age group have grips of only 101 and 99 pounds, respectively. And it's not limited to that particular age bracket; in fact, men between the ages of twenty-five and twenty-nine posted losses of 26 and 19 pounds, too. Grip strength is important, as it is an indicator of overall good health, since weakness is a sign of frailty. Particularly as adults age, grip strength is also an important predictor of certain health outcomes, including mortality, disability, health complications, and increased lengths of hospital stays.[64] Additionally, a weak grip is associated with increased risks of heart attacks and strokes, and shorter survival times.[65]

A lack of physical activity has also led to an increase in obesity and a rise in metabolic syndrome, which is a cluster of symptoms that includes increased blood pressure, high blood sugar, excess body fat around the waist, and abnormal cholesterol or triglyceride levels. Metabolic syndrome has been linked to an increase in the risk of heart disease, stroke, and diabetes;[66] furthermore, it raises the likelihood of death by cardiovascular disease by 52 percent.[67] People who spend more time in front of computers have a higher obesity risk, even if they think they get enough exercise during the week. Researchers asked adults about their levels of physical activity, internet and computer use during leisure time, and other sedentary activities (such as reading, talking on the phone, playing video games, or watching television). They found that those with the highest levels of computer use were one and a half times more likely to be overweight, and two and a half times more likely to be obese, than were people who didn't use a computer at all. Those who had high levels of computer use were also more likely to report lower levels of physical activity and were two and a half times more likely to engage in more than five hours a day of other sedentary activities.[68] Likewise, teens who spend a lot of time at the computer or on devices are more likely to be overweight or obese than are those who spend no time in front of the computer.[69] This is likely due to increased eating of unhealthy foods, high-calorie soft drinks, and sleep deprivation, all of which are risk factors that increase the likelihood of obesity, especially combined with the sedentary activity of spending high amounts of time in front of a screen.

Another aspect of the body that digital devices impact is sleep. Sleep is important because it allows the brain to rest and restore itself. Sleep deprivation can actually lead to psychosis and even death. Other impacts of sleep deprivation include an inability to process glucose as efficiently as those who get eight hours of sleep, which means that the sleep-deprived have an increased likelihood of developing type 2 diabetes.[70] A 2014 National Sleep Foundation poll found that 72 percent of teens bring their cell phones into their bedrooms and use them when they are trying to go to sleep, with texting being the most popular activity before bedtime.[71] Twenty-eight percent leave their phones on while sleeping, only to be awakened at night by texts, calls, or emails.[72] Another study found that 98 percent of teens are sending texts after 8:00 p.m., and 70 percent sent a text between 10:00 p.m. and 5:59 a.m.[73] Those who texted in the hour before bed were most likely to say that they were sleepy, and that they woke up unrefreshed after a night's sleep.[74] Teens who lost sleep due to cell phone use at night ended up with increased depressive symptoms, lowered self-esteem, and a decrease in coping skills.[75] As we face a crisis of mental health in the United States, solutions like getting more sleep by removing devices from kids' and teens' (and even adults') bedrooms at night, to allow for restful sleep, may have a major influence on mental and physical health.

Overall, the message is that despite living in an increasingly digital world, bodies still matter. In spite of utopian sci-fi writing that presents a future in which everyone is jacked into a pleasing virtual-reality matrix and freed of "annoying" physical labor (as tech utopists often seem to frame it), we are still, at the core, embodied creatures. Our situational awareness has evolved to protect those bodies, to keep us alive in times of threat. Situational awareness is composed of three components: perception, comprehension, and anticipation.[76] In essence, we are aware of what's around us in the environment; we comprehend whether or not it's a threat; then we anticipate the next steps (e. g., we see something near us, realize it's a bear, anticipate whether it may attack us, and then plan our escape). Two terrifying viral videos on social media illustrate the importance of situational awareness: In the first, a woman, distracted by texting on her cell phone, walks unaware into an automated car garage, which raises or lowers cars automatically to store them on various floors.[77] She suddenly panics as the garage door rolls down, locking her in. The floor then begins to lower. It takes her down to the next story, where another car is queued up and ready to enter the car elevator. The woman tries to escape, but the car plows ahead, running her over and pinning her to the back wall. In the second video, a young woman is filmed jaywalking across a busy highway, with her cell phone glued to her ear.[78] She crosses in front of three lanes of cars, then, rushing into the final lane without looking, she is slammed by a fast-moving van. She is thrown into the air like a rag doll, spinning and flying at least three car lengths before she lands. The video gives no indication to viewers whether or not she survived the frightful accident. Other such accidents have occurred due to distracted drivers, pedestrians, train conductors, and others. Lack of situational awareness has also led to a spate of robberies of cell phones from distracted users. Many victims, mesmerized by their phones, don't notice the robber riding up beside them on a skateboard or bicycle to steal those very phones that have so enraptured their owners. One man in Pasadena was actually punched in the face while talking on his cell phone and walking on the sidewalk; the robber escaped with the phone in a nearby getaway car driven by a teen girl.[79] Our immersion in digital worlds and the hypnotic effect these technologies have over us do not negate our embodied selves. Bodies exist outside digital connectivity. A key to surviving this era with our bodies and possessions intact is to find some kind of balance between our embodied selves and our disembodied minds swept up in digital technologies. Situational awareness, particularly on city streets, is clearly compromised by the mesmerizing qualities of our devices; a "heads up / eyes up" approach to navigating urban life will likely raise the odds people get to their destinations with both their devices and their well-being intact.

HIGH TECH/HIGH TOUCH

Futurist John Naisbitt has said that "the more high technology around us, the more the need for human touch. High Tech/High Touch. The principle symbolizes the need for balance between our physical and spiritual reality."[80] Some people are already attempting to strike a mind/body balance. These countertrends are attempts at tonics to our digital immersion and to the intensification of civilizing factors constraining the body. One of these is a rise of tribalism, in a movement called *neotribalism*. Our societies used to be organized by tribes, which provided protection to members against other tribes, and opportunities for teaching, learning, and sustenance. Some argue that, now, the family unit has taken the place of the tribe, and the corporation (and its related brands) now stands in for the tribal unit. Yet neither of these quite take the place of the tribe, with the family unit being too small and the corporation too big and imper-sonal. What's lost is tribal laws, customs, and identity. A such, there has been a return to neotribalism and "high touch" activities, from crafting to drumming circles, that bring the body and the sense of touch back to center stage. Once again, it's all about tactility.

One salient example of the rise of neotribalism is the culture emanating out of rave life in Ibiza or a myriad of music festivals, like Ultra in Miami, com-plete with their shamanistic drug use and quasi-spiritual experience.[81] Another is Burning Man. Burning Man exists as a kind of respite for the overcivilized. On the playa of Black Rock Desert, situated 120 miles outside of Reno, Nevada, a giant sculpture of a couple in a romantic embrace is set afire. Mark Magellan writes in his blog about it: "The sexless giants stood erect over the world; they gazed into each other's eyes, saying goodbye to the world that was, and embracing what was bound to come; their shadows formed dark tentacles that were nailed to the desert floor, mocking the light from the blazing fire."[82]

Last year, Mark and other "burners," many hailing from Silicon Valley, co-created the pop-up Black Rock City, which emerges from the Nevada desert each year. Burning Man's website says that "day-to-day life on the playa is tricky, but it's beautiful. It breaks the routines of civilization and makes us re-learn fundamental skills."[83] Elaborate handmade wood or metal sculptures dot the dusty playa, and colorful, whimsical, and even outlandish "art cars" pass by like desert floats, many lit with neon and loaded with burners. A relentless beat of electronic dance music provides the soundtrack for it all. The 2017 theme for Burning Man art—"Radical Ritual"—emphasized tribalism, spiritualism, and the human desire to *make* as a pleasurable activity:

> Beyond the dogmas, creeds, and metaphysical ideas of religion, there is imme-diate experience. It is from this primal world that living faith arises. In 2017, we will invite participants to create interactive rites, ritual processions, elaborate images, shrines, icons, temples, and visions. Our theme will occupy the ambig-uous ground that lies between reverence and ridicule, faith and belief, the absurd and the stunningly sublime. The human urge to make events, objects, actions, and personalities sacred is protean. It can fix on and inhabit anyone or anything. This year our art theme will release this spirit in the Black Rock Desert.[84]

Burning Man's website stating that life on the playa "breaks the routines of civilization" is reminiscent of the pastoral experience we visited earlier. These kinds of neo-tribal experiences put particular emphasis on nature and the body, freeing "burners" from the normal strictures of civilization and putting them back in touch with some of the basic survival needs of earlier tribal life. Victor Jeffreys II, a photo editor for Gawker Media, described his first "burn:"

> You can roller skate topless, ride mustaches, paint your fingernails, dance inside of sharks, watch/do suspensions (imagine a 180-pound man hanging, 20 feet above the ground, from two meat hooks going through his nipples), accept candy from strangers dressed in bunny suits sitting on the ground in the middle of the street, play fire Skee-Ball, join a 9 a.m. dance party in your underwear, do yoga, attend a small business workshop, learn to twerk, give hugs (or blow jobs), receive advice (or blow jobs), build castles (in the dust … not sand), jump on trampolines, re-birth (literally through a birth canal made of rope suspended in the air), be a Barbie, read books, drink kava, not shower for a week, pee in bottles (that have to be emptied into the Porta-Potty, kiss (consenting adult) men, kiss (consenting adult) women, wear wings and pretend to be a fairy, dance, dance, and dance some more.[85]

Depending on others on the playa also re-evokes the communal sense of the tribe, something that has been lost in modern civilization, since we've largely left tribal life behind. Although the Burning Man "network of dreamers and doers" is the digerati's version of the Summer of Love, civilization is never far away, since this time "turn on, tune in, and drop out" means always being jacked into Wi-Fi, so you can upload pics, videos, and stories of the event to Facebook, Instagram, and elsewhere—much to the chagrin of some burners, who see the festival as an opportunity to disconnect from digital life. Perhaps not surprisingly, untethered Millennials make up approximately 52 percent of the attendees and are the largest age group that attends.[86]

Although the playa ostensibly is a kind of "back to the land" tribal experience, people have begun dragging civilization along with them to the desert—and the creature comforts that it can entail. One of the rules of Burning Man is that no money can be exchanged, and no commerce is allowed at Burning Man, which has fostered a system of bartering or free-spirited giving, or "gifting" of everything from massages to Jell-O shots. Yet despite the intentional lack of a traditional capitalistic economy, a clear "have and have nots" vibe has emerged in recent years, as wealthy Silicon Valley scions "burn" in rented, fully stocked luxury RVs for the week to ten days of their stay. A 2017 census of Burning Man found that the majority (70 percent) of burners did not stay in these kinds of RVs or campers, choosing tents or yurts instead.[87] Tesla CEO Elon Musk was one of the "glampers," spending $10,000 or more for an RV loaded up with food, booze, and enough water for a week in the desert, plus paid help that would come by at regular intervals to drain the septic tanks.[88] The appearance of commercial turnkey or "plug and play" camps after 2012, where "vacationer burners" could just show up, get a wristband, and party in secluded, VIP environments, prompted the organizers to have a moral discussion about whether these kinds of camps were in the spirit of Burning Man, or whether they even belonged there. In the end, the Burning Man organizers decided that they didn't:

> Bringing a VIP lifestyle experience—with velvet ropes and wristbands—introduces an element of exclusivity into a culture that values inclusion, and those that opt in to these kinds of camps miss out on the transformative power of the event. . . . Coming to Burning Man and living in an area that's self-contained while avoiding engagement with the broader community directly contradicts the spirit of the event.[89]

In a sense, then, the glampers committed the fundamental sin of bringing the city to the playa—along with its social demarcations of class (e.g., the "VIP lifestyle"), which is the opposite of this attempt to retribalize the many.

The 2018 theme for Burning Man turned away from the neo-tribal theme and looked toward the future, as it explored the concept of "iRobot." The Burning Man website asked about the rise of robots and AI algorithms, "Are we entering a Golden Age that frees us from mindless labor?"[90] (In other words, do AI and robotics eliminate embodied labor?) And it posited that "this is a context between wet intelligence, something that we barely understand that has evolved on earth over a span of billions of years, and dry intelligence, which was invented in 1936."

Clearly, these are the most pressing questions we face at this time, as human society itself is challenged by the rapid advances of AI and automation. Yet while technology marches on, the efforts to retribalize continue as a persistent countertrend. The neotribalism experiment that is Burning Man is expanding to other areas around the globe, where there are local attempts to re-create the Burning Man spirit. These include Blazing Swan in Australia, Fuego Astral in South America, Element 11 in Utah in the United States, and, finally, the Love Burn in Miami, whose 2019 theme is the "Lost Island of Taboo."

Others have sought to reclaim the body in a different way, namely, through a return to simpler occupations common in pre-industrial times, and to making things by hand, as part of a "tribe" at which handcrafted items are on display and where lessons are given on making things—aptly named the maker movement. Beginning around 2005 with the founding of *Make* magazine, the maker movement encompasses the tinkerer, hacker, and DIY crowd in a steampunk-inspired mash-up of skills seemingly inspired by Jules Verne's book *Twenty Thousand Leagues Under the Seas*.[91] As of 2017, nearly two hundred "Maker Faires" had sprung up in forty-five countries, including flagship events in New York and San Francisco, and those in Bangkok, Cairo, Nantes, Beijing, and other locations.[92] Attendees tend to skew male, with an average age in the midthirties, meaning they are older Millennials or younger Gen Xers. Many attend the fairs with children, family, or friends.

The maker movement is driven by two seemingly opposing forces: on the one hand, the promise of digital technologies, robotics, and 3-D printing; on the other, a certain nostalgia for days gone by, a longing for simpler days when body and environment were more strongly connected. Dale Doughtery, the founder of *Make* magazine and also Maker Faire, while talking about the origin of making in his TED talk, emphasized the reintegration of the body and the world around it, in a world where the body has become alienated from its surroundings:

> So it goes on to show you people making things out of wood, a grandfather making a ship in a bottle, a woman making a pie—somewhat standard fare of the day. But it was a sense of pride that we made things, that the world around us was made by us. It didn't just exist. We made it, and we were connected to it that way. And I think that's tremendously important.[93]

At one of the Maker Faires, the body was reasserted on a bigger-than-life scale, in the form of a three-story mechanical ballerina who dances to the tinkling songs of a children's music-box. Animal bodies showed up as well, like the massive praying mantis configured as a workable marionette, with its decidedly low-tech/high-touch ropes that animate it just waiting to be pulled by curious passersby. The stars of the show, though, were both a gigantic, seventy-foot-long, two-story-high steampunk elephant with articulated legs that allow it to "walk" around the park with people riding atop it as it sprayed others with water from its trunk, and a five-story-high spider, which carried people on its back like a camel.[94]

Other makers showed off other handicraft skills, such as blacksmithing.

Many children are fascinated by these lost arts, and they take part in the making. At a recent maker fair in San Mateo, one middle-schooler came all the way from Australia to show off the particle accelerator she had built. David Strehlow, former vice president of marketing at Huawei, said about Maker Faires: "Girls are an equal and abundant part of it. That was one of the things I was most happy to see last year. And even more than high touch, the event is characterized by a pure joy and enthusiasm I haven't seen around tech since it became big money."[95] In a move to engage the youth, graduate student Andrew Milne has started Maker Mobile, a mobile maker/invention workshop, so they can join this tribe and learn new skills.[96]

The maker trend tends to focus on earlier technologies (like blacksmithing or the pulleys and ropes used to animate marionettes) or handmade modern technologies (like robots, drones, and 3-D printing). A parallel but slightly different trend is the resurgence of "crafts" and the handcrafted. One expression of this is the "craft cocktails" poured by specially trained bartenders. YouTube offers videos on how to make specialty cocktails at home or how to locate or even make ingredients that are hard to find, like gum syrup; and a variety of mixology podcasts are available on different platforms. Barbering is another old-school, high-touch "craft" seeing a revival. Waxed mustaches and product-infused 1800s miner haircuts have made a comeback in the last few years, accompanied by a myriad of well-coiffed beards. Shops offering straight-razor shaves and barbering have cropped up in cities from New York to Los Angeles and San Francisco; the Blind Barber in the East Village of New York is one of these. From its mechanical red-and-blue vintage barber pole out front, to its restored vintage barber chairs, to the "speakeasy"-style bar inside, shops like this one evoke nostalgia and give harried city dwellers a respite, providing them an opportunity to step back in time and experience a simpler, hands-on, low-tech world.[97] Many of these craft bartenders and barbers sport multiple tattoos that are displayed below rolled-up sleeves, in another nod to tribalism and a repatriating of the body and physicality. There is also a resurgence in the use of black-and-white photography, specifically using film and "baths" for photo developing. Each step is processed by hand, from putting the film in a can and shaking it back and forth to develop the film, to exposing the photo paper and developing it through the series of baths, to finally hanging it on a clothes line to dry. Vinyl records, played on old-time record players, are making a comeback too. For example, in the up-and-coming Highland Park neighborhood of LA, a hip bar called the Gold Line, founded by Stone's Throw Records founder

Peanut Butter Wolf, has the shelves behind the bar lined with his personal collection of vinyl records and a vintage Rock-Ola jukebox. The records are spun by the bartenders for appreciative customers on weeknights and by guest DJs on the weekends. The brick walls, leather-and-wood barstools, and wood-paneled walls definitely lend this place a high-touch vibe; and its simple, no-nonsense, three-ingredient cocktails give visitors the feeling that it sprang from simpler times.[98] In the steady march forward of the digital, the desire for tactility and the analog is starting to express itself in these kinds of countermovements.

Still others are bringing the body and tactility back into their lives by leaving cities altogether, pursuing a hands-on life via the back-to-the-land movement. These "back-to-the-landers" are bolstered by blogs and magazines like *New Pioneer*, which teach new or aspiring farmers how to live in a style reminiscent of *Little House on the Prairie* again. One of farms highlighted in the magazine is nineteenth-century Stone Garden Farm and Village, whose farm wife is, ironically, named Laura. Its website describes a host of handmade items and farm-raised livestock and foodstuffs for sale in its gift shop, giving us a glimpse into the lives of the family members:

> Stone Garden is a nearly self-sufficient farm. We produce our own eggs, meats, dairy and vegetables. In our general store, we sell a variety of homemade soaps, handcrafted herbal teas, honey, maple syrup, metal garden art, many crafts, free range multi-colored eggs, and lots more according to season. In October, we sell pumpkins, corn stalks, folk art, harvest crafts, our own bottled sodas and cider. For Christmas, we offer trees, wreathes, roping and local handmade Christmas decorations and gifts.[99]

The couple is also restoring the buildings in a nearby town, returning them to their original purpose, including a general store and a bakery. As outlined on Stone Garden's website, the family lives a simpler life of homeschooling the kids, tending the farm animals, making food from scratch, and honing traditional skills. Laura's bio ends with this imagery of them having achieved their version of the American Dream: "Though Laura can certainly fill up a day milking their Jersey cow, making soap and cheese, homeschooling the kids and caring for the gardens and animals, she always has time to stop for a cup of tea and a chat with those who wish to hear some of their stories. As many people often comment, she really is 'living the dream.'"[100]

Trends are showing that some who are interested in this kind of lifestyle but want to retain the amenities of living in cities are exploring a hybrid back-to-the-land movement via urban gardening and beekeeping. Meetup groups and groups like Honey Love in Los Angeles have sprung up to mentor urban and suburban dwellers who are curious about the art of beekeeping. Part of this is a reaction to news of bee-colony collapse due to the use of pesticides across the country. Urban and suburban beekeepers keep beehives on their rooftops, on balconies, or in their backyards. On the weekends, experts teach novice beekeepers everything from how to smoke a hive before opening it to how to process the honey. Similar to the novice beekeepers, there are urban gardening and farming enthusiasts who plant container gardens in available spaces or grow their own food on apartment balconies. Hundreds of Pinterest boards on the topic have emerged as inspiration for these small-scale urban farmers, showing everything from carrots and lush tomatoes grown in pots to whimsical rows of recycled square tea cans, each planted with a single herb inside a kitchen window.

Farmers and flea markets have been transformed by the "maker" aesthetic as well. Though they traditionally host small farm wares from local farmers—ranging from fresh eggs to fruits and vegetables, fresh-baked breads, and honey—these markets have transformed recently; now they are not just flea markets but also a gathering site for producers of artisanal food and food trucks. One example of this change is seen in the hipster market Artists & Fleas in Williamsburg, New York, which is now replicated in Los Angeles both in Venice and in the arts district Downtown. Digital-native shopkeepers there are embodying the high-touch countermovement to the high tech permeating their lives. African American and Millennial soap maker Thaka (one of the vendors who sells at Artist & Fleas) describes the hands-on approach she and her husband, Mo, take to their artisanal soapmaking:

> Sheawa is a natural and hand crafted "Bath & Body Patisserie" created to rekindle the romantic feel of bathing, and to nurture the body. Their products contain their own imported shea butter and all organic ingredients.[101]

Their Instagram account, @sheawa.inc, is filled with photos of natural textures and colors, emphasizing high touch—from wooden spoons filled with pink Himalayan sea salt or activated charcoal crystals, to yellow-and-white plumeria blossoms floating in a wooden bowl filled with water, to soaps that are sprinkled with crushed red English roses. The photos make you want to reach out and enjoy the beautiful textures of natural ingredients in their products.

Merging digital natives' innate connectivity with images evoking a high-touch experience, Thaka and Mo's Instagram account is a sensual delight.

Another set of entrepreneurial Millennials focusing on tactility and returning to a high-touch lifestyle is Real Bearded Men. Theirs is a shop founded by a group of bearded young men, and it provides all-natural balms for beard grooming. The Artist & Fleas website describes them as follows:

> Do you love beards? We do! But we truly have yet to meet anyone who loves beards as much as the best-friend duo behind Real Bearded Men. This line of all-natural beard oils, balms and more will have your beard (or the beards in your life) in tip-top shape in no time.[102]

The maker movement and these kinds of "farmers-market-meets-handmade-artisanal-goods" folks provide small-scale, high-touch, handmade, unique items in a world that has become increasingly high-tech, homogenized, branded, and mass-produced from cheap-quality ingredients. These kinds of tactile, sensory proclivities among Millennials and others are both a response to and a tonic for the increasing march of civilization and the cold glass screens that have come to dominate the lives of both digital natives (those who grew up in a world where there always was an internet) and digital immigrants (those who came to the internet later in life). In a society that is progressively dominated by technology, these countertrends remind us of both simpler times and what it means to be human.

Untethering isn't limited to the United States—as devices proliferate around the world, other countries are experiencing some of the same social patterns we are beginning to see in this country. Hyperconnectivity to digital devices presents problems, but it also holds the potential for new forms of work and enhanced relationships across borders. Some countries are scrambling to address the various configurations and unintended outcomes of digital connectivity, with China using firewalls to block out Western social media sites like Facebook and Twitter altogether. Where some see threat, others see opportunity; some countries are rolling out the welcome mat by offering digital workers passports, visas, and other incentives to attract innovation. Still others are struggling with falling birth rates and a growing number of singles, which is not only changing the complexion of both families and cultures but also leaving their future workforce unable to meet demands, all while the support of an aging population is in question. Overall, though, the signs are all there: We are becoming an untethered world.

CHAPTER 9

THE UNTETHERED WORLD

In a word, they failed to take into account man's almost infinite appetite for distractions.
—Aldous Huxley, *Brave New World*, 1932

"**S**cientists can be awfully bright. But they're human, and they have blind spots like everyone else. They're often nerds—people who are blind or nearly blind to subtexts—and they try (mostly successfully) to compensate by mastering texts," said economist Ethan Anderson. He and I were talking about the fact that it seems sometimes that the human impacts of technology are an afterthought, are overlooked altogether, or are realized after it's too late. When Ethan mentioned *texts*, he was referring to the overt messages in any conversation, book, advertisement, film, and so on; texts carry the intentionality of whatever message is being put forward. The *subtext*, on the other hand, is the unwritten rules, the unsaid, the message *within* a message that can be easily overlooked in communication. Body language, for example, is the subtext of the words being spoken in conversation. Body language can vastly change the meaning of what is being said. Overlook it, and you can miss the true message altogether.

Dr. Robert J. Oppenheimer was one of these scientists who was blind to the subtext of his work until later. As the head of the Los Alamos Lab, he was tapped to lead the Manhattan Project, which was tasked with creating the world's first nuclear bomb. The debut of his creation would be in New Mexico, the culmination of a project he would code-name Trinity, inspired by the John Donne poem, "Holy Sonnet XIV: Batter My Heart, Three-Person'd God." Here's a bit of it:

> Batter my heart, three-person'd God, for you
> As yet but knock, breathe, shine, and seek to mend;
> That I may rise, and stand, o'erthrow me, and bend
> Your force to break, blow, burn, and make me new.[1]

The nod to Donne at the dawn of the atomic age is likely a subliminal memorial to Oppenheimer's lost love, psychiatrist Jean Tatlock.[2] Tatlock was the daughter of a noted professor at University of California at Berkeley, where Oppenheimer had taught and where they had become acquainted. Oppenheimer had been involved with her romantically from 1936 to at least 1941. They'd gotten engaged twice, yet never married. Oppenheimer continued an affair with Tatlock even after marrying someone else in 1940. She unfortunately suffered from clinical depression, and on January 5, 1944, her father, after receiving no reply to knocks on her door, climbed into her house through a window and discovered her dead in her bathroom; Jean had been the victim of a lethal combination of barbiturates and drowning. Tatlock had introduced Oppenheimer to the poetry of John Donne.[3]

After Jean's tragic death, Oppenheimer continued with this work, ultimately testing his bomb's ability to "break, blow, burn" in the Jornada del Muerto desert, thirty-five miles southeast of Socorro, New Mexico, on the US Air Force's Alamogordo Bombing and Gunnery Range. Oppenheimer's Gadget was an implosion-type nuclear bomb, the same type as the Fat Man later dropped over Nagasaki, Japan. The Gadget was estimated to be the equivalent of 13 kilotons of TNT. Dr. Isidor Rabi, physicist and winner of the Nobel Prize in Physics in 1944 for his discovery of nuclear magnetic resonance (now used in MRIs) was there to witness this first nuclear test on July 16, 1945. He also worked on the Manhattan Project. Rabi described what happened on that cold desert morning:

> Nine miles away from where we were, there was a tower about 100 feet high. On the top of that tower was a little shack about ten by ten. In that shack was a bomb. At first, the announcer said: "Thirty seconds ..." "Ten Seconds ..." We were lying there, very tense, in the early dawn, and there were just a few streaks of gold in the east; you could see your neighbor very dimly. Those ten seconds were the longest ten seconds that I ever experienced. Suddenly, there was an enormous flash of light, the brightest light I have ever seen or that I think anyone has ever seen. It blasted; it pounced; it bored its way right through you. It was a vision which was seen with more than the eye. It was seen to last forever. You would wish it to stop; altogether it lasted about two seconds. Finally it was over, diminishing, and we looked toward the place where the bomb had been; there was an enormous ball of fire which grew and grew and it rolled as it grew; it went up into the air, in yellow flashes and into scarlet and green. It looked menacing. It seemed to come toward one. A new thing had just been born.[4]

In the 1965 documentary *The Decision to Drop the Bomb*, Oppenheimer, looking down and away from the camera in subdued penitence, reflected on that day, saying:

> We knew the world would not be the same. A few people laughed, a few people cried, most people were silent. I remembered the line from the Hindu scripture, the Bhagavad Gita. Vishnu is trying to persuade the Prince that he should do his duty and to impress him takes on his multi-armed form and says, "Now, I am become Death, the destroyer of worlds." I suppose we all thought that one way or another.[5]

Oppenheimer became the Hindu god Shiva, the destroyer, the day the Little Boy bomb was dropped over Hiroshima. When the second atomic bomb, known as the Fat Man, was dropped above Nagasaki, he felt remorse. At his farewell ceremony in October of 1945 at Los Alamos, he told those assembled these words, which resonate to this day:

> In years to come we may look at this scroll, and all that it signifies, with pride. Today that pride must be tempered with a profound concern. If atomic bombs are to be added as new weapons to the arsenals of a warring world, or to the arsenals of nations preparing for war, then the time will come when mankind will curse the names of Los Alamos and of Hiroshima.
>
> The peoples of this world must unite or they will perish. This war, that has ravaged so much of the earth, has written these words. The atomic bomb has spelled them out for all men to understand. Other men have spoken them, in other times, of other wars, of other weapons. They have not prevailed. There are some, misled by a false sense of human history, who hold that they will not prevail today. It is not for us to believe that. By our works we are committed, to a united world, before this common peril, in law, and in humanity.[6]

Oppenheimer this time was acting as another god from the Hindu *Trimurti*, or trinity; now as the face of Vishnu, the preserver. It drove him to travel to Washington, DC, after the second bomb was dropped over Nagasaki. On October 25, 1945, Oppenheimer was welcomed into the Oval Office by President Harry Truman. He implored the president to enact controls on nuclear weaponry, saying, "Mr. President, I feel I have blood on my hands."[7] The remark infuriated Truman, who ejected Oppenheimer posthaste. President Truman later told Secretary of State Dean Acheson never to bring "that son of a bitch in this office ever again."

In a sense, Mark Zuckerberg is the Oppenheimer of our untethered era, not fully realizing the impact his technology would have on the world until after the damage has been done. Zuckerberg was called before the Senate and Congress in 2017 to testify about the impact his platform, Facebook, had had in facilitating Russian meddling in the 2016 presidential election. During the election, Facebook was filled with fake news stories that were posted and shared, mostly aimed at right-leaning voters, with headlines like: "Hillary Clinton Calling for Civil War If Trump Is Elected"; "Pope Francis Shocks World, Endorses Donald Trump for President"; "Barack Obama Admits He Was Born in Kenya"; and "FBI Agent Who Was Suspected of Leaking Hillary's Corruption Is Dead." The pope's "endorsement" story alone garnered 868,000 shares.[8]

Facebook also allowed advertisers to target anti-Semitic users who had very specific interests, like "Jew Haters," or "History of 'Why Jews Ruin the World,'" categories that Facebook later said were created by an algorithm rather than by a human.[9] This kind of targeting enabled Russian operatives to send people fake stories that confirmed the very beliefs and fears they already held, triggering a psychological tendency called *confirmation bias*. Confirmation bias is the tendency to search for, interpret, favor, and recall information in a way that confirms one's preexisting beliefs or hypotheses.[10] Information that is counter to one's strongly held beliefs is usually ignored or discounted. Confirmation bias can cause people to make poor decisions on an individual level; but when taken to a societal level like this, amplified by social media, the results can be devastating. It enables bad actors to remotely manipulate people on a scale heretofore unknown, using fake people ("bots") to spread the messages and persuade others to share them.

When the charges were first leveled against Facebook, Zuckerberg initially dismissed the idea that his platform might be culpable in election meddling, saying that fake news surely had no impact on whom voters chose to be president and calling it a "pretty crazy idea" to think fake news had influenced the election.[11] He followed that by saying, "I think there is a certain profound lack of empathy in asserting that the only reason why someone could have voted the way they did is because they saw some fake news." Yet research after the fact showed that Russians did indeed run a concerted ad campaign to sway votes, particularly those of nonwhite voters. They did this by first sending benign messages to them, drawing them in and building trust by promoting racial identity, community, and affinity. Later, these same Russian-controlled accounts flipped, working to suppress likely Hillary Clinton voters by attacking the candidate they supported, by sending messages aimed at suppressing voter turnout at the polls (for example, by telling them to boycott the election in protest), and by promoting a third-party candidate. These ads generated 1,262,068 "impressions," or displays on web pages.[12] They were paid for by the Internet Research Agency, a Kremlin-linked Russian political group. The information on these activities was released by the US House Intelligence Committee on May 10, 2018.[13] According to written testimony provided to DC lawmakers, Facebook admitted that Russia-based operatives published about 80,000 posts online between June 2015 and August 2017 in an attempt to influence the presidential election. The posts may have reached as many as 126 million Americans.[14] The platform has since disabled targeting based on certain offensive search terms.

On April 10, 2018, Mark Zuckerberg sat stone-faced and emotionless in front of a panel of senators, ready to answer questions about Facebook's role in Russian election meddling. Clearly, he'd been extremely prepared. Facing folks old enough to be his grandparents, he calmly answered question after question posed to him about Facebook and how it works, questions like, "Mr. Zuckerberg, how is it you can provide this service for free?"[15] "Senator, we run ads," came the bemused reply. Undeniably, most of the digital immigrants interrogating him had no idea—even at a basic level—how the platform works. In hindsight, Facebook's impact is clear: The social network has had a transformative impact on the world. The unintended consequences of creating such a massive network are just beginning to show up now. Facebook, Google, and Twitter have all been weaponized to sway elections across the globe. Fake political ads based out of Russia and designed to create divisions in the United States may have been shared hundreds of millions of times.[16] Follow-on studies found that older people (those over sixty-five) and Republicans were the most likely to share fake news.[17] Overall, at least 470 Russian-run pages have been identified, traceable back to a Russian troll farm in St. Petersburg.[18] Facebook has since shut down all of them.

Although Zuckerberg had originally brushed off the charge that Facebook had potentially supported interference in the 2016 election, he later had second thoughts. Reflecting back on his comments, he said: "After the election, I made a comment that I thought the idea of misinformation on Facebook changed the outcome of the election was a crazy idea. Calling that crazy was dismissive and I regret it. This is too important an issue to be dismissive."[19] Corporate officers for Facebook, Twitter, and Google were all called in to testify before the Senate Judiciary Subcommittee. Admitting culpability after the fact, Facebook's general counsel, Colin Stretch, said to the senators, "The foreign interference we saw was reprehensible."[20]

The election meddling was noticed early on by a Facebook insider, early investor Roger McNamee. He noticed something was amiss when misogynistic memes about Hillary Clinton kept popping up on Bernie Sanders's Facebook page. Because of his understanding of how the platform works, he knew these weren't simply organic posts but instead were paid advertising originating from— somewhere, likely a well-organized campaign, intent on fomenting hatred and mistrust. McNamee said, "Those people have all been Zucked. They've all had their brains altered, and they've come to believe things that weren't true. And I want Facebook to contact every one of them."[21] He went on to discuss the harm done by internet companies like Facebook:

> This entire scandal occurred because the big Internet companies know more about you than you know about yourself, which gives them huge power to influence you, to persuade you to do things that serve their economic interests. Facebook, Google and others compete for each consumer's attention, reinforcing biases and reducing the diversity of ideas to which each is exposed. The degree of harm grows over time. Consider a recent story from Australia, where someone at Facebook told advertisers that they had the ability to target teens who were sad or depressed, which made them more susceptible to advertising. In the United States, Facebook once demonstrated its ability to make users happier or sadder by manipulating their news feed. While it did not turn either capability into a product, the fact remains that Facebook influences the emotional state of users every moment of every day. Former Google design ethicist Tristan Harris calls this "brain hacking."[22]

Unintended network effects like these are beginning to show up in our untethered world. In Facebook's case, what began as a clever way to micro-target advertising to consumers, using behavioral, demographic, and psychographic data (i.e., data that describe consumers' psychological attributes, like their values, attitudes, interests, personalities and lifestyles) gathered through likes or via fun "quizzes" that, for example, rate your personality. This same system was later used by bad actors to identify and then target those most vulnerable to manipulation, namely, the anxious and the fearful. Network effects were used to proliferate these messages of division and fear throughout people's social networks, as people shared fake news on their newsfeeds. Since people usually associate and are Facebook friends with those who are similar to themselves in beliefs and values, amplifying these messages quickly via viral-ready memes wasn't hard to do, as they confirmed what people already believed. The distribution of these messages went much further than what many initially believed: Jonathan Albright of Harvard's Berkman Klein Center for the Internet and Society found that of six Russian-bought sites on Facebook (with the unlikely names of Blacktivists, United Muslims of America, Being Patriotic, Heart of Texas, Secured Borders, and LGBT United), the content they generated had been shared 340 million times.[23] Russian interference and new, persuasive advertising using the same techniques via social media has been successful in swaying voters, whipping up negative sentiment and fear, and polarizing members of the two major political parties, causing rifts in friendships and families in its wake. This is exactly what these ads were designed to do.

This kind of "divide and conquer" strategy using social media is not just happening in the States, and it was not confined to the 2016 US presidential election—Cambridge Analytica, the now-defunct firm behind the Trump campaign that was operating in the shadows, also worked to sway the Brexit Leave. EU campaign, and, according to its former website, one hundred other campaigns across five continents.[24] Evidence also points to Russian interference in other countries around the world, including Germany, where messages by the Alternative for Germany (AfD) party, which is a nationalist, anti-immigration group that advocates for closer ties with Moscow, were amplified. Sweden, too, fell victim to Russian cybersecurity attacks and dissemination campaigns aimed at spreading falsehoods to polarize the country, as well as a number of other Western European countries.[25] Yet despite mounting evidence, a significant number of people in the United States and elsewhere still believe that none of this is happening: According to an NPR/Marist poll, as late as July 2017, a quarter of US voters overall and 41 percent of Republicans believed there was no Russian meddling in the presidential election.[26] The fact that the United States and other governments were caught off guard by election meddling within their borders show that it is a major threat.

Online, Russian bots continue to take on an active role in dividing groups of people by taking advantage of public confusion, fear, and a thirst for information in the wake of disasters. After the Florida shooting at Marjory Stoneman Douglas High School in February 2018, bots were mobilized to promote an extremist gun position. A researcher at New Knowledge, a group that is following Russian trolls online, says trolls responded quickly after the shooting, taking advantage of people's desire for knowledge about the attack, their fears, and their feelings of helplessness and vulnerability. This seems to be a common thread among these trolls: Build trust first, then steer the conversation toward divisive topics. Aarti Shahani of NPR talked with a researcher at New Knowledge about the trolls that appeared after the Florida high-school shooting; he reports:

> By 2:30 p.m. Eastern that day [the researcher] saw an uptick of messages by this one troll network. And they just started sharing breaking news, OK? But by 3 p.m. Eastern, a half hour later, they quickly pivoted to conspiracy theories, speculating it was a Democrat conspiracy and also advancing an extreme pro-gun position, saying teachers need to carry concealed handguns to protect students.[27]

The story about teachers carrying handguns later made it onto the evening news, showing how these bots can reshape the national conversation about school shootings and other issues, potentially emboldening more extreme reactions.

Given that the vast majority of people are online now, and the fact that many are spending the bulk of their time there, how to deal with these kinds of issues of swaying public opinion and dividing people from one another is a vexing and complex issue. One group of journalists—funded by the founder of Craigslist, Craig Newmark's foundation, and the Knight Foundation—is addressing them via a new venture called the Markup, whose aim is to uncover some of the negative consequences of technology on society, including the aforementioned Russian election meddling. The Markup describes its mission as follows:

> The Markup is a nonpartisan, nonprofit newsroom that produces meaningful data-centered journalism that illuminates how powerful institutions are using technology in ways that impact people and society. We aim to hold the powerful to account, raise the cost of bad behavior and spur reforms.[28]

The social media and search platforms themselves—Facebook, Google, and Twitter—are also making efforts post-election to root out Russian fake accounts and disable bots responsible for spreading misinformation. The American public is cynical about their ability to do anything about it, though, so the damage may well be done. By fall 2018, although the majority (76 percent) thought that big tech companies like Facebook, Google, and Twitter have a responsibility to prevent the misuse of their platforms, only a third said that they were very or somewhat confident that these companies can achieve that objective.[29] Sixty-six percent said they are not too confident or not at all confident. The outcome may be that voters don't come out to vote, which is one of the key objectives of these fake-news campaigns. At the very least, political polarization has widened. Data from the American National Election Studies shows that warm feelings toward the Democratic Party by Republicans, and of Democrats toward the Republican Party, have plummeted when compared to 1980 levels, thereby straining negotiations, conversations, or even relationships "across the aisle."[30] These are the kinds of divides that fake-news purveyors are driving wedges into and amplifying. Living in a connected world now means that we are all subject to targeting and influence using social media, leveraging our trust networks. We need better trust signals as to the provenance of data (i.e., knowing its source) and identity signals (i.e., whom the ad or story is coming from). We also need to become better consumers of data, such as fact-checking by reading laterally across platforms to confirm the veracity of news before sharing items that might quite literally be "too good to be true," as they were conjured up for us out of our worst fears and served up to us on a digital platter by algorithms designed just for that purpose.

OUR INCREASINGLY UNTETHERED WORLD

The unintended network effects of living in an untethered world will continue to grow as digital connectivity becomes an increasingly global phenomenon. Two springs ago, I went to Shanghai with a delegation from the University of Southern California, hosted by the US-China Institute, to speak on untethering and US Millennials. It was my first visit to Asia. Unlike the vision many seem to have in their imaginations of China as an agrarian or "developing" nation, Shanghai is a very modern city—there is nothing "ancient" or historical about it. Its skyline is filled with skyscrapers. In fact, it is so futuristic-looking that it was chosen as the backdrop for the sci-fi movie *Her*, the film that explored our increasingly complicated relationship with artificially intelligent digital agents. It is a city of newfound wealth, where Western brands signifying luxury and conspicuous consumption abound. The French Concession is a particularly concentrated area of this: a mixture of haute couture and arty coffee shops with fledgling baristas busying themselves cranking out cafe lattes and espressos that rival those in Milan. Upscale Western brands like Gucci, Vera Wang, Harry Winston, Godiva, and many others line the streets, beckoning to aspirational shoppers. Shanghai seems to be a cultural mash-up of East and West: Outside a mall store

I saw a full-size cardboard cutout of an Asian boy styled like Justin Bieber, with the tag line, "New York Tough." He looked anything but tough, but "street cred" and Western hip-hop cool is in fashion there. On the streets, the boys are killing the fashion game, looking punk tough in skinny leather jeans and spiked tennies or seeming Saville Row preppy cool; whatever the style, these boys are putting in the effort—and winning. Their style is highly derivative of Western fashions, yet they wear it with effortless swag.

Just like in the West, cell phones and digital connectivity is everywhere here, perhaps even more so. I ended up in a stylish cafe for lunch on my last afternoon in the French Concession. It was painted Tiffany blue and white, and this was clearly not by accident; the owners used the familiar color scheme to hint at resplendent luxury. Everything in the place was highly curated, down to the menus and matching bowl and spoon holder, which were white, with red lips and a pink flower. It was a "see and be seen" kind of place, designed to be perfectly Instagram-mable. I was seated at the window table, which enabled me to watch the people of Shanghai go by. In the booth on my left sat two very stylish Chinese girls, likely part of Shanghai Fashion Week. One looked like a Chinese Gwen Stefani, with bright-red matte lipstick, fashionable cat eyes, and a pink ponytail. At another table, a family sat down—a husband, wife, daughter, and perhaps an aunt. Everyone in the entire restaurant had cell phones in their hands. The aunt at the next table answered two calls, while the others sat in silence, looking at their phones and texting. The two stylish girls also looked at their phones. No one spoke to one another. Electronic ambient music clanged hollowly around the room, fighting off the otherwise awkward silence. Outside, young men walked by, gripping their iPhones; people in pairs texted or talked to someone else while walking together. Few people had their attention devoted to their in-person companions—it would seem that "presence" is becoming a relic of the analog age. Attention is passé. Multitasking on digital devices has become everything.

After Shanghai, I traveled to Bali, in an effort to write this book with the clarity of some critical distance away from constant connectivity. In Bali, too, like in China, American brands were everywhere, visible both in the cities and in the tiny wooden shacks that lined the roadsides, where bottles of Coca-Cola were neatly displayed for sale. Little family-run *warangs* sell a selection of grilled mahi-mahi and other fish—alongside burgers, pizza, and spaghetti bolognese for tourists who are "sick of rice," as one tourist put it on her Yelp review for a restaurant in hip Seminyak. The unspoiled, exotic island of Bali has largely disappeared, although you can catch glimpses of it in the people's kind smiles, in a beautiful plate of mie goreng (a dish of traditional stir-fried ramen noodles and fried egg), or in the fruit pancakes the locals love to make for breakfast. The wares, often aggressively hawked by resident roadside sellers, are Chinese. Much of the food and culture is American. Signs everywhere advertise "free Wi-Fi," indicating that Bali is catering to a new kind of tourist—a wired, always-on tourist—who, though in a tropical paradise where life (apparently) slows down for a while, wants to keep up with Facebook, chat on Weibo, or post Instagram selfies in front of ancient temples. This tourist *needs* to be connected. "Picture, or it didn't happen" is their mantra. Read the Airbnb reviews of inns and restaurants: Most make some reference to the "fast Wi-Fi." It is a critical concern among tourists. Reviews will be docked stars if the Wi-Fi stumbles. Innkeepers are under pressure to provide it. The Bali of old is still available— via pre-packaged Balinese ritual dances designed for consumption by tourists, photographable or live-streamable, on Wednesday and Friday nights at 7 p.m., for an hour, for a price. This Bali has become commodified and trotted out like a kind of Off-Off-Broadway play, where actors' costumes are shed at the end of the evening, as scores of Balinese dancers and actors ride home at high speed, wind in their hair, on a million scooters. Each has a glowing cell phone in his or her pocket or purse. You can't blame the Balinese for this display; it's what the tourists expect. These photo ops offer up the Bali of tourists' imaginations, the one they came to see, and this is the Bali they will post on social media to elicit FOMO in their followers. The Balinese are happy to oblige. In this way, Bali has disappeared; it has become a simulacra—existing more as the Bali of your dreams on Instagram and Facebook, in the photos and videos of these staged events captured and posted by tourists online than it does in real life.

Having grown up in a touristy beach town, I expected this kind of typical tourist experience in Seminyak, which is known for its luxury hotels, beach bars, and hot clubs. After seeing it and Ubed, I made my way to the far side of the island, to a little fishing village called Amed, thinking I'd get away from it all for a bit to write. There's not really any *there* there in Amed, just a few little inns that serve meals on site, and a handful of stores. I thought here, at the quiet end of this island, I could escape technology for a few days, think, and write. On my second warm, humid evening there, I decided to sit out on my veranda and look out to sea. On the horizon, I saw the lights of gigantic container ships that I imagined were full of freshly minted iPhones and other electronics, heading for the Port of Los Angeles. As I scanned the horizon in front of me, something caught my eye: below me, behind a bush at the entrance to the open-air restaurant at my inn, I saw the blue glow of a cell-phone screen lighting up a face in the dark. I realized then that the tentacles of digital connectivity have reached everywhere; that the notion of some "unspoiled tropical island" without devices and things like Facebook are probably gone now. Digital connectivity is encroaching to the farthest and most remote regions on Earth: Five billion people, or two-thirds of Earth's population, now have a cell phone.[31] Eighty percent of the US population has a cell phone, as do 86 percent of Europeans, 68 percent of Asians, and 63 percent of Northern Africans and Middle Easterners. Even in remote Sub-Saharan Africa, the penetration of cell phones is nearing half (44 percent); this is helping to propel its impressive growth, which is expected to outpace that of Asia over the next five years. We truly are living in an untethered world now, which brings with it both new opportunities and new challenges.

THE DIGITAL PANOPTICON

One of the unintended consequences of our increasing global connectivity emerging, related to our "always on" behaviors, is the growth of surveillance in our everyday lives. For example, China has developed a "social-credit" system for its citizens.[32] Using facial-recognition software and vast computer databases documenting consumer activities, China is pursuing the goal of promoting "trustworthiness" among its 1.4 billion citizens by gamifying it. You do good things, you score points. You do something bad—perhaps you're late on a payment or you're caught jaywalking or smoking in a nonsmoking area—and you're docked points. This is a new, technologically driven way to establish social control. People's behavior will be monitored via a system of sophisticated CCTV cameras installed on city streets and linked to a number of facial-recognition tools, plus surveillance of people's activities on their mobile devices. The plan is to enlarge the sphere of surveillance and control to include AI and Big Data. This system is designed to provide feedback to citizens on not just the lawfulness of their behavior but also the morality of it. There, your social-credit score is based not only on your own conduct but also on both the friends with whom you associate and your social media posts. Within this system, citizens are rated, using a numerical scoring system similar to our credit score. The government's intention is to manage social unrest and quell any potential uprisings among China's 1.4 billion citizens. As China's Communist Party put it, the system will "allow the trustworthy to roam freely under heaven while making it hard for the discredited to take a single step."[33]

Being "trustworthy" under the Chinese social-credit system can lead to a citizen "winning" a wide variety of benefits, from cheaper rent on apartments to lower energy bills, to no-deposit rentals of things like bicycles or apartments. Demerits or a lower social-credit score can have wide-ranging negative impacts, ranging from difficulty getting a job or receiving government subsidies, to being barred from purchasing real estate, to having one's ability to travel limited. In particular, low scorers cannot travel first-class, visit luxury hotels, frequent nightclubs, visit golf courses, purchase cars, or even send their children to high-quality private schools. Lists of "blacklisted" people are published publicly and on social media to further shame them into better behaviors.[34]

China's system is a modern kind of digital surveillance, with built-in negative and positive feedback to shape behaviors. Philosopher Michel Foucault, in his book *Discipline and Punish*, described how surveillance can move from the body to the mind; to explain this, he used Jeremy Bentham's prison, called the panopticon, as a metaphor for these new techniques of maintaining power.[35] Bentham's design can be used for prisons, schools, hospitals, or any other type of building where control of the occupants is needed. The design is simple yet ingenious: A central guard tower with windows is encircled by the various "cells," each of which has windows facing the tower. The guard tower is fitted with a system of blinds that can be tipped closed, so the guard can see out but the prisoners (or other inhabitants) cannot see in. In this way, they never know for sure whether or not they are being watched; since they do not know if they are being watched, they feel as if they are always being watched, so they modify their behavior as if they are. Thus, "the gaze" of the guard becomes internalized within every prisoner. In this system, control moves from the external control of the guard over the prisoners to internal control by the prisoners themselves. In the panopticon, no guard need even be in the tower at all for it to work, since eventually all of the prisoners will control their own behavior.[36]

China's social-credit score is a kind of digital panopticon: Because people are aware of the placement of surveillance cameras and facial-recognition software, the cell-phone monitoring and collection and archiving of all their activities, and the monitoring of their social media, China's citizens will likely internalize this all-encompassing digital gaze. They can then be expected to reorient their behavior to align with the state-sanctioned actions the government is trying to encourage. With the ability to monitor behavior and "gamify" trust via rewards and punishments in this way, large-scale behavioral monitoring, and increasingly control, becomes possible. In China, the negative impacts of the social-credit system can be devastating to one's livelihood. Journalist Liu Hu recently tried to book a flight and was told he couldn't fly because he was on a list of untrustworthy individuals. Liu had been ordered by a court to apologize for a series of tweets he had written. Now, he says, "I can't buy property. My child can't go to a private school."[37] Hinting at the panoptic nature of China's social-credit system, he continued, "You feel you're being controlled by the list all the time." Given Hu's account, China's surveillance system is already being internalized by its citizens, who are then, perhaps unwittingly, setting the stage for their own self-control in adherence with the government's behavioral goals.

In the United States, Elon Musk and his team have been working on our own version of a digital panopticon: an implantable brain/machine interface Musk calls a "neural lace." His stated goal is to create cyborgs of us all such that we are permanently jacked into the Matrix.[38] "Creating a neural lace is the thing that really matters for humanity to achieve symbiosis with machines," Musk said.[39] Should he succeed, panoptic surveillance and its potential for control will be total, and inescapable. Along with the panoptic aspects of the neural lace, other troubling mental-health factors may be unintentionally amplified. Already, as we have seen, our hyperconnection to devices is driving anxiety and depression, particularly among the young, who use them the most. A recent global study by Gallup found that across the globe, of 154,000 people surveyed in 145 countries, the Negative Experiences Index—an average of people's reported physical pain, sadness, anger, worry, and stress—is the highest it has been since 2006, likely not coincidentally corresponding with the development of the connected iPhone and social media.[40] Our connectivity to devices and social media—with its competitive and fantastical aspects of the virtual mirror, which allows people to curate their lives, thereby presenting a narrow, highly filtered version of events and themselves—contribute to these rising anxiety and depression rates, as people compare their lives to the artificially "happy" and perfect-looking lives of others, and inevitably fall short.[41] Studies have found that our contexts help drive negative feelings: When we experience social pressure not to feel sad (e.g., seeing that everyone on social media is seemingly happy all of the time) but then we inevitably do experience sadness, we feel like a failure, which creates a whirlpool of negative thoughts and emotions that drag us down further into depression and anxiety.[42] For our own wellness, then, and particularly so for those most connected to social media, the ability to disconnect for a time is key. A neural lace will preclude such disconnection, locking users into an inescapable panopticon. Implanted in the brain, the idea of the neural lace is to create a kind of "augmented human" who is by design untethered, a cyborg of human and machine, allowing a plugged-in "super-human" to emerge. As such, augmented humans will be essentially unable to unplug—ever. Futurist thinkers, like Dr. Michio Kaku, professor of theoretical physics at the City University of New York, and others, argue that a "brain net" will be able to send our thoughts or feelings instantly across the planet, which he sees as the future of the mind.[43] Others argue that those unwilling to subject themselves to such augmentation will fall behind. Chris Smedley, the CXO of Digital Habitats, is one of these. In a private Facebook Messenger conversation with me, argued that, over time, un-augmented humans will be at a disadvantage compared to those who are augmented with implantable devices like a neural lace. Yet if current trends are any indication, implanted, wearable devices like the one Musk proposes could amplify the mental-health issues we are already seeing, as mentioned above; this is especially likely because they are related to constant connectivity. In fact, there is an already-existing market opportunity to identify people who are struggling with mental-health issues and—rather than getting them help—push them to make specific purchases. Interestingly, Amazon has filed a patent for its virtual assistant, Alexa, to recognize when someone is depressed and then offer to sell that person drugs.[44] It will work by detecting "abnormal" physical or emotional conditions by using a voice-analysis algorithm that will assess a user's emotional state, including "happiness, joy, anger, sorrow, sadness, fear, disgust, boredom, stress, or other emotional states."[45] By addressing symptoms of the growing mental-health problems caused by too much connectivity, people can stay jacked into the Matrix while companies monetize their mental illness that is exacerbated by that very connection to the system. Certainly, some will see this as a benefit, yet it also suggests new and possibly troubling privacy issues on the horizon.

Apart from growing device connectivity globally, some of the related patterns of untethering we're seeing emerge in the United States—like unhooking from the traditional social structures of marriage, religion, long-term careers, home buying, and so on—are beginning to emerge in other parts of the world. One of the key issues materializing is that younger digital natives in various countries aren't marrying and having children, thereby threatening to throw off what's called the "replacement rate" of their society.[46] One-fifth of American women remain childless, as do women in Germany, Spain, and the United Kingdom. Some would no doubt argue that with escalating global population rates, and the pressure on the environment, this is a good thing. Yet on a case-by-case basis, a population that dips below replacement faces a number of social and economic challenges, including a shrinking labor force and a disproportionate number of elderly people without enough younger folks to support them. The trouble is, once population stalls, it tends to remain there, which can be a challenge to a country's economy as the number of available workers dwindles. There are benefits, of course, including less strain on natural resources, and higher labor-force participation for workers who are able and ready to work. Some countries turn to immigration to shore up the unmet demand for workers, a tactic that itself can cause other unintended problems. Japan is one of the countries now struggling with fertility rates dipping below replacement. Their digital natives are untethering from traditional marriage and aren't having children, much like young people in the United States. This leaves Japan in the tenuous position: it has a rapidly aging population and lacks a large-enough younger generation to step up and fulfill work and other societal roles. In the 1970s, Japan's women had an average of 2.1 children; now, the average is 1.4, far below the rate needed to maintain Japan's population. The birth rate is the lowest it has been since the country began compiling the statistics in 1899. As a result, Japan is now selling more adult diapers than baby diapers.[47] Untethering is happening across western Europe as well, as more people are living single, and fewer are becoming parents. In England and Wales, marriage has hit a record low.[48] Similar to the United States, many in these countries are likely to reach their forties having never had children. In 1946, only 9 percent of English and Welsh women had no children; now that number has about doubled, to 17 percent. In Germany, 22 percent of women reach their early forties without having children; in Hamburg, 32 percent do.[49] In almost all of the countries that compose the Organization for Economic Cooperation and Development (OECD), marriage rates have plum-meted compared to those recorded in both 1970 and 1995.[50] The always-on demand of work facilitated by device connectivity is one possible reason for these changes. Another may well be the notion of unlimited choice of partners, explored earlier—the idea that there is an unlimited sea of possible romantic partners available as online dating finds its way into these areas. The increasing lure of an untethered, digital-nomad lifestyle of travel spelled out on Instagram is a third possible reason for the decline in putting down roots. These kinds of social impacts of global untethering, including the growth of digital surveil-lance, and a waning workforce as fertility falls below replacement, are beginning to surface. Their long-term impacts still remain to be seen.

POWERING THE UNTETHERED WORLD

Setting aside the social implications for a moment, we must remember that it takes electricity to power all of these devices and to keep an increasingly networked society of "smart" devices going. As one of the untethered generation's cornerstone values, technology defines their age group. Yet 24/7 connectivity for mobile devices and internet access means their devices need constant charging. Young people are not above "stealth charging," that is, plugging into any and every available electrical socket to keep their device powered on. I live in a building with a doorman: At Christmastime last year, a young man with a KFC bag and a large soda pushed in behind me after the doorman buzzed me into the building. He wasn't someone I'd seen before in the building, so he caught my eye. Having seen the lit-up Christmas tree in the atrium, he figured there was a plug nearby. I watched him carefully set his bag and drink on the floor, pull out his phone, unroll a charge cord, and plug in. The doorman went over to him, to get him out, but he encountered pushback: "I'm just charging my phone!" he said angrily, as if that were reason enough to let him into a private, locked building.

People like this young man will do almost anything for a charge: According to my friend who works in streaming media, people regularly try to plug into the onstage power outlets of bands and performers during live shows. Even more appalling, an unruly and possibly intoxicated passenger on an IndiGo flight tried to force his way into the cockpit of the plane, stating that his mobile phone needed to be charged.[51] One young man even jumped up onto the stage at a Broadway play, where he tried to plug his phone into a fake outlet. An audience member who was present that night, Chris York, described what happened on his Facebook page:

> At "Hand to God" tonight, I saw an audience member climb onto the stage right before the show and plug his cell phone into a (fake) electrical outlet on the set. ON. THE. SET. The crew had to stop the pre-show music, remove the cell phone, and make an announcement as to why you can't do that. Truly. Moron. Has theatre etiquette—heck, Common Sense—[really] fallen that far??[52]

Of course, the entire incident was filmed by another theater patron and shared on social media, since filming has become everyone's first reaction when an incident happens.[53] This isn't limited to airplanes and stage performances, though. At work, people have accidently unplugged their boss' computers while trying to get a charge; one young man even shut down a flight-schedule screen at the airport in his desperation to plug in, saying:

> Once I shut off the flight schedule screen unknowingly at Peshawar airport when I pulled out the cord and tried to put my charger in the socket. The security personnel rushed at me and I was greatly ashamed when told that I had switched off the screen.[54]

A librarian in the United Kingdom said he's even seen fights break out over charging issues:

> I work for public libraries and I regularly see fights breaking out due to phone charging. In addition, people often unplug our devices. The most dangerous was someone who had shoved a screwdriver into the earth socket, so they could plug a European plug straight in, without an adapter.[55]

Another fellow saw a woman's attempt to find a charge at a children's hospital, perhaps to keep in touch with relatives about a sick or injured child. In her haste, she chose an unfortunate thing to unplug:

> I once sat in the waiting area in Bristol children's hospital with my little girl. We saw a woman go up to the fish tank and unplug it in order to plug her phone charger in! She was aghast when the receptionist told her to remove it and plug the fish tank back in.[56]

Clearly, this need for constant connectivity leads to a demand for "roaming energy," energy on the go for the untethered. I've even seen "emergency charges," single-use disposable charges, for sale on the counter of my local package-and-shipping store to meet this growing requirement. These devices plug right into phones or other electronics and are powered to release an "emergency" charge when no outlet is available; they are then discarded when used up. To satisfy this appetite for an opportunity to charge one's devices, it seems that charging as a service may be needed, perhaps provided as a perk by local businesses inside coffee shops, or as an incentive to frequent other small businesses, which can be advertised with a "Charging Inside" sign on the front window, or perhaps with a new category on Yelp to indicate that chargers are available. The availability of an outlet or charging station may attract people who will stay long enough to garner a significant charge. People may also likely be willing to pay a premium for energy on demand at kiosk charging stations in order to maintain connectivity. Inductive charging may also become an attractive solution to the charging problem—through which phones and other devices can be charged from thirty feet away. Retail settings or business settings like trade shows could let shoppers or potential clients charge while spending time at the shop or trade-show booth. Providing charging facilities for people for whom always-on connectivity is a core value may prove to be a successful lure for businesses trying to attract younger consumers. Also, more green, renewable energy will be needed to power not only our devices but also the datacenter infrastructure behind it all that keeps the networks up and running.

THE UPSIDES OF AN UNTETHERED WORLD

All is not lost. Clearly there are positive effects emerging alongside the drawbacks of global connectivity. A majority of Millennials (72 percent) now value experiences over the acquisition of things. Their new American Dream is to make a difference in the world. In some ways, their motto might be "better living through technology," as they find new and unique ways to deploy technology for social impact. The ability to amplify social impact is related to the ability of a network to exceed any individual's personal knowledge and social connections, allowing him or her to leverage skills, goods, services, and opportunities on a global scale by virtue of digital connectivity. Three significant areas of positive societal impact that are coming out of global connectivity and social media include: (1) global learning, philanthropy, and employment; (2) citizen journalism; and (3) global citizenship.

(1) Global Learning, Philanthropy, and Employment

In places like sub-Saharan Africa, mobile phones are now more common than is the access to electricity to operate them, which sometimes means they have to walk for miles to get a charge.[57] In other parts of the world, there are more cell phones than there are toilets.[58] This is partly because poorer countries whose populations were late to the game in developing infrastructure were able to leapfrog over older landline technologies and go straight to mobile phones.[59] As such, services and goods like philanthropic aid can be sent directly to recipients in need, possibly with the use of cryptocurrencies; this process bypasses potentially corrupt governmental or business entities. Clean Water Coin is one such cryptocurrency, which was designed to raise money for the nonprofit called Charity: Water, an organization that works to provide clean water to families around the world.[60] Another philanthropy, the Pineapple Fund, has donated $56 million in Bitcoin to fifty-six hand-selected charities.[61] Additionally, some philanthropic organizations and individuals are creating their own digital platforms to achieve positive social change. For example, Lalit Gautam, an Indian Millennial tech entrepreneur now living in Paris, is creating opportunity for impoverished artisans in rural India through his social-impact platform Handscart.com. In a private Facebook Messenger conversation with me, he describes its development:

> The condition of Indian rural communities is very bad. Seventy percent of the population depends on agriculture which is seasonable and then the rest are producers of crafts. They are in high demand all over the world but still, the condition of artisans is bad—why? Because middle men and commission agents take all the profits. . . . The artisans then started making products that are poor quality with machines, so they think the demand is lower (as sales drop for these cheaper quality objects). Another reason that artisans in rural areas are very poor and illiterate is they don't have power: no TV, no smartphone, no Internet, so they are not aware of marketing and selling and the demand for [their] products. I decided to start something to make them sustainable and employed. I created a platform where they can sell with the help of us. We eliminate commission and the middle man and make them self-sustainable, so they can afford their own homes and toilets by self-funding. We also help them become educated [via] skills education.

Access to a global marketplace and education at levels above their local area's resources are both important positive social innovations enabled by a digital connectivity that can help lift people out of poverty the world over. Other such high-impact digital businesses will continue to develop, as evidenced by an entire sector of social-impact investing that has emerged to support them as they do, and whose sole aim is to fund prosocial business ventures, including education for girls.[62]

(2) Citizen Journalism

A second and very important good to emerge out of global connectivity is citizen journalism. With "fake news" spreading virally, it becomes critical to have alternative stories from verifiable local sources. The ability to report news through connected cell phones, be it through Twitter, uploaded videos on YouTube, or something as simple as a short message service (SMS) text message, means that people who previously did not have a voice can be heard, adding to media diversity. Citizen journalists have agitated for change around the globe; one example of this is the Arab Spring that began in Tunisia in 2010, sparked by twenty-six-year-old fruit vendor Mohamed Bouazizi, who set himself on fire after refusing to give in to a governmental inspector's pressure for bribes.[63] His helplessness and desperation evoked a wave of sympathy, and protesters rose up, aided by hashtags on Twitter and other social media. The movement quickly spread to Libya, Egypt, Yemen, Syria, and Bahrain, leading to the toppling of long-standing governmental regimes.[64] It's worth noting that nearly a third of the population in the Middle East is between the ages of fifteen and twenty-nine, and all are digital natives.[65] Another recent social movement fueled by social media is the #MeToo campaign, begun in 2017. This movement calls attention to sexual harassment, originally centered in the tech and media industries. It has resulted in the resignation of and in some cases litigation against powerful men, ranging from venture capitalists in Silicon Valley to movie producer Harvey Weinstein, comedian and senator Al Franken, and former host of *The Today Show* Matt Lauer.[66] The 2018 #WhiteWednesday movement is yet another; it surfaced among Iranian youth and women. Seeking gender equality and better social conditions, young women wore white and some even removed their hijabs in protest, posting photos of themselves on social media and demanding equal rights.[67] Roxana Dumitrache, the Cultural Programs Coordinator for International Affairs at the Romanian Cultural Institute, expressed her solidarity with the protesters by posting a dramatic black-and-white photo on Twitter of an Iranian woman protester in Mashhad, with her loose, long blond hair flowing down her back and her hijab in hand. Dumitrache wrote:

> Solidarity with the Iranian waving her hijab on the sidewalk of a crowded Mashhad street, risking her freedom and perhaps her life. An almost cinematic frame: on a busy boulevard, in the hysterical murmur of horns and street noise, her hijab becomes a white flag.[68]

Platforms are emerging to encourage and support citizen journalism, with training, tools, and other support, like the communications agency On Our Radar, which allows isolated communities or individuals to share their experiences. Cofounded in 2012 by digital native, journalist, and activist Libby Powell, On Our Radar has so far trained at least four hundred citizen journalists to report and share their stories from the ground in their communities, using nothing more than voicemail and text messaging.[69] The agency's work ranges from issues around poverty and public health (including youth homelessness, the Ebola virus, and dementia) to political accountability. In the year of its founding, On Our Radar's citizen journalists reported on the election in Sierra Leone, which helped bring about changes in the voting process there.

Global connectivity and communications networks like Twitter or Facebook mean that social movements are unhooked from geographic place. As a result, social and environmental movements are likely to mobilize a much larger audience of supporters, creating a much wider oculus of visibility and a "ripple effect" of activism and rallying of support across the global stage. Issues are no longer localized in this connected world of ours, and citizen journalists can help get the word out, even helping out in disaster recovery and relief efforts, such as in the drone photography for earthquake relief work being done by Dr. Gonzalo Bacigalupe in Chile.[70]

(3) Global Citizenship

Being untethered represents a paradigm shift for understanding life in the digital era. Yuval Noah Harari's thesis from his book *Sapiens* is that religion was a fiction that helped us live together without killing each other. Capitalism is a newer fiction, the idea that we can specialize in one thing and get paid so we don't have to master every skill we would otherwise need to learn to stay alive, much less feed and provide great lives for our families. Now, social spaces on digital networks are a third-generation fiction within which we increasingly live. Digital social networks broaden our horizons beyond the provincial bounds that constricted us in the past. We can find support—be it financial, emotional, skills-related, or otherwise—from people around the world, knowing we are not alone. Digital connectivity is a force multiplier. It presents us with options on how to live, and where. We can see others' lifestyles and learn from how they solve problems, rather than stumbling through life, reinventing the wheel every single time.

Via connected mobile devices, global Wi-Fi, and social media, the world has grown both smaller and more complex simultaneously. This necessitates a new way of thinking, one that takes into account the broader systems and the context in which people and organizations exist. Younger, untethered digital natives already understand this; they see themselves as part of a much larger, global network when compared to previous generations. In fact, Millennials are the generation most likely to see themselves as "citizens of the world," according to long-term pollster John Zogby, who refers to them as "First Globals."[71] Picking up and living somewhere else in the world, backpacking through Europe or Asia, or lending a hand for a humanitarian project in sub-Saharan Africa over college spring break makes all the sense in the world to them.

Many of the grand challenges that we face, not only as citizens of a country but as citizens of the world, require cooperation and collaboration across national boundaries. These include climate change, emergency responses to natural or human-made disasters, public-health challenges, overfishing of the seas, pollution, lifting people out of poverty through education, clean energy usage, and other large-scale problems. Yet many of these issues are so far beyond the everyday human scale that, for many people, they are too abstract and too hard to grasp. For example, climate change and any efforts we make to counteract it may take generations to see results. Yet putting a human face on these issues through getting to know those who are being affected by them right now can increase empathy as well as philanthropy and charitable giving. Seeing a face and becoming acquainted with someone else through his or her stories humanizes large-scale, esoteric global issues and increases the likelihood that people will get involved. We are at our core a social species; as a cornerstone of being human, we are curious about one another and in need of connection. Without being connected to others, we as a species would have died off long ago. Digital connectivity holds the promise of facilitating people reaching out and making or maintaining cross-cultural connections, more fully realizing our human potential and putting a face people can empathize with on the most pressing issues of our time.

At an energy and technology conference in Paris, I ended up seated next to a charming young woman named Wafa. We could not be more different: I'm a city dweller, and I was dressed in a business suit, pearls, and a scarf, with my blonde hair in a cascade of curls. Wafa's hair was completely covered; she was dressed modestly, head to toe, in the traditional Muslim garb of a chocolate-brown abaya and tan hijab. She conversed easily with our various table members, in Arabic, French, and very good English, and she was delighted at my attempts (albeit elementary) at speaking both French and Italian, since "most Americans only speak one language!" she exclaimed with a laugh. She was a young Muslim who was also a trained engineer. Her warm smile immediately drew me in, and I asked her where she was from. She replied, "Algeria, in the middle of the Sahara Desert!" She was there to present a paper on ways to use solar technology to help her people survive the brutal conditions in which they find themselves. She was exploring how solar ovens could be used to feed her people the camel meat that is a dietary staple. I asked her about the temperature in Algeria, to which she said with a laugh, "It is the hottest place on the planet!" Wafa told me about life in her tiny town outside Algiers, describing it in the most glowing terms. With a light in her eyes and a warm smile, she said, "It's not luxury . . . but we're happy. At night, we go out and everyone is smiling, and there's music. We eat good food, and we're happy. Look at my kids." She showed me her son, buried neck deep in the sand with a funny smile on his face, and her little girl, playing with another girl outside in the early-evening on deep-red sand. She told me about a nearby oasis, and how beautiful it is. She said, "You should come see!" Then she surprised me with, "Are you on Facebook?" I said yes, and she immediately friended me. Even in the middle of the Sahara Desert, Facebook. Wafa then asked me about my work. When I told her that I look at the impact of technologies on society, she looked down, then with some hesitation asked me, "With all these technologies, do you think people are really happy? We have a simple life. But we are happy. Come visit me in the desert. I will show you." Her question made me stop and think. *Are* we really happier with all our devices?

Franklin Vagnone, the historic preservationist friend in New York whom I introduced you to earlier—while he was banging away on the little vintage Olivetti typewriter, typing out his thank-you notes—also made me think about our connection to our devices in a different way. He sent me a link to his blog recently, with pictures and reflections of a trip he took to a historic home in Australia. First of all, it really is a modern-day technological marvel that we can send photos and videos around the world instantaneously, and we simply take it for granted. Not long ago, this alone would have been nearly impossible, or it would have taken a half hour or more for a single photo to download on a dial-up modem connection to a computer bulletin board. Now, these kinds of experiences across time and space have become an unremarkable part of our daily routines. One of the photos Franklin sent was of a riotous array of colors of a garden in full bloom, later echoed in a colorful display of food on his plate at lunch. Photos of the vista outside showed far-off mountains towering over a green plain. Inside, a golden light bathed the inviting but worn sitting room, awash with saturated colors of oranges, reds, and sunflower yellows. Looking at the pictures, I imagined Franklin—and myself as well—touching the antique and well-worn sofa, feeling the smooth texture of its fabric contrasted with the raised stitching of the jacquard pattern that covered the sturdy arms. I realized, while looking at the photos and seeing the world through Franklin's eyes, that he's not only preserving "history" but also, in his own quiet way, he is on a mission to preserve something else: In a world where experiences are increasingly virtualized and take place on a cold glass screen, Franklin reminds us of the gentle art of tactility, the restorative qualities of nature, the sensual joy of a meal together, the quiet and peace and joy of a garden in full bloom. Instead of merely history, he's preserving what it means to be human.

Wafa's question continued to eat at me after we parted, and it still does: "With all these technologies, do you think people are really happy?" It is probably because there was a ring of truth to her question. Could it be that maybe we *aren't* happier with all of these devices? Despite their benefits, I think maybe she's onto something when she talks about how her life lived unplugged from technology—at least sometimes—is a happier way of living. The increasing lack of analog experiences, combined with overprotective parenting, has left many younger digital natives ill prepared to take on the challenges of everyday life. Living sheltered from an analog life, young adults are suffering a lack of resiliency, that special quality that comes from overcoming obstacles in life, often through a painful process of trial and error. This bears out in college, as universities are now seeing a notable decline in grit among their students. The increasingly virtualized lives led by young people that has left them with a lack of practical experience and a lack of the skills needed to cope with predicaments as minor as finding a mouse in a dorm room—a problem that drove one student to call the police for help.[72] And, don't get me wrong, it's not about the mouse here. This is merely one example of a raft of issues for which younger digital natives lack the fortitude to face. With the anxiety their lack of preparedness causes them, some are seeking to comfort themselves in ways that are not healthy, like consuming alcohol or opioids or engaging in lots of random hookups, which ultimately leaves them feeling even more lonely and disconnected—especially the girls—which, in turn, drives more alcohol consumption, drug-taking, and risky behavior. Others are seeking a return to the analog, tactility, affection, and connection through pets, which are increasingly taking the place of humans in "comforting" people. On any given day, you will see at least a few "comfort dogs" walking across many college campuses. In the United States, there were 98 million pets in 1980; by 2014, that number had grown to 179 million, an 83 percent increase.[73] According to the American Animal Hospital Association

(AAHA), more than 80 percent of pet owners think of themselves as their pets' moms and dads. As of 2016, Millennials became the most likely of all generations to own a pet, with 35 percent of them saying that they have a dog and 35 percent reporting that they have a cat.[74] They are also adopting their pets at a younger age, with the average Millennial getting his or her first pet at age twenty-one; for Boomers, it was twenty-nine, typically after marriage and kids. As a result, Millennials are more likely to have a pet as a single person, contrasted with the "family pet" of before, which was part of the American Dream.[75] Consequently, Americans' spending on pets reached a new high of $70 billion in 2017, up $3 billion from 2016.[76] This trend is not confined to America, though, as countries across the world—including China, Russia, India, Brazil, Japan, and Vietnam—see booming growth in the pet market.[77] Pets are becoming humanized, seen as a beloved member of the family. In effect, among digital natives, pets are taking the place of the missing human connection, including children or committed romantic partners.

Our pets are a way to bring comfort, and also a way to bring tactility back to our lives. Their love and attention bring us simple joy. Thinking back on my conversation with Wafa about the happiness of her more analog life, our discussion reminded me—and should remind us all—to consciously make an effort to unplug from our devices for a bit, to create some "sacred spaces" where we reconnect with our family, friends, nature, and ourselves.[78] I'm not suggesting a return to Thoreau's *Walden Pond*, or a neo-Amish way of living sans electronics. I like the fun of texting or checking Instagram or Facebook as much as the next person. But the research gives me pause: It shows us that the more time we spend on devices and social media, ultimately, the unhappier and unhealthier we are.[79] Somehow, we need to rebalance our lives, reconciling our desire to connect digitally with the remembrance that we are at our core still *embodied* creatures, and that the full excitation of our senses of touch, taste, and smell—that is, those senses that are largely left behind in a digital world—need to be a part of our regular, lived experience. We need to bring the body back into our lives via face-to-face communication, forays into nature, holding each other's hands, and seeking out more analog, hands-on experiences. As digital as our lives have become, tactility and the senses are a part of our embodied experience of the world, and they are a source of pleasure, comfort, and inspiration. A life without them is dull, devoid of the full array of sensual experiences we are capable of. A simulated life is simply a thin veneer of all we are and can be. Perhaps we need to take a page from the slow-food movement's playbook to figure this out.

Slow food is a social movement created to counteract the growing dominance of fast food, to resist the technologies of industrial food production and instead to make and eat "slower," savoring better-quality, flavorful food that is healthier.[80] In a similar fashion, maybe we need to create a "slow device" movement to counterbalance our device obsession. Following such a countermovement, we would take time offline to connect, undistracted, with others; to sleep uninterrupted; to dream; to venture into the peacefulness and beauty of nature unmediated. To do so would be good for the body and the spirit.

Paradoxically, while individually we need to rebalance our personal use of devices, on a grander scale, our connectivity may just save us. The subtext Oppenheimer learned in the aftermath of the devastation wrought by the atomic bomb was that we must unite as peoples of this world, or we will perish; this unity may well be realizable, finally, through Zuckerberg's Facebook and other social media like it. Connected digital "citizens of the world" have the opportunity to link us all, through an ever-widening network of global friendships and connections, as more people come online across the world. These cross-cultural experiences can foster a more nuanced understanding of other people's lives, cultures, and circumstances. They offer us a new perspective on the issues that confront us all, by putting a human face on the greater challenges that need our help and attention—such as providing access to healthful food, clean water, education, and opportunity. Further, this may encourage us to adopt new practices to mitigate climate change and poverty and their harmful effects, to help others around the world.

My relationship with Wafa is an example of these global connections. My mind wanders to her, and I wonder what she is doing over there in the desert in that little town of hers on the other side of the world. In my mind, I can see her warm brown eyes and luminous smile radiating happiness from within. I like to imagine her with her arms encircling her children on the red sands of the Sahara on a moonlit night. What can her life teach us? "I'm waiting for you in the Sahara!" she said to me recently on Facebook Messenger, "And if one day, you come to join our caravan for an escapade for a time, the time of a dream? You will feel a little at home, because all souls yearn for serenity and silence and our Sahara is a real haven of peace."[81] Her life hints at a truth we may not have wanted to admit before: that the serenity and peace we seek will never be found online.

The friendship I have with Wafa—and with many others around the globe—would have been near impossible (and certainly improbable) years ago. Yet these kinds of relationships will become increasingly unremarkable, the everyday purview of digital natives who are becoming global citizens living in an untethered world. Experiences like this mark a new era of the globalization of the self, living a new dream on a much larger stage. These experiences offer us a different paradigm, as we learn to live not completely unbounded, but certainly less constrained by traditional bounds of nations and cultures, which in prior times were the purview of only the rich during their global travels. Digital connectivity virtualizes world travel, democratizing the experiences of other cultures as never before. Travel is still important, but digital connectivity gives us a glimpse and makes the world seem perhaps a bit more accessible a place.

Yet as we have seen, there is a cost to untethered living: Living online means that a broader spectrum of our behaviors are traceable and trackable, leaving us open to persuasion, manipulation, surveillance, and control. Our past is never past anymore: digital natives may strive to "live in the now," but the network never forgets. Other negative impacts are surfacing, including declining mental and physical health, waning social skills, and a lack of accountability, which encourages behaviors like "ghosting" on romantic or work relationships, as well as other nefarious exploits. The illusion of thousands of romantic choices leads people not to choose at all, often enhancing loneliness as they wait for perfection on the horizon, perfection that will never come. Comparisons to lives that don't exist on social media fuel anxiety and depression. Yet despite these drawbacks, social media and device connectivity continue to entice us, precisely because they digitize and serve up to us with greater ease than ever before many of our most basic social and psychological needs—the needs for affiliation and friendship, the need for approval, and opportunities for work or romance to which we might never have had access before. They satisfy our curiosity and our sense of adventure, providing hours of entertainment and leisure, both physical and virtual. They allow us to stay in touch with our family, near or far. And, increasingly, they provide us our most basics on Maslow's hierarchy of needs, like food, shelter, transportation, and clothing.[82] Can we learn to live in harmony with our digital lives? Can we balance our analog, embodied selves with the digital—the virtual with the face-to-face? Can we consciously connect, rather than simply being left to our own devices? If we can, then the untethered world's promise of cooperation, collaboration, and new opportunities is only just beginning.

NOTES

INTRODUCTION

1. Rory Reid, "Most Under-25s Can't Read a Map Because They Rely on Sat-Navs," CNet, July 11, 2011, https://www.cnet.com/roadshow/news/most-under-25s-cant-read-a-map -because-they-rely-on-sat-navs/.

2. Michael Winnick, "Putting a Finger on Our Phone Obsession," *DScout* (blog), June 16, 2016, https://blog.dscout.com/mobile-touches.

3. Rurik Bradbury, *Research Report: The Digital Lives of Millennials and Gen Z* (New York: LivePerson, September 2017), https://www.liveperson.com/resources/reports/ digital-lives-of-millennials-genz/.

4. "Swimming Pools (Drank)," written by Kendrick Lamar and Tyler "T-Minus" Williams, performed by Kendrick Lamar, released July 31, 2012, single, Top Dawg Entertainment; lyrics available at https://genius.com/Kendrick-lamar-swimming-pools-drank-lyrics.

5. Joe Keohane, "What News-Writing Bots Mean for the Future of Journalism," *Wired*, February 16, 2017, https://www.wired.com/2017/02/robots-wrote-this-story/.

6. Greg Dool, "Newsstand Sales Drop Another 12.4 Percent in 2016," *Folio*, March 7, 2017, https://www.foliomag.com/newsstand-sales-drop-another-12-4-percent-2016/.

7. "Once-Endangered Bookstores Are Booming Again," CBS News, April 23, 2018, https://www.cbsnews.com/news/once-endangered-bookstores-are-booming-again/.

8. Alley Wilson, "Dutch City Installs Lights in Sidewalk to Help Distracted Phone Users Cross the Street Safely," Global News, February 20, 2017, https://globalnews.ca/news/3257580/ dutch-city-installs-lights-in-sidewalk-to-help-distracted-phone-users-cross-the-street-safely/.

9. Cisco, "Air, Food, Water, Internet: Cisco Study Reveals Just How Important Internet and Networks Have Become as Fundamental Resources in Daily Life," news release, September 21, 2011, https://newsroom.cisco.com/press-release-content?articleId=474852.

10. Retired Sgt. Brink (@LASDBrink), "#Facebook is not a Law Enforcement issue, please don't call us about it being down, we don't know when FB will be back up!!" Twitter, August 1, 2014, 9:37 a.m., https://bit.ly/2DrTn6y.

11. Neetzan Zimmerman, "Teen Commits Suicide after Parents Ban Her from Facebook," *Gawker* (blog), https://bit.ly/1bDjb4W.

12. Sarah Manski and Ben Manski, "No Gods, No Masters, No Coders? The Future of Sovereignty in a Blockchain World," *Law & Critique* 29, no. 2 (July 2018): 151–62, https:// link.springer.com/article/10.1007/s10978-018-9225-z.

13. T. Smith, "Coming of Age in Twenty-First Century America: Public Attitudes Towards the Importance and Timing of Transitions to Adulthood," *Ageing International* 29, no. 2 (2004): 136–48.

14. For more on Coboat see: Coboat, Facebook, https://www.facebook.com/Coboat.

15. "20Mission: San Francisco," 20Mission, http://www.20mission.com/.

16. Cory Doe, in interview with the author, June 15, 2015, in Portland, OR.

17. Michael Hurwitz and Jason Lee, "Grade Inflation and the Role of Standardized Testing," in *Measuring Success: Testing, Grades, and the Future of College Admissions*, ed. Jack Buckley, Lynn Letukas, and Ben Wildavsky (Baltimore, MD: Johns Hopkins University Press, 2018).

18. Anthony P. Carnevale, Nicole Smith, and Jeff Strohl, "Recovery: Job Growth and Education Requirements through 2020," CEW Georgetown, January 31, 2018, https://bit.ly/2n9ECba.

19. Drew DeSilver, "U.S. Students' Academic Achievement Still Lags That of Their Peers in Many Other Countries," Pew Research Center, Washington, DC, February 15, 2017, http://www.pewresearch.org/fact-tank/2017/02/15/u-s-students-internationally-math-science/.

20. Jamie Varon, "This Is How We Date Now," *Thought Catalog* (blog), last updated October 23, 2018, https://thoughtcatalog.com/jamie-varon/2014/12/this-is-how-we-date-now/.

21. Cory Doe, "Untethered Millennial Lifestyle," interview by the author, June 8, 2015.

22. Ibid.

23. For more on the Summer of Love, see Sheila Weller, "Suddenly That Summer," *Vanity Fair*, July 2012, https://bit.ly/2IVbhB1.

24. Adrienne Rich, "Song." Copyright © 2016 by the Adrienne Rich Literary Trust. Copyright © 1973 by W. W. Norton & Company, Inc., from *Collected Poems: 1950–2012* by Adrienne Rich. Used by permission of W. W. Norton & Company, Inc.

25. Noelle Hancock, "Why I Gave Up a $95,000 Job to Move to an Island and Scoop Ice Cream," *Cosmopolitan*, October 9, 2017, https://www.cosmopolitan.com/lifestyle/a39772/why-i-gave-up-a-95k-job-to-move-to-an-island/.

26. Matthew Townsend, "Gump's Survived the San Francisco Earthquake—But Not E-Commerce," Bloomberg, August 4, 2018, https://bloom.bg/2M7lpHM.

27. Gabby Noone, "Kanye West's Latest Yeezy Collection Sold Out in 5 Minutes," MTV News, March 29, 2017, https://on.mtv.com/2OdeiLk.

28. Ismael Hermosillo Jr., in interview with the author, August 4, 2018.

29. Alexis Pankerson, in interview with the author, August 4, 2018.

30. Lauren Debter, "McDonald's Profit Drops 13% as Sales Slump Persists," *Forbes*, July 23, 2015, https://www.forbes.com/sites/laurengensler/2015/07/23/mcdonalds-second-quarter-earnings/.

31. Nancy Luna, "Chipotle Same-Store Sales Up on Higher Checks, Digital Sales Gains," *Nation's Restaurant News*, July 27, 2018, https://bit.ly/2R91zeG.

32. America's Health Rankings, "Disconnected Youth in United States in 2018" (Minneapolis, MN: United Health Foundation, 2018), https://bit.ly/2NOOGbL.

33. Michael Suh, "Millennials: Unmoored from Institutions," Pew Research Center: Social and Demographic Trends, Washington, DC, March 5, 2014, https://pewrsr.ch/2nZW3f4.

34. Kevin Granville, "Facebook and Cambridge Analytica: What You Need to Know as Fallout Widens," *New York Times*, March 19, 2018, https://www.nytimes.com/2018/03/19/ technology/facebook-cambridge-analytica-explained.html.

35. For more on the Bolt lightbulb from Misfit, see "Welcome, Misfit," Misfit, https:// misfit.com/go/bolt.

36. Nurfilzah Rohaidi, "IBM's Watson Detected Rare Leukemia in Just 10 Minutes," *Asian Scientist Magazine*, August 15, 2016, https://bit.ly/2mzdlzL.

CHAPTER 1: BECOMING TETHERED

1. Jon Meacham, *Franklin and Winston: An Intimate Portrait of an Epic Friendship* (New York: Random House, 2003), p. 356.

2. Walter Isaacson and Evan Thomas, "The Wise Men: Six Friends and the World They Made," in *The Wise Men: Six Friends and the World They Made* (New York: Simon & Schuster, 2013), p. 270.

3. "Winston Churchill and the Queen on VE Day," Winston Churchill on May 8, 1945, posted on November 23, 2010, YouTube video, 9:25, https://youtu.be/rePb2NadxQw.

4. Ibid.

5. Steven James Hantzis, *Rails of War: Supplying the Americans and Their Allies in China-Burma-India* (Lincoln, NE: Potomac Books, 2017).

6. John Bush Jones, *All-Out for Victory! Magazine Advertising and the World War II Home Front / John Bush Jones*, 1st ed. (Lebanon, NH: University Press of New England, 2009).

7. Cari Romm, "The World War II Campaign to Bring Organ Meats to the Dinner Table," *Atlantic*, September 25, 2014, https://www.theatlantic.com/health/archive/2014/09/ the-world-war-ii-campaign-to-bring-organ-meats-to-the-dinner-table/380737/.

8. Amy Bentley and Drew Gilpin Faust, *Eating for Victory: United States Food Rationing and the Politics of Domesticity during World War Two* (PhD Diss., ProQuest Dissertations and Theses, University of Pennsylvania, 1992).

9. E. M. Collingham, *The Taste of War: World War II and the Battle for Food*, 1st American ed. (New York: Penguin, 2012).

10. Roger A. Bruns, *Zoot Suit Riots*, Landmarks of the American Mosaic (Santa Barbara, CA: Greenwood, 2014).

11. "General Paul Tibbets: Reflections on Hiroshima," interview by Tom Ryan, Manhattan Project Voices, 1989, https://www.manhattanprojectvoices.org/oral-histories/ general-paul-tibbets---reflections-hiroshima.

12. Richard Sisk, "Here's How the Crew of the Enola Gay Crew Recalled the First Atomic Weapons Attack in History," *Business Insider*, August 7, 2015, https://read.bi/2PRVTEl.

13. To hear recordings of the big band remotes, see "The Big Bands on One Night Stand Volume 3," Radio Archives, 2018, https://www.radioarchives.com/The_Big_Bands_on_One _Night_Stand_Volume_3_p/ra163.htm.

14. "African-American Soldiers in World War II Helped Pave Way for Integration of US

Military," Voice of America News, October 31, 2009, https://www.voanews.com/a/a-13-2005
-05-10-voa47-67929177/396374.html.

15. Although certainly black and women's rights still lagged behind white men's during this
time, both of these groups benefited by their participation in the war effort. The same processes
and effects that I have detailed for whites were also at work for blacks during the war, just greatly
reduced/handicapped by racism. They lagged whites in terms of mobility and opportunities, but
they still began to see similar possibilities. The same with women, though it is notable that women's
workforce participation never went back to pre-World War II levels. Civil rights and women's
rights movements soon followed on the heels of the war, as they struggled to maintain and expand
their newfound status and freedoms established during their wartime participation.

16. Jean-Francois Pitet, "Zanzibar Cafe, New York: Home of Cab Calloway,"
HiDeHoBlog (blog)," http://www.thehidehoblog.com/blog/2009/10/zanzibar-cafe
-new-york-home-of-cab-calloway.

17. For more on the history of the Cafe Zanzibar, see ibid.

18. To hear the original recording of the announcement of Japan accepting the Potsdam
Resolution during the Big Band Remote from Cafe Zanzibar, listen online at https://bit.ly/
2OzcEET.

19. "Victory Over Japan," Radio Days, April 5, 2014, http://www.otr.com/vj.html.

20. Adams first coined the phrase "the American Dream" in *The Epic of America*, 2nd ed.
(Greenwood, 1931), p. 404.

21. *Keeping Up with the Kardashians*, created by Ryan Seacrest and Eliot Goldberg
(Calabasas, CA: Bunim-Murray Productions, 2007).

22. "He Who Does with the Most Toys Wins Steel Metal License Plate Frame Auto Tag #
49," Amazon, https://www.amazon.com/Steel-Metal-License-Plate-Frame/dp/B00F8RYBS2.

23. Andrew Marks, "Cracking the Kindergarten Code," *New York Magazine*, December
29, 2016.

24. Gavin Wright, *Sharing the Prize: The Economics of the Civil Rights Revolution in the
American South* (Cambridge, MA: Belknap Press of Harvard University Press, 2013).

25. C. I. Jones, "Chapter 1: The Facts of Economic Growth," in *Handbook of
Macroeconomics*, ed. John B. Taylor, Harald Uhlig, vol. 2 (Amsterdam: Elsevier 2016), pp. 3–69,
https://doi.org/10.1016/bs.hesmac.2016.03.002.

26. US Department of Labor, "Chapter 3: The Department in the New Deal and World
War II, 1933–1945," History of the Department, https://www.dol.gov/general/aboutdol/
history/dolchp03.

27. Daniel Fetter, "How Do Mortgage Subsidies Affect Home Ownership? Evidence from
the Mid-Century GI Bills" (working paper, National Bureau of Economic Research, Cambridge,
MA, 2011).

28. Betty Friedan, "The Problem That Has No Name," *American Journal of Public Health*
100, no. 9 (2010): 1582–84.

29. Michael Callahan, "The Sorority on 63rd Street," *Vanity Fair*, April 2010, http://www
.vanityfair.com/culture/2010/04/barbizon-hotel-201004.

30. Steven Meloan, "Jeri and Taylor Meloan," interview by Julie M. Albright, January 19,
2015.

31. Jack Kerouac, *On the Road* (New York: Penguin, 2018), p. 86.

32. Steven Meloan, "Googies," *Sonoma Valley Sun*, September 28, 2015, http://sonomasun.com/2015/09/28/googies-steve-meloan/.

33. Zillow, "Hawthorne CA Home Prices & Home Values," Premier Agent Resource Center, data through September 30, 2018, https://www.zillow.com/hawthorne-ca/home-values/.

34. "Tailor Salaries in Los Angeles, CA," Indeed, last updated October 24, 2018, https://www.indeed.com/salaries/Tailor-Salaries,-Los-Angeles-CA.

35. "Born of Controversy: The GI Bill of Rights" (Washington, DC: US Department of Veterans Affairs, June 24, 2008).

36. William Schneider, "The Suburban Century Begins," *Atlantic* 270, no. 1 (1992): 33.

37. "Median Age at First Marriage, 1890–2006," Infoplease, 2018.

38. Sandra L. Colby and Jennifer M. Ortman, "The Baby Boom Cohort in the United States: 2012 to 2060" (Washington, DC: United States Census Bureau, May 2014), https://binged.it/2vvkyWO.

39. Douglas Charles, "From Subversion to Obscenity: The FBI's Investigations of the Early Homophile Movement in the United States, 1953–1958," *Journal of the History of Sexuality* 19, no. 2 (2010): 262–87, 386.

40. Matthew Josephson, *The Robber Barons: The Great American Capitalists, 1861–1901* (New York: Harcourt, Brace, 1934).

41. Michael D. Carr and Emily E. Wiemers, "The Decline in Lifetime Earnings Mobility in the U.S.: Evidence from Survey-Linked Administrative Data" (working paper; Washington Center for Equitable Growth, Washington, DC, May 2016), https://equitablegrowth.org/working-papers/the-decline-in-lifetime-earnings-mobility-in-the-u-s-evidence-from-survey-linked-administrative-data/.

42. "Milken Set to Pay a $600 Million Fine in Wall St. Fraud," *New York Times*, April 21, 1990.

43. Chris Serico, "Drew Barrymore Opens Up about How Her 'Odd Childhood' Made Her a Better Mom," Today, October 28, 2015, https://www.today.com/series/secrets-of-success/drew-barrymore-opens-about-how-her-odd-childhood-made-her-t52466.

44. Michael E. Eidenmuller, "Wall Street (1987): Gordon Gekko; Address to Teldar Paper Shareholders," American Rhetoric: Movie Speeches, 2001, https://bit.ly/2LGqrLX.

45. Adam Smith, *The Wealth of Nations* (Scotland: W. Strahan and T. Cadell, London, 1776), available online at https://www.goodreads.com/ebooks/download/25698?doc=749.

46. Boston Record Commissioners, *A Report of the Record Commissioners of the City of Boston* (Boston: Rockwell and Churchill, 1876).

47. Betty Friedan, *The Feminine Mystique* (New York: W. W. Norton, 1963).

48. Jesse Bering, "Half Dead: Men and the 'Midlife Crisis,'" *Scientific American* (blog), https://blogs.scientificamerican.com/bering-in-mind/half-dead-men-and-the-mid-life-crisis/.

49. *American Beauty*, directed by Sam Mendes (Glendale, CA: DreamWorks, 2018).

50. T. Fahy, ed., *Alan Ball: Conversations* (Jackson, MS: University Press of Mississippi, 2013), p. 9.

51. Hugo Martin, "L.A. County Sets Another Tourism Record with 48.3 Million Visitors

Last Year," *Los Angeles Times*, January 10, 2018, http://www.latimes.com/business/la-fi-la
-tourism-20180110-story.html.

52. Laura Barton, "Boulevard of Broken Dreams," *1843*, November/December 2013,
https://bit.ly/2PqXHb7.

53. Émile Durkheim, *Suicide: A Study in Sociology* (London: Routledge, 2006).

54. For more on this, see Stephanie Cardwell's "Reckless Reevaluated: Containment
Theory and Its Ability to Explain Desistance Among Serious Adolescent Offenders" (thesis,
University of Alabama at Birmingham, 2013), https://bit.ly/2Ked8wy.

55. Durkheim, *Suicide*. Durkheim also explored this theme in an earlier book, Émile
Durkheim, *The Division of Labor in Society*, trans. W. D. Halls (New York: Free Press, 1984).

56. See the 2016 film *I, Daniel Blake*, directed by Ken Loach (London: Sixteen Films;
Wild Bunch; BBC Films, 2016), for an exploration of this.

57. Émile Durkheim, *Suicide: A Study in Sociology*, trans. John A. Spaulding and George
Simpson; ed. and intro. by George Simpson (New York: Free Press, 1966), p. IV.

58. "Suicide," National Institute of Mental Health, May 2018, https://www.nimh.nih
.gov/health/statistics/suicide.shtml.

59. David M. Downes and Paul Elliott Rock, *Understanding Deviance: A Guide to the
Sociology of Crime and Rule-Breaking*, 5th ed. (Oxford; New York: Oxford University Press,
2007).

60. W. Reckless, "A New Theory of Delinquency and Crime," *Federal Probation* 25, no. 4
(1961): 42.

61. "United States Forecast on Urbanization 2000–2050," Statista, May 2018, https://bit
.ly/2OlHDqx.

62. *The Unprecedented Opioid Epidemic* (Washington, DC: Police Executive Research
Forum, September 2017), https://binged.it/2n1cDNf.

63. Ruben Castaneda, "Millennials Hit Hard by Opioids," *US News & World Report*,
March 12, 2018, https://bit.ly/2vv9vjL.

64. "Drug Overdose Death Data," Centers for Disease Control and Prevention, December
19, 2017, https://www.cdc.gov/drugoverdose/data/statedeaths.html.

65. Diana Henriques, "Andrew Madoff, Who Told of His Father's Swindle, Dies at 48,"
New York Times, September 3, 2014, https://nyti.ms/2M872zv.

66. Diana Henriques, "Madoff Is Sentenced to 150 Years for Ponzi Scheme," *New York
Times*, June 29, 2009, http://www.nytimes.com/2009/06/30/business/30madoff.html.

67. Carl Benedikt Frey and Michael A. Osborne, "The Future of Employment: How
Susceptible Are Jobs to Computerization?" (working paper, University of Oxford, Oxford, UK,
September 17, 2013), https://www.oxfordmartin.ox.ac.uk/downloads/academic/The_Future
_of_Employment.pdf.

68. Zack Friedman, "Student Loan Debt Statistics in 2018: A $1.5 Trillion Crisis," *Forbes*,
October 26, 2018, https://bit.ly/2UYztok.

69. P. H. Lindert and J. G. Williamson, *Unequal Gains: American Growth and Inequality
Since 1700* (Princeton: Princeton University Press, 2016).

70. J. Guo, "Income Inequality Today May Be Higher Today Than in Any Other Era,"
Washington Post, July 1, 2016, http://wapo.st/2q4YvU2.

71. *Requiem for the American Dream*, directed by Peter D. Hutchison, Kelly Nyks, and Jared P. Scott, featuring Noam Chomsky (Naked City Films, 2015). Trailer available at "Noam Chomsky—'Requiem for the American Dream' Trailer," Noam Chomsky, April 6, 2015, YouTube video, 2:20, https://www.youtube.com/watch?v=zI_Ik7OppEI.

CHAPTER 2: SYNCHRONIZATION AND HARMONIZATION

1. Gus Lubin, "The 13 Richest Americans of All Time," *Business Insider*, April 17, 2011, http://www.businessinsider.com/richest-americans-ever-2011-4#1-john-d-rockefeller-13. In comparison, the richest man in modern history, Jeff Bezos of Amazon, was worth $150 billion in 2018. "#1 Jeff Bezos," *Forbes*, July 19, 2018, https://www.forbes.com/profile/jeff-bezos/#845a3171b238.

2. "Financier's Fortune in Oil Amassed in Industrial Era of 'Rugged Individualism,'" *New York Times*, May 24, 1937, https://nyti.ms/2LIniLq.

3. Laura Schillington, "Graffiti, Space, and Gender," Nature of Cities, March 23, 2016, https://bit.ly/2lg32Tc.

4. Jeff Beer, "Shepard Fairey: Obey Obama," *Ad Age*, January 30, 2008, https://bit.ly/2MdFiJN.

5. Peter Schjeldahl, "Hope and Glory," *New Yorker* 85, no. 2 (2009): 79.

6. Michael Cooper and Michael Powell, "McCain Camp Says Obama Is Playing 'Race Card,'" *New York Times*, August 1, 2008, https://www.nytimes.com/2008/08/01/us/politics/01campaign.html.

7. "At Least 80 Electoral Votes Depended on Youth," Center for Information & Research on Civic Learning and Engagement, Tufts University, November 7, 2012, http://civicyouth.org/at-least-80-electoral-votes-depended-on-youth/.

8. Tom Rosentiel, "Inside Obama's Sweeping Victory," Pew Research Center, Washington, DC, November 5, 2008, https://pewrsr.ch/1QU0zo5.

9. Linda Qui, "Barack Obama's Top 25 Campaign Promises: How'd He Do?" PolitiFact, January 5, 2017, https://bit.ly/2zNh2uz.

10. "Exit Polls 2012: How the Vote Has Shifted," *Washington Post*, November 6, 2012, http://www.washingtonpost.com/wp-srv/special/politics/2012-exit-polls/table.html.

11. Thom File, "Young-Adult Voting: An Analysis of Presidential Elections, 1964–2012" (Washington, DC: US Department of Commerce, US Census Bureau, April 2014), https://bit.ly/1PiiLpa.

12. Julie Beck and Caroline Kitchener, "Early Signs of a Youth Wave," *Atlantic*, November 7, 2018, https://www.theatlantic.com/politics/archive/2018/11/youth-turnout-midterm-2018/575092/.

13. Michael Suh, "Millennials: Unmoored from Institutions," Pew Research Center, Washington, DC, March 5, 2014, https://pewrsr.ch/2nZW3f4.

14. A. Carfagna, "The First Globals: Understanding, Managing, and Unleashing the Potential of Our Millennial Generation," *International Educator* 23, no. 5 (2014): 16, 18.

15. Tom Hayden et al., *The Port Huron Statement* (Chicago: Students for a Democratic Society, 1962).

16. Tom Hayden, "Two, Three, Many Columbias," Hippyland, 1968, https://bit.ly/2OvlSEU.

17. A case could be made that these privileged young people are generous with wealth that is not their own, and that they may tend toward fiscal conservatism as they grow older and control their own wealth.

18. Daniel Fox, Robert P. Jones, and Thomas Banchoff, "A Generation in Transition: Religion, Values, and Politics among College-Age Millennials," Public Religion Research Institute, April 19, 2012, https://bit.ly/2OsYOX4.

19. Harvard Kennedy School Institute of Politics, "Harvard IOP Summer 2016 Poll," news release, July 18, 2016, http://iop.harvard.edu/survey/details/harvard-iop-summer-2016-poll.

20. Marshall McLuhan, *Understanding Media: The Extensions of Man*, ed. W. Terrence Gordon, critical ed. (Corte Madera, CA: Gingko Press, 2003).

21. Christopher H. Sterling and John Michael Kittross, *Stay Tuned: A History of American Broadcasting*, 3rd ed. LEA's Communication Series (Mahwah, NJ: Lawrence Erlbaum Associates, 2002).

22. William Seaver Woods, Isaac K. Funk, and E. J. Wheeler, *Literary Digest* 73 (April–June 1922): 28.

23. Jason Loviglio, *Radio's Intimate Public: Network Broadcasting and Mass-Mediated Democracy* (Minneapolis: University of Minnesota Press, 2005).

24. Jack Lule, *Understanding Media and Culture: An Introduction to Mass Communication* (Boston, MA: FlatWorld, 2018).

25. Neil Postman, *Amusing Ourselves to Death: Public Discourse in the Age of Show Business* (New York: Viking, 1985).

26. Samantha Smith, "Less Overlap in the Political Views of Republicans and Democrats Than in the Past," Pew Research Center, Washington, DC, October 4, 2017, https://pewrsr.ch/2vrcqre.

27. Business Wire, "Frisch's Big Boy Restaurants Reveals Secrets of the Drive-Through Window," news release, August 23, 2016, http://bit.ly/2rlQNHf.

28. Mike Pomranz, "Millennials Just Don't Want to Deal with Restaurant Employees," *Food & Wine*, June 22, 2017, http://bit.ly/2sohbP9.

29. Amanda Lenhart, "Chapter 1: Meeting, Hanging Out and Staying in Touch: The Role of Digital Technology in Teen Friendships," Pew Research Center, Washington, DC, August 6, 2015, http://www.pewinternet.org/2015/08/06/chapter-1-meeting-hanging-out-and-staying-in-touch-the-role-of-digital-technology-in-teen-friendships/.

30. "Survey Shows 14–16 Year Olds Spent Summer in Their Bedroom," OnSide Youth Zones, September 25, 2016, https://www.onsideyouthzones.org/news/survey-shows-14-16-year-olds-spent-summer-in-their-bedroom/.

31. *The Cisco Connected World Technology Report* (San Jose, CA: Cisco, December 12, 2012).

32. "For Most Smartphone Users, It's a 'Round-the-Clock' Connection," Report Linker Insight, January 26, 2017, https://www.reportlinker.com/insight/smartphone-connection.html.

33. *Cisco Connected World Technology Report*.

34. A. Kleinman, "Nearly 20 Percent of Young Adults Use Their Smartphones During Sex: Survey," *HuffPost*, July 12, 2013, http://bit.ly/1faWIBO.

35. T. Veblen, *The Theory of the Leisure Class* (Worcestershire: Read Books, 2015).

36. Uptin Saiidi, "Millennials: Forget Material Things, Help Us Take Selfies," CNBC, May 6, 2016, https://cnb.cx/2Di1ORk.

37. Gavin Haines, "A Third of Millennials Say Posting Pictures on Social Media Is as Important as the Holiday Itself," *Telegraph*, August 23, 2018, https://bit.ly/2o46AIb.

38. Z. Y. Tan, "What Happens When Fashion Becomes Fast, Disposable And Cheap?" NPR, April 10, 2016, http://n.pr/1oOfJlN.

39. Vivian Hendriksz, "How the Selfie Effect Is Disrupting the Industry," Fashion United, August 4, 2016, https://bit.ly/2OX8UfV.

40. Maria Halkias, "Neiman Marcus Holds Tight to Top Standing in Luxury Retailing," *Dallas News*, April 26, 2016, https://bit.ly/2MaZEUh.

41. "Burning Man Event FAQ," Burning Man, 2018, https://burningman.org/event/preparation/faq/.

42. "Couchsurfing: Our Story," Couchsurfing, 2017, http://www.couchsurfing.com/about/about-us/.

43. "Millennials and Ride Hailing Services & Apps, Paving a New Path for Mobility," ReportLinker, September 20, 2017, https://bit.ly/2yrYGwc.

44. Flip: The Easiest Way to Sublet or Get Out of Your Lease, https://flip.lease/.

45. "The Assemblage: NoMad," GarysGuide, https://www.garysguide.com/spaces/b5ovmoz/The-Assemblage-NoMad.

46. Ryan Merkley, "A Transformative Year: State of the Commons 2017," Creative Commons, May 8, 2018, https://creativecommons.org/2018/05/08/state-of-the-commons-2017/.

47. Jim Giles, "Internet Encyclopaedias Go Head to Head," *Nature*, December 14, 2005, https://www.nature.com/articles/438900a.

48. D. Etherington, "People Now Watch 1 Billion Hours of YouTube Per Day," TechCrunch, February 28, 2017, https://techcrunch.com/2017/02/28/people-now-watch-1-billion-hours-of-youtube-per-day/.

49. Kif Leswing, "Postmates Is Scrapping Its 15-Minute Food Delivery Service for the Summer," *Business Insider*, June 30, 2016, https://read.bi/2LOmOUi.

50. Leanne Reis, "Breakthrough Offering from Mobile-Commerce Pioneer Tapingo Unlocks Revenue Stream for Universities," BusinessWire, August 3, 2015, https://www.businesswire.com/news/home/20150803005316/en/Breakthrough-Offering-Mobile-Commerce-Pioneer-Tapingo-Unlocks-New.

51. Ibid.

52. *2018 College Hopes & Worries Survey Report* (Princeton, NJ: Princeton Review, 2018), https://bit.ly/2nhikV2.

53. Kevin Chan, "SAE 515: My Views on Sustainability" (class report, SAE Institute, University of Southern California, Los Angeles, 2016).

54. *Consumer Pulse and Market Segmentation Study–Wave 6* (Atlanta, GA: Smart Grid Consumer Collaborative, 2017), https://binged.it/2Kj06xX.

55. G. Ritzer, *McDonaldization: Chicago, America, the World* (Thousand Oaks: Sage, 2003).

56. Monique, "Customization Online," class project, November 3, 2018, Cal State Los Angeles.

57. Alton Y. K Chua and Snehasish Banerjee, "Customer Knowledge Management via Social Media: The Case of Starbucks," *Journal of Knowledge Management* 17, no. 2 (2013): 237–49.

58. Y. N. Harari, *Sapiens: A Brief History of Humankind* (Toronto, Ontario: Signal, McClelland & Stewart, 2016).

59. Robert F. Kennedy Jr., *Crimes against Nature: How George W. Bush and His Corporate Pals Are Plundering the Country and Hijacking Our Democracy*, 1st ed. (New York: HarperCollins, 2004).

60. Thomas Houser, "The Fairness Doctrine: An Historical Perspective," *The Notre Dame Lawyer* 47 (1971): 550.

61. Mary Ann Cusack, "The Emergence of Political Editorializing in Broadcasting," *Journal of Broadcasting* 8, no. 1 (1963): 53–62.

62. "Supreme Court Upholds FCC 'Fairness Doctrine,'" *Back Stage* 10, no. 24 (1969): 1, 10.

63. Ford Rowan, *Broadcast Fairness: Doctrine, Practice, Prospects; A Reappraisal of the Fairness Doctrine and Equal Time Rule*, Longman Series in Public Communication (New York: Longman, 1984).

64. Edmund Sanders, "FCC Rules Are Dealt Setback in Senate; Committee Votes to Keep TV Station Owners from Reaching More Than 35% of the National Market," *Los Angeles Times*, September 5, 2003, pp. C-1.

65. Stuart Minor Benjamin, "Evaluating the Federal Communications Commission's National Television Ownership Cap: What's Bad for Broadcasting Is Good for the Country," *William and Mary Law Review*, November 2004, http://link.galegroup.com.libproxy2.usc.edu/apps/doc/A126684726/AONE?u=usocal_main&sid=AONE&xid=1fbae2bb.

66. Kenneth B. Noblespecial, "Reagan Vetoes Measure to Affirm Fairness Policy for Broadcasters," *New York Times*, June 21, 1987, p. 1.

67. Ashley Lutz, "These 6 Corporations Control 90% of the Media in America," *Business Insider*, June 14, 2012, https://read.bi/2vd7YfM.

68. Art Swift, "Americans' Trust in Mass Media Sinks to New Low," Gallup, Washington, DC, September 14, 2016, http://bit.ly/2cVRrpZ.

69. Garrett Hardin, "Tragedy of the Commons," *Science*, December 13, 1968.

70. Swift, "Americans' Trust in Mass Media."

71. Deep Patel, "How to Reach and Engage Millennial Audiences," *Forbes*, July 4, 2017, https://bit.ly/2KkFqFD.

72. John Herrman, "Inside Facebook's (Totally Insane, Unintentionally Gigantic, Hyperpartisan) Political-Media Machine," *New York Times Magazine*, August 24, 2016, https://nyti.ms/2mcTpT7.

73. Keith Wagstaff, "Oculus Co-Founder Palmer Luckey Is Putting His Money behind Trump," Mashable, September 23, 2016, https://mashable.com/2016/09/23/palmer-luckey-trump-supporter-memes/#3SIVe0kY6Oq7.

74. Lisa De Moraes, "Bill Clinton Tells Trevor Noah United States 'Less Racist, Less Sexist, Less Homophobic' But More Siloed," *Deadline*, September 16, 2016, https://deadline.com/2016/09/bill-clinton-donald-trump-trevor-noah-daily-show-hillary-1201820791/.

75. "Lawmakers Publish Evidence That Cambridge Analytica Work Helped Brexit Group," Reuters, April 16, 2018, https://reut.rs/2vkbxmI.

76. Bryan Logan, "Twitter Found More Than 50,000 Russia-Linked Accounts That Actively Shared Election-Related Material—and Trump Interacted with Them Hundreds of Times," *Business Insider*, January 19, 2018, https://read.bi/2M0lLAI.

77. J. Winston, "How the Trump Campaign Built an Identity Database and Used Facebook Ads to Win the Election," Startup Grind, November 18, 2016, http://bit.ly/2nBKko4.

78. Christopher Mims, "How Facebook Is Dominating the 2016 Election," *Wall Street Journal*, October 2, 2016, https://www.wsj.com/articles/how-facebook-is-dominating-the-2016-election-1475429365.

79. Jane Wakefield, "Cambridge Analytica: Can Targeted Online Ads Really Change a Voter's Behaviour?" BBC News, March 30, 2018, https://bbc.in/2KxAL3j.

80. Morton Deutsch and Harold B. Gerard, "A Study of Normative and Informational Social Influences upon Individual Judgment," *Journal of Abnormal and Social Psychology* 51, no. 3 (1955): 629–36, http://dx.doi.org/10.1037/h0046408.

81. Luis, "Impact of Fake News Online," class project, November 3, 2018, Cal State Los Angeles.

82. Catherine Collin et al., "How Strong Is the Urge Toward Social Conformity? Solomon Asch (1907–1996)" in *The Psychology Book: Big Ideas Simply Explained*, Big Ideas (London; New York: Dorling Kindersley Publishing, 2012).

83. "Here's the Personality Test Cambridge Analytica Had Millions of Facebook Users Take," MSN, March 19, 2018, https://www.msn.com/en-us/health/wellness/here's-the-personality-test-cambridge-analytica-had-millions-of-facebook-users-take/ar-BBKrwct.

84. Ibid.

85. J. Toohey, "Can Big Data Analysis Swing a Political Election?" Fox5, May 23, 2017, http://www.fox5ny.com/news/256571281-story.

86. Marshall McLuhan, "The Playboy Interview: Marshall McLuhan," interview by Eric Norden, *Playboy Magazine*, March 1969, https://binged.it/2qQOlVw.

87. Craig Timberg and Elizabeth Dwoskin, "Twitter Is Sweeping out Fake Accounts, Suspending More Than 70 Million in 2 Months," *Chicago Tribune*, July 7, 2018, https://trib.in/2ASSen8.

88. Alex Hern and Olivia Solon, "Facebook Closed 583m Fake Accounts in First Three Months of 2018," *Guardian*, May 15, 2018, https://bit.ly/2IBOp8T.

CHAPTER 3: THE UNTETHERED ADULT

1. Tim Henderson, "More Americans Living Alone, Census Says," *Washington Post*, September 28, 2014, https://wapo.st/2CFalfd.

2. Ibid.

3. Richard A. Settersten Jr. and Barbara Ray, "What's Going on with Young People

Today?" *Future of Children* 20, no. 1 (Spring 2010), https://files.eric.ed.gov/fulltext/EJ883077
.pdf.

    4. Julie Beck, "When Do You Become an Adult?" *Atlantic*, January 5, 2016, http://
theatln.tc/2mjh1cI.

    5. Quoctrung Bui and Claire Cain Miller, "The Typical American Lives Only 18
Miles from Mom," *New York Times*, December 23, 2015, https://www.nytimes.com/
interactive/2015/12/24/upshot/24up-family.html.

    6. Annie Nova, "A Growing Share of Millennials Are Living with Mom," CNBC, May
11, 2018, https://www.cnbc.com/2018/05/10/nearly-25-percent-of-millennials-live-with
-their-mom-.html.

    7. Amy J. Rauer, Gregory S. Pettit, Jennifer E. Lansford, et al., "Romantic Relationship
Patterns in Young Adulthood and Their Developmental Antecedents," February 18, 2013,
https://www.ncbi.nlm.nih.gov/pmc/articles/PMC3830676/.

    8. "Parenting in America," Pew Research Center, Social & Demographic Trends,
Washington, DC, June 20, 2018, http://www.pewsocialtrends.org/2015/12/17/1
-the-american-family-today/.

    9. D'Vera Cohn, Jeffrey S. Passel, Wendy Wang, and Gretchen Livingston, "Barely Half
of U.S. Adults Are Married—A Record Low," Pew Research Center, Washington, DC,
December 14, 2011, http://www.pewsocialtrends.org/2011/12/14/barely-half-of-u-s
-adults-are-married-a-record-low/.

    10. US Census Bureau, "The Majority of Children Live with Two Parents, Census Bureau
Reports," release no. CB16-192, November 17, 2016, https://bit.ly/2BE0jZp.

    11. Jenna Marbles, "My Thoughts on Marriage," YouTube video, 6:14, May 9, 2012,
https://bit.ly/2DPoKsa.

    12. Henya Mania, "Why Not to Get Married," YouTube video, 22:57, October 30, 2017,
https://bit.ly/2Opwoxh.

    13. Richard Fry, "5 Facts about Millennial Households," Pew Research Center,
Washington, DC, September 6, 2017, https://pewrsr.ch/2vPkrbK.

    14. Wendy Wang, Kim Parker, and Paul Taylor, "Breadwinner Moms," Pew Research
Center, Social and Demographic Trends, Washington, DC, May 29, 2013, http://www
.pewsocialtrends.org/2013/05/29/breadwinner-moms/.

    15. Andrew J. Cherlin, Elizabeth Talbert, and Suzumi Yasutake, "Changing Fertility
Regimes and the Transition to Adulthood: Evidence from a Recent Cohort" (paper presented
at the Annual Meeting of the Population Association of America, Boston, MA, May 3, 2014),
http://citeseerx.ist.psu.edu/viewdoc/download?doi=10.1.1.687.2273&rep=rep1&type=pdf.

    16. Sara McLanahan and Christopher Jencks, "Was Moynihan Right? What Happens to
the Children of Unmarried Mothers," *Education Next* 15, no. 2 (Spring 2015), https://www
.educationnext.org/was-moynihan-right/.

    17. Single Mothers by Choice, https://www.singlemothersbychoice.org/.

    18. Prelude Fertility, https://www.preludefertility.com/.

    19. Scott Neuman, "Generation Rent: Slamming Door of Homeownership," NPR, June 7,
2012, https://n.pr/2MpWGvd.

    20. Reid Cramer and Elliot Schreur, "Millennials and Homeownership," Millennials

Rising Resource Center, October 16, 2014, https://www.newamerica.org/millennials/
millennials-rising-resource-center/.

21. Jamie Varon, "This Is How We Date Now," *Thought Catalog* (blog), October 23, 2018,
https://thoughtcatalog.com/jamie-varon/2014/12/this-is-how-we-date-now/.

22. Christopher Kurz, Geng Li, and Daniel Vine, "The Young and the Carless? The
Demographics of New Vehicle Purchases," Board of Governors of the Federal Reserve System,
June 24, 2016, http://bit.ly/2Ees0IX.

23. BOOK by Cadillac, 2018, https://binged.it/2JIoad6.

24. Common Living, https://www.common.com/why-common/.

25. Kate Hakala, "This Is Why Men Outnumber Women Two-to-One on Tinder," Mic,
October 24, 2015, https://mic.com/articles/110774/two-thirds-of-tinder-users-are-men-here
-s-why#.gIeV7Ejhz.

26. Katy Winter, "Death of the Seven Year Itch: Average Relationship Is Now Just 2 Years
and 9 Months . . . and Social Media Is to Blame," *Daily Mail Online*, February 6, 2014.

27. "Number of Paid Subscribers Registered to the Match Group from 1st Quarter
2014 to 3rd Quarter 2018 (in 1,000s)," Statista, November 2018, https://www.statista.com/
statistics/449465/paid-dating-subscribers-match-group/.

28. Lea Rose Emery, "The Most Popular Dating App for Millennials Is . . ." Bustle, April
25, 2018, https://bit.ly/2KubLeK.

29. Kerry Flynn, "How eHarmony Stays Relevant in the Age of Tinder and Match Group,"
International Business Times, February 16, 2016, https://www.ibtimes.com/how-eharmony
-stays-relevant-age-tinder-match-group-2306810.

30. Varon, "This Is How We Date Now."

31. Sheena S. Iyengar and Mark R. Lepper, "When Choice Is Demotivating: Can One
Desire Too Much of a Good Thing?" in *The Construction of Preference*, ed. Sarah Lichtenstein
and Paul Slovic (New York: Cambridge University Press, 2006), pp. 300–22.

32. Scott J. South and Kim M. Lloyd, "Spousal Alternatives and Marital Dissolution,"
American Sociological Review 60, no. 1 (1995): 21, http://doi.org/10.2307/2096343.

33. Niraj Chokshi, "What Is an Incel? A Term Used by the Toronto Van Attack Suspect,
Explained," *New York Times*, April 25, 2018, https://www.nytimes.com/2018/04/24/world/
canada/incel-reddit-meaning-rebellion.html.

34. "About the Mystery Method," The Mystery Method, 2013, http://www.the
mysterymethod.com/.

35. Neil Strauss, *The Game: Penetrating the Secret Society of Pick-up Artists* (Melbourne,
Victoria: Text Publishing Company, 2015), p. 486.

36. Ibid.

37. Varon, "This Is How We Date Now."

38. Ashley Madison, https://www.ashleymadison.com/.

39. Sugarbook, "What Is a Sugar Baby: How to Be a Sugar Baby," Sugarbook, https://
sugarbook.com/what-is-a-sugar-baby.

40. Sebastián Valenzuela, Daniel Halpern, and James E. Katz, "Social Network Sites,
Marriage Well-Being and Divorce: Survey and State-Level Evidence from the United States,"
Computers in Human Behavior 36 (2014): 94–101, http://doi.org/10.1016/j.chb.2014.03.034.

41. American Academy of Matrimonial Lawyers, "Big Surge in Social Networking Evidence Says Survey of Nation's Top Divorce Lawyers," press release, February 10, 2010, http:// aaml.org/about-the-academy/press/press-releases/e-discovery/big-surge-social-networking -evidence-says-survey; Erica Briscoe, "The Hague Convention on Protection of Children and Co-Operation in Respect of Intercountry Adoption: Are Its Benefits Overshadowed by Its Shortcomings?" *Journal of the American Academy of Matrimonial Lawyers* 22 (2009): 437–60.

42. Slater and Gordon Lawyers, "Social Media Is the New Marriage Minefield," press release, April 30, 2015, https://bit.ly/2Qcyxcx.

43. Amanda Lenhart, "Teens, Technology and Romantic Relationships," Pew Research Center, Internet & Technology, Washington, DC, February 1, 2016, http://www.pewinternet .org/2015/10/01/teens-technology-and-romantic-relationships/.

44. American Psychological Association, "College Students' Mental Health Is a Growing Concern, Survey Finds," *Monitor on Psychology* 44, no. 6 (June 2013): 13, https://bit.ly/ 1kn79VT.

45. N. H. Nie, D. S. Hillygus, and L. Erbring, "Internet Use, Interpersonal Relations, and Sociability: A Time Diary Study," in *The Internet in Everyday Life*, ed. B. Wellman and C. Haythornthwaite (Oxford: Blackwell, 2002), pp. 215–43.

46. Andrew Lepp, Jacob E. Barkley, and Aryn C. Karpinski, "The Relationship between Cell Phone Use, Academic Performance, Anxiety, and Satisfaction with Life in College Students," *Computers in Human Behavior* 31 (February 2014): 343–50, https://www .sciencedirect.com/science/article/pii/S0747563213003993.

47. José De-Sola Gutiérrez, Fernando Rodríguez de Fonseca, and Gabriel Rubio, "Cell-Phone Addiction: A Review," *Frontiers in Psychiatry* 7 (2016), http://doi.org/10.3389/ fpsyt.2016.00175.

48. Laura M. Holson, "A Curious Midlife Crisis for a Tech Entrepreneur," *New York Times*, June 13, 2015, https://nyti.ms/2qqebEv.

49. Ibid.

50. Gizmo, "An Unexpected Twist," *Modern Gypsy Tales* (blog), July 25, 3017, https://bit .ly/2R9h1aN.

51. Richard Fry, "Millennials Overtake Baby Boomers as America's Largest Generation," Pew Research Center, Washington, DC, March 1, 2018, http://pewrsr.ch/1Ta1G2l.

52. Sarina Trangle, "More Micro-Apartments Could Be Coming to the City," AM New York, August 2, 2017, https://bit.ly/2KDOAgU.

53. Brock Keeling, "Spend Your Entire Paycheck on This 240-Foot Apartment," Curbed San Francisco, March 30, 2016, http://bit.ly/2F5ECmI.

54. Yanan Wang, "Man Moves to San Francisco, Pays $400 a Month to Sleep in Wooden Box in Friends' Living Room," *Washington Post*, March 29, 2016, https://www.washingtonpost .com/news/morning-mix/wp/2016/03/29/man-moves-to-san-francisco-pays-400-a-month-to -sleep-in-wooden-box-inside-friends-living-room/.

55. L. Shen, "Adult Dorms Could Be the Future of City Living," *Fortune*, March 16, 2016, doi:http://fortune.com/2016/03/16/adult-dorms-funded-by-venture-capital.

56. Common Living.

57. "What Did Mies Van Der Rohe Mean by Less Is More?" Phaidon, https://bit.ly/1skwepe.

58. More on the Living Cube can be found at http://tillkoenneker.work/living cubefurniture/.

59. IKEA, "Welcome to the World's Smallest Ideas," https://bit.ly/2OMqGTw.

60. "Millennials: Technology = Social Connection," Nielsen Company, http://www .nielsen.com/us/en/insights/news/2014/millennials-technology-social-connection.html.

61. Leslie Josephs, "Hotels Are Shrinking Rooms and Adding More Places to Be Alone with Other People," *Quartz*, June 13, 2017, https://qz.com/999947/hotels-are -shrinking-rooms-forcing-guests-to-talk-to-each-other-in-common-areas/.

62. B. Wormald, "America's Changing Religious Landscape," Pew Research Center, Washington, DC, May 12, 2015, http://www.pewforum.org/2015/05/12/americas -changing-religious-landscape/

63. Jana Riess, "Why Millennials Are Really Leaving Religion (It's Not Just Politics, Folks)," Religion News Service, June 26, 2018, https://bit.ly/2DHXPOJ.

64. Michael Suh, "Millennials: Unmoored from Institutions," Pew Research Center, Social and Demographic Trends, March 5, 2014, http://www.pewsocialtrends.org/2014/03/07/ millennials-in-adulthood/sdt-next-america-03-07-2014-0-01/.

65. Jennifer L. Lawless and Richard Logan Fox, *Running from Office: Why Young Americans Are Turned Off to Politics* (Oxford: Oxford University Press, 2015).

66. "Gatebox - Promotion Movie 'OKAERI'_English," YouTube video, 2:00, December 13, 2016, https://bit.ly/2hmdgPP.

67. Anonymous user, "Gatebox Wife," Facebook, September 16, 2017, https://www .facebook.com/pg/gatebox/posts/. This comment has since been removed.

68. V. Vinge, *The Coming Technological Singularity*, Kindle ed. (1993).

69. Joaquin Phoenix, *Her*, directed by Spike Jonez (Los Angeles: Annaperna Pictures, 2013).

70. "R/Vive - I Am Building a VR Dating App and I Just Had My First VR Date!" Reddit, https://bit.ly/2DP02rw.

71. Ibid.

72. Ibid.

73. "VR Kanojo Gameplay Full Game (English Subs No Commentary)," RobertCram1, YouTube video, 14:11, February 28, 2017, https://www.youtube.com/watch?v =-OAmhAu25qE.

74. "The World's First Ever VR Date—Weekly Product Update," Arnaud Betrand, YouTube video, 8:43, February 12, 2017, https://bit.ly/2y4bDwL.

75. Alicia Vikander, *Ex Machina*, directed by Alex Garland (Los Angeles: Universal Pictures International, 2014).

CHAPTER 4: GROWING UP DIGITAL

1. Andy Grignon, "I Can't Speak for the Original iPhone Team," Facebook, August 17, 2017, https://www.facebook.com/search/str/andy+grignon+and+iPhone+team/ keywords_blended_posts.

2. Barbara H. Fiese, Marcia A. Winter, and Joanna C. Botti, "The ABCs of Family Mealtimes: Observational Lessons for Promoting Healthy Outcomes for Children with Persistent Asthma," *Child Development* 82, no. 1 (2011): 133–45.

3. "Dinnertime with XFINITY XFi," YouTube video, 0:30, August 31, 2017, https://youtu.be/KzMhNuHJMbA.

4. Carol Moser, Sarita Y. Schoenebeck, and Katharina Reinecke, "Technology at the Table: Attitudes about Mobile Phone Use at Mealtime," *Proceedings of the 2016 CHI Conference on Human Factors in Computing Systems* (May 7, 2016): 1881–92, https://bit.ly/1Nqg61T.

5. LivePerson Inc., "Gen Z and Millennials Now More Likely to Communicate with Each Other Digitally Than in Person," LivePerson, October 17, 2017, http://bit.ly/2xThHLw.

6. Here is a sample baby with iPad video: "A Magazine Is an iPad That Does Not Work," YouTube video, 1:25, October 6, 2011, https://bit.ly/1GKp1T6.

7. Tim Kaucher, comments on author's Facebook page, October 13, 2017.

8. "Zero to Eight: Children's Media Use in America 2013," Common Sense Media, October 28, 2013, https://tinyurl.com/y73dufbw.

9. "Connection and Control: Case Studies of Media Use among Lower-Income Minority Youth and Parents," Common Sense Media, October 24, 2016, https://bit.ly/2f9p7jM.

10. Jacqueline Howard, "Report: Young Kids Spend over 2 Hours a Day on Screens," CNN, October 19, 2017, http://cnn.it/2yDHXZ0.

11. A. Lenhart, "Mobile Access Shifts Social Media Use and Other Online Activities," April 8, 2015, http://pewrsr.ch/1DMho1V.

12. Common Sense Media, "Connection and Control: Case Studies of Media Use among Lower-Income Minority Youth and Parents | Common Sense Media," October 24, 2016, https://www.commonsensemedia.org/research/connection-and-control -case-studies-of-media-use-among-lower-income-minority-youth-and.

13. "Media Use by Tweens and Teens: Infographic," Common Sense Media, November 3, 2015, bit.ly/1RO21Ze.

14. Aaron Smith, "U.S. Smartphone Use in 2015," Pew Research Center, Internet & Technology, Washington, DC, April 1, 2015, http://www.pewinternet.org/2015/04/01/ us-smartphone-use-in-2015/.

15. Janet Adamy, "Gen Z Is Coming to Your Office. Get Ready to Adapt," *Wall Street Journal*, September 6, 2018, https://www.wsj.com/graphics/genz-is-coming-to-your-office/.

16. "Would Your Kids Respond in the Same Way as These Kids? Raises an Interesting," YouTube video, 3:01, July 25, 2015, https://youtu.be/1XDVDyDJ3s0.

17. LivePerson "Gen Z and Millennials Now More Likely to Communicate."

18. "YouTube, Instagram and Snapchat Are the Most Popular Online Platforms among Teens," Pew Research Center, Washington, DC, May 29, 2018, https://pewrsr.ch/2LP5CdC.

19. Author anonymous upon request, private Facebook Messenger conversation with the author, August 23, 2017.

20. Sherry Turkle, *Alone Together: Why We Expect More from Technology and Less from Each Other* (New York: Basic Books, 2017).

21. "Millennials Would Rather Go Without House or Car Keys Than Mobile Phone for 2 Days," Marketing Charts, October 1, 2013, https://www.marketingcharts.com/digital-37059.

22. Adam Alter, *Irresistible: Why We Can't Stop Checking, Scrolling, Clicking and Watching* (London: Bodley Head, 2017).

23. Nir Eyal and Cory Hoover, *Hooked: How to Build Habit-Forming Products* (London: Portfolio Penguin, 2014).

24. AVG Technologies, "Kids Competing with Mobile Phones for Parents' Attention," *Journal of Engineering* (2015): 792.

25. "Most Preschoolers Use Tablets, Smartphones Daily: New Study Suggests an Income-Based 'Digital Divide' Is Narrowing," HealthDay, last updated November 2, 2015.

26. Rachel Pells, "Giving Your Child a Smartphone Is Like Giving Them a Gram of Cocaine," *Independent*, June 7, 2017, http://ind.pn/2rVyCZG.

27. Kelly Flanagan, "This Is How Kids Will React to Taking Away Their Electronics (in Sequence)," UnTangled, January 27, 2016, https://drkellyflanagan.com/2016/01/27/this-is-how-kids-will-react-to-taking-away-their-electronics-in-sequence/.

28. BBC Trending, "The Disturbing YouTube Videos That Are Tricking Children," BBC News, March 26, 2017, https://bbc.in/2NjW8Xi.

29. Laura June, "YouTube Has a Fake Peppa Pig Problem," *Outline*, March 16, 2017, https://theoutline.com/post/1239/youtube-has-a-fake-peppa-pig-problem?zd=1&zi=exh4qpi5.

30. "Paw Patrol Babies Pretend to Die Suicide by Annabelle Hypnotized Ghost Pranks! Paw Patrol Cartoon #," posted by "TerrenceBeck," YouTube video, 9:52, August 18, 2017, https://youtu.be/2GsaoIm_IeU.

31. Sapna Maheshwari, "On YouTube Kids, Startling Videos Slip Past Filters," *New York Times*, November 4, 2017, http://nyti.ms/2AeFKB7.

32. "PlayDoh Butt Doctor Syringe Injection Learning Colors with Finger Family Nursery Rhymes," YouTube video, 2:01, March 22, 2017, https://bit.ly/2DWDK7z.

33. Sexual predators may take advantage of a child's natural curiosity about sex by telling "dirty" jokes, showing him or her sexualized imagery or pornography, or by playing sexual games, a known precursor to sexual abuse. Amanda Grossman-Scott, "8 Ways a Predator Might Groom Your Child," EducateEmpowerKids.org, http://bit.ly/2iuKXyq.

34. Simon Hill, "From J-Phone to Lumia 1020: A Complete History of the Camera Phone," Digital Trends, August 12, 2013, https://bit.ly/2q2H7yU.

35. Margaret Kane, "Say What? 'Young People Are Just Smarter,'" CNET, March 28, 2007, https://cnet.co/2KBMTAg.

36. Steven Meloan, private Facebook Messenger conversation with the author, July 23, 2017.

37. Steven Meloan, "No Way to Run a Culture," *Wired*, June 5, 2017, https://www.wired.com/1998/02/no-way-to-run-a-culture/.

38. Jonathan Zittrain, Kendra Albert, and Lawrence Lessig, "Perma: Scoping and Addressing the Problem of Link and Reference Rot in Legal Citations," Legal Information Management, June 12, 2014.

39. Kurt Wagner, "Snapchat Is Still Bigger Than Instagram for Younger U.S. Millennials," *Recode*, August 24, 2017, http://bit.ly/2jdz4NJ.

40. Terry Sullivan, "How Film Saved an Infamous Photo," *Professional Artist*, January 18, 2016, https://professionalartistmag.com/how-film-saved-now-infamous-clintonlewinsky-photo/.

41. John Walters, "Free BASEing, Wing Suits and the Man Who Could Fly; Dean Potter Always Wanted to Fly. And for a While, He Did," *Newsweek* 164, no. 24 (June 19, 2015).

42. E. van der Klashorst and K. Cyrus, "Train Surfing: Apposite Recreation Provision as Alternative to Adolescent Risk-Taking and Sensation-Seeking Behaviour," *Journal of Science and Medicine in Sport* 15 (2012): S318.

43. "Video Shows Baby Put in Refrigerator; Teens Charged," CNN, August 10, 2017.

44. Beth Spotswood, "Stockton Teenager Live-Streams the Fatal Crash That Killed Her Sister," *SFist*, July 24, 2017, https://bit.ly/2vax52Q.

45. AnneClaire Stapleton, "Teens Accused of Putting a Crying Baby in a Fridge and Posting the Video on Snapchat," CNN, August 10, 2017, https://cnn.it/2KniQfD.

46. Nathalie Granda and KFSN, "Judge Sentences Teen Who Live Streamed Crash That Killed Sister to 6 Years, 4 Months in Prison," ABC30 Fresno, February 9, 2018, https://abc30 .tv/2OCcM9o.

47. Anneta Konstantinides, "Obdulia Sanchez Speaks Out about Crash That Killed Sister," *Daily Mail*, August 21, 2017, http://www.dailymail.co.uk/news/article-4808236/Teen -filmed-crash-killed-sister-speaks-out.html.

48. Amanda Lenhart, Monica Anderson, and Aaron Smith, "How Teens Meet, Flirt With and Ask Out Potential Romantic Partners," chap. 2 of *Teens, Technology, and Romantic Relationships*, Pew Research Center, Internet & Technology, Washington, DC, October 1, 2015, http://www.pewinternet.org/2015/10/01/how-teens-interact-with -potential-romantic-partners/.

49. Joyce C. Abma and Gladys M. Martinez, "Sexual Activity and Contraceptive Use among Teenagers in the United States, 2011–2015," *National Health Statistics* no. 104, June 22, 2017, http://bit.ly/2tRUN0y.

50. Alan W. Silberberg, "Your Family and Your Kids Need Cyber Security Training, Now," *Huffington Post*, October 12, 2016, http://bit.ly/2gq5pil.

51. Lenhart, Anderson, and Smith, "How Teens Meet, Flirt with and Ask Out Potential Romantic Partners."

52. Anne Preble, "The Essential Guide to Social Media Geofilters," *Volume Nine* (blog), November 15, 2017, https://bit.ly/2QqUuVA.

53. Michael Smith, conversation with the author, May 20, 2017.

54. Alan Silberberg, interview with the author, Santa Monica, CA, October 27, 2017.

55. "Eighth Grade (2018)," IMDb, https://www.imdb.com/title/tt7014006/.

56. Kevin Driscoll, "Social Media's Dial-Up Ancestor: The Bulletin Board System," *IEEE Spectrum*, October 24, 2016, https://spectrum.ieee.org/tech-history/cyberspace/ social-medias-dialup-ancestor-the-bulletin-board-system.

57. *Gagapedia*, s.v. "Little Monsters (Fanbase)," Fandom, https://bit.ly/2xWwZgq.

58. J. Lorber, *Paradoxes of Gender* (New Haven: Yale University Press, 1994).

59. K. Steinmetz, "Gender and Sexuality: Beyond He or She," *Time*, March 16, 2017, http://time.com/4703309/gender-sexuality-changing/.

60. Angel Haze, "Angel Haze, Interview: 'At Home, I'm Dead. But on Stage, I'm God.'" *Evening Standard*, January 15, 2016, https://bit.ly/2robnsz.

61. Neal A. Palmer et al., *Out Online: The Experience of Gay, Lesbian, Bisexual*

and Transgender Youth on the Internet (New York: Gay, Lesbian & Straight Education Network, 2013), https://www.glsen.org/sites/default/files/Out%20Online%20FINAL .pdf.

62. Renée Fabian, "6 of the Safest Spaces for LGBT Youth to Hang Online," *Daily Dot*, February 25, 2017, https://www.dailydot.com/irl/lgbt-youth-safe-spaces/.

63. G. Beemyn, "Coloring Outside the Lines of Gender and Sexuality: The Struggle of Nonbinary Students to Be Recognized," *Educational Forum* 79, no. 4 (September 10, 2015): 359–61, http://doi.org/10.1080/00131725.2015.1069518.

64. A. Oakley, "Disturbing Hegemonic Discourse: Nonbinary Gender and Sexual Orientation Labeling on Tumblr," *Sage Journals*, August 17, 2016, http://journals.sagepub.com/doi/10.1177/2056305116664217.

65. Russell Goldman, "Here's a List of 58 Gender Options for Facebook Users," ABC News, February 13, 2014, https://abcn.ws/2DTF6zG.

66. L. Kann, E. O. Olsen, T. McManus, et al., "Sexual Identity, Sex of Sexual Contacts, and Health-Related Behaviors among Students in Grades 9–12—United States and Selected Sites, 2015," Centers for Disease Control and Prevention, *Morbidity and Mortality Weekly Report, Surveillance Summaries* 65, no. 9 (August 12, 2016): 1–202.

67. Paz, "You Are Super Valid," *Tumblr*, https://pazwrites.tumblr.com.

68. Jenseia, "It's Okay to Be Questioning," We're All Queer Here, *Tumblr*.

69. Rebecca Greenway, "Kids Aspire to High-Profile Careers as YouTube Personalities," NBC Bay Area, June 1, 2017, https://bit.ly/2OFUwJu.

70. John Lynch and Travis Clark, "A 7-Year-Old Boy Is Making $22 Million a Year on YouTube Reviewing Toys," *Business Insider*, December 3, 2018, https://www.businessinsider .com/ryan-toysreview-7-year-old-makes-22-million-per-year-youtube-2018-12.

71. Taylor Ferber, "Disney Child Stars Who Met with Incredibly Tragic Fates," VH1 News, February 27, 2016, http://www.vh1.com/news/246620/disney-stars-tragic-fate/.

72. Francis Ford Coppola, "Apocalypse Now - I Love the Smell of Napalm in the Morning," YouTube video, 0:59, filmed in 1979, posted August 1, 2007, https://www.youtube .com/watch?v=bPXVGQnJm0w.

73. J-14 Magazine, "Jake Paul's Neighbors Accuse the Team 10 House of Turning the Neighborhood into a Literal 'War Zone,'" *J-14*, July 18, 2017, bit.ly/2xZwVON.

74. Ibid.

75. J. Lynch, "Meet the YouTube Millionaires: These Are the 10 Highest-Paid YouTube Stars of 2017," *Business Insider*, December 8, 2017, https://read.bi/2RoqsDi.

76. For an example of the Army's *Harlem Shake* video, see: "Harlem Shake (Original Army Edition)," YouTube video, 0:33, February 10, 2013, https://bit.ly/1imdLV3.

77. Chris Molanphy, "Why Rae Sremmurd's 'Black Beatles' Is No. 1 (Hint: It's Not Just the Mannequin Challenge)," *Slate*, November 22, 2016, https://slate.me/2fBmQut.

78. Malcolm Gladwell, *The Tipping Point: How Little Things Can Make a Big Difference* (London: Abacus, 2015).

79. "Shower Fire Challenge Gone Wrong," YouTube video, 1:01, September 3, 2014, https://bit.ly/2KnQqlI.

80. "Salt & Ice Challenge," YouTube video, 2:14, May 1, 2012, https://bit.ly/2LXIWe9.

81. Inside Edition, "Teens Suffer Crazy Injuries Attempting 'Kylie Jenner Lip Challenge,'" YouTube video, 2:04, April 21, 2015, https://bit.ly/2na6Tk9.

82. "Kylie Jenner, 17, FINALLY Admits to Lip Fillers," *Daily Mail*, May 8, 2015, https://dailym.ai/1EQZhoU.

83. "Kids Are Jumping Out of Cars for Drake's New Challenge," Rahny Taylor Morning Show, July 18, 2018, https://973now.iheart.com/content/2018-07-18-kids-are-jumping-out-of-cars-for-drakes-new-challenge/.

84. Madison Malone Kircher, "11-Year-Old Hangs Himself in Failed YouTube-Inspired 'Prank,'" *Intelligencer*, September 19, 2016, https://slct.al/2vc4jic. Gloria Steinem, "After Black Power, Women's Liberation," *New York Magazine*, April 4, 1969, http://nymag.com/news/politics/46802/.

85. Chery Rodewig, "Geotagging Poses Security Risks," US Army, March 7, 2012, https://bit.ly/2P4En0e.

86. Business Wire, "Digital Birth: Welcome to the Online World," news release, October 6, 2010, https://bit.ly/2RRcskZ.

87. Nikki Williams, "Digital Kidnapping—A New Kind of Identity Theft," Center for Digital Ethics & Policy, September 2, 2015, http://www.digitalethics.org/essays/digital-kidnapping-new-kind-identity-theft.

88. Scott Jaschik, "Social Media as 'Fair Game' in Admissions," Inside Higher Ed, April 23, 2018, https://www.insidehighered.com/admissions/article/2018/04/23/new-data-how-college-admissions-officers-view-social-media-applicants.

89. Adrienne LaFrance, "When Bad News Was Printed on Milk Cartons," *Atlantic*, February 14, 2017, http://theatln.tc/2D0PC3Q.

90. Barry Glassner, *Culture of Fear: Why Americans Are Afraid of the Wrong Things* (New York: Basic Books, 2018).

91. "Annual Report 2017," Center for Collegiate Mental Health, July 27, 2018, http://ccmh.psu.edu/publications/.

92. James Doe, interview with the author on Facebook Messenger, August 24, 2017.

93. Jane Doe, interview with the author via text message, August 13, 2018.

94. Doug Criss, "Who Needs Santa? 6-Year-Old Orders Dollhouse and Cookies from Amazon's Alexa," CNN, January 5, 2017, https://www.cnn.com/2017/01/05/health/amazon-alexa-dollhouse-trnd/index.html.

95. Rachel Metz, "Alexa, Are You Turning the Kids into Spoiled Brats?" *MIT Technology Review*, August 25, 2017, www.technologyreview.com/s/608430/growing-up-with-alexa/.

96. Lance Ulanoff, "Turing Test Winner Eugene Goostman: The Inside Story," Mashable, June 12, 2014, https://mashable.com/2014/06/12/eugene-goostman-turing-test/#BgRhfyPTYPqq.

97. Metz, "Alexa, Are You Turning the Kids into Spoiled Brats?"

98. Ibid.

99. R. Gonzalez, "Hey Alexa, What Are You Doing to My Kid's Brain?" *Wired*, May 11, 2018, https://bit.ly/2IPtTBO.

100. Heather Nolan, "Brands Are Creating Virtual Influencers, Which Could Make the Kardashians a Thing of the Past," *Adweek*, May 11, 2018, https://bit.ly/2syH0xP.

101. Lilly Pace, "Lil Miquela Drops 'Hate Me,'" *V Magazine*, August 17, 2018, https://vmagazine.com/article/lil-miquela-drops-hate-me/.

102. University of Plymouth, "Robots Have Power to Significantly Influence Children's Opinions," *Science Daily*, August 15, 2018, https://bit.ly/2nInXOH.

103. "UnGlue: End Screen Time Battles. Start Better Habits," UnGlue, https://www.unglue.com/.

104. Stephanie W. Marcy, "Kids and Screen Time" (lecture, *LA Weekly*'s Screen Time Debate, Los Angeles, CA, August 9, 2018).

105. Ibid.

CHAPTER 5: YOUR BRAIN ON DIGITAL

1. Tom Wolfe, *Electric Kool-Aid Acid Test* (New York: Vintage Classics, 2018).

2. Others trace the origin of the *Just Say No* slogan to a student contest run by social psychology professor Richard I. Evans at USF, won by Jordan Zimmerman. The attribution to Nancy Reagan was made in remarks by President Reagan at a drug-abuse-center benefit dinner. Ronald Reagan Presidential Foundation and Institute, "Nancy Reagan: Her Causes—Just Say No," https://www.reaganfoundation.org/ronald-reagan/nancy-reagan/her-causes/

3. Stephanie Pappas, "This Is Your Brain on Drugs (Really)," LiveScience, April 20, 2018, https://bit.ly/2Fo7Z2t.

4. Marc Santora, "Drug 85 Times as Potent as Marijuana Caused a 'Zombielike' State in Brooklyn," *New York Times*, December 22, 2017, https://www.nytimes.com/2016/12/14/nyregion/zombielike-state-was-caused-by-synthetic-marijuana.html.

5. For an example of the Excision Robokitty graphics and electronic dance music, see "Excision—Robo Kitty Live in Dallas 2/14/15," YouTube video, 1:58, March 4, 2015, https://www.youtube.com/watch?v=BVBvouxRFtM.

6. Marisa Kendall, "'Hacking' the Brain: Silicon Valley Entrepreneurs Turn to Fasting and 'Smart Drugs,'" *Mercury News*, October 4, 2016, http://bayareane.ws/2Br6Xpl.

7. "PsychonautWiki," https://psychonautwiki.org/.

8. Andy Greenberg, "Silk Road Creator Ross Ulbricht Loses His Life Sentence Appeal," *Wired*, June 3, 2017, https://bit.ly/2qC2B5s.

9. Karen Kaplan, "More Than a Third of Infants Are Using Smartphones, Tablets, Study Says," *Los Angeles Times*, April 25, 2015, https://lat.ms/1HL3qgk.

10. "The Common Sense Census: Media Use by Kids Age Zero to Eight 2017," Common Sense Media, October 19, 2017, https://bit.ly/2y5N05V.

11. "Mattel and Fisher-Price Apptivity Seat," released 2013, Mattel and Fisher-Price Customer Service, https://bit.ly/2Nl5L8c.

12. "A Magazine Is an iPad That Does Not Work," YouTube video, 1:25, October 6, 2011, https://bit.ly/1GKp1T6.

13. Yolanda (Linda) Reid Chassiakos, Jenny Radesky, Dimitri Christakis, Megan A. Moreno, Corinn Cross, and the Council on Communications and Media, "Children and

Adolescents and Digital Media—Pediatrics," *American Academy of Pediatrics Technical Report* 138, no. 5 (November 2016), http://pediatrics.aappublications.org/content/early/2016/10/19/peds.2016-2593.

14. American Academy of Pediatrics, "American Academy of Pediatrics Announces New Recommendations for Children's Media Use," news release, October 21, 2016, https://bit.ly/2eUUttI.

15. Stuart Wolpert, "The Teenage Brain on Social Media," UCLA Newsroom, May 31, 2016, https://bit.ly/1TY0TWP.

16. Jamie Doward, "The Lure of Tall Buildings: A Guide to the Risky but Lucrative World of 'Rooftoppers,'" *Guardian*, February 26, 2017, https://bit.ly/2m2zdFx.

17. Susruthi Rajanala, "Selfies: Living in the Era of Filtered Photographs," *JAMA Facial Plastic Surgery* 20, no. 6 (August 2, 2018), https://jamanetwork.com/journals/jamafacialplasticsurgery/fullarticle/2688763.

18. Gary W. Small and Gigi Vorgan, *iBrain: Surviving the Technological Alteration of the Modern Mind* (New York: Harper, 2009).

19. Kep Kee Loh and Ryota Kanai, "How Has the Internet Reshaped Human Cognition?" *Neuroscientist*, July 13, 2015.

20. M. Hsu, M. Bhatt, R. Adolphs, D. Tranel, and C. F. Camerer, "Neural Systems Responding to Degree of Uncertainty in Human Decision-Making," *Science* 310 (2005): 1680–83.

21. Nicholas G. Carr, *The Shallows: How the Internet Is Changing the Way We Think, Read and Remember* (London: Atlantic, 2011).

22. Small and Vorgan *iBrain*.

23. Julie Albright, interview with Don Paul, November 16, 2016, Los Angeles, CA.

24. Joseph M. Vitolo, "History of Penmanship," Washington Calligraphers Guild, https://www.calligraphersguild.org/penmen.html.

25. Platt R. Spencer, *Spencerian Handwriting: The Complete Collection of Theory and Practical Workbooks for Perfect Cursive and Hand Lettering* (Berkeley, CA: Ulysses, 2016).

26. Eddie Wrenn, "Could We Forget How to WRITE? The Typical Adult Has Not Scribbled Anything by Hand for Six Weeks," *Daily Mail*, June 22, 2012, dailym.ai/2z5esfT.

27. Lyndsey Layton, "Elementary Students Learn Keyboard Typing ahead of New Common Core Tests," *Washington Post*, October 13, 2013, https://wapo.st/2KpaODd.

28. Anne Mangen and Jean-Luc Velay, "Digitizing Literacy: Reflections on the Haptics of Writing," *Advances in Haptics*, April 1, 2010, http://doi.org/10.5772/8710.

29. Ibid.

30. Anne Mangen and Lillian Balsvik, "Pen or Keyboard in Beginning Writing Instruction? Some Perspectives from Embodied Cognition," *Trends in Neuroscience and Education* 5, no. 3 (n.d.): 99–106.

31. Timothy W. Curby and Abby G. Carlson, "Fine Motor Skills and Academic Achievement," *Psychology Today*, February 5, 2014, https://www.psychologytoday.com/blog/psyched/201402/fine-motor-skills-and-academic-achievement.

32. Anne Chemin, "Handwriting vs Typing: Is the Pen Still Mightier Than the Keyboard?" *Guardian*, December 16, 2014, www.theguardian.com/science/2014/dec/16/cognitive-benefits-handwriting-decline-typing.

33. Marieke Longcamp et al., "Neuroanatomy of Handwriting and Related Reading and Writing Skills in Adults and Children with and without Learning Disabilities: French-American Connections," *Pratiques*, US National Library of Medicine, December 2016, www.ncbi.nlm.nih .gov/pmc/articles/PMC5297261/.

34. Gunther R. Kress, *Literacy in the New Media Age* (London: Routledge, 2010).

35. Faye Linda Wachs, Juliana Lynn Fuqua, Paul M. Nissenson, et al., "Successfully Flipping a Fluid Mechanics Course Using Video Tutorials and Active Learning Strategies: Implementation and Assessment" (paper presented at the 2018 ASEE Annual Conference & Exposition, Practice III: Multimedia Learning), https://www.asee.org/public/conferences/106/ papers/23046/view.

36. Neil Harris, "John Philip Sousa and the Culture of Reassurance," Library of Congress, https://www.loc.gov/item/ihas.200152753/.

37. Stephen L. Rhodes, "The American School Band Movement," chap. 9 in *A History of the Wind Band: The American School Band Movement* (2007), https://bit.ly/2nedQkm.

38. Michael L. Mark and Charles L. Gary, *A History of American Music Education* (Lanham, MD: Rowman & Littlefield, 2007).

39. Estelle R. Jorgensen, "Justifying Music Instruction in American Public Schools: A Historical Perspective," *Arts Education Policy Review* 96, no. 6 (1995): 31–38, http://doi.org/10 .1080/10632913.1995.9934570.

40. "How to Play Guitar Hero Like a Pro," *WikiHow*, June 26, 2017, www.wikihow.com/ Play-Guitar-Hero-Like-a-Pro. Also see YouTube for videos of kids playing Guitar Hero songs.

41. The YouTube "play along" Queen *Bohemian Rhapsody* video can be seen here: "Queen—Bohemian Rhapsody 100% Expert FC Guitar Hero: Warriors of Rock," posted by "StarSlay3r," YouTube video, 6:17, October 14, 2010, https://tinyurl.com/y8d4fyxu.

42. Associated Press, "Piano Stores Closing across US as Kids Snub Lessons for Other Activities," *Guardian*, January 2, 2015, https://www.theguardian.com/us-news/2015/jan/02/ piano-stores-closing-kids-snub-lessons-compete-technology.

43. "The Sound of Silence: The Unprecedented Decline of Music Education in California Public Schools; A Statistical Review" (Warren, NJ: Music for All Foundation, September 2004), https://artsedresearch.typepad.com/SoundofSilence.pdf.

44. Javier C. Hernández, "Steinway's Grand Ambitions for Its Pianos in China," *New York Times*, July 23, 2016, https://nyti.ms/2MnHGRz.

45. John Noble Wilford, "Flutes Offer Clues to Stone-Age Music," *New York Times*, June 24, 2009, https://www.nytimes.com/2009/06/25/science/25flute.html.

46. Christopher J. Steele et al., "Early Musical Training and White-Matter Plasticity in the Corpus Callosum: Evidence for a Sensitive Period," *Journal of Neuroscience*, January 16, 2013, http://www.jneurosci.org/content/33/3/1282.

47. E. G. Schellenberg, "Music and Cognitive Abilities," *Current Directions in Psychological Science* 14, no. 6 (February 2, 2006): 317–20.

48. John Noble Wilford, "Stone Age Flutes Found in Germany Offer Clues to Early Music," *New York Times*, June 24, 2009, https://www.nytimes.com/2009/06/25/science/ 25flute.html.

49. Emily Gersema, "Music Training Can Change Children's Brain Structure and Boost

the Decision-Making Network," USC Dornsife, November 28, 2017, https://dornsife.usc.edu/news/stories/2711/music-training-can-change-childrens-brain-structure-and-boost-th/.

50. National Endowment for the Arts, "New NEA Research Report Shows Potential Benefits of Arts Education for At-Risk Youth," news release, March 30, 2012, https://www.arts.gov/news/2012/new-nea-research-report-shows-potential -benefits-arts-education-risk-youth.

51. *2012 College-Bound Seniors: Total Group Profile Report* (New York: College Board, September 24, 2012), http://media.collegeboard.com/digitalServices/pdf/research/ TotalGroup-2012.pdf.

52. T. White-Schwoch et al., "Older Adults Benefit from Music Training Early in Life: Biological Evidence for Long-Term Training-Driven Plasticity," *Journal of Neuroscience* 33, no. 45 (June 2013): 17667–74, https://doi.org/10.1523/jneurosci.2560-13.2013.

53. Eames Yates, "Here's Why Steve Jobs Never Let His Kids Use an iPad," *Business Insider*, March 4, 2017, https://www.businessinsider.com/heres-why-steve-jobs -never-let-his-kids-use-ipad-apple-social-media-2017-3.

54. Chris Weller, "Bill Gates and Steve Jobs Raised Their Kids Tech-Free—and It Should've Been a Red Flag," *Business Insider*, January 10, 2018, https://read.bi/2CS03da.

55. Waldorf School of the Peninsula, "Media & Technology Philosophy," http:// waldorfpeninsula.org/curriculum/media-technology-philosophy/.

56. More on the Waldorf School of the Peninsula can be found here: http:// waldorfpeninsula.org.

57. Waldorf School of the Peninsula, "Media & Technology Philosophy."

58. "Connection and Control: Case Studies of Media Use among Lower-Income Minority Youth and Parents," Common Sense Media, October 24, 2016, https://bit.ly/2f9p7jM.

59. Tristan Harris, "How Technology Is Hijacking Your Mind: From a Former Insider," Medium, May 18, 2016, https://bit.ly/2ILHmH6.

60. Kristen Purcell et al., "How Teens Do Research in the Digital World," Pew Research Center, Internet & Technology, Washington, DC, October 31, 2012, https://www.pewinternet .org/2012/11/01/how-teens-do-research-in-the-digital-world/.

61. Bernard McCoy, "Digital Distractions in the Classroom: Student Classroom Use of Digital Devices for Non-Class Related Purposes," *Journal of Media Education*, October 15, 2013, http://digitalcommons.unl.edu/journalismfacpub/71.

62. Jeffrey H. Kuzenekoff and Scott Titsworth, "The Impact of Mobile Phone Usage on Student Learning," *Communication Education* 62, no. 3 (February 12, 2013), https://binged .it/2mNb4Ck.

63. "U.S. Teen Mobile Report Calling Yesterday, Texting Today, Using Apps Tomorrow," Nielsen Company, October 14, 2010, https://www.nielsen.com/us/en/insights/news/2010/ u-s-teen-mobile-report-calling-yesterday-texting-today-using-apps-tomorrow.html.

64. Amanda Lenhart, Rich Ling, Scott Campbell, and Kristen Purcell, "Teens and Mobile Phones," Pew Research Center, Internet & Technology, Washington, DC, July 28, 2015, http:// www.pewinternet.org/2010/04/20/teens-and-mobile-phones/.

65. Cal Newport, *Deep Work* (London: Piatkus, 2016).

66. Kit Eaton, "How One Second Could Cost Amazon $1.6 Billion In Sales," *Fast*

Company, July 30, 2012, https://www.fastcompany.com/1825005/how-one-second
-could-cost-amazon-16-billion-sales.

67. Steven Meloan, personal communication with the author, May 20, 2017, Facebook
Messenger.

68. "Digital Video and Connected Consumer," Accenture, https://accntu.re/1UfJlno.

69. Ibid.

70. Derek Thompson, "Hollywood Has a Big Millennial Problem," *Atlantic*, June 9, 2016,
https://bit.ly/2lgSfFY.

71. Janna Anderson and Lee Rainie, "Main Findings: Teens, Technology, and Human Potential
in 2020," Pew Research Center, Internet & Technology, Washington, DC, February 29, 2012, http://
www.pewInternet.org/2012/02/29/main-findings-teens-technology-and-human-potential-in-2020/.

72. Angela J. Hanscom and Richard Louv, *Balanced and Barefoot: How Unrestricted
Outdoor Play Makes for Strong, Confident, and Capable Children* (Oakland, CA: New Harbinger
Publications, 2016).

73. Kimberly Marselas, "Losing Our Grip: More Students Entering School without Fine
Motor Skills," Lancaster Online, October 26, 2015, https://bit.ly/2QtZgBP.

74. Alfred Korzybski, *Science and Sanity: An Introduction to Non-Aristotelian Systems and
General Semantics*, 4th ed., with a new preface by Russell Meyers (Lakeville, CT: International
Non-Aristotelian Library, 1958).

75. "The Rise of the Mirror as Commonplace," Joukowsky Institute for Archaeology
& the Ancient World, 2009, https://www.brown.edu/Departments/Joukowsky_Institute/
courses/13things/7306.html.

76. Charlie Sorrel, "How the Invention of the Mirror Changed Everything," *Fast
Company*, November 15, 2016, https://www.fastcompany.com/3065643/how-the-invention
-of-the-mirror-changed-everything.

77. Bice Benvenuto, Roger Kennedy, and Jacques Lacan, *The Works of Jacques Lacan: An
Introduction* (New York: St. Martin's, 1986).

78. Charles Horton Cooley, *Human Nature and the Social Order* (New York: Scribner's,
1902), p. 152.

79. John Brunner, *Stand on Zanzibar* (London: Gollancz, 2014).

80. Bernadette Wegenstein, *The Cosmetic Gaze: Body Modification and the Construction of
Beauty* (Cambridge: MIT Press, 2012).

81. "Dangerous Selfies Have Killed 259 People," BBC News, October 4, 2018, https://
bbc.in/2Rpi5r7.

82. Tom Dart, "Houston Teenager Fatally Shoots Himself while Taking a Selfie with a
Gun," *Guardian*, September 2, 2015, https://www.theguardian.com/us-news/2015/sep/02/
houston-man-selfie-gun-shoots-self-deleon-alonso-smith.

83. Katharine Lackey, "'Safety over Selfie': National Park Visitors Can't Seem to
Stop Getting Too Close to Wildlife," *USA Today*, https://www.usatoday.com/story/news/
nation/2018/08/20/national-park-visitor-safety-wildlife-selfies/973656002/.

84. Caroline Moss, "This Teenager Is Getting Harassed after Her Smiling Selfie at
Auschwitz Goes Viral," *Business Insider*, July 20, 2014, https://www.businessinsider.com/
selfie-at-auschwitz-goes-viral-2014-7.

85. Bianca Bosker, "New 'Selfie-Help' Apps Are Making All Your Friends Better Looking Than You," *Huffington Post*, December 7, 2017, https://www.huffingtonpost.com/2013/12/05/selfie-instagram_n_4391220.html.

86. Julie M. Albright and Mary Andres, "'Because Choice': The Internet as Other in Personal Relationships," in *Quickies: The Handbook of Brief Sex Therapy*, vol. 3 (New York: Norton, 2018).

87. Émile Durkheim, *Suicide: A Study in Sociology* (Glencoe, IL: Free Press, 1951). Originally published 1897.

88. "Tinder: Swiping Self Esteem?" American Psychological Association, August 4, 2016, https://www.apa.org/news/press/releases/2016/08/tinder-self-esteem.aspx.

89. American Psychological Association, "Tinder: Swiping Self Esteem?" press release, August 4, 2016, http://www.apa.org/news/press/releases/2016/08/tinder-self-esteem.aspx.

90. H. B. Shakya and N. A. Christakis, "Association of Facebook Use with Compromised Well-Being: A Longitudinal Study," *American Journal of Epidemiology* 185, no. 3 (February 1, 2017), https://www.ncbi.nlm.nih.gov/pubmed/28093386.

91. Sherry Ametenstein, "Not So Social Media: How Social Media Increases Loneliness—PsyCom," PsyCom.net, May 16, 2018, https://www.psycom.net/mental-health-wellbeing/mental-health-wellbeing-mental-health-wellbeing-how-social-media-increases-loneliness/.

92. César G. Escobar-Viera, Ariel Shensa, Nicholas D. Bowman, Jaime E. Sidani, Jennifer Knight, A. Everette James, and Brian A. Primack, "Passive and Active Social Media Use and Depressive Symptoms among United States Adults," *Cyberpsychology, Behavior, and Social Networking* 21, no. 7 (2018): 437–43, doi:10.1089/cyber.2017.0668.

93. *The Association for University and College Counseling Center Directors Annual Survey* (Indianapolis, IN: AUCCCD, 2018).

94. American Psychological Association, "The State of Mental Health on College Campuses: A Growing Crisis," December 11, 2012, https://binged.it/2Lc9msW.

95. Centers for Disease Control and Prevention, "Antidepressant Use among Persons Aged 12 and Over: United States, 2011–2014," NCHS Data Brief No. 283, August 15, 2017, https://www.cdc.gov/nchs/products/databriefs/db283.htm.

96. Center for Drug Evaluation and Research, "Postmarket Drug Safety Information for Patients and Providers - Suicidality in Children and Adolescents Being Treated with Antidepressant Medications," U.S. Food & Drug Administration, Center for Biologics Evaluation and Research, last updated February 5, 2018, https://bit.ly/2LKeiou.

97. Daniel Boyatzis and Richard E. Goleman, "Emotional Intelligence Has 12 Elements. Which Do You Need to Work On?" *Harvard Business Review*, December 5, 2017, https://bit.ly/2jV5xWK.

98. Bopha Phorn, "Teens Who Mocked, Filmed and Failed to Help Drowning Florida Man Won't Face Charges," ABC News, June 25, 2018, https://abcn.ws/2MoUNyu.

99. Faith Karimi, "Teens Who Laughed and Recorded a Drowning Man in His Final Moments Won't Face Charges," CNN, June 26, 2018. https://cnn.it/2MXZ394.

100. CBS / Associated Press, "LeBron James, Others Laud Good Samaritan Who Stopped Teen Fight," March 22, 2017, https://cbsn.ws/2LurWwJ.

101. Tanja S. H. Wingenbach, Chris Ashwin, and Mark Brosnan, "Sex Differences in Facial Emotion Recognition across Varying Expression Intensity Levels from Videos," *PLOS One* 13, no. 1 (2018), doi:10.1371/journal.pone.0190634.

102. Daniel Goleman, *Emotional Intelligence* (London: Bloomsbury, 2014).

103. Barry Caplan, Facebook post.

104. Itiel E. Dror and Stevan Harnad, "Offloading Cognition onto Cognitive Technology," in *Cognition Distributed: How Cognitive Technology Extends Our Minds*, ed. Itiel E. Dror and Stevan Harnad (Amsterdam: John Benjamins, 2008), pp. 1–23.

105. Henry H. Wilmer, Lauren E. Sherman, and Jason M. Chein, "Smartphones and Cognition: A Review of Research Exploring the Links between Mobile Technology Habits and Cognitive Functioning," *Frontiers in Psychology* 8 (2017), http://doi.org/10.3389/fpsyg.2017.00605.

106. Rory Reid, "Most Under-25s Can't Read a Map Because They Rely on Sat-Navs—Roadshow," CNET. July 11, 2011, https://cnet.co/2IIMsFe.

107. Kirsten M. Beyer, Aniko Szabo, and Ann B. Nattinger, "Time Spent Outdoors, Depressive Symptoms, and Variation by Race and Ethnicity," *American Journal of Preventive Medicine* 51, no. 3 (September 2016): 281–90.

CHAPTER 6: UNTETHERED FROM NATURE

1. Julie Jargon and David Kesmodel, "Bona Fide Fans Chase Rib-Free Rib Sandwich," *Wall Street Journal*, October 11, 2010, https://on.wsj.com/2PrOYl4.

2. Jonathan Taylor, "What Goes Up . . ." *The Osbournes* (MTV) December 3, 2002.

3. "The McRib Is Back," *The Colbert Report*, Comedy Central video, 3:47, October 28, 2010, http://www.cc.com/video-clips/ea746g/the-colbert-report-the-mcrib-is-back.

4. U/untimelyreferences, "It's Happening: The McRib Returns at Select McDonald's Locations on November 7, 2017," Reddit, https://bit.ly/2MIltPd.

5. "McRib Is Back," *Colbert Report*.

6. Although McDonalds seems to have removed the full ingredient list from the McRib website (likely because they are not offering the product at this time), a previous version of the ingredient list can be found at Ben Popken, "What's a McRib Made Of?" Consumerist, November 2, 2011, https://consumerist.com/2011/11/02/whats-a-mcrib-made-of/.

7. Hayley Peterson, "McDonald's Reveals How It Makes the McRib Sandwich," *Business Insider*, June 19, 2015, https://www.businessinsider.com/how-mcdonalds-makes-the-mcrib-2015-6.

8. Meredith Melnick, "Why Lovin' the McRib Isn't Heart Smart," *Time*, October 27, 2011, http://ti.me/2lq2OrL.

9. Vani Hari, "Subway: Stop Using Dangerous Chemicals in Your Bread," *Food Babe* (blog), https://foodbabe.com/subway/.

10. Ian Crouch, "Fast Food Doubles Down," *New Yorker*, April 25, 2014, https://bit.ly/2H3OiOp.

11. Stephen Colbert, quoted in ibid.

12. Nate Silver, "Double Down by the Numbers: Unhealthiest Sandwich Ever?" FiveThirtyEight, April 19, 2010, https://fivethirtyeight.com/features/double-down-by-numbers-unhealthiest/.

13. "Louis' Lunch: Burger Restaurant in New Haven, CT," Louis' Lunch, 2019, http://louislunch.com/.

14. Bruce Horovitz, "Down to a Science," *QSR Magazine*, August 12, 2015, https://www.qsrmagazine.com/exclusives/down-science.

15. The exceptions to this are Latin markets more prevalent in the West and Southwest, where pig's heads, trotters, and offal of all sorts can be found on display.

16. Christian Hetrick, "Whole Foods Still Hasn't Shed Its Whole Paycheck Status," *SF Gate*, August 24, 2018, https://bit.ly/2E2wIOA.

17. Bonnie Ghosh-Dastidar, Deborah Cohen, Gerald Hunter, et al., "Distance to Store, Food Prices, and Obesity in Urban Food Deserts," *American Journal of Preventive Medicine*, 47, no. 5 (November 2014): 587–95, https://bit.ly/2C1TeEO.

18. Sarah Treuhaft and Allison Karpyn, *The Grocery Gap: Who Has Access to Healthy Food and Why It Matters* (New York; Philadelphia, PA: PolicyLink, the Food Trust, February 22, 2017), http://thefoodtrust.org/uploads/media_items/grocerygap.original.pdf.

19. Andrew Dugan, "Fast Food Still Major Part of U.S. Diet," Gallup, August 6, 2013, https://news.gallup.com/poll/163868/fast-food-major-part-diet.aspx.

20. Cheryl D. Fryar, Jeffery P. Hughes, Kirsten A. Herrick, and Namanjeet Ahluwalia, "Fast Food Consumption among Adults in the United States, 2013–2016," National Center for Health Statistics, data brief no. 322 (Washington, DC: Centers for Disease Control and Prevention. October 30, 2018), https://www.cdc.gov/nchs/products/databriefs/db322.htm.

21. Dugan, "Fast Food Still Major Part of U.S. Diet."

22. Marianne Quinlan-Sacksteder, "How 'Grocerants,' Millennials and Technology Are Changing the Shopping Landscape," SmartBrief, May 26, 2016, https://www.smartbrief.com/original/2014/02/how-%E2%80%9Cgrocerants%E2%80%9D-millennials-and-technology-are-changing-shopping.

23. Eric Schlosser, *Fast Food Nation: The Dark Side of the All-American Meal* (Boston: Mariner/Houghton Mifflin Harcourt, 2012).

24. Harvey A. Levenstein, *Paradox of Plenty: A Social History of Eating in Modern America* (Berkeley, CA: University of California Press, 2010).

25. "Consumer Spending in the Quick Service Restaurant (QSR) Sector in the United States from 2004 to 2017 (in Billion U.S. Dollars)," Statista, February 2018, https://bit.ly/2oSplyE.

26. Alexandra Sifferlin, "34% of Kids Eat Fast Food on a Given Day, Study Says," *Time*, September 16, 2015, http://time.com/4035490/fast-food-kids/.

27. Lydia Saad, "Americans' Dining-Out Frequency Little Changed from 2008," Gallup, January 11, 2017, https://bit.ly/2MfxyGy.

28. Dugan, "Fast Food Still Major Part of U.S. Diet."

29. Abigail Okrent and Aylin Kumcu, "U.S. Households' Demand for Convenience Foods," United States Department of Agriculture, Economic Research Service, July 2016, https://www.ers.usda.gov/publications/pub-details/?pubid=80653.

30. Surabhi Bhutani, Dale A. Schoeller, Matthew C. Walsh, and Christine McWilliams, "Frequency of Eating out at Both Fast-Food and Sit-Down Restaurants Was Associated with High Body Mass Index in Non-Large Metropolitan Communities in Midwest," *American*

Journal of Health Promotion 32, no. 1 (January 2018): 75–83, https://www.ncbi.nlm.nih.gov/pmc/articles/PMC5453830/.

31. Sharon Palmer, "Young Vegetarians on the Rise," *Environmental Nutrition* 40, no. 2 (February 1, 2017).

32. Michael Pellman Rowland, "Millennials Are Driving the Worldwide Shift Away from Meat," *Forbes*, April 2, 2018, https://www.forbes.com/sites/michaelpellmanrowland/2018/03/23/millennials-move-away-from-meat/.

33. Porch, "Cooking Nightmares: A Generational Look at Capabilities in the Kitchen," Porch, 2018, https://porch.com/resource/cooking-nightmares.

34. "Food Expenditure Series," US Department of Agriculture, Economic Research Service, last updated October 2, 2018, https://www.ers.usda.gov/data-products/food-expenditure-series/.

35. "Television Watching and 'Sit Time,'" Harvard T. H. Chan School of Public Health, Obesity Prevention Source, April 13, 2016, https://www.hsph.harvard.edu/obesity-prevention-source/obesity-causes/television-and-sedentary-behavior-and-obesity/.

36. C. Erik Landhuis, Richie Poulton, David Welch, and Robert J. Hancox, "Programming Obesity and Poor Fitness: The Long-Term Impact of Childhood Television," *Obesity* 16, no. 6 (2008): 1457–59, http://doi.org/10.1038/oby.2008.205.

37. John Muir, *John of the Mountains: The Unpublished Journals of John Muir* (Reprint Services Corp., 1991).

38. John Muir, *Our National Parks* (Layton, UT: Gibbs Smith, 2018).

39. Ibid.

40. "Exposure to Greenness and Mortality in a Nationwide Prospective Cohort Study of Women," *Environmental Health Perspectives* 124 (2016): 1344–52, https://ehp.niehs.nih.gov/doi/10.1289/ehp.1510363.

41. Sherry Turkle, *Alone Together* (New York: HarperCollins, 2014).

42. Lord Byron, *Poetry of Byron, Chosen and Arranged by Matthew Arnold* (London: Macmillan, 1881), "I. Personal, Lyric, and Elegiac Nature the Consoler, II" (Childe Harold, canto iii, stanzas 71–75, available at https://www.bartleby.com/205/17.html.

43. Peter Lindenbaum, "Shakespeare's Golden Worlds," in *Changing Landscapes: Anti-Pastoral Sentiment in the English Renaissance* (Athens: University of Georgia Press, 1986), pp. 91–135.

44. Phillip Huscher, "Program Notes: Gustav Mahler; Symphony No. 3 in D Minor," Chicago Symphony Orchestra, 2009, https://cso.org/uploadedFiles/1_Tickets_and_Events/2009-2010/Program_Notes/ProgramNotes_Mahler_Symphony3.pdf.

45. M. H. Stevens, T. Jacobsen, and A. K. Crofts, "Lead and the Deafness of Ludwig Van Beethoven," *Laryngoscope* 123, no. 11 (2013): 2854–58.

46. Peter Gutmann, "Ludwig van Beethoven Symphony No. 6 ('Pastoral')," Classical Notes, 2012, http://www.classicalnotes.net/classics4/pastoral.html.

47. Dictionary.com, s.v. "Sublime," last updated January 2019, https://www.dictionary.com/browse/sublime.

48. "Vans Partners with the Van Gogh Museum Amsterdam," Vans, https://bit.ly/2OmatnH.

49. "America's Best Idea Today," National Parks Service, https://www.nps.gov/americasbestidea/.

50. National Parks Service Office of Communications, "Follow the American Dream in National Parks," news release, August 4, 2017, https://bit.ly/2wXjWdd.

51. Ken Burns, quoted in, "Who Was John Muir?" Sierra Club, https://vault.sierraclub .org/john_muir_exhibit/about.

52. John Muir, *Our National Parks* (Boston and New York: Houghton, Mifflin; Cambridge: Riverside Press, 1901), p. 56, available at Sierra Club, https://vault.sierraclub.org/ john_muir_exhibit/writings/our_national_parks/.

53. Peter Matthiessen, *Courage for the Earth: Writers, Scientists, and Activists Celebrate the Life and Writing of Rachel Carson* (Boston: Mariner Books, 2007), p. 135.

54. Neil E. Klepeis et al., "The National Human Activity Pattern Survey (NHAPS): A Resource for Assessing Exposure to Environmental Pollutants," *Journal of Exposure Science & Environmental Epidemiology* 11, no. 3 (2001): 231–52, http://doi.org/10.1038/sj.jea.7500165.

55. Stephen Moss, *Natural Childhood* (Swindon, UK: National Trust, 2016) https:// www.nationaltrust.org.uk/documents/read-our-natural-childhood-report.pdf.

56. Stephen R. Kellert, "Interest–Action Gap: Americans Face a Significant Gap between Their Interests in Nature and Their Efforts, Abilities, and Opportunities to Pursue Those Interests in Their Lives," Nature of Americans, 2018, https://natureofamericans.org/findings/ interest-action-gap.

57. Timothy Egan and Casey Egan, "Can the Selfie Generation Unplug and Get into Parks?" *National Geographic*, November 20, 2017, https://on.natgeo.com/2wIh97E.

58. *Yellowstone Visitor Use Study* (White River Junction, VT: National Parks Service, August 2017), https://www.nps.gov/yell/getinvolved/visitorusestudy.htm.

59. "Cuyahoga Valley National Park Visitor Use Study," National Parks Service, https:// bit.ly/2y8a0PB.

60. Carolyn Finney, *Black Faces, White Spaces: Reimagining the Relationship of African Americans to the Great Outdoors* (Chapel Hill: University of North Carolina Press, 2014), p. 213.

61. D. C. Martin, "Apartheid in the Great Outdoors: American Advertising and the Reproduction of a Racialized Outdoor Leisure Identity," *Journal of Leisure Research* 36, no. 4 (2004): 513–35.

62. "Ever See a Black Hiker Before?" Outdoor Afro, http://outdoorafro.com/2009/11/ ever-see-a-black-hiker-before/.

63. Egan and Egan, "Can the Selfie Generation Unplug and Get into Parks?"

64. Ibid.

65. K. C. Madhav, Shardulendra Prasad Sherchand, and Samendra Sherchan, "Association between Screen Time and Depression among US Adults," *Preventive Medicine Reports* 8 (2017): 67–71, http://doi.org/10.1016/j.pmedr.2017.08.005.

66. N. A. Cheever, L. D. Rosen, L. M. Carrier, and A. Chavez, "Out of Sight Is Not Out of Mind: The Impact of Restricting Wireless Mobile Device Use on Anxiety Levels among Low, Moderate and High Users," *Computers in Human Behavior* 37 (2014): 290–97.

67. Darrell Huff and Irving Geis, *How to Lie with Statistics* (New York: W.W. Norton, 2006).

68. Thomas H. Stevens, Thomas A. More, and Marla Markowski-Lindsay, "Declining National Park Visitation," *Journal of Leisure Research* 46, no. 2 (2014): 153–64, http://doi.org/ 10.1080/00222216.2014.11950317.

69. Egan and Egan, "Can the Selfie Generation Unplug and Get into Parks?"

70. Ryan Bergeron and Sean Redlitz, "Does National Park Service Have a Youth Problem?" CNN, March 20, 2015, https://www.cnn.com/2015/03/19/us/im-national-parks-older-visitors-morgan-spurlock/index.html.

71. T. E. Bunting and L. R. Cousins, "Environmental Dispositions among School-Age Children," *Environment and Behavior*, 17, no. 6 (1985).

72. *Yellowstone Visitor Use Study*.

73. Danny Bernstein, "The Numbers Behind National Parks Visitation," National Parks Traveler, https://tinyurl.com/y8p2c4ny.

74. "Number of Overnight-Camping Stays Declines in National Parks," Leave No Trace Center for Outdoor Ethics, https://bit.ly/2MeGMCT.

75. Bernstein, "Numbers Behind National Park Visitation."

76. Carolyn Gregoire, "The New Science of the Creative Brain on Nature," *Outside*, March 18, 2016, https://tinyurl.com/ycnumwyj.

77. S. Kaplan, "The Restorative Benefits of Nature: Toward an Integrative Framework," *Journal of Environmental Psychology* 15 (1995): 169–82.

78. "Thinking in Nature," *Hedgehog Review* 15, no. 1 (2013): 59.

79. "History of EMDR," EMDR Institute—Eye Movement Desensitization and Reprocessing, 2019, http://www.emdr.com/history-of-emdr/.

80. Peter Dockrill, "Doctors in Scotland Are Literally Prescribing Nature to Their Patients," Science Alert, October 9, 2018, https://bit.ly/2Pr63ft.

81. R. Kaplan and S. Kaplan, *The Experience of Nature: A Psychological Perspective* (Cambridge: Cambridge University Press, 1995); Kaplan, "Restorative Benefits of Nature."

82. F. Thomas Juster et al., "Changing Times of American Youth: 1981–2003" (Ann Arbor, MI: Institute for Social Research, University of Michigan, 2004), http://bit.ly/2CgGoDM.

83. Craig M. Hales, Margaret G. Carroll, Cheryl D. Fryar, and Cynthia L. Ogden, "Prevalence of Obesity among Adults and Youth: United States, 2015–2016," National Center for Health Statistics data brief no. 288 (Washington, DC: Centers for Disease Control and Prevention, October 2017), https://www.cdc.gov/nchs/data/databriefs/db288.pdf.

84. "Childhood Obesity Facts," Centers for Disease Control and Prevention, last updated August 13, 2018, https://www.cdc.gov/obesity/data/childhood.html.

85. Louise Jack, "Children Spend Less Time Outdoors Than Prisoners, According to New Persil Ad," *Fast Company*, March 22, 2016, https://bit.ly/2y4C9XF.

86. Laura Donnelly, "'iPad Generation' Means Nine in 10 Toddlers Live Couch Potato Lives," *Telegraph*, January 20, 2016, https://www.telegraph.co.uk/news/health/news/12108895/iPad-generation-means-nine-in-10-toddlers-live-couch-potato-lives.html.

87. "Polarization Abounds in the U.S., But We Universally Agree on the Value of Nature," DJ Case & Associates, March 20, 2018, https://djcase.com/case-in-point/united-nature-americans.

88. "Connecting America's Youth to Nature," Nature Conservancy poll, July 28–August 4, 2011, http://bit.ly/2CsJCnb.

89. "Media and Technology Use Predicts Ill-Being among Children, Preteens and

Teenagers Independent of the Negative Health Impacts of Exercise and Eating Habits," *Computers in Human Behavior* 35 (June 2014): 364–75, https://bit.ly/2EbYbh0.

90. Frances E. Kuo and Andrea Faber Taylor, "A Potential Natural Treatment for Attention-Deficit/Hyperactivity Disorder: Evidence From a National Study," *American Journal of Public Health* 94, no. 9 (September 2004), https://www.ncbi.nlm.nih.gov/pmc/articles/PMC1448497/.

91. Richard Louv, *Last Child in the Woods: Saving Our Children from Nature-Deficit Disorder* (London: Atlantic, 2010).

92. Angela Hanscom, "The Unsafe Child: Less Outdoor Play Is Causing More Harm Than Good," Children & Nature Network, May 12, 2015, http://bit.ly/1RzGXqW.

93. Paula S. Nurius, Christopher M. Fleming, and Eleanor Brindle, "Life Course Pathways from Adverse Childhood Experiences to Adult Physical Health: A Structural Equation Model," *Journal of Aging and Health* (2017), http://doi.org/10.1177/0898264317726448.

94. Jay Mechling, *On My Honor: Boy Scouts and the Making of American Youth* (Chicago: University of Chicago Press, 2004).

95. Bryan Wendell, "Gone but Not Forgotten: Beekeeping and 9 Other Discontinued Merit Badges," *Bryan on Scouting* (blog), April 28, 2014, https://blog.scoutingmagazine.org/2014/04/28/gone-but-not-forgotten-beekeeping-and-9-other-discontinued-merit-badges/.

96. "Merit Badges," Boy Scouts of America, last updated 2018, https://www.scouting.org/programs/boy-scouts/advancement-and-awards/merit-badges/.

97. Sean Lester, "Girl Scouts' Membership Continues to Decline, but Americans Still Bought a Ton of Cookies in 2015," *Dallas News*, December 8, 2015, https://www.dallasnews.com/business/business/2015/12/08/girl-scouts-membership-continues-to-decline-but-americans-still-bought-a-ton-of-cookies-in-2015.

98. "Research Reports and Materials," Nature of Americans, April 26, 2017, https://natureofamericans.org/research.

99. Kellert, "Interest–Action Gap."

100. Ben Quiggle, "KOA Study: Tech Can Distract While Camping," Woodall's Camp-ground Management, April 13, 2018, http://www.woodallscm.com/2018/04/koa-study-tech-distracts-from-camping-fun/.

101. "Ansel Adams National Parks," Ansel Adams Gallery, September 18, 2017, http://anseladams.com/ansel-adams-national-parks/.

102. Quiggle, "KOA Study: Tech Can Distract While Camping."

103. Joseph Coughlin, "Greener Than You: Boomers, Gen X & Millennials Score Themselves on the Environment," *Forbes*, May 5, 2018, https://bit.ly/2MXHPfU.

104. Howard and Matthew Greene, "Sustaining Admissions," *University Business Magazine*, July 1, 2008, https://www.universitybusiness.com/article/sustaining-admissions.

105. "The Sustainability Imperative," Nielsen Company, October 12, 2015, https://www.nielsen.com/us/en/insights/reports/2015/the-sustainability-imperative.html.

106. Adamantios Diamantopoulos, Bodo B. Schlegelmilch, Rudolf R. Sinkovics, and Greg M. Bohlen, "Can Socio-Demographics Still Play a Role in Profiling Green Consumers? A Review of the Evidence and an Empirical Investigation," *Journal of Business Research* 56, no. 6 (2003): 465–80.

107. Lee Ann Head, "My Not-So-Green Millennial," GreenBiz, May 29, 2015, https://bit.ly/2N0KTb7.

108. Jean M. Twenge, W. Keith Campbell, and Elise C. Freeman, "Generational Differences in Young Adults Life Goals, Concern for Others, and Civic Orientation, 1966–2009," *Journal of Personality and Social Psychology* 102, no. 5 (2012): 1045–62, http://doi.org/10.1037/a0027408.

109. Chloe Brice, "Tiny Dolphin 'Horrifically' Killed by Beachgoers for Selfie," ABC News, February 18, 2016, http://www.abc.net.au/news/2016-02-18/baby-dolphin-killed-by-crowd-of-beachgoers-in-argentina/7182070.

110. Chloe Lyme, "Yunnan Wild Animal Park Peacocks 'Shocked to Death' after Tourists Pluck Their Feathers," *Daily Mail*, February 22, 2016, https://dailym.ai/2Ni2avP.

111. Ibid.

112. Amy Schellenbaum and Erika Owen, "We're Begging You: Stop Taking Selfies with Wild Animals," *Travel Leisure*, March 4, 2016, www.travelandleisure.com/articles/selfies-killing-animals.

113. "Shark Dragged from the Ocean for a Photo by Man in Florida," ABC News, February 22, 2016, https://ab.co/1oCKKKy.

114. *Time* Staff, "Tourists Get in the Way of Sea Turtles Laying Eggs in Costa Rica," *Travel and Leisure*, https://www.travelandleisure.com/articles/tourists-costa-rica-sea-turtles.

115. Doug Criss and Samira Said, "Three Florida Men Charged in Shark-Dragging Video," CNN, December 13, 2017, https://www.cnn.com/2017/12/13/us/shark-dragged-video-arrests-trnd/index.html.

116. "Florida Men Plead Not Guilty in Shark Dragging Case," NBC Universal, January 10, 2018, https://bit.ly/2Pkbv3G.

117. *A Close up on Cruelty: The Harmful Impact of Wildlife Selfies in the Amazon* (London: World Animal Protection, 2017), https://d31j74p4lpxrfp.cloudfront.net/sites/default/files/africa_files/amazon_selfies_report.pdf.

118. Ibid.

119. "What Is CITES?" CITES, https://www.cites.org/eng/disc/what.php.

120. "Casey Nocket Pleads Guilty to Defacing Rocks at Rocky Mountain National Park, Other Parks," Denver Channel, June 14, 2016, www.thedenverchannel.com/news/state-news/casey-nocket-pleads-guilty-to-defacing-rocks-at-rocky-mountain-national-park-other-parks.

121. Kriston Capps, "Graffiti Artist 'Creepytings' Is Defacing National Parks," CityLab, October 24, 2014, https://tinyurl.com/yacluxhh.

122. Ryan Grenoble, "Boy Scout Leaders Topple Ancient Rock Formation in Utah's Goblin Valley State Park," *HuffPost*, December 6, 2017, https://tinyurl.com/y7ujn6pt.

123. Eyder Peralta, "Ex-Scouts Who Toppled Ancient Rock Formations Reach Plea Deal," NPR, March 18, 2014, https://tinyurl.com/ycoqak96.

124. Jethro Mullen, "Bison Attacks Woman Taking Selfie in Yellowstone Park," CNN, July 23, 2015, https://www.cnn.com/2015/07/22/travel/yellowstone-woman-bison-attack-selfie/index.html.

125. Andrew Bisharat, "Why Are So Many BASE Jumpers Dying?" *National Geographic*, August 30, 2016, https://on.natgeo.com/2Lj2Hxc.

126. Ben Guarino, "Man Who Dissolved in Boiling Yellowstone Hot Spring Slipped While Checking Temperature to Take Bath," *Washington Post*, November 17, 2016, http://wapo.st/2zjpm1G.

127. "Fake Nature," British Computer Society, April 2013, https://bit.ly/2C6cH8E.

128. "Jillian Michaels Talks about the X22i Incline Trainer from NordicTrack," Nordic Track, June 12, 2017, YouTube video, https://youtu.be/3WkLHZ9rvgA.

129. For an example, see Michael Seeley's "Hypnosis for Life Healing Sleep ~ Manifesting Health & Cleansing Chakras (Rain Sounds Sleep Music)," Michael Seeley, June 24, 2018. YouTube video, 2:00:37, https://bit.ly/2PRtqzm.

130. Sarah Perez, "Self-Care Apps Are Booming," TechCrunch, April 2, 2018, https://tcrn.ch/2HcqCcc.

131. Ibid.

132. Steve Paulson, Richard Davidson, Amishi Jha, and Jon Kabat-Zinn, "Becoming Conscious: The Science of Mindfulness," *Annals of the New York Academy of Sciences* 1303, no. 1 (n.d.): 87–104.

133. "Mindful USC Mobile App," University of Southern California, 2019, http://mindful.usc.edu/mindful-usc-mobile-app/.

134. Stoyan R. Stoyanov, Leanne Hides, David J. Kavanagh, et al., "Mobile App Rating Scale: A New Tool for Assessing the Quality of Health Mobile Apps," *Advances in Pediatrics* 3, no. 1 (2015), https://www.ncbi.nlm.nih.gov/pmc/articles/PMC4376132/.

135. "Calm.com Launches First Offline Product—Sleep Mist," Business Wire, July 27, 2017, https://bit.ly/2QfExT9.

136. Alex Panish, "Meet the Gay Ranger Who Is Helping Make the National Park Service a Little More Queer," *Out Magazine*, April 22, 2015, http://bit.ly/2BZbmMC.

137. "Chesapeake Bay Watershed Agreement," Chesapeake Bay Program, 2014, https://www.chesapeakebay.net/what/what_guides_us/watershed_agreement.

138. Alexis Dickerson, "Relationship with Nature," Facebook, October 6, 2018.

139. Ibid.

140. "Get Your Pass," Every Kid in a Park, https://everykidinapark.gov/get-your-pass/.

141. Jessica Plautz, "Do National Parks Need Wi-Fi to Stay Relevant?" Mashable, November 3, 2014, https://bit.ly/2NIapOs.

142. Eva Barrows, "7 Instagrammers to Follow for Camping & RV Inspiration," *KOA Camping Blog*, https://koa.com/blog/instagram-camping-rv-inspiration/.

143. *2018 North American Camping Report* (Billings, MT: KOA Camping Blog, 2018), https://koa.com/north-american-camping-report/.

144. T. Ruiz, D. Havlick, C. Holder, and E. Skop, "The Future of Our National Parks: How Do Millennials Feel about America's Greatest Idea?" (thesis, University of Colorado Boulder, Colorado Springs, 2008), http://search.proquest.com/docview/1899598465.

145. Ibid.

146. *Engaging and Retaining Millennial Consumers Attitudes Toward Outdoor Activities and Brands* (Boulder, CO: Outdoor Industry Association, 2012), https://www.outdoorindustry.org/pdf/MillennialsActivitiesAndBrands-OutdoorIndustryAssociation-FINAL.pdf.

147. Michael Roberts, "The Outdoor Industry Has a Millennial Problem," *Outside*, August 20, 2016, https://www.outsideonline.com/1998221/youths.

148. Luke Kilpatrick, Facebook post, October 17, 2018.

149. Justin Housman, "Tesla Just Made the World's Hottest Surfboard," *Surfer*, July 30, 2018, https://bit.ly/2NqVyXS.

150. Paul Lang and Ryan Riccitelli, "Bill Tai: The Kite Guy of Silicon Valley," *Kiteboarder Magazine*, November 24, 2009, https://www.thekiteboarder.com/2009/11/bill-tai-the-kite-guy-of-silicon-valley/.

151. "Events," ACTAI Global, 2018, http://actai.global/events/.

152. "Join the World's Biggest Happiness Study," Mappiness, https://www.mappinessapp.com/.

153. Leigh Gallagher, *The End of the Suburbs: Where the American Dream Is Moving* (New York: Portfolio/Penguin, 2014).

154. Chris Park and Michael Allaby, "New Urbanism," in *A Dictionary of Environment and Conservation* (Oxford: Oxford University Press, 2017), https://bit.ly/2ODZqth.

155. "Urban Green Spaces," World Health Organization, August 4, 2016, http://www.who.int/sustainable-development/cities/health-risks/urban-green-space/en/.

156. Paul Boutin, Facebook Messenger conversation with the author, November 18, 2018.

157. Sarah Perez, "A Majority of U.S. Teens Are Taking Steps to Limit Smartphone and Social Media Use," TechCrunch, August 24, 2018, https://tcrn.ch/2MJESP5.

158. Krishna Thakker, "Meal Kit Subscriptions Grew 67% Over the Past Year: Report," Grocery Dive, October 15, 2018, https://bit.ly/2RfD6s3.

159. Nick Wells, "Everyone's into Meal Kits Like Blue Apron . . . Until They're Not: Sobering Numbers Underlie Food Subscription Services," CNBC, May 27, 2017, https://cnb.cx/2VAwiU8.

160. Mary Ellen Shoup, "Move Over Millennials, Gen Z Is Now Shaping the Food and Beverage Landscape," Food Navigator-USA, July 17, 2018, https://bit.ly/2Li6Cte.

161. "Connecting Kids and Nature," National Wildlife Federation, https://bit.ly/2SOzYQk.

162. "LifeSail," LifeSail Community Sailing Center, 2017, https://www.lifesail.org/.

163. David Baddiel (@Baddiel), Twitter post, April 13, 2018, https://twitter.com/baddiel/status/984843868859486210?lang=en.

CHAPTER 7: THE UNTETHERED WORKER

1. "News Reporter Chooses Vanlife after Hiking Pacific Crest Trail," Dylan Magaster, April 30, 2018, YouTube video, 10:24, https://www.youtube.com/watch?v=sCTBbb1kWlU.

2. Ibid.

3. "Solo Female Van Life: Where to Park," Liz Bryant, August 5, 2018, YouTube video, 6:12, https://bit.ly/2QAxrbV.

4. Julia Reinstein, "Teachers Are Moonlighting as Instagram Influencers to Make Ends Meet," BuzzFeed News, August 31, 2018, https://bit.ly/2wzsE1V.

5. Ibid.

6. "Estimated Probability of Competing in Professional Athletics," NCAA, April 23, 2018, https://on.ncaa.com/21wK3jx.

7. "Average Playing Career Length in the National Football League (in Years)," Statista, April 2011, https://bit.ly/2oUUDXJ.

8. Aric Jenkins, "Tom Brady Isn't the Highest-Paid NFL Player by a Long Shot. Here Are the Top 5," *Time*, January 29, 2018, https://ti.me/2znhcbF.

9. Angela Chen, "Brain Injury Found in 99 Percent of Donated Brains of NFL Players in New Study," Verge, July 25, 2017, https://bit.ly/2v4O6gb.

10. Mark Murray, "Poll: 48 Percent Want Their Child to Play a Sport Other Than Football," NBC News, February 2, 2018, https://nbcnews.to/2DXoVB0.

11. Jeanine Poggi, "Nearly Half of Millennials and Gen Xers Don't Watch Any Traditional TV: Study," AdAge, September 22, 2017, https://bit.ly/2NW64uj.

12. "Twitch TV," Twitch, 2017, https://www.twitch.tv/p/about/.

13. Ibid.

14. "eSports Audience Size Worldwide from 2012 to 2021, by Type of Viewers (in Millions)," Statista, February 2018, https://bit.ly/2rU1xOt.

15. Michelle Quah, "eSports Goes from Gaming to Big Money League," *Business Times*, April 24, 2017, https://bit.ly/2ISrcgk.

16. "Collegiate eSports Governing Body," NAC eSports, 2019, https://nacesports.org/.

17. John Koetsier, "eSports: The New Football Scholarship? Gaming Scholarships for College Grew 480% Last Year," Forbes, May 12, 2018, https://bit.ly/2ONbOUI.

18. Jessica Spitz, "Fortnite, Which Is Free to Play, Has Pulled in More Than $1 Billion, Report Says," NBC News, July 19, 2018, https://nbcnews.to/2L8O2o4.

19. Ibid.

20. "Paris 2024 Olympics: eSports 'in Talks' to Be Included as Demonstration Sport," BBC News, https://bbc.in/2vK5nfT.

21. Julia Alexander, "Ninja's 12-Hour Streaming Schedule Isn't What Mentally Exhausts Him," Polygon, April 24, 2018, https://bit.ly/2Re0XIo.

22. "Meet Ninja: Fortnite Sensation Sits down for Interview with Ariel Helwani | E:60 | ESPN," ESPN, September 18, 2018, YouTube video, 5:38, https://www.youtube.com/watch?v=yqqhC4DCO-w.

23. Ibid.

24. "How This 26 Year Old Gamer 'Ninja' Makes $500,000 a Month Playing Video Games from His Bedroom," Urban Leak, September 18, 2018, https://bit.ly/2pm8THf.

25. James Vincent, "Drake Drops in to Play Fortnite on Twitch and Breaks the Record for Most-Viewed Stream," Verge, March 15, 2018, https://bit.ly/2pdVaCF.

26. Gianpiero Petriglieri, Susan J. Ashford, and Amy Wrzesniewski, "The 4 Things You Need to Thrive in the Gig Economy," *Harvard Business Review*, April 11, 2018, https://bit.ly/2FiRq9Z.

27. Jennifer Calfas, "A Startling Number of Teachers Are Renting Their Homes Out to Help Pay Bills," *Time*, August 16, 2018, https://ti.me/2BlNcA6.

28. Jon Yongfook, interviewed in *One Way Ticket: The Digital Nomad Documentary*, directed and produced by Youjin Do (2017), https://digitalnomaddocumentary.com/.

29. Jon Yongfook (@yongfook), "Remembering the Beautiful Blue Town," Instagram photo, July 22, 2018, https://www.instagram.com/p/BlieUgTHrRw/.

30. Kristen Pope, "How One Writer Used Crowdfunding to Raise $12,775 in 30 Days," Write Life, June 29, 2015, https://thewritelife.com/crowdfunding-a-book/.

31. Marco Torregrossa, "How the Platform Economy Gives Superpowers to Freelancers," Medium, August 31, 2018, https://bit.ly/2MkI9Qm.

32. Ryan Lawler, "Eight Months after Merger, Elance-oDesk Raises Another $30 Million Led by Benchmark," TechCrunch, November 25, 2014.

33. "Airbnb Experiences," Airbnb, https://bit.ly/2Aq1Hyz.

34. "Exceptional Culinary Experiences Worldwide," Eatwith, 2019, https://bit.ly/2xBqBKs.

35. Erica E. Phillips, "Digital Freight Startup Convoy Raises $185 Million, Surpasses $1 Billion in Value," *Wall Street Journal*, September 21, 2018, https://www.wsj.com/articles/digital-freight-startup-convoy-raises-185-million-surpasses-1-billion-in-value-1537524002.

36. Reid Hoffman (@reidhoffman), "Automation Is Happening in Transportation Today, It's Just Not in the Way You Think. Convoy Is Helping Truck Drivers Run Their Own Business and Experience the American Dream," Twitter, September 21, 2018, https://twitter.com/reidhoffman/status/1043187375906598912.

37. *Freelancing in America: 2017* (survey; New York: Edelman Intelligence; Mountain View, CA: Upwork and Freelancers Union, September 2017), https://www.upwork.com/i/freelancing-in-america/2017/.

38. Upwork, "Freelancers Predicted to Become the U.S. Workforce Majority within a Decade, with Nearly 50% of Millennial Workers Already Freelancing, Annual 'Freelancing in America' Study Finds," press release, October 28, 2017, https://bit.ly/2yArgOF.

39. Yuki Noguchi, "Freelanced: The Rise of the Contract Workforce," NPR, January 22, 2018, https://n.pr/2n2oVoU.

40. *Freelancing in America: 2017*.

41. Ibid.

42. Kaytie Zimmerman, "Work-Life Balance Becoming Unattainable Goal for Millennials," *Forbes*, December 13, 2017, https://bit.ly/2NPfoQH.

43. Danielle Paquette, "Workers Are Ghosting Their Employers Like Bad Dates," *Washington Post*, December 12, 2018, https://wapo.st/2GaXN3b.

44. Natalie Wong and Ellen Huet, "WeWork Fails to Reach a Deal for Offices at 1 World Trade Center," *Bloomberg*, September 5, 2018, https://www.bloomberg.com/news/articles/2018-09-05/wework-fails-to-reach-a-deal-for-offices-at-1-world-trade-center.

45. Eddie Small, "Durst Snubs WeWork, Says There Are Better Offers for 1 WTC Space," Real Deal, September 5, 2018, https://bit.ly/2OsRbgh.

46. *Freelancing in America: 2017*.

47. Katie Lobosco, "66% of Millennials Have Nothing Saved for Retirement," CNNMoney, March 7, 2018, https://cnnmon.ie/2NvojGP.

48. Megan Leonhardt, "Why a 33-Year-Old Turned to a Risky Loan When His Baby's Premature Birth Left Him Broke," CNBC, August 14, 2018, https://cnb.cx/2CXxiuv.

49. Maria LaMagna, "More Banks Are Trying to Get a Piece of the Payday Loan Pie," MarketWatch, September 16, 2018, https://on.mktw.net/2N73IJD.

50. Jeffrey R. Young, "How Many Times Will People Change Jobs? The Myth of the Endlessly-Job-Hopping Millennial," EdSurge, July 20, 2017, https://bit.ly/2uxw9FQ.

51. Jay Shepherd, *Firing at Will: A Manager's Guide* (Berkley, CA: Apress Media, 2011), pp. 3–4.

52. Emily Grace Buck (thread by @emilybuckshot), Twitter, September 21, 2018, https://twitter.com/emilybuckshot/status/1043321927299813377:

> To clarify some questions people have been asking (and keep in mind I am NOT a company rep)
>
> - Around 250 people are jobless, not 225
> - We did not get any kind of severance
> - Our healthcare only lasts for one more week
> - Many former employees were contract & can't get unemployment.

53. Brandon Cebenka (@binysaur), Twitter, September 21, 2018, https://bit.ly/2xxPgAG.

54. "Amazon CamperForce," Amazon Delivers Jobs, 2018, https://www.amazondelivers.jobs/about/camperforce/.

55. Jessica Bruder, "What Is CamperForce? Amazon's Nomadic Retiree Army," *Wired*, September 14, 2017, https://www.wired.com/story/meet-camperforce-amazons-nomadic-retiree-army/.

56. Cherie Ve Ard, "Workamping at Amazon.com Pre CamperForce: Was It Worth It?" *Technomadia* (blog), July 17, 2018, https://bit.ly/2NwacRz.

57. Ibid.

58. Ibid.

59. Ibid.

60. Ella Morton, "The Mechanical Chess Player That Unsettled the World," *Slate*, August 20, 2015, https://bit.ly/1HYbbeX.

61. "FAQs," Amazon Mechanical Turk, 2018, https://www.mturk.com/worker/help.

62. Jonathan Zittrain, "The Internet Creates a New Kind of Sweatshop," *Newsweek*, March 14, 2010, https://www.newsweek.com/internet-creates-new-kind-sweatshop-75751.

63. Daniel Dylan Wray, "The Companies Cleaning the Deepest, Darkest Parts of Social Media," Vice, June 26, 2018, https://bit.ly/2yVWdOR.

64. Katie Burke, "Airbnb Proposes New Perk for Hosts: A Stake in the Company," *San Francisco Business Times*, September 21, 2018, https://bit.ly/2I7mcUD.

65. Ingrid Lunden and Romain Dillet, "Airbnb Aims to Be 'Ready' to Go Public from June 30, 2019, Creates Cash Bonus Program for Staff," TechCrunch, June 29, 2018, https://techcrunch.com/2018/06/29/airbnb-ipo/.

66. Maggie Overfelt, "20-Somethings Would Take Less Pay if They Had These 5 Job Perks," CNBC, May 31, 2017, https://cnb.cx/2OKT87Z.

67. *State of the American Workplace* (Washington, DC: Gallup, 2017), https://bit.ly/2xL6ae6.

68. Brie Weiler Reynolds, "2017 Annual Survey Finds Workers Are More Productive at Home, and More," FlexJobs, August 21, 2017, https://bit.ly/2vZx9S5.

69. Carol Kinsey Goman, "Why IBM Brought Remote Workers Back to the Office—and Why Your Company Might Be Next," *Forbes*, October 12, 2017, https://bit.ly/2NeSuCS.

70. Ibid.

71. Julie Bort, "$1 Billion Startup Automattic Is Closing Its San Francisco Office and Having Everyone Work from Home," *Business Insider*, June 12, 2017, https://read.bi/2OtfbzM.

72. Cisco, "Are Consumer Devices, Social Media and Video Causing Company IT Policies to Bend, or Break?" news release, November 8, 2010, https://bit.ly/2pLYjcK.

73. Martin De Wulf, "The Stress of Remote Working," Hacker Noon, January 9, 2018, https://bit.ly/2ELjXTZ.

74. Joseph Grenny and David Maxfield, "A Study of 1,100 Employees Found That Remote Workers Feel Shunned and Left Out," *Harvard Business Review*, November 2, 2017, https://bit.ly/2z6LIY5.

75. Ibid.

76. James Manyika, Susan Lund, Michael Chui, et al., "Jobs Lost, Jobs Gained: What the Future of Work Will Mean for Jobs, Skills, and Wages," McKinsey & Company, November 2017, https://mck.co/2J5pBqO.

77. "Robot Doctors Will 'Absolutely' Replace Surgeons | Health | WIRED," Wired UK, May 11, 2016, YouTube video, 14:47, https://youtu.be/Sg-RHZipKnw.

78. Ian Steadman, "IBM's Watson Is Better at Diagnosing Cancer Than Human Doctors," *Wired*, February 11, 2013, https://www.wired.co.uk/article/ibm-watson-medical-doctor.

79. Nancy J. Wei, Bryn Dougherty, Aundria Myers, and Sherif M. Badawy, "Using Google Glass in Surgical Settings: Systematic Review," *JMIR MHealth and UHealth* 6, no. 3 (2018), http://doi.org/10.2196/mhealth.9409.

80. Josh Constine, "Atrium Raises $65M from A16z to Replace Lawyers with Machine Learning," TechCrunch, September 10, 2018, https://tcrn.ch/2CFtYpv.

81. Ryan Watson, "Accounting for AI," *Insight*, Summer 2017, https://bit.ly/2MTzIfr.

82. Lance Mayfield, private Facebook conversation with the author, 2017.

83. Tom Kaiser, "Why Domino's Will Eat Pizza Hut's Lunch," *Franchise Times*, January 26, 2017, https://www.franchisetimes.com/February-2017/Why-Dominos-will-eat-Pizza-Huts-lunch/.

84. "Robot Bartenders Shake Things Up at Sea," Royal Caribbean International, September 20, 2016, https://bit.ly/2GRs7uX.

85. Tom Stillwell, "I Always Did Chores for My Dad," Facebook Messenger conversation with the author, January 7, 2019.

86. Mark J. Perry, "The US Produces 40% More," AEI, July 24, 2017, https://bit.ly/2STsKeh.

87. Dan Sewell and Christopher S. Rugaber, "Lots of High-Tech Factory Jobs in U.S., but Skilled Workers Are Lacking," *Seattle Times*, August 16, 2017, https://bit.ly/2PRGjJ0.

88. Jeffrey J. Selingo, "Wanted: Factory Workers, Degree Required," *New York Times*, January 30, 2017, www.nytimes.com/2017/01/30/education/edlife/factory-workers-college-degree-apprenticeships.html?_r=0.

89. Richard Fry, Ruth Igielnik, and Eileen Patten, "How Millennials Today Compare with Their Grandparents 50 Years Ago," Pew Research Center, Washington, DC, March 16, 2018, https://pewrsr.ch/2FRBfQp.

90. Christopher Mullins and David Kauzlarich, "The Ghost Dance and Wounded Knee: A Criminological Examination," *Social Pathology* 6, no. 4 (n.d.): 264–83.

91. "Elon Musk Quits AI Ethics Research Group," BBC News, February 22, 2018, https://bbc.in/2I8nIGa.

92. Patrick Gillespie, "Truck Drivers Wanted. Pay: $73,000," CNN Money, October 9, 2015, https://cnnmon.ie/2LhBkyy.

93. "About Y Combinator," Y Combinator, https://www.ycombinator.com/.

94. Kate McFarland, "Overview of Current Basic Income Related Experiments (October 2017)," Basic Income Earth Network, October 19, 2017, https://bit.ly/2OAQzso.

95. "Cost of Living in Finland," Numbeo, January 2019, https://bit.ly/2RkDbKQ.

96. McFarland, "Overview of Current Basic Income Related Experiments."

97. William Julius Wilson, *When Work Disappears: The World of the New Urban Poor* (New York: Knopf, 1999).

98. Peter S. Goodman, "The Robots Are Coming, and Sweden Is Fine," *New York Times*, October 10, 2018, https://nyti.ms/2DKWIsQ.

99. John Ydstie, "Robust Apprenticeship Program Key to Germany's Manufacturing Might," NPR, January 4, 2018, https://n.pr/2lSa92M.

100. Sebastian Buck, "As Millennials Demand More Meaning, Older Brands Are Not Aging Well," *Fast Company*, October 5, 2017, https://bit.ly/2xjSapy.

101. Umair Haque, "Eudaimonics: The Art of Realizing Genuinely Good Lives," Eudaimonia and Co., September 14, 2017, https://bit.ly/2EfdaGO.

102. Ibid.

103. "The First EOS Wallet Built for Everyday Use," EOS Lynx, 2018, https://eoslynx.com/.

104. "Puerto Rico Increases Hurricane Maria Death Toll to 2,975," BBC News, August 29, 2018, https://www.bbc.com/news/world-us-canada-45338080.

105. "Assessing the U.S. Climate in 2017," National Centers for Environmental Information (NCEI), July 30, 2018, https://www.ncei.noaa.gov/news/national-climate-201712.

106. "Is There a Revolution Brewing in Puerto Rico?" ABC News (Australia), July 23, 2018, YouTube video, 25:35, https://youtu.be/bdW1UbsWp28.

107. Dean Takahashi, "Blockchain Billionaire Brock Pierce on Saving Puerto Rico, Cryptocurrency Games, and Fighting Controversy," Venture Beat, October 29, 2018, https://bit.ly/2Fwl4L9.

108. Ibid.

109. Neil Strauss, "Brock Pierce: The Hippie King of Cryptocurrency," *Rolling Stone*, July 26, 2018, https://bit.ly/2QKbF4Z.

110. Steven Buchko, "How Many Bitcoins Remain? | Quick Guide to Bitcoin Supply," CoinCentral, January 3, 2018, https://bit.ly/2QGu56s.

111. Sudhir Khatwani, "9 Most Profitable Proof of Stake (POS) Cryptocurrencies," CoinSutra: Bitcoin Community, March 10, 2018, https://coinsutra.com/proof-of-stake-cryptocurrencies/.

112. Jeff John Roberts, "The Diamond Industry Is Obsessed with the Blockchain," *Fortune*, September 12, 2017, http://fortune.com/2017/09/12/diamond-blockchain-everledger/.

113. Linda-Eling Lee, Ric Marshall, Damion Rallis, and Matt Moscardi, *Women on Boards: Global Trends in Gender Diversity on Corporate Boards* (New York: MSCI, November 2015), https://www.msci.com/documents/10199/04b6f646-d638-4878-9c61-4eb91748a82b.

114. "Elephant in the Valley," Women in Tech, 2017, https://www.elephantinthevalley.com/.

115. Geo Star, ".:RAW:. To All of You Who Have Risen from the Ashes, This One's for You . . ." Facebook, October 8, 2018, https://bit.ly/2QHfxD8.

116. Ibid.

117. "Crystal Rose - Sensay - World Blockchain Forum," posted by Keynote, October 14, 2017, YouTube video, 14:54, https://bit.ly/2QyszD3.

118. Sherry Turkle, *Alone Together* (New York: HarperCollins, 2014).

119. Richard Kastelein, "Guardian Circle Turns to Blockchain for Global Decentralized 9-1-1 Emergency Response," Blockchain News, October 10, 2017, https://bit.ly/2sqj2nH.

120. "Hyperledger: Blockchain Collaboration Changing the Business World," IBM, 2018, https://www.ibm.com/blockchain/hyperledger.

121. BuroHQ, https://www.burohq.co/.

122. Nielson Company, "Consumer-Goods' Brands That Demonstrate Commitment to Sustainability Outperform Those That Don't," news release, December 10, 2015, https://bit.ly/2x94Gds.

123. Sasha Lekach, "Volvo's 360c Autonomous Concept Car Is for Sleeping, Working, and Hanging Out," Mashable, September 5, 2018, https://bit.ly/2I70LTD.

124. Jean François Lyotard, *The Postmodern Condition: A Report on Knowledge* (Minneapolis: University of Minnesota Press, 1984).

CHAPTER 8: UNTETHERED FROM THE BODY

1. T. J. Prescott, M. E. Diamond, and A. M. Wing, "Active Touch Sensing," *Philosophical Transactions of the Royal Society B: Biological Sciences* 366, no. 1581 (2011): 2989–95.

2. Marshall, W. McLuhan, Terrence Gordon, Elena Lamberti, and Dominique Scheffel-Dunand, *The Gutenberg Galaxy: The Making of Typographic Man* (Toronto: University of Toronto Press, 2017).

3. "National Citizen Service Teenage Adventure Survey," OnePoll, London, UK, June 15, 2016, http://www.onepoll.com/national-citizen-service-teenage-adventure-survey/.

4. Margaret L. McLaughlin et al., *Touch in Virtual Environments: Haptics and the Design of Interactive Systems* (Upper Saddle River, NJ: Prentice-Hall, 2002).

5. "Is It the End for the Paperback? Kindle e-Book Outsells Print Versions for First Time Ever," *Daily Mail*, May 20, 2011, www.dailymail.co.uk/sciencetech/article-1388779/The-end-paperback-Kindle-ebook-sales-exceed-print-sales-time-ever.html.

6. Zoe Wood, "Paperback Fighter: Sales of Physical Books Now Outperform Digital Titles," *Guardian*, March 17, 2017, https://www.theguardian.com/books/2017/mar/17/paperback-books-sales-outperform-digital-titles-amazon-ebooks.

7. Brandon Keim, "Why the Smart Reading Device of the Future May Be . . . Paper," *Wired*, Conde Nast, May 1, 2014, https://www.wired.com/2014/05/reading-on-screen-versus-paper/.

8. Donavan Freberg, Facebook page, https://www.facebook.com/donavanfreberg. Reproduced with permission.

9. Michel Foucault, *Discipline and Punish: The Birth of the Prison* (New York: Vintage, 2011).

10. "2018 Greater Los Angeles Homeless Count Presentation," LAHSA, May 31, 2018, https://www.lahsa.org/documents?id=2059-2018-greater-los-angeles-homeless-count -presentation.pdf.

11. "Attempts to Get Homeless into Shelters Fail 99 Percent of Time, Data Show," CBS New York, August 29, 2016, https://newyork.cbslocal.com/2016/08/29/homeless-shelter -failure/.

12. Juliet Bennett Rylah, "Bridge Between DTLA Luxury Apartments Allows Residents to Avoid Their Homeless Neighbors," LAist, May 16, 2014, http://bit.ly/2CJyp2w.

13. "DSM History," American Psychiatric Association, 2018, https://www.psychiatry.org/ psychiatrists/practice/dsm/history-of-the-dsm.

14. Ibid.

15. Keith Tester, *The Inhuman Condition* (London: Routledge, 1995), p. 92.

16. The superego is the part of a person's mind theorized by Sigmund Freud that acts as a self-critical conscience, reflecting social standards learned from parents and teachers.

17. Sigmund Freud, "Civilized Sexual Morality and Modern Nervous Illness," *Sexual-Probleme*, 1908, http://doi.org/10.1037/e417472005-228.

18. Michel Foucault and Alan Sheridan, *Discipline and Punish: The Birth of the Prison* (London: Penguin, 1977).

19. Jean Baudrillard and Sheila Faria Glaser, *Simulacra and Simulation* (Ann Arbor: University of Michigan Press, 2014).

20. Ibid.

21. Steve Redhead and Claire Abel, *The Jean Baudrillard Reader* (New York: Columbia University Press, 2014), p. 128.

22. "2018 Revision of World Urbanization Prospects," United Nations Department of Economic and Social Affairs, May 16, 2018, https://bit.ly/2KwBaDE.

23. Mark Poster, "Swans Way: Care of Self in the Hyperreal," *Configurations* 15, no. 2 (2009): 151–75, http://doi.org/10.1353/con.0.0029.

24. Davey Alba, "The Logan Paul Suicide Video Shows YouTube Is Facing a Crucial Turning Point," BuzzFeed, January 4, 2018, https://www.buzzfeednews.com/article/daveyalba/ youtubes-logan-paul-debacle-highlights-its-content#.migXmJpGd9.

25. Miles Klee, "'2 Girls, 1 Cup': An Investigation into the Web's Shittiest Mystery," *MEL Magazine*, May 15, 2017, https://bit.ly/2qPDCiQ.

26. T. Koops, A. Dekker, and P. Briken, "Online Sexual Activity Involving Webcams—An Overview of Existing Literature and Implications for Sexual Boundary Violations of Children and Adolescents," *Behavioral Sciences & the Law* 36, no. 2 (2018): 182–97.

27. Albert Mehrabian, *Silent Messages: Implicit Communication of Emotions and Attitudes* (Belmont, CA: Wadsworth, 1981).

28. Daniel Goleman, *Emotional Intelligence* (London: Bloomsbury, 2014).

29. Mark Bauerlein, "Why Gen-Y Johnny Can't Read Nonverbal Cues," *Wall Street Journal*, August 27, 2009, https://www.wsj.com/articles/SB10001424052970203863204574348493483201758.

30. R. Kraut, M. Patterson, V. Lundmark, et al., "Internet Paradox: A Social Technology

That Reduces Social Involvement and Psychological Well-Being?" *American Psychologist* 53, no. 9 (1998): 1017–31.

31. Gary W. Small and Gigi Vorgan, *iBrain: Surviving the Technological Alteration of the Modern Mind* (New York: Harper, 2009).

32. N. H. Nie, D. S. Hillygus, L. Erbring, "Internet Use, Interpersonal Relations, and Sociability: A Time Diary Study," in *The Internet in Everyday Life*, ed. B. Wellman, and C. Haythornthwaite (Malden, MA: Blackwell, 2002), pp. 215–43.

33. Cecilia Brown, "Are We Becoming More Socially Awkward? An Analysis of the Relationship Between Technological Communication Use and Social Skills in College Students" (honors paper, Connecticut College, New London, 2013), https://bit.ly/2AI1c49.

34. Tara Kraft, "The Role of Positive Facial Feedback in the Stress Response" (master's thesis, University of Kansas, Lawrence, 2011), https://pdfs.semanticscholar.org/2ccd/afb6a03329f727c56c5d8042c75d4568d0a2.pdf.

35. J. P. Harman, C. E. Hansen, M. E. Cochran, and C. R. Lindsey, "Liar, Liar: Internet Faking but Not Frequency of Use Affects Social Skills, Self-Esteem, Social Anxiety, and Aggression," *Cyberpsychology and Behavior* 8, no. 1 (2005): 1–6.

36. G. J. Feist and F. Barron, "Emotional Intelligence and Academic Intelligence in Career and Life Success" (paper presented at the Annual Convention of the American Psychological Society, San Francisco, CA, June 1996).

37. S. Blakemore and S. Choudhury, "Development of the Adolescent Brain: Implications for Executive Function and Social Cognition," *Journal of Child Psychology and Psychiatry* 47 (2006): 296–312.

38. V. P. Mathews, W. G. Kronenberger, Y. Wang, et al., "Media Violence Exposure and Frontal Lobe Activation Measured by Functional Magnetic Resonance Imaging in Aggressive and Nonaggressive Adolescents," *Journal of Computer Assisted Tomography* 29 (2005): 287–92; N. Birbaumer, R. Veit, M. Lotze, et al., "Deficient Fear Conditioning in Psychopathy: A Functional Magnetic Resonance Imaging Study," *Archives of General Psychiatry* 62 (2005): 799–805.

39. Ibid.

40. Brad J. Bushman and Craig A. Anderson, "Comfortably Numb," *Psychological Science* 20, no. 3 (2009): 273–77, http://doi.org/10.1111/j.1467-9280.2009.02287.x.

41. Laura Stockdale, Robert G. Morrison, Robert Palumbo, et al., "Cool, Callous and in Control: Superior Inhibitory Control in Frequent Players of Video Games with Violent Content," *Social Cognitive and Affective Neuroscience* 12, no. 12 (October 4, 2017), https://bit.ly/2ke2xro.

42. Erving Goffman, *The Presentation of Self in Everyday Life* (New York: Anchor, 2008).

43. Owen Hargie, *Skilled Interpersonal Communication: Research, Theory and Practice* (New York: Routledge, 2017), p. 47.

44. J. K. Mullen, "The Impact of Computer Use on Employee Performance in High-Trust Professions: Re-Examining Selection Criteria in the Internet Age," *Journal of Applied Social Psychology* 41, no. 8 (2011): 2009–43.

45. Julie M. Albright, "How Do I Love Thee and Thee and Thee: Self-Presentation, Deception, and Multiple Relationships Online," in *Online Matchmaking*, ed. Monica T. Whitty (New York: Palgrave Macmillan, 2007), pp. 81–93, http://doi.org/10.1057/9780230206182_7.

46. "Woman Discovers She Has Spent $1.4 Million in Possible Love Scam -- Dr. Phil," Dr. Phil, June 1, 2015, YouTube video, 4:03, https://bit.ly/2vtbsKv.

47. Ned Zeman, "Manti Te'o on the Hoax and Life After: 'Honestly, I'm Never Going to Be Completely Normal,'" *Vanity Fair*, September 12, 2017, https://bit.ly/2vy7SAI.

48. Judy Battista, "At Scouting Combine, Te'o Faces First Interview Test," *New York Times*, February 23, 2013, https://nyti.ms/2CnIL58.

49. Brendan I. Koerner, "Online Dating Made This Woman a Pawn in a Global Crime Plot," *Wired*, October 5 2015, http://bit.ly/1MaSYgM.

50. Kyung Lah, "Tokyo Man Marries Video Game Character," CNN, December 17, 2009, https://cnn.it/2D5ah8W.

51. Ibid.

52. William Kremer and Claudia Hammond, "Hikikomori: Why Are so Many Japanese Men Refusing to Leave Their Rooms?" BBC News, July 5, 2013, https://www.bbc.com/news/magazine-23182523.

53. "Mystery of the Missing Million," Documentary Films TV, November 3, 2016, YouTube video, 46:57, https://bit.ly/2VPhAsI.

54. Jeremy Berke, "Japan's Demographic Time Bomb Is Getting More Dire, and It's a Bad Omen for the Country," *Business Insider*, June 5, 2018, https://read.bi/2xLj6S9.

55. Chris Weller, "'This Is Death to the Family': Japan's Fertility Crisis Is Creating Economic and Social Woes Never Seen Before," *Business Insider*, May 21, 2017, https://www.businessinsider.com/japan-fertility-crisis-2017-4.

56. Cathy Hackl, "The Rise of CGI Influencers and Digital Humans," *Public Relations Journal* 10, no. 1 (August 1, 2018), https://bit.ly/2vHt6e4.

57. Miranda Katz, "CGI 'Influencers' Like Lil Miquela Are About to Flood Your Feeds," *Wired*, May 2, 2018, https://www.wired.com/story/lil-miquela-digital-humans/.

58. Jamie Ducharme, "People Are Getting Plastic Surgery to Look Like Snapchat Filters," *Time*, August 3, 2018, http://time.com/5357262/snapchat-plastic-surgery/.

59. *The Hunchback of Notre Dame*, directed by William Dieterle, written by Sonya Levien, Bruno Frank, and Victor Hugo, featuring Charles Laughton, Cedric Hardwicke, Thomas Mitchell, and Maureen O'Hara (Los Angeles, CA: Universal Pictures, 1939).

60. Homa Khaleeli, "Text Neck: How Smartphones Are Damaging Our Spines," *Guardian*, November 24, 2014, http://bit.ly/2lZeamT.

61. Eugenia Hoi Ci Woo et al., "Effects of Electronic Device Overuse by University Students in Relation to Clinical Status and Anatomical Variations of the Median Nerve and Transverse Carpal Ligament," *Muscle & Nerve* 56, no. 5 (November 2017): 873–80, http://onlinelibrary.wiley.com/doi/10.1002/mus.25697/abstract.

62. "UPDATE! Are Kids Learning to Ride Bikes Later?" Free-Range Kids, August 23, 2017, http://bit.ly/2E6nr3i.

63. Michael Hollmann and Frank Schifferdecker-Hoch, "Comparative Study of Millennials (Age 20–34 Years) Grip and Lateral Pinch with the Norms," *Journal of Hand Therapy* 30, no. 1 (2017), http://doi.org/10.1016/j.jht.2016.10.002.

64. Richard W. Bohannon, "Hand-Grip Dynamometry Predicts Future Outcomes in

Aging Adults," *Journal of Geriatric Physical Therapy* 31, no. 1 (2008): 3–10, https://www.ncbi.nlm.nih.gov/pubmed/18489802.

65. Darryl P. Leong, Koon K. Teo, Sumathy Rangarajan, et al., "Prognostic Value of Grip Strength: Findings from the Prospective Urban Rural Epidemiology (PURE) Study," *Lancet* 386, no. 9990 (July 18, 2015): 266–73.

66. "Metabolic Syndrome," Mayo Clinic, March 6, 2018, http://mayocl.in/2COg3tO.

67. Jaspinder Kaur, "A Comprehensive Review on Metabolic Syndrome," *Cardiology Research and Practice* 2014 (January 1, 2014), http://dx.doi.org/10.1155/2014/943162.

68. C. Vandelanotte, T. Sugiyama, P. Gardiner, et al., "Associations of Leisure-Time Internet and Computer Use with Overweight and Obesity, Physical Activity and Sedentary Behaviors: Cross-Sectional Study," *Journal of Medical Internet Research* 11, no. 3 (2009): e28.

69. Erica L. Kenney and Steven L. Gortmaker, "United States Adolescents' Television, Computer, Videogame, Smartphone, and Tablet Use: Associations with Sugary Drinks, Sleep, Physical Activity, and Obesity," *Journal of Pediatrics* 182, no. C (n.d.): 144–49.

70. Mustafa Afifi, "Habitual Sleep Deprivation Is Associated with Type 2 Diabetes: What Comes First?" *Oman Medical Journal* 32, no. 3 (2017): 261.

71. "2014 Sleep in America Poll—Sleep in the Modern Family," *Sleep Health* 1, no. 2 (2014): e13.

72. "2015 Sleep in America Poll," *Sleep Health* 1, no. 2 (2015): e14–e375.

73. Wendy M. Troxel, Gerald Hunter, and Deborah Scharf, "Say 'GDNT': Frequency of Adolescent Texting at Night," *Sleep Health* 1, no. 4 (n.d.): 300–303.

74. "2011 Poll, Technology and Sleep," National Sleep Foundation, Washington, DC, 2011, https://www.sleepfoundation.org/sleep-polls-data/sleep-in-america-poll/2011-technology-and-sleep.

75. Lynette Vernon, Kathryn L. Modecki, and Bonnie L. Barber, "Mobile Phones in the Bedroom: Trajectories of Sleep Habits and Subsequent Adolescent Psychosocial Development," *Child Development* 89, no. 1 (2018): 66–77.

76. M. Endsley, "Toward a Theory of Situation Awareness in Dynamic Systems," *Human Factors: The Journal of Human Factors and Ergonomics Society* 37, no. 1 (1995): 32–64, http://doi.org/10.1518/001872095779049543.

77. "A Terrifying Example of Why You Shouldn't Walk and Text," Newsflare, December 8, 2017, Facebook video, 1:24, https://bit.ly/2Me9Ejr.

78. "Listening to the Phone While Crossing the Street, the Woman Got a Terrible Accident," Feedytv.com, August 12, 2018, https://bit.ly/2KS09kH.

79. Ruby Gonzales, "Man Punched in Face, Phone Stolen, While Making Call on Pasadena Sidewalk," *Pasadena Star News*, June 20, 2018, https://bit.ly/2OFkLyX.

80. John Naisbitt et al., *High Tech High Touch: Technology and Our Accelerated Search for Meaning* (London: Nicholas Brealey, 2001).

81. Christina Goulding and Avi Shankar, "Club Culture, Neotribalism and Ritualised Behaviour," *Annals of Tourism Research* 38, no. 4 (2011): 1435–53.

82. Tales from the Playa, "Embrace," Burning Man Journal, April 28, 2015, https://bit.ly/2Oa826L.

83. "Playa Living," Burning Man, https://burningman.org/event/preparation/playa-living/.

84. Aimee Groth, "Burning Man Just Moved One Step Closer to Becoming a Religion," *Quartz*, December 7, 2016, https://qz.com/857275/burning-mans-2017-theme-announced-by-larry-harvey-indicates-the-festival-is-becoming-more-like-a-religion/.

85. Victor Jeffreys II, "Burning Man: Sex Drugs Sex Drugs Sex and More Drugs and Sex," *Gawker*, September 11, 2013, https://bit.ly/1iDBrRX.

86. "2017 Burning Man Census Archive," Burning Man, 2018, https://burningman.org/culture/history/brc-history/census-data/.

87. "Census Archive," Burning Man: The Culture Historical Archives, 2017, https://burningman.org/culture/history/brc-history/census-data/.

88. Stu Woo and Justin Scheck, "At Burning Man, Air-Conditioning, RVs Make Inroads," *Wall Street Journal*, September 3, 2011, https://on.wsj.com/2MeCzjf.

89. "Turnkey Camping," Burning Man: The Event Camps and Placement, https://burningman.org/event/camps/turnkey-camping/.

90. "2018 Art Theme: I, Robot," Burning Man: The Culture Historical Archives, https://bit.ly/2AJcRzT.

91. Alan Foster, "20,000 Leagues Under the Sea-DVD Special Edition," *Chronicle* 25, no. 6 (2003): 46.

92. "About Maker Faire," *Make:*, 2019, https://makerfaire.com/media-center/#fast-facts-collapse.

93. Dale Dougherty, "Transcript of 'We Are Makers,'" TED, January 2011, https://www.ted.com/talks/dale_dougherty_we_are_makers/transcript?language=en.

94. "This Giant Mechanical Elephant Is a Steampunk Fever Dream," Insider, September 27, 2016, YouTube video, 0:44, https://youtu.be/U9fl9RqGjXo.

95. David Strehlow, Facebook page.

96. "What Makes a Maker? Habits, Attitudes and Skills That You Can Teach Aspiring Makers," Maker Faire, 2014, https://bit.ly/2smHGpx.

97. Blind Barber (@blindbarber), "Instagram Photos and Videos," Instagram, https://www.instagram.com/blindbarber/?hl=en.

98. Farley Elliott, "Highland Park's Groovy New Vinyl Bar Hits All the Right Notes," Eater LA, October 2, 2018, https://bit.ly/2NwCmYO.

99. "Who We Are Village," Stone Garden Farm & Village, https://stonegardenfarm.com/who-we-are.

100. Ibid.

101. Bath and Body Patisserie Sheawa, 2019, https://www.sheawa.com/.

102. "New Right Now at Chelsea: August 1," Artists & Fleas, August 2, 2016, https://bit.ly/2VWY7qa.

CHAPTER 9: THE UNTETHERED WORLD

1. John Donne, "Holy Sonnets: Batter My Heart, Three-Person'd God by John Donne," Poetry Foundation, https://bit.ly/2TS9VrU.

2. Alex Wellerstein, "The First Light of Trinity," *New Yorker*, July 16, 2015, https://bit.ly/2Gp1myg.

3. Ibid.

4. John S. Rigden, *Rabi: Scientist and Citizen* (Cambridge, MA: Harvard University Press, 2000).

5. As quoted in Jason Pontin, "Oppenheimer's Ghost," *MIT Technology Review*, October 15, 2007, https://bit.ly/2NJzMDx.

6. Paul Ham, "As Hiroshima Smouldered, Our Atom Bomb Scientists Suffered Remorse," *Newsweek*, April 12, 2016, https://www.newsweek.com/hiroshima-smouldered-our-atom-bomb-scientists-suffered-remorse-360125.

7. Peter J. Kuznick, "A Tragic Life: Oppenheimer and the Bomb," *Arms Control Today*, July 1, 2005, https://bit.ly/2DwWZ7x.

8. Joshua Benton, "The Forces That Drove This Election's Media Failure Are Likely to Get Worse," Nieman Lab, November 9, 2016, https://bit.ly/2fZZMJU.

9. Julia Angwin, Madeleine Varner, and Ariana Tobin, "Facebook Enabled Advertisers to Reach 'Jew Haters,'" ProPublica, September 14, 2017, https://bit.ly/2h62JGP.

10. Scott Plous, *The Psychology of Judgment and Decision Making* (New York: McGraw-Hill Higher Education, 2007).

11. Olivia Solon, "Facebook's Fake News: Mark Zuckerberg Rejects 'Crazy Idea' That It Swayed Voters," *Guardian*, February 9, 2018, https://bit.ly/2eOsoDZ.

12. Young Mie Kim, "Beware: Disguised as Your Community, Suspicious Groups May Target You Right Now for Election Interference Later" (Project DATA, University of Wisconsin-Madison, August 8, 2018), https://journalism.wisc.edu/wp-content/blogs.dir/41/files/2018/08/nonwhite-recruitment-and-suppression.Russia.Kim_.v.3.080818.pdf.

13. Ibid.

14. David Ingram, Reuters, "Facebook Now Says 126 Million Americans Probably Saw Russian Posts That Tried to Sway US Politics," *Business Insider*, October 30, 2017, https://read.bi/2ITaOfl.

15. "Senator Asks How Facebook Remains Free, Mark Zuckerberg Smirks: 'We Run Ads,'" NBC News, Mark Zuckerberg testifies before the Senate, April 10, 2018, YouTube video, 1:00, https://bit.ly/2xVL7Wo.

16. Craig Timberg, "Russian Propaganda May Have Been Shared Hundreds of Millions of Times, New Research Says," *Washington Post*, October 5, 2017, https://www.washingtonpost.com/news/the-switch/wp/2017/10/05/russian-propaganda-may-have-been-shared-hundreds-of-millions-of-times-new-research-says/?utm_term=.71355d05357f.

17. Laura Hazard Owen, "Old People Are Most Likely to Share Fake News on Facebook. They're Also Facebook's Fastest-Growing U.S. Audience," Nieman Lab, January 11, 2019, http://www.niemanlab.org/2019/01/old-people-are-most-likely-to-share-fake-news-on-facebook-theyre-also-facebooks-fastest-growing-u-s-audience/.

18. Timberg, "Russian Propaganda May Have Been Shared."

19. Brennan Weiss, "From 'Crazy' to 'Regret': Here's How Facebook's Positions on Russian Interference Evolved over Time," *Business Insider*, November 1, 2017, https://read.bi/2EkNN6r.

20. Cecilia Kang et al., "Tech Executives Are Contrite about Election Meddling, but Make

Few Promises on Capitol Hill," *New York Times*, October 31, 2017, https://www.nytimes .com/2017/10/31/us/politics/facebook-twitter-google-hearings-congress.html?_r=0.

21. Anita Balakrishnan, CNBC, "Facebook Investor Says He Wants the Company to Contact Everyone Who Saw Fake News during Election," Yahoo! Finance, November 14, 2017, https://sg.finance.yahoo.com/news/russian-election-interference-reveals-danger-173400746.html.

22. Roger McNamee, "I Invested Early in Google and Facebook. Now They Terrify Me," *USA Today*, August 10, 2017, https://usat.ly/2hE0VIu.

23. Timberg, "Russian Propaganda May Have Been Shared."

24. "Cambridge Analytica: The Data Firm's Global Influence," BBC News, March 22, 2018, https://www.bbc.com/news/world-43476762.

25. Erik Brattberg and Tim Maurer, "Russian Election Interference: Europe's Counter to Fake News and Cyber Attacks" (paper, Carnegie Endowment for International Peace, Washington, DC, May 23, 2018), https://carnegieendowment.org/2018/05/23/ russian-election-interference-europe-s-counter-to-fake-news-and-cyber-attacks-pub-76435.

26. "NPR/Marist Poll Results September 2018: Election Security," Marist Poll, September 2018, http://maristpoll.marist.edu/npr-marist-poll-results-september-2018-election-security/.

27. Aarti Shahani, "Russian Bots Are Spreading False Information after the Florida Shooting," NPR, February 20, 2018, https://n.pr/2Cd3meK.

28. Christine Schmidt, "Watch Out, Algorithms: Julia Angwin and Jeff Larson Unveil the Markup, Their Plan for Investigating Tech's Societal Impacts," Nieman Lab, September 24, 2018, https://bit.ly/2zsHKIK.

29. "Elections in America: Concerns over Security, Divisions over Expanding Access to Voting," Pew Research Center, US Politics & Policy, Washington, DC, October 29, 2018, http://www.people-press.org/2018/10/29/elections-in-america-concerns-over -security-divisions-over-expanding-access-to-voting/.

30. Hunt Allcott and Matthew Gentzkow, "Social Media and Fake News in the 2016 Election," *Journal of Economic Perspectives* 31, no. 2 (2017): 211–36, http://doi.org/10.3386/w23089.

31. Paul Sawers, "5 Billion People Now Have a Mobile Phone Connection, According to GSMA Data," VentureBeat, June 13, 2017, https://bit.ly/2s5JORj.

32. Peter Dockrill, "China's Chilling 'Social Credit System' Is Straight Out of Dystopian Sci-Fi, and It's Already Switched On," ScienceAlert, September 20, 2018, https://bit.ly/2pquAGg.

33. Ibid.

34. Rogier Creemers, "Chinas Social Credit System: An Evolving Practice of Control," *SSRN Electronic Journal*, May 9, 2018, http://doi.org/10.2139/ssrn.3175792.

35. Michel Foucault and Alan Sheridan, *Discipline and Punish: The Birth of the Prison* (London: Penguin Books, 1977).

36. Ibid.

37. "China Assigns Every Citizen a 'Social Credit Score' to Identify Who Is and Isn't Trustworthy," CBS New York, April 24, 2018, https://cbsloc.al/2wbfBCR.

38. *The Matrix*, directed by Lana Wachowski and Illy Wachowski (Burbank, CA: Warner Brothers, 1999).

39. Elon Musk (@elonmusk), "Creating a neural lace is the thing that really matters for humanity to achieve symbiosis with machines," Twitter, June 4, 2016, https://bit.ly/2DzPPPF.

40. *Gallup 2018 Global Emotions Report* (Washington, DC: Gallup, 2018), https://bit.ly/2Om0sd6.

41. Jean M. Twenge, Thomas E. Joiner, Megan L. Rogers, and Gabrielle N. Martin, "Increases in Depressive Symptoms, Suicide-Related Outcomes, and Suicide Rates among US Adolescents after 2010 and Links to Increased New Media Screen Time," *Clinical Psychological Science* 6, no. 1 (2017): 3–17, http://doi.org/10.1177/2167702617723376.

42. Brock Bastian, "So Many in the West Are Depressed Because They're Expected Not to Be," *Conversation*, August 1, 2017, https://bit.ly/2uoq0bp.

43. Michio Kaku, *The Future of the Mind: The Scientific Quest to Understand, Enhance, and Empower the Mind* (New York: Anchor, 2015).

44. James Cook, "Amazon Patents New Alexa Feature That Knows When You're Ill and Offers You Medicine," *Telegraph*, October 9, 2018, https://bit.ly/2ys1NoH.

45. Jon Brodkin, "Amazon Patents Alexa Tech to Tell If You're Sick, Depressed and Sell You Meds," Ars Technica, October 11, 2018, https://bit.ly/2A6qhG1.

46. Joseph Chamie, "Replacement Fertility Declines Worldwide," Yale Global Online, July 12, 2018, https://bit.ly/2DbFOWN.

47. Jeremy Berke, "Japan's Demographic Time Bomb Is Getting More Dire, and It's a Bad Omen for the Country," *Business Insider*, June 5, 2018, https://read.bi/2xLj6S9.

48. May Bulman, "Marriages between Men and Women Hit Lowest Rate on Record in England and Wales," *Independent*, February 28, 2018, https://ind.pn/2livyIN.

49. "The Rise of Childlessness," *Economist*, July 27, 2017, https://econ.st/2zEGbYb.

50. "SF3.1: Marriage and Divorce Rates," OECD Family Database, last updated July 25, 2018, https://www.oecd.org/els/family/SF_3_1_Marriage_and_divorce_rates.pdf.

51. Michael Safi, "Man Removed from Indian Plane after Entering Cockpit to Charge Phone," MSN, September 26, 2018, https://bit.ly/2OOeJfE.

52. Quoted in Robert Viagas, "Audience Member Tries to Use Stage Outlet to Charge Phone at Hand to God," *Playbill*, July 6, 2015, https://bit.ly/2QhyOv5.

53. "Moron Jumps on Stage on Broadway to Try and Charge His Phone in a Fake Outlet," posted by "Garruba1," July 6, 2015, YouTube video, 0:10, https://www.youtube.com/watch?v=YVt9K0YhhLM.

54. "Weird Places Readers Charge Phones," BBC News, July 22, 2015, https://www.bbc.com/news/magazine-33561851.

55. Ibid.

56. Ibid.

57. "In Much of Sub-Saharan Africa, Mobile Phones Are More Common Than Access to Electricity," *Economist*, November 8, 2017, https://econ.st/2KwpQHk.

58. "Greater Access to Cell Phones Than Toilets in India: UN," United Nations University, April 14, 2010, https://bit.ly/2RXb29g.

59. "In Much of Sub-Saharan Africa, Mobile Phones Are More Common."

60. Clean Water Coin, 2014, http://www.cleanwatercoin.org/.

61. "How Cryptocurrency and Blockchain Are Changing Philanthropy: Expert Take," Cointelegraph, March 3, 2018, https://bit.ly/2Flvihx.

62. "The World Bank Group (WBG) and Adolescent Girls' Education Factsheet," World

Bank, April 13, 2016, https://bit.ly/2dVbb8G.

63. Frank Gardner, "Tunisia One Year On: Where the Arab Spring Started," BBC News, December 17, 2011, https://www.bbc.com/news/world-africa-16230190.

64. Steven A. Cook and Eni Enrico Mattei Fellow, "The Arab Spring's Aftermath, in 7 Minutes," *Atlantic*, January 26, 2016, https://bit.ly/2IpbmJI.

65. "Middle East and North Africa: Youth Facts," YouthPolicy.org, https://bit.ly/1O4LJap.

66. "You Are Not Alone," Me Too, https://metoomvmt.org/.

67. Nassim Hatam, "Why Iranian Women Are Wearing White on Wednesdays," BBC News, June 14, 2017, https://bbc.in/2NPBN1g.

68. Roxana Dumitrache (@roxdumitrache), Twitter, January 5, 2018, https://bit.ly/2DzYpOn.

69. Mark Wilding, "This Journalist Is Helping Isolated Communities Share Their Stories Using Cell Phones," Vice, March 1, 2016, https://bit.ly/2xCrEuA.

70. Gonzalo Bacigalupe and Lautaro Ojeda, "Drones for Community Disaster Risk Reduction in Chile" (paper to be presented at the Fifteenth International Conference on Technology, Knowledge & Society, Barcelona, Spain, March 11–12, 2019), https://cgscholar.com/cg_event/events/T19/proposal/36930/proposal_details.

71. John Zogby and Joan Snyder Kuhl, *First Globals: Understanding, Managing and Unleashing, the Potential of Our Millennial Generation* (self pub., 2013).

72. Peter Gray, "Declining Student Resilience: A Serious Problem for Colleges," *Psychology Today*, September 22, 2015, https://bit.ly/2waHYB5.

73. "National Pet Owner Survey Finds People Prefer Pet Companionship over Human," American Animal Hospital Association, 1995, https://faunalytics.org/wp-content/uploads/2015/05/Citation1338.pdf.

74. Julie Springer, *The 2017–2018 APPA National Pet Owners Survey Debut* (Greenwich, CT: American Pet Products Association, 2018), https://americanpetproducts.org/Uploads/MemServices/GPE2017_NPOS_Seminar.pdf.

75. "National Pet Owner Survey."

76. Kerry Lengyel, "American Pet Spending Reaches New High," *Veterinarian's Money Digest*, March 24, 2018, https://bit.ly/2RJ3kj8.

77. Alissa Wolf, "Here's a Look at the Pet Markets Trends Around the World," Balance Careers, December 15, 2018, https://bit.ly/2sv5BTK.

78. Kim Painter, "Kids Are Spending More Time Staring at Phones, Tablets Than Ever Before," *USA Today*, October 19, 2017, https://www.usatoday.com/story/news/2017/10/19/media-goes-mobile-for-young-kids/776652001/.

79. Jean M. Twenge, *iGEN: Why Today's Super-Connected Kids Are Growing up Less Rebellious, More Tolerant, Less Happy and Completely Unprepared for Adulthood*: *And What That Means for the Rest of Us* (New York: Atria, 2017).

80. "Our Philosophy," Slow Food International, 2015, https://www.slowfood.com/about-us/our-philosophy/.

81. Wafa Braham Chaouch, "The Sahara," Facebook, September 29, 2018.

82. Neel Burton, "Our Hierarchy of Needs," *Psychology Today*, May 23, 2012, https://bit.ly/2JeiOuR.